Free Expression in
the Age of the Internet

Free Expression in the Age of the Internet

Social and Legal Boundaries

Jeremy Harris Lipschultz

University of Nebraska at Omaha

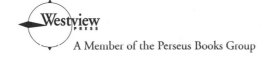

Westview PRESS

A Member of the Perseus Books Group

Published in 2000 in the United States of America by Westview Press, 5500 Central Avenue, Boulder, Colorado 80301-2877, and in the United Kingdom by Westview Press, 12 Hid's Copse Road, Cumnor Hill, Oxford OX2 9JJ

Find us on the World Wide Web at www.westviewpress.com

Library of Congress Cataloging-in-Publication Data
Lipschultz, Jeremy Harris, 1958–
    Free expression in the age of the Internet : social and legal
boundaries / Jeremy Harris Lipschultz.
        p.   cm.
    Includes bibliographical references and index.
    ISBN 0-8133-9108-3 (hc). — ISBN 0-8133-9113-X (pbk.)
    1. Freedom of speech—United States.   2. Internet (Computer
network).   3. Mass media—Social aspects.   I. Title.
KF4772.L57   1999
342.73'0853—dc21   99-41536
                                                                                                  CIP

The paper used in this publication meets the requirements of the American National Standard for Permanence of Paper for Printed Library Materials Z39.48-1984.

10   9   8   7   6   5   4   3   2   1

Contents

Illustrations

Boxes

Preface

This book would not have been possible without the encouragement and constant support of my family. In particular, my spouse, Sandy, provided many tips and ideas as we discussed the content of the manuscript. Our children, Jeff and Elizabeth, and their use of and interest in the personal computer have sparked many thoughts about what has been called the age of the Internet. Their grandmother, Faye Shepherd, assisted our family in viewing the technological innovations of the moment in a larger context. This was the social setting that became fertile ground for growing a synthesis of the many views of free expression.

Westview Press has been incredibly supportive in moving forward with this project. Senior Editor Catherine Murphy has been detail-oriented yet open enough to giving me the necessary "space" to finish this project in a timely manner. Cathy understood that a book about freedom of expression required open-mindedness in the editorial process. Lisa Wigutoff and Joan Sherman were excellent in helping this book to press in a timely manner. Additionally, freelance editor Anne Scanlan-Rohrer was helpful in synthesizing comments provided from reviewers Clay Calvert of Pennsylvania State University, Hazel Dicken-Garcia of the University of Minnesota, Elliot King of Loyola College of Maryland, and James Leonhirth of Florida Institute of Technology. Their comments were very constructive in providing additional sources for material not included in the first draft of the manuscript.

The genesis of this project came during a generous periodic professional leave from my teaching responsibilities at the University of Nebraska at Omaha. As such, I want to personally thank Dean John Flocken and the College of Arts and Sciences, Communication Chair Deborah Smith-Howell, Interim Graduate Chair Warren Francke, my coauthor on numerous other projects Michael Hilt, and the University of Nebraska Board of Regents for their patience. My colleagues in the Department of Communication have been very supportive of my research agenda, and this is appreciated. Additionally, Chelle Williams provided valuable technical support at key moments during the editing and printing of this manuscript.

Several teachers and scholars have directly influenced my views about free expression and media technology, including Robert Spellman, L. Erwin Atwood, Dennis Davis, Kyu Youm, David Pritchard, Michael

Sherer, Bruce Johansen, Warren Francke, Hugh Cowdin, Sherrie Wilson, Chris Allen, H. B. Jacobini, Walter Jaehnig, Stuart Bullion, Gary Whitby, and Mark Rousseau.

The challenge of this book was to try to place in some historical and theoretical context a subject that appeared to be changing daily. It is my hope that this book serves as a starting point for serious discussions about free expression in the age of the Internet.

Jeremy Harris Lipschultz
Omaha, Nebraska

Acronyms

ACLU	American Civil Liberties Union
AOL	America Online
CDA	Communications Decency Act
CEO	chief executive officer
CMC	computer-mediated communication
COPA	Child Online Protection Act
CTW	Children's Television Workshop
ECPA	Electronic Communications Privacy Act
FCC	Federal Communications Commission
FDA	Food and Drug Administration
FOI	freedom of information
FTC	Federal Trade Commission
GUI	graphical user interface
HTML	hypertext markup language
IEG	Internet Entertainment Group
IM	instant message
IRS	Internal Revenue Service
ISP	Internet service provider
LAN	local area network
MIT	Massachusetts Institute of Technology
MSN	Microsoft Network
NTIA	National Telecommunications and Information Administration
PC	personal computer
POV	point of view
ProComp	Project to Promote Competition in the Digital Age
RIAA	Recording Industry Association of America
SPLC	Southern Poverty Law Center
TOS	terms of service

Congress shall make no law respecting an establishment of religion, or prohibiting the free exercise thereof; or abridging the freedom of speech, or of the press; or the right of the people peaceably to assemble, and to petition the Government for a redress of grievances.

—United States Constitution, Amendment 1 (1791)

1

Social Communication Theory of Free Expression:

Politics and the Internet

"One thing that will not change in a world of vastly increased inter-personal communications networks is that the day has only 24 hours."

—Ithiel de Sola Pool, media scholar (1990)

"The penetration of time, the use of time as a mechanism of control, the opening of time to commerce and politics has been radically ex-tended by advances in computer technology."

—James W. Carey, cultural theorist (1992)

"The beauty of the Net is that one does not have to screen everything through a publisher and editor before reaching the audience."

—Fred Lawrence, law professor (1997)

"Such a decentralized system . . . resonates with . . . the central American credo of liberal individualism. Its great virtue is that it is designed to allow everyone to do his own thing. And that, according to some, is its great vice."

—Glen O. Robinson, law professor (1996)

1

"The Internet is clearly the political football of the nineties. The Communications Decency Act (CDA) *as well as presidential pledges to wire all schools to the Internet are representations of this idea."*

—**Henry E. Crawford, lawyer (1997)**

"The Supreme Court should provide clear guidance that we do not forfeit our First Amendment rights when we go on-line."

—**Patrick Leahy, U.S. senator (1997)**

"In my ignorance, I have to accept the possibility that if we had to decide today just what the First Amendment should mean in cyberspace, we would get it fundamentally wrong."

—**David Souter, U.S. Supreme Court justice (1997)**

"The Internet is presenting us with some cases we have never seen before."

—**Al Gore, U.S. vice president (1999)**

The great threat to free expression today, it has been argued, is not the power of government but rather the control and manipulation of information exercised by private industry: "Even in a democracy, even with all the late-twentieth-century panoply and paraphernalia of real-time worldwide communication (into every home), it is entirely possible to create a virtual screen of reverse reality between the great majority of all human beings alive on the planet and a small but powerful minority" (Childers, in Gerbner, Mowlana, and Schiller, 1996, p. 176). Reformers make the case that we need "a measure of autonomy from the state without delivering the press totally and completely to the vicissitudes of the market" (Fiss, 1996, pp. 157–158). Such critical perspectives on mass media raise obvious yet minimally explored questions about traditional First Amendment thinking and its emphasis on the "search for truth," "social responsibility," and "the marketplace of ideas." If mass media exist primarily to promote commerce in the marketplace and if social management and control are central to that end (Noelle-Neumann, 1995), then we need to reexamine the frameworks we use to understand free expression in light of the social, political, and economic realities.

From a cultural perspective, "social life is more than power and trade"—it involves the sharing of values and ritual: "Our existing models of communication are less an analysis than a contribution to the chaos of modern culture, and in important ways we are paying the penalty for long abuse of fundamental communicative processes in the service of politics, trade, and therapy" (Carey, 1992, p. 34). Historically, most mass technologies have not been used as tools to improve communication in meaningful ways, but the Internet has the potential to, in James Carey's words, *reshape* "our common culture" (p. 35). In this sense, free expression is at an important crossroads. The important question for individuals today is whether the new communication tools will be utilized for sharing between peoples or whether they will be manipulated and abused in the name of power and commerce. R. Williams's (1966) thesis is that society traditionally has been seen in terms of power, government, property, production, and trade but that there is a new emphasis today: "Society is a form of communication, through which experience is described, shared, modified, and preserved" (p. 18).

The information age has been forged in a social context: "Because we have seen our cities as the domain of politics and economics, they have become the residence of technology and bureaucracy" (Carey, 1992, p. 34). Just as in the politics of land, in which geography and growth work in the interest of a real estate market, the politics of cyberspace has much to do with the interests of those developing and "homesteading" this new electronic "frontier" through computer-mediated communication (CMC) (Fernback, in Jones, 1997, p. 36): "Cyberspace is an arena of power; CMC users act every day on the assumption that the tyranny of geography can be overcome within cyberspace. . . . Cyberspace is essentially a reconceived public sphere for social, political, economic, and cultural interaction" (p. 37).

The assumption is that communication involves more than a simple transmission of ideas and that language is what makes us human: "To grasp hold of the popular arts with terms like *myth, ritual, pilgrimage, liminality, story, narrative, chronicle* . . . is to see in a miraculously discontinuous world persistent practices by which that world is sedimented and held together" (Carey, 1988, p. 15). Traditional free-expression thought, however, has been dominated by legal scholars, with their emphases on the marketplace of ideas, clear-and-present danger tests, national security and prior restraint issues, literalist interpretations of the First Amendment versus balancing models, and legal issues involving subsequent (e.g., libel and invasion of privacy case law) punishment for speech (Fraleigh and Tuman, 1997). Although the legal model has successfully served to restrain government abuses against free speech, it denies the power of multinational corporations. The normative legal model objectifies ideas in a way that makes no real distinctions between society, culture, democracy, understanding, and community.

The postindustrial world in which telecommunication takes place involves a fundamental political struggle, particularly for the developing nations: "Electronic colonialism is the dependency relationship established by the importation of communication hardware, foreign-produced software, along with engineers, technicians, and related information protocols, that vicariously establish a set of norms, values, and expectations which, in varying degrees, may alter the domestic cultures and socialization processes" (McPhail, 1981, p. 20). Today, we must go further and say that a global information order may be as much the source of control as the source of liberation. The social communication theory of free expression should give us a way in which to think about how and why people choose to speak out or not; under what circumstances mass media amplify, muffle, and distort free expression; and what roles public opinion, mass persuasion, marketing, advertising, and consumer behavior play in the development and movement of "ideas." We must address not only government and private control of free expression but also economic and social components. Individuals communicate in a social world—one with both legal and social boundaries. The Internet, in this sense, is a metaphor for our desire to "connect" with one another. Consumption and entertainment, however, demand our most precious resources—time and money.

An appropriate starting point for the discussion of social theory is Nick Stevenson's (1995) eloquent synthesis of political economy and ideological theories of mass communication. In his view, the Marxist emphasis of "social reproduction of the status quo" is contrasted with the assumptions of classical liberalism:

> Whereas liberalism has argued that the mass media have an essential role to play in the maintenance of free speech, Marxism has charged that unequal social relations have helped form the ideological images and representations of society. . . . Marxists have rightly criticized liberal accounts for assuming that the free exchange of ideas could take place in conditions of class domination (p. 9).

In the broadest sense, social theory, as C. Lemert (1999) described it, is "the normal accomplishment of adept human creatures figuring out what other creatures of the same sort are doing with, to, or around them" (p. 2). It inevitably deals with the observation of power. In this sense, it is a theory that can be applied to real life, particularly under conditions of social change. Lemert selected French theorist Jean Baudrillard's 1983 work as an example of how social theory is utilized as a critique of modern culture. Baudrillard wrote, "Representation starts from the principle that the sign and the real are equivalent. . . . Conversely, simulation starts from the Utopia of this principle of equivalence . . . simulation envelops the who edifice of representation as itself a simulacrum" (Lemert, 1999, p.

484). The hyperreal or imaginary world of Disneyland is one of Baudrillard's examples of confusion about what is "real."

Likewise, I will argue that cyberspace serves to confuse reality for people by placing value in virtual space. One group has suggested that we live in a time of "transformation politics"—an era that demands that scholars employ theory, study, *and* practice (Woolpert, Slaton, and Schwerin, 1999). This book will actively mix theory, study, and practice in order to depict free expression on the Internet as a culturally transforming process and one that inevitably involves a struggle.

A social communication theory of free expression should evolve from the following challenges to normative tradition:

1. Free expression is not the product of an idealistic search for "truth" or objective reality but rather is subjective by its very nature. Individuals interpret (encode and decode) speech, which must be studied in a social context. "Society-wide mass communication" resides along with institutional, organizational, intergroup, interpersonal, and intrapersonal processes: "Alternative society-wide and public networks are now rare [but] may still develop, especially informally, under conditions of restricted access to mass media channels" (McQuail, 1994, p. 7).

2. Free expression is not only understood in terms of its presumed psychological value to individuals but also is a component in a social, political, and economic system. In the shift from traditional to contemporary society, we see "increases in *social differentiation* and *psychological isolation* in urban-industrial populations brought about by such factors as bureaucracy, contracts, migration, stratification, and the spread of innovation" (Lowery and DeFleur, 1995, p. 11, emphasis in source). We communicate to have identity.

3. That which passes for "free expression" in no way resembles what might be at the fringes because all speech is limited by a variety of social constraints, both real and imagined. E. Noelle-Neumann (1984) contended that we attend to the social world around us and check our speech: "It is fear of isolation, fear of disrespect, or unpopularity; it is a need for consensus" (p. 62).

4. Popular concepts such as "social responsibility" and "the marketplace of ideas" have no utility in learning about free expression, except to the extent that individuals adopt and use these notions as tools of political power or as a way to make democracy function in the search for consensus. W. L. Bennett (1996) framed the central question: "*How will democracy cope with news that is ever more standardized and politically managed at its source, while becoming ever more*

personalized and socially isolated at its destination?" (p. XI, emphasis added).

The purpose of this book is to examine free expression in a broad social, cultural, and legal context and to relate thinking to dramatic technological changes in recent decades. As N. Negroponte (1995) noted, "being digital" means being affected by both technological and social change. It has been predicted that the twenty-first century will bring "a distinct psychological shift from a dependence on visual, uniform, homogenous thinking . . . to a multi-faceted configurational mentality" (McLuhan and Powers, 1989, p. 86). The Internet is one vehicle for understanding the nature of free expression.

It is also important to relate the new technologies to a historical context of marketplace thinking, traditional print and broadcast models, normative versus social theories, current legal issues, Internet content, personal forms of free expression, privacy issues, commercial rights, global concerns, and the future of expression *after* the Internet. The technological focus of Marshall McLuhan is instructive: "McLuhan insists, again and again, that the study of the way technical forms of media shape human perception constitutes the most important theoretical issue facing media studies today" (Stevenson, 1995, p. 117). Although the medium may not entirely turn out to be the message in a deterministic sense, Stevenson found that it may come to affect the very structuring of private and public life. In the case of the Internet, it will be argued here that though message content has significance, the *acts* of daily checking one's e-mail and Listservs also are important. This is because the Internet serves the postmodern requirements to magnify social differentiation. When we use the globally connected hardware and software to communicate with others alienated by conditions of the information age, we search for communities linked by interest rather than geography. The harshness of a consumer-based culture is thus softened by open communication in a way that reminds us that "we are not alone." Still, we ultimately must retreat to the dominant cultural values found in the materialistic "needs" of the day; the marketing of needs through social codes, as exercised on commercial World Wide Web pages, is "used to signify distinctions of status and prestige"—distinctions that help to socially define us (Stevenson, 1995, p. 149).

Howard Rheingold's (1994) mostly optimistic view of the electronic frontier was tempered by the emergence during the 1990s of corporate web sites: "The big players in business and government are newer at CMC [computer-mediated communication] than the Internet pioneers and BBSers [electronic bulletin board users], but they bring a lot more weight to bear on the market and on political regimes when they devote their resources to it" (pp. 301–302). The Internet offered a "potential" for unbridled free expression, but regulatory efforts and court cases challenged notions that cyberspace would be a lawless frontier (Foerstel, 1998, p. 42). The United States Supreme Court's 1999 decision to uphold a section of the Communications Decency Act of 1996 that makes it a crime to send obscene e-mails was evidence that existing legal tests would apply to the Internet. Annoy.com, a site that had allowed people to send anonymous and lewd electronic mail to public officials, unsuccessfully argued that the law was confusing. Rather than interpret the law, the Supreme Court simply sided with a lower court ruling: "The justices' one-sentence order affirmed the lower court and effectively endorsed the constitutionality of the e-mail provision" (Biskupic, 1999). In *Apollomedia v. Reno*, a San Francisco company challenged the section, 47 U.S.C. Sec. 223(a)(1)(A)(ii), that made it "a felony to use a telecommunications device to communicate anything that is 'obscene, lewd, lascivious, filthy or indecent, with intent to annoy, abuse, threaten, or harass another person.'" At issue was whether obscene and unprotected speech, as defined by *Miller v. California* (1973), should apply to the Internet and other digital technology. The conclusion that indecent but not obscene speech is protected by the First Amendment follows earlier broadcast decisions that attempted to limit media available to children. It also guaranteed that there would be legal efforts to treat cyberspace as geography open to zoning restrictions. At least two members of the Supreme Court have previously argued unsuccessfully that because computer servers exist in physical space, cyberspace is no different from the world around it. This book is about how cyberspace has become the legal battleground over the meaning of free expression in democratic and open societies.

Each chapter in this book begins with key ideas in the field of communication. The reader will then be guided to the prime concerns of the chapter. After each analysis, I will summarize the main points and raise discussion questions that the reader may explore with fellow "Netizens"—citizens of the digitally connected worldwide community, reflecting "the new non-geographically based social membership" (Hauben and Hauben, 1997, p. X).

The Internet in the late 1990s will be used as a case study to show how social communication theory can assist in understanding free expression as a component of political power. The purpose is to challenge traditional normative views and to substitute an empirically based view of free expression—one centered on our observations of the digital age. Some would say that "technology is now carrying us into the greatest age of mass communication the world has ever known" (Emord, 1991, p. XIII), yet we barely understand the devices used in the communication process:

Deep inside a computer are circuits that do those things by transforming them into mathematical language. But most of us never see the equations, and few of us would understand them if we did. Most of us, nevertheless, participate in this digital culture. . . . As far as the public face is concerned, "computing" is the least important thing that computers do (Ceruzzi, 1998, p. 1).

In this book, *freedom of expression* is defined broadly as the freedom of individuals to communicate openly without obstruction from legal, governmental, corporate, or social forces. As I. S. Pool (1983) noted: "The onus is on us to determine whether free societies in the twenty-first century will conduct electronic communication under the conditions of freedom established for the domain of print through centuries of struggle, or whether the great achievement will become lost in a confusion about new technologies" (p. 10). However, I go further here by recognizing that even where legal and governmental restrictions do not exist, certain social conditions will tend to limit absolute free expression by individuals—a point highlighted by critical legal and social theorists. Traditional mass media have enjoyed rather broad rights of free expression, but these are communicators who may be manipulated and even controlled by existing power structures. It remains to be seen what will happen when the powerful must deal with millions or billions of "publishers" communicating through complex and unpredictable computer networks. It is understood that the definition of free expression places the bar on a high rung—perhaps even on the top rung. Therefore, rather than marveling at the successes of the system, we are more likely to be disappointed by its failings. The approach I offer in this volume is intended to counter the blind faith and enthusiasm that ordinarily accompanies the study of new technologies.

This book defines the Internet as simply the first generation of interlocking networks of computers that have allowed individuals at the end of the twentieth century to engage in worldwide communication in forms that know no geographic borders. Such communication began with text and progressed through a range of multimedia forms typified by the World Wide Web, the most common partition of cyberspace. We speak of "the age of the Internet" because the Internet is the media form that has come to define social change. Much as turn-of-the-century newspapers, newsreels, pre–World War II radio, television in the 1960s, and cable media in the 1980s did, the Internet represents the struggles in society between maintenance of the status quo and agents of social change. By the beginning of 1999, more than a third of American adults were online, according to Nielsen Media Research; the estimated 70.5 million Internet users represented a whopping 340 percent increase in just three years. Further, more than half of those in the targeted eighteen-to-thirty-four-year-old age bracket, the group coveted by advertisers, regularly used the Internet. The survey also found that:

- One in ten adults had made an online purchase on the Internet.
- About one-fourth of all adults used the Internet to shop for purchases, but a majority still bought offline from traditional stores.
- More men than women used the Internet, and 71 percent of all online purchases were made by men.
- Nearly one in five people over age fifty used the Internet.
- Nearly half of Asian adults used the Internet, but less than one-fourth of African Americans and Native Americans were online.

According to Media Metrix, the top three World Wide Web properties were America Online, Yahoo! and Microsoft. Each reached 46 to 48 percent of all web users, or an estimated 29 million unique visitors each month (communication from Media Metrix, November 23, 1998). The top five web sites for the same period were Yahoo.com, AOL.com, Microsoft.com, Netscape.com, and Geocities.com, raising monopoly concerns about the $4.21-billion merger between America Online and Netscape (Associated Press, November 23, 1998), as well as a Yahoo! $4.58-billion purchase of GeoCities, the largest web site location. The deal made Yahoo a top web gateway. At the same time, the audience for Internet news has shifted from technology-centered to "ordinary" subjects such as weather—now the most popular web topic among 41 percent of adults using the web (The Pew Center for the People and The Press, January 14, 1999).

These Internet data were published at a time when researchers were exploring concerns about the effects of heavy Internet usage. A Carnegie Mellon University study suggested that the Internet may be a place that contributes to depression—especially among those who spend a lot of time on e-mail and in chat rooms. Although some scholars raised methodological issues about the study, others wondered how the Internet contributed to an increasingly complex social communication environment, even as the technology becomes easier to use. The diffusion of home computers has been sparked by their new simplicity, computing power, and decreasing costs: "Home computers became more user friendly, and their rate of adoption rose gradually" (Rogers, 1995, p. 243).

The Internet as a Vehicle for Understanding Free Expression

In terms of legal issues, the Internet provides unique opportunities to better unveil the limitations of and constraints on free expression: "Historically, technological innovations in communications have worked revolutions in law and policy, often triggering cycles of robust free expression followed by official regulation, or even censorship, followed in turn by protest and eloquent pleas for freedom. Censorship is a human instinct" (Smolla, 1992, p. 337).

The following four principles, then, are advanced:

1. The Internet is neither an entirely "print" nor an entirely "electronic" mass media form, and it violates artificial legal dichotomies imposed by the courts. Speech that might be controlled in the broadcast context (*Red Lion v. FCC*, 1969) may not be controlled in the print media arena (*Tornillo v. Miami Herald*, 1973). As the Internet matures from a text-based to a multimedia-driven medium, this point becomes a key one. "The new technologies have not inherited all the legal immunities that were won for the old" (Pool, 1983, p. 1). Further, the Internet blurs the three legal domains—print media law, common-carrier (telephone) law, and broadcast-telecommunication regulation. "Although the first principle of communications law in the United States is the guarantee of freedom in the First Amendment, in fact this country has a trifurcated communications system" (Pool, 1983, p. 2). During the 1990s, the online system labeled "the information superhighway" was being driven more by market forces than by legal rules as "many companies [were] poised to pour hundreds of thousands and even millions of dollars into new media advertising budgets" (Alexander, Owers, and Carveth, 1998, p. 247). The Internet began with "pioneers," was defined by academic "settlers," and was exploited by "people of capital" (p. 249). Its future, however, remained open to redefinition at the turn of the century. It has been argued that the First Amendment should neither prevent convergence nor force governmental categorization. "Rather, the latest advances in telecommunications provide federal courts the opportunity to discard the inherently silly notion that freedom of speech depends on the configuration of the speaker's voicebox or mouthpiece" (Krattenmaker and Powe, 1995, p. 1720).

2. The Internet is both a "broadcast" and "common-carrier" medium, and it defies traditional regulatory models. At the same time, in free-expression terms, individuals have the power to be their own publishers. Speech that might be prohibited on the broadcast airwaves (*Pacifica v. FCC*, 1978) may be allowable on the telephone, where children can be technologically locked out (*Sable v. FCC*, 1989), and in newspapers and magazines, which hold rather full First Amendment freedoms. To this point, computerized ratings and blocking devices have proven to be ineffective in limiting access by children to so-called adult material. Print media zoning models are being tested. The technology creates the possibility to develop adult zones in cyberspace.

3. The Internet is a vehicle for core, "raw" political speech, as well as managed public relations, marketing, and advertising. The professionalization of the Internet by the shifting away from simple "HTML"-coded documents to complex dynamic "DHTML," "Java," and "ActiveX" scripting served to standardize content and limit discourse. In other words, technology "requires expertise" (Jones, 1997, p. 7). However, graphical user interface (GUI) software offered the potential to make it easier for individuals to create Internet publications by doing on-screen point-and-click editing rather than having to write complex code.

Historically, political speech has been protected under the law by the U.S. Supreme Court, even when the speech advocated violence or terrorism in the name of racism (*Brandenburg v. Ohio*, 1969). Traditional legal tests, such as the clear-and-present-danger standard, are difficult to apply in cyberspace. Regardless of the medium, however, the government has been limited by the courts from engaging in prior restraints against publication (*Near v. Minnesota*, 1931; *New York Times v. United States*, 1971). These limits may apply even to instructions on how to build bombs when the information floodgates are opened by numerous competing media (*United States v. The Progressive*, 1979)—perhaps explaining why one can now find such instructions on the Internet. Likewise, the courts' definition of the *fighting words* that might be regulated has been severely limited, and people offended by a message have been instructed to "avoid further bombardment of their sensibilities simply by averting their eyes" (*Cohen v. California*, 1971). Presumably, offensive messages on the Internet should likewise be avoided by leaving and staying away from such sites.

Attempts by the government to outlaw "hate speech," such as that exemplified by cross burnings, have been rejected by the Supreme Court. In *R.A.V. v. City of St. Paul* (1992), the Court interpreted the First Amendment to mean that ideas could not be restricted because of content. Language in the state statute about speech that "arouses anger, alarm or resentment in others" was found to be unconstitutional because it amounted to "viewpoint discrimination."

The notion that we protect even offensive speech did not stop Planned Parenthood and abortion doctors from winning a $107-million judgment against antiabortion activists operating the Nuremberg Files web site, called a "hit list" because it lined out the names of doctors who have been killed. (See Figure 1.1.) "Free speech is not in jeopardy," physician Elizabeth Newhall said, "women and their providers are" (Associated Press, February 3, 1999). The case, filed under racketeering and violence statutes, was appealed. Defenders of the site said its offerings were protected political speech. Days after the decision, the Internet service provider Mindspring "pulled the plug" on the pages (*Washington Post*,

THE NUREMBERG FILES

.new. Horrible Pictures Smuggled From Baby-Butcher Lab!

Nuremberg Files Web Site Overview

A coalition of concerned citizens throughout the USA is cooperating in collecting dossiers on abortionists in anticipation that one day we may be able to hold them on trial for crimes against humanity.

Why This Must Be Done
One of the great tragedies of the Nuremberg trials of Nazis after WWII was that complete information and documented evidence had not been collected so many war criminals went free or were only found guilty of minor crimes.

We do not want the same thing to happen when the day comes to charge abortionists with their crimes. We anticipate the day when these people will be charged in PERFECTLY LEGAL COURTS once the tide of this nation's opinion turns against the wanton slaughter of God's children (as it surely will) . *If you are not perfectly clear on what we are talking about, click the hyperlink in the preceding sentence.*

How You Can Help
In order to facilitate this effort, you can help collect evidence against:

1) Persons who perform abortion (doctors, nurses, etc.);

2) Persons who own or direct abortion clinics;

3) Persons who provide protection to abortion clinics (security guards, escorts, law enforcement

FIGURE 1.1   The Nuremberg Files

ALLEGED ABORTIONISTS AND THEIR ACCOMPLICES

We are updating this section weekly. Our goal is to record the name of every person working in the baby slaughter business across the United States of America. Email us with your evidence.

- Click Here If You Need Pictures To Remind You Why These People Must Be Brought To Justice

- This link takes you to a list of recent national news stories about this site.

- We are **testing a new format** for the baby butchers' list! Click here and see what you think. We can do this for every State in these presently united States of America with your help.

Legend: **Black font (working)**; Greyed-out Name **(wounded)**; ~~Strikethrough~~ (fatality)

ABORTIONISTS: the baby butchers

Lawson Akpalonu (CA)	Ben Graber (FL)	Norman M. Neches (DC)
Edward Allred (CA)	William Graham (LA)	James Newhall (OR)
Kevin W. Alexander (DC)	Marshall Grandy (TX)	Richard S. Newman (DC)
Eduardo Aquino (TX)	Richard P. Green (DC)	Mark Nichols (OR)
Gostal Arcelin (FL)	Thomas H. Gresinger (VA)	Mario Ochoa (TX)
(SEND US MORE NAMES!)	David A. Grimes	(SEND US MORE NAMES!)
Carl L. Armstrong (OH)	Jay M. Grodin (MD, VA)	Soo-Young Oh (MD)
Ali Azima (FL)	~~David Gunn (FL)~~	Tati I. Okereke (NY)
(SEND US MORE NAMES!)	R.V. Guggemheim (OR)	(SEND US MORE NAMES!)
Fritz Bailey (CA)	Tom Gunter (CA)	Kathleen A. Olson
Carlos Baldocedas (IL)	Moshe Hacamovitch (TX)	G.W. Orr (NE)
Faith E. Barash (MD)	Martin Haskell (OH)	Nadar Ostovartz (CA)
Martin Barke (CA)	Liam Haim (MD)	Olusoji Oyesanya (WI)
Scott Barrett, Jr. (MO)	Jae E. Han (IL)	Ronald Julian Orleans (MD)
Jan Barton (IL)	George Hansen (TX)	Oluhenga Oredein (VA)

FIGURE 1.1 (continued)

Box 1.1   Nuremberg Files Case:
Judge Denies Free Expression

In Portland, Oregon, a judge "banned a group of abortion foes from contributing to an anti-abortion Internet site." U.S. District Judge Robert E. Jones called the Nuremberg Files site and the related printed posters "blatant and illegal communication of true threats to kill."

Jones wrote, "I totally reject the defendants' attempts to justify their actions as an expression of opinion or as a legitimate and lawful exercise of free speech." Jones's opinion came three weeks after a jury awarded a $107-million judgment against those backing the web site. Three abortion doctors who were murdered were listed on the site, and their names were crossed out hours after the killings. Judge Jones said he has no jurisdiction over the Nuremberg Files because its creator, Neal Horsley, was not a defendant. An Internet service provider has twice shut down the World Wide Web site, but its content appeared on numerous mirror sites.

"We are doing nothing that the constitution forbids," Horsley said. "All of these actions are proving that people who are doing nothing more than exercising their First Amendment rights to resist and protest legalized abortion are being prevented from even speaking about the injustice."

The antiabortion movement's most controversial web site, the Nuremberg Files featured dripping blood and tiny baby arms and legs. It also listed doctors who perform abortions, a group increasingly under physical threat. Family-planning clinics, politicians, judges, and entertainers who take a prochoice stance were also identified.

In the most controversial aspect of the site, the names of seven people killed since 1993 were crossed out, and the names of another fifteen who had been wounded appeared in "ghostly gray type." Brenda Cummings of the Women's Health Rights Coalition said, "What was a list of doctors became a clear directory of violence."

There were at least 150 such antiabortion web sites worldwide. Computer programmer Horsley, who edited the Nuremberg Files, claimed he was collecting evidence for the day when abortion will be illegal and providers will face trial, "akin to the post World War II Nazi trials at Nuremberg."

(Source: Adapted from Associated Press, February 25, 1999; Scripps Howard News Service, November 14, 1998)

February 7, 1999, p. A-15), but other "mirror" sites continued to post similar information.

4. The Internet's "scarcity" lies not in limits on the numbers of people who can communicate at one time per se but rather on the speed of data transfer and the capacities of individual computers. As such, existing models for the regulation of electronic mass media, which fail in their own right, do not apply to global computerized communication. Although e-commerce has been slowed and even halted by Internet traffic bottlenecks, we should expect that improvements such as the next-generation Internet will provide better traffic management. The position taken here is that it is social rather than normative legal theory that is most useful in building predictive models about communication behavior.

C. R. Sunstein (1993) refocused the legal analysis on questions such as "whether unregulated markets actually promote a well-functioning system of free expression" (p. 18). He proposed support for a "deliberative democracy" in which there is "political equality," or a focus on the power of the idea: "The identity, the resources, and the power of the speaker do not matter" (p. 20). Thus, the government has been seen as not only an enemy of free expression but also a "friend"—a power source that has the ability to promote free expression (Fiss, 1996, p. 20).

The Boundaries of Free Expression

A key problem for free expression in the digital age stems from the fact that employees of private companies do not have free-speech rights in the workplace (Sixel, 1998). Thus, Internet communication by an employee can lead to her or his firing by an employer. The First Amendment is problematic in this regard because it protects individuals from government control in an age when government seems less important than corporate culture. The workplace, totally apart from issues of cyberspace, has become legally restricted in terms of speech by sexual harassment laws.

Employees, especially those of private companies, face real and imagined threats in regard to free expression because employers can wield the anvil of termination. Cameron Barrett learned this the hard way. He was fired for having a personal web page that included sexually explicit material and for suggesting that women staff members look at it (Associated Press, January 16, 1998). In another case, Lizz Summerfield quit after her Virginia employer asked her to remove company references from her private "SexyChyck" page. In a consumer-based society, the threat of not having a job and thus not having money becomes the most serious of feared consequences. "The American model is supported by advertising that precludes creation of other kinds of programming and socializes populations to become neurotic in their need to buy advertised commodities (Bagdikian, in Gerbner, Mowlana, and Schiller, 1996, p. 10).

Elizabeth Noelle-Neumann's *Spiral of Silence: Public Opinion—Our Social Skin* (1984) is central to the view of social theory advanced in this book. Noelle-Neumann contended that individuals in *any* society face pressures to conform based on the perceived "climate of opinion" at any given time (p. 4). This climate is the social environment, which changes slowly along with the agents of social change. It is the "fear of isolation" that drives social conformity: "To run with the pack is a relatively happy state of affairs; but if you can't, because you won't share publicly in what seems to be a universally acclaimed conviction, you can at least remain silent, as a second choice, so that others can put up with you" (p. 6). Speech, then, is more confident or silent depending on the public perception of the ideas being expressed and the fear of incurring the cost associated with expression. Likewise, critical race theory supports the view that minorities may fall silent when faced with hate speech or other racism.

The empirical question raised by this book involves the role that geographic proximity plays in exercising social control when the technology of choice has no geographic boundaries. Will social controls on free expression be a function of spheres of influence, as well as message content? It is predicted that the fear of isolation relates to one's local community rather than one's virtual community. In the one case, a loss of social connections leaves few options: One can exit the community or face living in an isolated condition. In the other case, one has many more options, afforded by cyberspace's worldwide population. If communication degrades into caustic speech, leaving involves only the click of a mouse. Moving from one's geographic home or quitting one's job, by contrast, can be time-consuming, costly, and complex. Therefore, it is proposed that the pressure to conform to local norms of behavior will outweigh the pressures in cyberspace. In free-expression terms, we would expect individuals to exercise a greater degree of latitude in cyberspace than in their neighborhoods, workplaces, and communities.

In effect, the Internet forces us to respond to the potential issues of power raised by changes in social control brought about by the information and consumer ages. Historically, cities have brought unlike peoples together, but the subcultures emerging in cyberspace bring "like" or "perceived like" peoples together in loosely knit social networks. Under such conditions, we would expect free expression to be more open because the threat of retaliation is limited by the homogeneity of the group, as well as by geographic distance between its members and the perceived anonymity. The physical (if not social) distance, however, remains. Space and distance are important because they remind us of our place, that is,

---

Box 1.2 Individual Communication in a Contemporary or "Mass" Society

1. Social differences are expected to be magnified by "division of labor, the bureaucratization of human groups, the mixing of unlike populations, and differential patterns of consumption."
2. Informal social control is predicted to be less effective because of declining norms and traditional values, "leading to increases in the incidence of deviant behavior."
3. Contracts, civil and criminal laws, and other formal rules become the dominant mechanisms for social control "as the new impersonal society develops."
4. Opposing lifestyles and values increase the levels of social conflict.
5. Open communication is less easy to achieve.
6. People in such a society become more media-dependent.

(Source: Lowery and DeFleur, 1995, pp. 11–12)

---

the social and cultural context of communication (Hoover, in Carey, 1988, p. 176).

Free expression is dependent on social conditions that seem to construct boundaries, just as modernization and technology lead to social barriers: "Open and easy communication as a basis for social solidarity between peoples becomes *more difficult* because of social differentiation, impersonality and distrust due to psychological alienation, the breakdown of meaningful social ties, and increasing anomie among the members" (Lowery and DeFleur, 1995, p. 12, emphasis in source). Social theory, then, stands in direct opposition to the technology cheerleaders who contend that cyberspace will help individuals, groups, organizations, and societies function better through improved communication networks.

It is sometimes easier to see the limitations of free expression in cyberspace as they exist in cultures with strong centralized governmental systems of control. Consider the Chinese government's controls on Internet access, designed to stop the leaking of state secrets and the spread of harmful information:

> The regulations cover a wide range of crimes, including revealing state secrets, engaging in political subversion, and spreading pornography and violence. They call for criminal punishment and fines of up to $1,800 for Internet providers and users. . . . Internet providers would be subject to supervision

by the Ministry of Public Security and would be required to help track down violators" (*Chronicle of Higher Education*, January 9, 1998, p. A-61).

The Chinese repression can be understood as, in part, an attempt by the government to shut down dissident exiles who protest the Beijing government through World Wide Web home pages, the first page that appears after typing in a web address. In fact, in 1998, China prosecuted a computer engineer for providing "30,000 Chinese e-mail addresses to a U.S.-based Internet democracy magazine" (Associated Press, July 29, 1998). The thirty-year-old founder of a Shanghai software company was charged with "inciting the overthrow of state power." He was convicted and sentenced to time in prison.

Elements of this sort of repressive thinking exist in most countries—including the United States. Despite America's role as the leader of democratic thought and as an innovator in communication technology, U.S. public- and private-sector entities have, since the mid-1990s, raised concerns about the content of the Internet.

On the one hand, there are public political products such as the Communications Decency Act (CDA), which was passed by Congress, signed by President Bill Clinton in 1996, and struck down by the U.S. Supreme Court in 1997. Likewise, there is the Child Online Protection Act (COPA) of 1998, which required adult sites to move content behind electronic barriers and made it a crime for "commercial" sites to be available to anyone under seventeen years of age. The measure, which forced sites to collect credit card numbers from users or face fines of up to $50,000 and six months in jail, faced legal challenges. In the meantime, librarians around the country struggled with the use of filtering software that tended to block more than just pornographic sites and in effect treated adults using the Internet in libraries as children.

On the other hand, there are quieter battles, such as the unexplained 1997 deletion of forum folders on educational topics by editors at America Online. At the same time, a former Music Television (MTV) programmer who had become an AOL content manager continued to expand entertainment offerings in the hopes of attracting subscribers and advertisers. In other words, the traditional American mass media model appeared to be prevailing in the digital age, as it was simply transferred to computers.

Consider the 1998 policy of a major public university system, titled "Executive Memorandum No. 16, Policy for Responsible Use of University Computers and Information Systems" (Smith, 1998). The school administration sought to "provide guidance" to its faculty, staff, and students by noting that computer usage was "a privilege, not a right." To the extent that computer usage is essential in modern communication, the policy effectively attempted to reduce free expression—supposedly a right grounded in the First Amendment—to the status of a privilege. The university claimed the right of redefinition because it was the "provider" of the technology. By accepting a computer account, then, the user was said to enter into an "agreement [to] abide and be bound by the provisions of this Policy." The agreement effectively invaded free expression by limiting speech that might be seen as "harassment," by regulating information that would be downloaded, and by placing stylistic requirements on "official" university World Wide Web pages (pp. 4–5).

Endicott College business professor Norman Becker echoed similar administrative worries at his university: "There is considerable concern about the potential misuse of computer resources. The exposure of a college to unfavorable publicity and to lawsuits from misuse can stall plans for expanding the use of computers and for providing unlimited access to the Internet" (*Chronicle of Higher Education*, January 16, 1998, p. B-12).

In a technological age of worldwide communication, it does not matter if you have free-speech rights if you do not also have the hardware and software to get your message out. This truth aligns the new computer technology and old problems associated with broadcast and print mass media.

Sometimes, the pressures to limit free expression have come from business interests. In June 1996, Massachusetts Institute of Technology (MIT) college student Manny Perez voluntarily shut down his acclaimed Morphing Grid World Wide Web home pages after receiving a letter from the powerful media law firm of Baker and Hostetler. Representing their client Saban Entertainment, producer of the popular children's television show *The Mighty Morphin Power Rangers*, lawyers claimed Perez had violated copyright law by using images, video, and audio from the show without permission: "Saban expressly reserves all of its rights to file a lawsuit against you to obtain both money and damages for all past acts of infringements and an injunction to prevent any future infringement and/or to refer this matter to the appropriate public authorities" (http://ic.www.media.mit.edu/Personal/manny/power/html_docs/disclaimer.html, June 1996). Perez wrote fans of his site: "I am a very poor college student and could not afford to pay any amount of money that Saban would request. Thus I am sorry to say that I must close down this site." He added, "I really can't understand why Saban would want to shut down this site." Saban, a multimillion-dollar enterprise, no doubt was moving to protect its economic turf. Following a letter-writing campaign by fans, Perez was allowed to continue—with conditions. By late 1997, his site had vanished into cyberspace, but in 1998, it returned, with this disclaimer:

> This is not an official Power Rangers WWW site. I am in no way associated with Saban Entertainment and/or the Power Rangers (well, I am a fan of the show, but I don't have an official seal). This site is intended as a resource for

fans of the Power Rangers. This is not intended to infringe on the copyrights held by Saban Entertainment (http://ic.www.media.mit.edu/ Personal/ manny/power/html_docs/disclaimer.html, October 10, 1998).

Perez explained to his site visitors how he was allowed to operate following his discussions with the Saban Interactive Department: "I was put in contact with the head of the Legal and Interactive Departments at Saban Entertainment. After a brief discussion, I was allowed to put the site back up."

Cyberspace can be more or less temporary, depending on how people archive files. In any case, however, the permanence of records seems to be out of the control of the author of those ideas. Cyberspace, then, has also come to be the place where debate over copyright law is most heated. The property rights of authors and publishers have been challenged by the technological ease of reproduction. The technological questions, too, are blending with the deeper ideological divides apparent in society. By late 1998, Congress had fashioned revisions to copyright law in an attempt to address problems associated with the ease of duplicating in a digital world. Most important, as will be discussed, the copyright extensions actually removed some material from the public domain.

The right to speak is sometimes confounded by the right of others to challenge that speech. Consider the case of a minister from Kansas named Joe Wright, whose opening prayer at the state capitol "sparked angry walkouts in two state legislatures, an unprecedented two readings on Paul Harvey's ABC Radio newscast, more than 6,500 phone calls to Wright's church and so many boxes of mail that the church staff doesn't know where to put them anymore" (*Omaha World-Herald*, May 1996). Although some praised the conservative prayer, others called it offensive, racist, and divisive: "We have endorsed perversion and called it an alternative lifestyle. . . . We have exploited the poor and called it the lottery. . . . We have rewarded laziness and called it welfare. . . . We have killed our unborn and called it choice. We have shot abortionists and called it justifiable" (from Wright's address, quoted in *Omaha World-Herald*, May 1996, p. 6). Internet chat rooms and web pages became places to debate the substance of the prayer as the mass media focused on the process of conflict.

The example illustrates support for the well-understood proposition that free expression appears to depend on self-interest and political concerns. If the speech conflicts with an individual's political or ideological position, then he or she is likely to oppose it. As the planet Earth enters the twenty-first century, the value of free expression is being challenged when the speech in question is objectionable to some. We seem to lack legal or social theories to help guide us through free-expression challenges, such as those involving hate speech, speech that attacks certain groups of people, or harassment, which is unwanted communication targeted at an individual who seeks to be left alone.

At the University of Wisconsin–Madison, where a campus speech code had been in place for seventeen years, a committee moved to narrow limitations on faculty expression in the classroom. But political science professor Donald Downs argued that a professor's speech should have to be more than thoughtless and insensitive to merit punishment: "[The words] should, at least, be harmful and derogatory" (*Chronicle of Higher Education*, October 2, 1998, p. A-14). Some had chided the harassment policies as an outgrowth of political correctness. Although no faculty member was ever punished under the rules, the code was used as a mechanism by which students could lodge complaints. It allowed for discipline against those on campus who made "racist or discriminatory comments," who demeaned others because of race, gender, origin, disability, or sexual orientation, or who intimidated others. A federal court refused to endorse the proposition that hate speech is unprotected by the First Amendment. Thus, the modern courts have consistently sided with a broad interpretation of First Amendment free expression. Normative declarations, however, fail to identify the social limitations of free expression.

That social conditions have an impact on the definition of free expression must be understood. It has already been noted that the so-called marketplace of ideas, on which much First Amendment thinking rests, has tended to be defined in the limited competition of a few major media players (Entman, 1989). In the case of news, for example, a "politics of illusion" dominates the landscape: "Dominant political images when acted upon can create a world in their own image—even when such a world did not exist to begin with" (Bennett, 1996, p. XV). The coming of the computer age has posed the threat that those with and without virtual communication will be in danger of "increasing isolation" (p. 218). And isolation itself can limit free expression. M. Parenti (1996) noted that free speech is "interpersonal behavior" that cannot be "detached from the socio-economic reality in which it might find a place" (p. 82). He argued that free-speech rights are the product of a "class struggle" in the country (p. 87): "Like other freedoms, free speech is situational. It exists in a social and class context, which is true of democracy itself . . . it is a dynamically developing process that emerges from the struggle between popular interests and the inherently undemocratic nature of wealthy interests" (pp. 87, 89–90).

Computer-mediated communication therefore involves social experimentation in free expression: "Social isolation becomes a difficult proposition for any contemporary community" (Jones, 1998, p. 17). It is often assumed that computers "break down boundaries" or "break down hierarchies" in cyberspace, "and yet computers can just as easily create boundaries and hierarchies" (p. 27). It is not well understood that the right to speak carries with it no guarantee of being heard in the marketplace. This becomes particularly clear in the case of the World Wide Web. Home pages may attract millions of computer users or barely any. The social utility of the information and entertainment is one factor; links to and from popular sites is another; and the listing or promoting of some sites by search engine software companies is still another. As the Internet matures, it remains to be seen whether it will follow the historical path of radio broadcasting in the United States. Amateur radio run by experimenters tended to fade away and become marginalized as the professional class defined the new industry. As the number of players in the industry was limited by professional considerations, the government defined conditions through a regulatory structure. Major players in the new industry sought protectionist governmental regulation. The few individuals who wanted to broadcast outside the ruling structure were labeled by government as "pirate" radio operators, and they faced legal and economic sanctions (Yoder, 1996). Still, many continued to operate "underground" in defiance of licensing procedures.

In speaking of the traditional mass media, we use the gatekeeping metaphor because only a small number of stories are selected as news and make it beyond the editors' closed "gates" (Shoemaker and Reese, 1996). Scholars in the field of media sociology make the case that the behavioral routines of news workers are important in understanding what is seen by the public. However, the Internet seems different in this regard because each of us can become a publisher. Ideas, then, are "out there" for immediate access by any computer user, but they may be withdrawn if they are subject to legal, social, political, or economic pressures. The gatekeeping on the Internet has more to do with how people find information through popular search engines such as Yahoo! or Lycos. "Hot" sites promoted by search engines are more likely to succeed: "No links = no hits = no ad dollars" (Wall Street Journal Reports, 1997). The *Wall Street Journal*'s special report on the Internet noted that some sites are rejected because they do not conform: "We don't want to compromise the integrity of the listings for users," said Yahoo's Andy Gems (Wall Street Journal Reports, 1997).

The extent to which the Internet deserves broad First Amendment protection rests, in part, on legal definitions of whether cyberspace communication should be considered print broadcast, a common carrier, or another form of speech.

The Internet as Print and Broadcast

Historical divisions between print and broadcast media come from government regulatory policy and court decisions upholding the notion of "scarcity" in broadcasting (*NBC v. U.S.*, 1943). Because no two individuals can use the same broadcast channel at the same time in the same location, the Federal Communications Commission (FCC) allocates frequencies to those licensees who propose to serve the public interest (Rowland, 1997), and records of proven performance guarantee a "renewal expectancy" to those who follow the rules. But no such system exists in print media. The paradigm has led to one line of legal thinking that supports the regulation of broadcasters (*Red Lion v. FCC*, 1969; *FCC v. Pacifica Foundation*, 1978; *Sable Communications v. FCC*, 1989) and another line of legal thinking that provides broad freedoms for newspapers and other printed forms (*New York Times v. Sullivan*, 1964; *Tornillo v. Miami Herald*, 1973; *Telecommunications Research & Action Center v. FCC*, 1987). So, though it has been legal to coerce broadcasters to be "fair," to provide time to legally qualified candidates for public office, and to avoid "dirty words," no such prohibitions have existed in the print media world.

To the extent that courts would be willing to treat Internet content as broadcasting, newspapers might face new limitations. D. R. Sheridan (1997) suggested that under indecency provisions of the Communications Decency Act, a newspaper "could have been held criminally liable for publishing indecent material in its electronic version that it could otherwise run with impunity in its print version" (p. 149, n. 15). He concluded that technological differences in electronic and print communication do not justify separate legal treatment. J. Wallace and M. Green (1997) argued that CDA proponents sought to extend broadcast regulation models to the Internet: "Supporters of the CDA argued that, though the Internet might lack scarcity, it was pervasive as required by the Court in *Pacifica*, and therefore its content was subject to government regulation" (p. 732). As will be shown later in this volume, the courts, to date, have opted for a legally open Internet despite political pressures to do otherwise.

Political Considerations of Internet Regulation

The attempts by a majority in Congress to embed indecency prohibitions into the law of cyberspace continued to be grounded in the old argument about protecting children (Field, 1997). These efforts appeared to be politically motivated, with the goal of attracting national media attention. For example, by one account, former Nebraska senator James Exon put the CDA ball into motion after watching a television account of Internet problems: "In 1994 NBC's news program *Dateline*, NBC aired a story concerning online pedophiles. . . . Senator James Exon's reaction to this program was the stimulus for what would become the CDA. . . . Although initial attempts to regulate online communications stalled, the idea found new life when a general overhaul of the telecommunications act began" (Dublinske, 1997).

As L. J. McKay (1996) noted, attempts by lawmakers to regulate in response to mediated reality can produce shortsighted cures: "Although the protection of children is certainly a valid purpose, the Communications Decency Act seems to have been approved in response to the public attention given to the issue. Such attention did not, however, consider the numerous alternatives to dealing with pornography on the Internet" (McKay, 1996, p. 502).

To treat the Internet as a print media means that individual Internet publishers, with little economic investment, may exercise wide free expression. However, legal or governmental freedoms provide no social guarantees. These forces may check free expression in complex and unseen ways.

Political Considerations in Understanding Free Expression

It can be said that all speech, such as that which might be defined as "indecent" by broadcast regulators and the courts (including the comedy of Howard Stern), has some political value to somebody (Lipschultz, 1997). In the broadcast context, the courts have been willing to support a channeling of "indecent" material to late-night hours when children are less likely to be in the audience (*Action for Children's Television v. FCC*, 1988). The courts have repeatedly found that political speech is the most worthy of protection, and the Federal Communications Commission has been unable to regulate indecency on the broadcast airwaves (*Action for Children's Television v. FCC*, 932 F.2d 1504, D.C. Cir. 1991, *cert. denied*, 503 U.S. 913, 1992; *Broadcast Indecency*, 8 F.C.C. Rcd. 704, 1993).

"Libelous" speech—speech that damages an individual or business reputation—can come from news stories, commercial speech, or Internet chat. In the most important legal interpretation of free expression, the U.S. Supreme Court in *New York Times v. Sullivan* (1964) upheld the newspaper's right to publish editorial advertisements: "It made it clearer than ever that ours is an open society, whose citizens may say what they wish about those who temporarily govern them" (Lewis, 1991, pp. 7–8). The opinion provided the same rights to the newspaper as were afforded to all citizens—what Justice William Brennan termed the "citizen-critic of government" (Lewis, 1991, p. 215). Such legal rights might become important as more people become their own publishers of web pages, news group postings, and e-mail exchanges on the Internet. But a legal right to speak is not free expression: It only creates an opportunity for such expression. And a right to criticize government is something short of a right to openly challenge corporate power and influence.

Despite a string of legal rulings since the 1960s that promote free expression as a core value in the United States, other forces are at work. In one descriptive set of accounts, writer Nat Hentoff (1992, p. 17) stated that "censorship—throughout this sweet land of liberty—remains the strongest drive in human nature, with sex a weak second." The point is that people seem willing to limit free expression when it does not serve their personal interests. What has been missing in the anecdotal accounts of limits on free expression is a linkage to those social theories that help explain why people behave as they do. Such an approach might predict that users of the Internet who once felt free to speak out will be less inclined to do so as the medium matures and becomes mainstreamed and as corporate and commercial powers exert more influence over it. At the very least, the maturation of the Internet means it is more likely that society's powerful will be aware of what is being said. What was once the province of a few on the leading edge of cyberspace has now become a main street. Only a few short years ago, it was uncommon for corporate managers to understand or use the Internet. Now, they recognize it as a tool to maintain their power bases. Any employee who does not take account of this fundamental change would risk his or her work life by using the Internet to speak out against the status quo.

The Trouble with Traditional Legal Thinking

Traditional legal perspectives on First Amendment theory are concerned with the doctrine of free expression and the interpretation of various aspects of the law (Emerson, 1966). Most come away from the normative legal exercise less than satisfied: "This failure to develop a satisfactory theory of the First Amendment is hardly surprising. The issues are controversial and the problems complex. The Supreme Court did not seriously commence the task of interpretation until a few decades ago, beginning with the *Schenk* case in 1919" (pp. VI–VII).

More than normative questions of social values, it is those controversial and complex issues and problems, I argue here, that are at the heart of the meaning of free expression; after all, free speech is grounded in societal notions of egalitarianism, justice, and fairness (Rescher, 1995, pp. 24–25). In one view, the concept of justice can be divided: "There is justice in the narrow sense of fairness, on the one hand, and on the other, justice in the wider sense, taking account of the general good" (p. 25). Freedom of expression in the Internet age is interpreted through what has been collectively assigned as "right" or "wrong." However, in a pluralistic culture, we may well fail to agree on such objectified standards. Thus, the courts and the culture float at sea without normative bearings. The value of free expression nonetheless appears to be fundamental to democratic thinking, and this high ideal has been central to the decisionmaking of most courts.

In the division of scarce public resources, including the time that our mass media consume, a simple fair-and-equal distribution may not lead to a wider just result. For example, in the business of journalistic news decisionmaking, all sources do not have something to say. T. I. Emerson (1970) argued that "to some extent [free expression] involves the right to remain silent" (p. 3). Similarly, many of those who want to speak offer only nonsense, repetition, or dull expression. Therefore, some contend that not every speaker is entitled to have equal access to the power of the mass media. Journalistic values—grounded in economic survival and prosperity—systematically ignore ideas that do not fit preexisting news patterns, themes, and conventions. Emerson found that individual free-expression rights must be "reconciled" with equal opportunities for others. If he was correct, the government must both hesitate to interfere with free expression and, at the same time, attempt to promote and encourage it (pp. 3–4). But more than that, social theory tells us that it is difficult for government to remove itself from the vast economic interests of the private-sector economy. The global, corporate world of the digital age operates under its own set of moral and ethical rules. Speech must navigate the choppy waters of that environment or risk being sunk or beached, and this is particularly true for the individual in postmodern society.

J. Cohen and T. Gleason (1990) found that individual rights were a twentieth-century invention. Before the 1900s, the law sided with the larger public good and limited free expression accordingly (p. 29). In a global and technologically driven world, however, it is unclear where the classic individual-public dichotomy falls. There are two countervailing forces at play: (1) the immense power of huge corporations that control many of the means to use mass communication and telecommunication tools in free expression, and (2) the ability of the computer-based tools of telecommunication, such as the Internet, to liberate individual free expression at a global level. Some would suggest the government (or, more specifically, the courts) must protect free expression. It can be argued that "the ultimate safeguard of the right to speak freely may not lie with the courts, but with the vigilance of the individual citizen who understands the value of free expression and the complex application of the First Amendment in the American judicial process" (Cohen, 1989, p. 120). Free expression is a concern that transcends national borders, and even within the borders of a modernized country, it is limited by people who are not adequately educated about the significance of expression in a free society.

One empirical model of free speech divided "protected" from "unprotected" speech (Van Alstyne, 1984, p. 35). The model proposed the measurement of two variables—the probability of a dangerous event and the gravity of "evil"—and this idea, originating from Judge Learned Hand, has been quoted by the U.S. Supreme Court (*Nebraska Press Assn. v. Stuart*, 427 U.S. 539, 562, 1976). A range of free-expression protection by subject has been proposed in which political candidates and issues would be at the core and pornographic and criminal expressions would be at the edge or fringe. Still, W. W. Van Alstyne concluded that American legal scholars have not "reconciled the interpretive difficulties" of free expression (p. 90).

For some, the answer is simple: Freedom of speech should be absolute. These thinkers argue that speech must be separated from harmful behavior that is open to punishment. For example, disseminating child pornography would not be regulated as a matter of speech but rather as a criminal behavioral act. Violent acts and not "fighting words" would be open to suppression. And terrorism or sedition would be punished rather than the speech involved in a subversive movement. For others, the rights of the larger public remain more important than those of any one individual. From this perspective, balancing theories emerge. It is left to the courts to define the standards of public interest.

The Role of Social Theories in Understanding Free Expression

The need for free expression is grounded in concerns about the individual in a modernized, postindustrial world. MIT professor Daniel Lerner confronted the problem of perceiving our reality through mediated communication:

> The mass media, by simplifying perception (what we "see") while greatly complicating response (what we "do"), have been great teachers of interior manipulation. They disciplined Western man in those emphatic skills which spell modernity. They also portrayed for him the roles he might confront and elucidated the opinions he might need. . . . There now exists, and its scope accelerates at an extraordinary pace, a genuine "world public opinion." This has happened because millions of people, who never left their native heath, now are learning to imagine how life is organized in different lands and under different codes than their own. That this signifies a net increase in human imaginativeness, so construed, is the proposition under consideration (Lerner, 1996, p. 328).

Socially constructed reality, whether "virtual reality" or "pseudocommunity," involves a ritual view of communication in which information sharing and understanding form the basis for development of critical perspectives. "The manner in which we seek to find community, empowerment, and political action all embedded in our ability to use CMC is troubling. No one medium, no one technology, has been able to provide those elements in combination" (Jones, 1998, pp. 15–21, 30). From a free-expression perspective, literacy and urbanization are factors in understanding communication.

Although it is fair to say that the term *postindustrial* falls short in explaining the current state of affairs, it is clear that social theorists have attempted to talk about trends such as an increased emphasis on the service economy, computer automation, and the decline of patriarchy (Block, 1990). Of particular interest here is the role that computers play in requiring people, particularly employees, to pay more attention to and concentrate harder on the screen. Likewise, computer users in the home may spend inordinate amounts of time in interpersonalized communication mediated through the computer. Under these circumstances of modernization, questions of social structure, social relationships, and social integration naturally surface (Calhoun, in Bourdieu and Coleman, 1991). Craig Calhoun argued persuasively that what has emerged are "imagined communities" furthered by mass media (p. 111). Information is passed, not as more rational, but rather legitimated by the media. He concluded that such information is "as dubious and untested as medieval myth" (p. 113): "Such tradition may appear more rational and may even offer a seemingly democratic sort of access. But it also enhances the oligopolistic character of the elite of message senders and removes most people from direct participation in—and therefore shaping of—the passing on of such traditions" (p. 113).

Calhoun's criticism was focused on television, but it is fair to say that our current preoccupation with the possibilities of the Internet is really no different. We may speak to people who wish to listen on the web, but political participation is in no way activated by this type of free expression. In the end, neither the free expression on the web nor the grassroots interpersonal communication of neighborhoods seems to matter much politically *unless* the movement gains status by attracting the attention of the traditional mass media.

C. Wright Mills (1963) would have suspected that such media attention would be the product of elite manipulation:

> The top of modern American society is increasingly unified, and often seems willfully coordinated: at the top there has emerged an elite whose power probably exceeds that of any small group of men in world history. The middle levels are often a drifting set of stalemated forces: the middle does not link the bottom with the top. The bottom of this society is politically fragmented, and even as a passive fact, increasingly powerless: at the bottom there is emerging a mass society (p. 38).

Although it can be argued that the elite do not "own" the Internet as Mills contended they owned other mass media (p. 226), the cultural conventions of the web are increasingly uniform and materialistic. Modern social conditions of rootlessness, impersonal relations, mobility, and the decline of family—all of which Mills (p. 333) identified—offer fertile ground for "imagined communities" in cyberspace that may distract the mass public rather than liberate it. The popular tendency to equate public opinion (and its presumed influence on elite decisionmaking) with the aggregate of individual opinions (Glasser and Salmon, 1995), as may be expressed in cyberspace, seems problematic in an age in which functional illiteracy and uninformed opinion are widespread.

What is remarkable, then, about the *Reno v. ACLU* case is the *reflex optimism* of both the district court and the U.S. Supreme Court for the use of the Internet as a democratic tool of free expression.

The Challenge to the Communications Decency Act: *Reno v. ACLU*

The case of *Janet Reno v. American Civil Liberties Union* (1997) is instructive in defining the current state of free-expression law in the age of the Internet. Following passage of a law to "protect" minors from "indecent" and "patently offensive" material on the Internet, a special three-judge district court had struck the measure down as unconstitutional (929 F.Supp. 824, E.D.Pa. 1996). Both the lower court and the U.S. Supreme Court were impressed by the rapid growth of the Internet, for there were nearly 10 million host computers by 1996, two-thirds of which were in the United States, and it was estimated that 200 million people would use the Internet by 1999:

> From the publishers' point of view, [the Internet] constitutes a vast platform from which to address and hear from a world-wide audience of millions of readers, viewers, researchers, and buyers. Any person or organization with a computer connected to the Internet can "publish" information. Publishers include government agencies, educational institutions, commercial entities, advocacy groups, and individuals. Publishers may either make their material available to the entire pool of Internet users, or confine access to a selected group, such as those willing to pay for the privilege. "No single organization controls any membership in the Web, nor is there any centralized point from which individual Web sites or services can be blocked from the Web" (521 U.S. 844, p. 853).

The use of the word *publisher* by the Court seemed to indicate a willingness to accept the print media First Amendment model for the Internet at

the same time that the scarcity rationale created for broadcasting continued to be applied to other new technologies such as direct broadcast
satellites (105 F.3d 723, D.C.Cir. 1997). Concerns over children's access to
"indecent" Internet material were weighed against the promise that parents would soon be able to use effective blocking software if they wished
to do so. The Telecommunications Act of 1996 was seen as a way to dereg-
ulate the marketplace so that new technologies could compete (Pub.L.
104-104, 110 Stat. 56). The Supreme Court cited (p. 863, n. 30) the lower
court's insistence on the lack of government intrusion into the Internet
because of four communication characteristics:

> First, the Internet presents very low barriers to entry. Second, these barriers
> to entry are identical for both speakers and listeners. Third, as a result of
> these low barriers, astoundingly diverse content is available on the Internet.
> Fourth, the Internet provides significant access to all who wish to speak in
> the medium, and even creates a relative parity among speakers (929 F.Supp.,
> p. 877).

If Judge Stewart Dalzell of the district court was correct, the Internet
might be "the most participatory form of mass speech yet developed,"
and it should be guaranteed "the highest protection from governmental
intrusion" (pp. 873, 883; also quoted in *Reno v. ACLU*). Though well intended, this simplistic thinking ignored the power of nongovernmental
intrusion by corporate and other entities, as the antitrust case against
computer software giant Microsoft has demonstrated. The Supreme
Court generally employed a strictly legal analysis, holding to the distinctions between radio and dial-a-porn telephone calls that it had drawn in
Pacifica and *Sable*. The *Reno v. ACLU* decision, in contrast, seemed to fashion medium-specific deregulation for the Internet: "Most Internet fora—
including chat rooms, newsgroups, mail exploders, and the Web—are
open to all comers" (p. 880). Justice John Paul Stevens's majority opinion
ultimately employed no First Amendment theory in the decision. Justice
Sandra Day O'Connor's partial dissent rested on zoning law: "Cyberspace is malleable. Thus, it is possible to construct barriers in cyberspace
and use them to screen for identity, making cyberspace more like the
physical world and, consequently, more amenable to zoning laws" (p.
880). Justice O'Connor, in fact, argued that cyberspace was making the
transition from an unzoned to "an extraordinarily well zoned" place. She
seemed to view such zoning through Internet controls as a good thing
and was concerned that zoning had not come to all corners yet. According to such a view, it is adults, not children, who need their rights protected—at least when it comes to the right to be indecent in cyberspace.

As will be discussed later in this book, new efforts aimed at regulating the Internet by identifying users have been advanced, and the courts have weighed in to invoke the First Amendment against such attempts. In October 1998, the Child Online Protection Act was attached to the government's omnibus spending bill, but the American Civil Liberties Union (ACLU) immediately challenged its constitutionality and won a preliminary injunction against the CDA II law. U.S. District Judge Lowell A. Reed Jr. wrote: "Perhaps we do minors of this country harm if First Amendment protections, which they will with age inherit fully, are chipped away in the name of their protection" (*American Civil Liberties Union, et al. v. Janet Reno,* United States District Court for the Eastern District of Pennsylvania, Memorandum, Civil Action No. 98-5591, February 1, 1999).

The Implications for Free Expression

There are no doubt more than two views of the digital revolution. One paradigm suggests that the remarkable technology will lead to communication breakthroughs by giving anyone with something to say a place to speak; clearly, the U.S. Supreme Court accepted this notion in *Reno v. ACLU.* An alternative paradigm is the much darker view that the new technology is simply another powerful means of manipulating the masses through the control of information and entertainment. This alternative offers the possibility that people are being led to believe freedom of expression is expanding while, in fact, it is contracting. The web, with all its potential, might turn out to be a rather uniform world in which messages must conform to the constraints of the medium—whatever they may become. One likely requirement to be "heard" by the public is that the commodities of "fame" and "celebrity" are employed by the web site (McQuail, 1994, p. 382). Such is the case with the telecommunication changes forged in the 1990s, which have rarely been assessed in terms of the merits of the First Amendment (Graber, 1997, p. 406). Still another middle-ground view is that the technology represents some degree of social change but not the dramatic change implied by futurists.

Focusing Social Understanding of Free Expression

We need to resist the temptation to be awed by the possibilities of the new technologies and instead see them for what they are—tools of human communication. As J. Carey and J. J. Quirk (in Carey, 1992) remarked, diverse futurists at the end of the twentieth century took on a religious dimension, just as individuals living at the dawn of industrialism or the Enlightenment period had:

What brings together this anomalous collection under the banner of the electronic revolution is that they are in a real sense the children of the "eighth day," of the millennial impulse resurfacing in response to social crises and technical change. They have cast themselves in the role of secular theologians composing theodicies for electricity and its technological progeny (Carey and Quirk, in Carey, 1992, pp. 114–115).

As with previous "gee-whiz" phenomena (radio, television, cable), our thinking should not be guided by the newness of the hardware, the speed or capabilities of the transmission lines, or the amusing nature of the marketing of the equipment—all of which have historically been of benefit to the "companies that presided over the new technologies" (Carey and Quirk, in Carey, 1992, p. 129). Free-expression thinking, rather, must address a hard question: Does any of this really change the ability of people to speak out *and* participate in a democratic sense? If we cannot answer affirmatively, then we must ask to what extent the elites utilize technology as a means of social control. If the powerful seek social control through communication technology, then we must wonder what they seek beyond money and the satisfaction of greed in its own right. Where, then, does free expression find itself in the age of the market and the consumer? We cannot answer that question without first noting that "hearing must be secured in a language of democracy that is demythologized and in which political words are again joined to political objects and processes" (pp. 140–141).

It has been argued here that social, political, and economic concerns should be merged with thinking about free expression in a digital age. In a sense, what is happening is that the traditionally "passive" mass media forum is being replaced by a more diverse and interactive one (Pool, 1990, p. 240). The political issue is whether this hyperdiversity will ultimately promote a disintegration of common bonds.

Free expression is a social issue because mass communicators embed social meanings into content (Berkowitz, 1997) and because technological innovation will continue to shape communication (Kaniss, 1991).

Politics is at issue for two reasons:

1. Government regulation of media technology is a political process impacted by a variety of forces inside and outside political institutions (Krasnow, Longley, and Terry, 1983), and
2. the tools of media technology are used as political weapons, as was the case when Internet gossip columnist Matt Drudge broke the story of an alleged affair between President Clinton and a White House intern (http://www.drudgereport.com, January 21, 1998) while *Newsweek* magazine held it, they said for one week, to gather more evidence.

Finally, economics is relevant because communication is altered by the market-driven nature of the economy (McManus, 1994). The First Amendment means that the government cannot mandate "quality" or a "healthier information diet" (p. 211). A bottom-line issue to be investigated is the potential for the Internet to be useful in altering existing democratic models of media driven by notions of market, advocacy, and trustee; even in the push for "civic" or "public" journalism, power remains in the hands of a few editors—the public is considered but not fully included in the process:

> Public journalism, in other words, stops short of offering a fourth model, one in which authority is vested not in the market, not in a party, and not in the journalist, but in the public. Nothing in public journalism removes power from the journalists or the corporations they work for. There are ways to grant the public greater authority in journalism. There are ways, in a sense, to democratize the practice of journalism (Schudson, 1998, p. 138).

Beyond the transformation of journalism itself, the Internet offers the *promise* of a new public sphere—one where ordinary people can take part in public dialogue. As will be shown, however, that promise is clouded by the realization that access to the new technology is not equal across class, race, and social groups. Moreover, access alone does not guarantee that an individual will have a say in a world flooded with messages that demand to be sorted, edited, and limited. Communication is contextual and influenced by other individual social and economic concerns.

The challenge for us is to see concepts such as the marketplace of ideas, social responsibility, and the public interest in light of social, political, and economic factors. If we do this, it will follow that new technologies such as the Internet may not fundamentally change the current balance of power. However, to the extent that the technology breeds new lines of communication and to the extent that interaction activates meaningful exchanges, group collaboration and evolutionary social change are possible. For example, in an increasingly mobile society, an extended family might use e-mail to adapt to the problems of social distance and rediscover each other through communication. Free expression, therefore, must be understood as a function of the speaker and the listener and their inclination to do anything beyond speech itself.

The discussions in this book will begin with normative concepts of free expression, such as the marketplace of ideas and its historical roots (Fraleigh and Tuman, 1997), and then challenge what *ought* to be with what has developed in a technological age in which time and space are altered (Wise, 1997). The Internet has cultural, political, and economic implications (Barrett, 1997). And the "virtual culture" or "cybersociety" of computer-mediated communication further suggests a blurring of tradition (Jones, 1998 and 1997). In such a world, free expression is altered as the technology leads to an entirely new language and communication form (Ihnatko, 1997). Rather than being bound by geography and nationalism, Netizens experiment with a "participatory global computer network" (Hauben and Hauben, 1997, p. 3). However, individuals in a modern or postmodern culture are not assured broader freedoms, because "cultural flows of information have swallowed up private space" (Stevenson, 1995, p. 157). So it is the contradictions about normative, legal, technological, and social-cultural perspectives that will drive this study of free expression in the age of the Internet.

Chapter Summary

This chapter introduced important notions, such as the significance of social conformity in understanding the boundaries of free expression in a digital age. It was argued that the Internet should be looked at through historical, social, legal, political, and economic windows. The optimism people have for the Internet was contrasted with the critical views of some who see the mass media as tools for the powerful.

Discussion Questions

1. Under what circumstances would you be willing to use the Internet to speak out against an employer, neighbor, or friend? What personal limitations of free expression exist for you?
2. Do you believe *all* ideas belong on the Internet? Are there any ideas that are too dangerous to be spread?
3. How influential are search engines in determining what you know about material on the Internet? How do you find out about new sites? How do major corporations such as Microsoft influence free expression?
4. Does the government have any business protecting children from pornography on the Internet? What about schools and parents?
5. Do you reside in any imagined communities online or elsewhere? What value does virtual reality have in a postmodern society?
6. Do you believe the Internet liberates us from the powerful or brings us under tighter social control? It has been said that the Internet in 1998 helped elect Minnesota governor Jesse "The Body" Ventura, a former professional wrestler. Can this be seen as empowerment?

2

A Historical Look at Traditional Legal Thought on Free Expression

"In the time before written history, it is doubtful that humans imagined themselves as individuals, with their own unique personalities."
—**Douglas M. Fraleigh and Joseph S. Tuman,**
free-expression scholars (1997)

"I have often regretted my speech, never my silence."
—**Publilius Syrus, philosopher (circa 100 B.C.)**

"The chiefs . . . shall be mentors. . . . The thickness of their skins shall be seven spans . . . they shall be proof against . . . criticism."
—**The Great Law, Iroquois (circa A.D. 1450)**

"Government became involved early, implementing a system of licensing in 1520 [to] preview material, thus controlling both content and distribution."
—**Paul E. Kostyu, media law researcher (1998)**

"Though all the winds of doctrine were let loose to play upon the earth, so Truth be in the field, we do injuriously by licensing. . . . Let her and falsehood grapple."
—**John Milton, writer (1644)**

"Every freeman has an undoubted right to lay what sentiments he pleases before the public . . . but if he publishes what is improper, mischievous, or illegal, he must take the consequences of his own temerity."
—**William Blackstone, legal interpreter (1769)**

"How do we know that the analogy of the market is an apt one? Especially when the wealthy have more access . . . how can we be sure that 'free trade of ideas' is likely to generate truth?"

—**Laurence Tribe, legal scholar (1978)**

"I am still convinced, however . . . that the theory of freedom of political expression remained quite narrow until 1798 . . . that the Bill of Rights . . . was in large measure a lucky political accident."

—**Leonard W. Levy, historian (1985)**

"From 1791 to the present . . . our society . . . has permitted restrictions upon the content of speech in a few limited areas, which are 'of such slight social value as a step to truth that any benefit that may be derived from them is clearly outweighed by the social interest in order and morality.'"

—**Antonin Scalia, U.S. Supreme Court justice (1991)**

Long before there was an information superhighway or cyberspace, traditions of free expression played an important role in social and legal thought: "Notwithstanding the modern fascination with the here and now of computers, satellites, cyberspace, and the information highway supposedly guiding us into the future, serious students of mass media must look back to their earliest roots" (Sloan and Startt, 1996, p. 1). The first writings of native peoples seem to be a logical starting point for any historical discussion, but writing grew from a long tradition of oral history: "That ability placed humans above animals and allowed them to share thoughts and feelings with others" (p. 1). But thoughts are protected only by fragile human memory, and so they are open to distortion and loss. It is known that "man-made scratchings" date to at least 400,000 years ago, and symbols are at least 135,000 years old (p. 2). Obviously, the ability to speak and record events had profound social and cultural implications: "From the earliest days of human history, communication was tied inextricably to transportation. Face-to-face communication was accomplished only when two people were in the same place. The continuation of the oral tradition of telling legends as well as the passing of current information was achieved only through travel" (Folkerts and Teeter, 1994, p. 3).

Carey (1992) identified historical contradictions of communication—"one that derives from modern advances in the printing press and transportation and one that is situated within the ancient theory and practice of the voice" (p. 6). In fact, transportation in America was seen as "communication between east and west" (p. 7). Thomas Jefferson, in Carey's view, sought to use transportation to promote communication for idealistic democratic purposes: "The technology of transport and communication would make it possible to erect the vivid democracy of the Greek city-state on a continental scale" (pp. 7–8). Today, the late-twentieth-century metaphor of the information superhighway invites the notion that communication may also be virtual transportation. The blending of transportation and communication is symbolic as a social construction of virtual geographies forged conceptually as new frontiers.

Although communication may have originated more than 2 million years ago and symbols began being used a few hundred thousand years ago, freedom of speech is considered a relatively new phenomenon:

> Imagine that you and your family are part of a nomadic band of hunters fifteen thousand years ago. The leader of your hunting pack indicates that you will move to the plains. . . . Would you challenge the orders of your leader, or would you accept the commands as part of the natural state of affairs?. . . If you lived in the days before written history, the answer . . . could be no (Fraleigh and Tuman, 1997, p. 30).

It is important to consider the oral roots of communication, but it is fair to say that the text-based Internet originally grew from written tradition. "Although writing in ancient Mesopotamia originated more than 5,000 years ago, Chinese writing has the distinction of being the oldest script which is still in use" (Sloan and Startt, 1996, p. 7). Recent findings suggest ancient Egypt may also lay claim to the earliest writings.

Writing grew from the first civilizations. The Sumerians about 3,000 B.C., who were thought to keep birth and financial records, developed the phonetic link between spoken and written language but failed to introduce an alphabet (Sloan and Startt, 1996). The people of Sumeria, located in what is now Iraq, believed in godlike kings who were not to be challenged. However, it is in their culture that the first known use of the word *freedom* has been found. The Sumerian city of Lagash dedicated a canal with text that said the king "established the freedom of the citizens" (Fraleigh and Tuman, 1997, p. 33). However, this referred to economic freedom from excessive taxation, not freedom of speech.

The Egyptians, borrowing from Sumerian thought, emerged with "sacred carved" hieroglyphic letters, hieratic "everyday" writing, and demotic "mundane" symbols (Fraleigh and Tuman, 1997, pp. 6–7). Phoenician and Greek alphabets followed. Written media are said to be about 2,000 years old: "The first systematic attempt to collect and distribute information was *Acta Diurna*, the hand-lettered 'daily gazette' posted reg-

---

Box 2.1   Egyptian Tablets May Be the Earliest Writing

Clay tablets that were found in the tomb of King Scorpion I appear to be 5,300 years old. German archeologist Gunter Dreyer told the Associated Press the writings record linen and oil deliveries—taxes paid to the king in an area that is now southern Egypt, 300 miles south of Cairo. The tablets have been carbon-dated to about 3300 B.C., which would challenge Sumerian writings as the first. The Egyptian writings are "line drawings of animals, plants and mountains . . . the first evidence that hieroglyphics used by later-day Pharonic dynasties did not 'rise as Phoenix from the ashes' but developed gradually." Researchers will continue to compare the findings at the Egyptian site with those from Mesopotamia, and it is possible that writing emerged in both locations about the same period.

(Source: Associated Press, December 16, 1998)

---

ularly in the Roman Forum between 59 B.C. and 222" (Emery, Emery, and Roberts, 1996, p. 1). The Romans received word of government actions and sporting contests, which seems to suggest a cross-cultural definition of news and public information. Distribution of written information was made possible because of technological advances by the Sumerians around 3500 B.C., which enabled them to seal symbols in clay tablets; movable type developed in Asia Minor before 1700 B.C., the Phoenicians' alphabet and the Egyptians' use of papyrus beginning around 500 B.C. (Emery, Emery, and Roberts, 1996). The Greeks, Romans, and Chinese are all credited with developing parchment writing surfaces around A.D. 100, which made books possible: "Wang Chieh published what is considered the world's oldest preserved book from wood blocks in A.D. 868. . . . Wood-block printing was introduced in Europe when Marco Polo returned from China in 1295" (p. 3). Movable type, which modernized printing, was introduced in Korea in 1241, prior to Johannes Gutenberg's introduction of it in Europe with the printing of the Bible in 1460: "William Caxton imported the first printing press into England in 1476, and by 1490 at least one printing press was operating in every major European city" (p. 3):

> The invention of movable type in Germany in the fifteenth century spurred a printing revolution that was to shatter social structures and encourage the spread of information among varied social classes. English kings and queens tried to restrain this democratization of knowledge because they feared that diversity of thought would lead to dissension. Such fears were carried to

British America in the 1600s, where British colonial officials also attempted to maintain control of information (Folkerts and Teeter, 1994, p. 5).

The business of printing would be more than an economic revolution of the marketplace: "Movable type contributed to a widespread diffusion of information that loosened the grip of the Catholic church on political, moral, and religious discussion" (Folkerts and Teeter, 1994, p. 8).

The technological drive toward free expression was coupled with changes in thinking that had allowed it to take root over the course of thousands of years. First, the Hebrews' theology that there was a direct covenant between people and their god, Yahweh, meant that law came from God through Moses, not from political leaders: "Even when the people of Israel came to be ruled by kings, the prophets (believed to be the messengers of Yahweh) often reminded officials that Yahweh was the true ruler, and they criticized the leaders for straying from God's will" (Fraleigh and Tuman, 1997, p. 35). Second, ancient Athenians went one step further in believing laws did not come from gods but rather were "of their own making" (p. 36). Debates, assembly, and comedy were allowed to cover previously restricted topics. Yet here, too, speech had its limits: "One type of forbidden speech was verbal abuse of the dead. Verbal abuse of the living was restricted *only* when it was inflicted in temples, courts, official buildings, and games.... Certain words were unsayable, and could not be used to attack the character of another person unless the charge were true" (p. 38).

Ancient Chinese also provided for free expression by reminding leaders that their right to rule came from higher sources and that the people mattered. Still, "legal philosophers countered with the claim that a strong government was necessary, because persons are selfish and can be motivated by a fear of strong punishments" (Fraleigh and Tuman, 1997, p. 42). Elsewhere throughout the world, the historical record seems to indicate that the freedom of individuals to speak varied widely based on legal, social, tribal, and religious differences. What does seem clear is that no early societies established formal structures that guaranteed free-expression rights, no matter what the wishes of a particular leader might be. The often noted European and American contributions, then, can be seen as being grounded in the more fundamental concerns over the rights of individuals that began with the Magna Carta in 1215. Considered "the cornerstone of English liberty" by most, it was forced on King John by English barons. Landowners sought rights and privileges that would not be afforded common people, but freemen for the first time were no longer under the absolute rule of the king under the language of the Magna Carta: "No freeman shall be taken or imprisoned ... or exiled or in anyway destroyed, nor will we go upon him or send upon him, except by the lawful judgment of his peers or by the law of the land." The language of the Magna Carta appears to recognize the value of both social and legal controls on individual behavior. Democratic thought, then, is not based in unlimited individual rights but rather in a system of law and social order imposed in effect, by peer norms.

Both in Europe and America, notions of individual rights and natural law questioned government authority. But though a philosophical desire to speak freely has flourished, the actual means to do so often has not been a reality. The historical significance of the Internet, as will be shown, may be that it provides a new opportunity for marginalized groups and individuals to get a message out and to do so because there are so many back alleys off the main highway; the highway is a more dangerous place because there is more traffic control on it.

It is somewhat difficult to separate social and legal thought, but in this chapter, the focus will be on legal ideas. Governments, through law, have defined free expression as a social value that is sometimes balanced against other interests. As a general rule, attempts have been made to protect an individual's right to speak at the same time that she or he may be held responsible for the effect of that expression. Implied in this is a balancing theory of free expression: "In any conflict between free speech and other social values, the weight of the speech interest is balanced against the weight of the competing interests, and the conflict is resolved under a straightforward cost/benefit analysis" (Smolla, 1992, p. 39). The shortcoming of balancing, however, is that it may lead to ad hoc determinations: "Under the pressure of the moment, there will be temptations for judges to find the harms great (or small) in particular cases" (Sunstein, 1993, p. 150).

In the United States, legal tradition grew from the common-law approach in England. There, judges "made" the law on a case-by-case basis.

Common-Law Approaches

The common law, which was distinguished in England from local law, came to be known to jurists through commentaries, or expert readings of the law at any given time. It is clear from these interpretations that those who spoke out did so at their own risk. In England, printing presses had been licensed in the sixteenth century, a stationers' company limited access to the new industry, and a star chamber pronounced guilt for those who committed, for example, blasphemy against the church:

> Under Elizabeth the government elaborated the system of prior restraints upon the press, dividing the administration of the complex licensing system among three Crown agencies: the Stationers' Company, a guild of master publishers chartered to monopolize the presses and vested with extraordi-

nary powers of search and seizure; the Court of High Commission, the highest ecclesiastical tribunal, which controlled the Stationers' Company and did the actual licensing; and the Court of Star Chamber which issued decrees defining criminal matter (Levy, 1985, p. 6).

The law reflected the ideology by offering subsequent punishment for free expression rather than imposing prior restraints on speech. D. M. Fraleigh and J. S. Tuman (1997) described the Star Chamber as "a room in England's Palace of Westminster where the King's Council met and meted out whatever punishments were deemed appropriate. The room was said to have stars painted onto the ceiling. Star Chamber proceedings were carried out in secret, and torture was one of the king's prerogatives. Parliament abolished the Star Chamber in 1642" (p. 364).

In this era, seditious libel law allowed for legal action against a speaker who criticized the king or any other officials in government. Libel could be punished as a crime because it was seen as having the potential to "provoke . . . a breach of the peace" (Fraleigh and Tuman, 1997, p. 7). In 1663, under the theory of treason, William Twyn was "sentenced to be hanged, cut down while still alive, and then emasculated, disemboweled, quartered, and beheaded" for printing a book that "endorsed the right of revolution" (p. 7). This was a standard punishment for use of words—a type of cruel sentence that was utilized until about 1720.

Parliament abandoned licensing in 1695, not because of public objection but rather because the system failed to adequately control the press. Still, without a formal licensing system, printers could explore the possibilities offered by a new world of media marketplaces—one in which news and information would be redefined: "The lapse of the licensing act in 1695 left controls by the king in place but signaled an open door for the proliferation of newspapers in London, the provinces, and the colonies. By 1704, London had nine newspapers, including a daily, that issued twenty-seven editions each week" (Folkerts and Teeter, 1994, p. 12).

The technology of the printing press would be a catalyst for social change, one that scholars associate with the dawning of the modern age:

> The spread of printing in the late fifteenth and sixteenth centuries ripped apart the social and structural fabric of the life of Western Europe and reconnected it in ways that gave shape to modern patterns. The availability of printed materials made possible societal, cultural, familial, and industrial changes facilitating the Renaissance, the Reformation, and the scientific revolution (Emery, Emery, and Roberts, 1996, pp. 3–4).

With licensing abandoned, the Crown turned to a legal system that allowed subsequent punishment for seditious libel against the government.

Prior Restraint

William Blackstone's *Commentaries on the Laws of England* during the 1765–1769 period helped define prior restraint doctrine: "The liberty of the press is indeed essential to the nature of a free state: but this consists in laying no *previous* restraints upon publications, and not in freedom from censure for criminal matter when published" (Blackstone, 1962, p. 161). The logic of the period was that a single censor could not be an "infallible judge of all converted points in learning, religion, and government." In Blackstone's widely accepted view, "every freeman has an undoubted right to lay what sentiments he pleases before the public; to forbid this is to destroy the freedom of the press, but if he publishes what is improper, mischievous or illegal, he must take the consequences for his own temerity." Therefore, the larger social good was achieved by placing responsibility in the hands of individuals. It would be somewhat more likely that individuals would challenge the order with new ideas than that a censor would allow such controversial ideas to be spread, and once available to the public, these could be judged. However, it is not clear that Blackstonian legal theory afforded any protection beyond the point of publication, even under the view of the Framers of the U.S. Constitution: "There is a major obstacle to free speech if someone who utters a criticism of the President is subject to a sentence of life imprisonment; but there is no prior restraint" (Sunstein, 1993, p. XII). Four types of expression that could be punished under common law were

- *Seditious libel*—words "designed to bring the government into dispute," which meant that truthful criticism was subject to greater punishment
- *Obscenity*—words that tended to corrupt people through "immoral influences," which meant that sexuality was taboo
- *Blasphemy*—words against the church were seen as "offenses to God," which meant that the state could inflict punishment.
- *Libel*—words against other individuals were thought to threaten peace, which meant that government would punish the offender rather than allow for retribution

The emergence of a two-party parliamentary system did not diminish the need for seditious libel trials. Under the system, truth was not a defense because the greater the truth was, the greater, too, was the libel. And if a criticism of officials was true, then it would be more likely to cause social unrest. Not until the passage of the Fox Libel Act in 1792 were juries allowed to decide what was and was not libelous.

The Framers of the U.S. Constitution reacted to the social conditions in England as the American system of free expression slowly emerged. However, "it seems clear that during the founding period, much of what we now consider 'free speech' was thought to be unprotected, and that the government could regulate much speech if it was harmful or dangerous" (Sunstein, 1993, p. XIV). Still, caution should be exercised here because the Framers were inconsistent in this regard, leading to what one scholar has termed "obstinate elusiveness of original intent in the free speech area" (Smolla, 1992, p. 28).

Not until the twentieth century did prior restraint become more fully defined. In *Near v. Minnesota* (1931), the Supreme Court concluded: "The fact that liberty of the press may be abused by miscreant purveyors of scandal does not make any less necessary the immunity of the press from prior restraint in dealing with official misconduct" (quoted in Flink, 1997, p. 22). The principle stands in opposition to the notion of government censorship, whereby censors stop information from getting out to the public: "No audience is able to assess for itself whether the material is quality or trash" (Redmond and Trager, 1998, p. 322). The *Near* case involved Jay Near, the publisher of the *Saturday Press*, who used his paper to attack the Minneapolis police chief for failing to arrest a "Jewish gangster": "Every vendor of vile hooch, every owner of a moonshine still, every snake-faced gangster and embryonic egg in the Twin Cities is a JEW," the anti-Semitic publisher wrote (Redmond and Trager, 1998, p. 323). A state law banned the newspaper from future publication, with Minnesota judges finding the content "malicious and scandalous" (Pool, 1983, p. 57). A minority of the court said freedom of the press did not include a right to be libelous, but the U.S. Supreme Court voted 5 to 4 to strike the statute down as unconstitutional. The Court left open the possibility for a narrow class of prior restraints: if national security in time of war was threatened, if publication might incite a violent overthrow of the government, and if fighting words or obscenities were published. Later analyses of the facts in the *Near* case in Fred Friendly's book *Minnesota Rag* concluded that there had been associations between Minneapolis police and organized crime figures, Jewish and not (Redmond and Trager, 1998, p. 323).

Colonial Influences

Only in recent years has it become understood that European notions of liberty flourished in America because they already existed there. "For roughly three centuries before the American Revolution, the ideas that made it [liberty] possible were being discovered, nurtured, and embellished in the growing English and French colonies of North America, as images of

America became a staple of European literature and philosophy" (Grinde and Johansen, 1991, p. XVII). The five nations of the Iroquois—the Mohawk, Onondaga, Oneida, Seneca, and Cayuga—were led by a council of chiefs who followed the Great Law: "The thickness of their skins shall be seven spans, which is to say they shall be proof against anger, offensive action and criticism" (Johansen, 1982, p. 27; Fraleigh and Tuman, 1997, p. 60). D. A. Grinde and B. E. Johansen (1991) quoted the writing of John Long to contrast Native American thought with the mindset of traditional European power groups: "The Iroquois laugh when you talk to them of obedience to kings; for they cannot reconcile the idea of submission with the dignity of man. Each individual is a sovereign in his own mind; and as he conceives he derivès his freedom from the Great Spirit alone, he cannot be induced to acknowledge any other power" (p. 16).

Thomas Jefferson held the view that the "general mass" of Native Americans enjoyed "an infinitely greater degree of happiness than those who live under European governments" (Grinde and Johansen, 1991, p. 17). Jefferson learned the ways of Indians, who, before the American Revolution, "were in the habit of coming often, and in great numbers to the seat of our government, where I was very much with them" (pp. 248–249). What has not yet been documented fully is the influence of Native American individualism on the constitutional form of government that came to include protection for the right to speak. We do know that provincial governors, including Benjamin Franklin, made alliances with Native groups, and "they returned with a taste for natural rights life, liberty, and happiness—that they saw operating on the other side of the frontier" (Johansen, 1982, p. 32).

James Madison's original language on free expression was: "The people shall not be deprived or abridged of their right to speak, to write or to publish their sentiments and freedom of the press, as one of the great bulwarks of liberty, shall be inviolable" (B. Schwartz, 1971, p. 1026, cited by Fraleigh and Tuman, 1997, p. 69, n. 67). There had been seditious libel laws in the colonies, such as the Stamp Act of 1765, and the Founders knew the importance of free expression as a political tool. Ultimately, what survived became the First Amendment:

> Congress shall make no law respecting an establishment of religion, or prohibiting the free exercise thereof; or abridging the freedom of speech, or of the press; or the right of the people peaceably to assemble, and to petition the Government for a redress of grievances.

The Iroquois, through the Great Law, already had the power to bring complaints about their chiefs, and their leaders could be removed for repeated problems (Johansen, 1982).

In looking at the way in which the new nation on the North American continent was formed, it is important to see how free expression through the press grew from humble beginnings and how social and political power was influential:

> In 1775 there were thirty-seven newspapers spread among the colonies, many of them opinionated and vituperative. Tom Paine's pamphlet *Common Sense,* which called for a complete separation from England, sold an astonishing 125,000 copies—reaching nearly everyone in the colonies who could read at the time—an estimated 60 percent of the white "citizens." Paine and others of like mind understood that the English concept of liberty was hierarchical—individual rights varied according to class, property, even location. . . . A mere change in residence might secure greater freedom (Flink, 1997, p. 21).

The European influences also can be seen in early developments in the United States. The Alien and Sedition Acts of 1798 made it criminal to "utter or publish" any "false, scandalous or malicious writings" against the government. Under the law, criticisms of the president intended to "excite" the public led to seditious libel convictions, although the law was never tested in the Supreme Court.

Throughout the nineteenth century, free expression in the United States was a matter of state law and social pressures, particularly as the antislavery abolitionist press gained steam. Events that overtook the offices of abolitionist Elijah Lovejoy's *St. Louis Observer* in 1833 were perhaps the best example of how a mob had the power to influence free expression:

> [Lovejoy's] office was stormed and his press burned down several times. He moved to Alton, Illinois, and published an abolitionist newspaper there until 1837, when he was shot and killed by an unidentified gunman who was part of a mob seeking to destroy all of Lovejoy's possessions. Lovejoy tried to protect his printing press and was known thereafter as the "martyred abolitionist" (Flink, 1997, pp. 118–119).

Less known were the years when Lovejoy fought proslavery activists who repeatedly tossed his printing press in nearby rivers. Lovejoy's *Observer* was anti-Catholic and antislavery, but his proximity to the North-South border made it difficult to practice liberty: "When a third press arrived, Lovejoy was determined to protect it, and so he armed himself; but he was nevertheless gunned down by a mob as his press went up in flames" (Folkerts and Teeter, 1994, p.179).

The end of the nineteenth century must also be understood as the era in which a technological revolution in mass media was born. The industrial revolution led to powered assembly-line printing presses, Linotype composition, free marketing through reduced taxes for rag paper, and the invention of wood pulp paper (Pool, 1983):

> The technologies and market developments that fostered the newspaper in the nineteenth century also helped magazines to proliferate. Monthlies or quarterlies could be distributed nationally by the mails, so second-class mail rates were particularly important to them. Before about 1970, subsidized postal delivery had been crucial to the economics of newspapers too, but eventually the mass commercial papers built their own metropolitan distribution networks, whereas national postal delivery remained vital to magazines (p. 20).

Technology, commerce, and market structure, it would seem, forged a powerful force: "The United States, with systems of mechanized communication and organized force, has sponsored a new type of imperialism imposed on common law in which sovereignty is preserved *de jure* and used to expand imperialism *de facto*" (Innis, 1972, p. 169).

Events in the nineteenth century raised more questions than were answered about the nature of free expression in a society whose First Amendment declared it a fundamental right. It was not until early in the twentieth century that the U.S. Supreme Court considered John Milton's concept of the marketplace of ideas, where truth and falsehood competed for acceptance. And again, technologies would make mass distribution of ideas possible, enabling them to reach groups that existed outside mainstream thought. The proliferation of printing press technology meant that it would become more difficult for the traditional powers to control free expression.

Conduct and Other Forms of Free Expression

World War I led to the Espionage Act of 1917 and amendments in 1918, and these forced the Supreme Court to begin to address the meaning of the First Amendment. A conviction for antiwar conspiracy by distributing a circular that recognized "your right to assert your opposition to the draft" was upheld by a unanimous Court in an opinion written by Justice Oliver Wendell Holmes:

> In many places and in ordinary times the defendants in saying all that was said in the circular would have been within their constitutional rights. But the character of every act depends upon circumstances in which it is done. The most stringent protection of free speech would not protect a man in falsely shouting fire in a theatre and causing panic. . . . The question in every case is whether the words used are in such circumstances and are of such a nature as to create a clear and present danger. . . . It is a question of proximity

and degree. . . . When a nation is at war many things that might be said in time of peace are such a hindrance to its effort that their utterance will not be endured (*Schenk v. United States*, 1919).

Former presidential candidate Eugene Debs found this out when he was convicted under the Espionage Act and sentenced to ten years in prison for giving an antiwar speech to Socialists in Ohio. He had said: "Don't worry about the charge of treason to your masters; but be concerned about the treason that involves yourselves." (*Debs v. United States*, 249 U.S. 211 (1919), at p. 214). The conviction was upheld in *Debs v. United States* (1919). In fact, Debs was in prison in 1920 when he again ran for president and received more than 900,000 votes.

In a surprising turn of events, Justice Holmes (joined by Justice Louis Brandeis) dissented in a conviction upheld in *Abrams v. United States* (1919). In one pro-Russian leaflet, the defendants had written: "We have more reason for denouncing German militarism than has the coward of the White House." In another, they had said: "Workers in the ammunition factories, you are producing bullets, bayonets, cannon to murder not only the Germans, but also your dearest, best, who are in Russia fighting for freedom" (p. 214). In this case, Holmes appeared to find that the government had gone too far in squelching opposing viewpoints:

Persecution for the expression of opinions seems to me perfectly logical. If you have no doubt of your premises or your power and want a certain result with all your heart you naturally express your wishes in law and sweep away all opposition. To allow opposition by speech seems to indicate that you think the speech impotent. . . . But when men have realized that time has upset many fighting faiths, they may come to believe even more than they believe the very foundations of their own conduct that the ultimate good desired is better reached by free trade of ideas—that the best test of truth is the power of the thought to get itself accepted in the competition of the market, and that truth is the only ground upon which their wishes safely can be carried out. That at any rate is the theory of our Constitution. It is an experiment, as all life is an experiment. . . . I think that we should be eternally vigilant against attempts to check the expression of opinions that we loathe and believe to be fraught with death, unless they so imminently threaten immediate interference with the lawful and pressing purposes of the law that an immediate check is required to save the country (*Abrams v. United States*, 1919).

After more than 100 years, the flame of free expression was beginning to be tested by the winds of change brought on by the urbanization and industrialization of the twentieth century. S. A. Lowery and M. L. DeFleur (1995) noted that "mass society" may be conceptualized in terms of the "master trends" that defined the early twentieth century:

- Industrialization: The factory system and corporation helped shape the social order. Social relationships "tended to be culturally rootless and personally anonymous" (Lowery and DeFleur, 1995, p. 7).
- Urbanization: As people moved to cities to work in factories, traditional family order gave way to civil and criminal law. Immigration brought unlike people together. "Trust is replaced by mistrust" (p. 10).
- Modernization: The times were marked by the development of thousands of technological innovations. This brought the diversity of goods, and the public increased its usage of mass media. "Modern societies, then, are media-dependent societies" (p. 11).

Justice Holmes's ideas would not be enacted in law for another half century. And in the interim, "the power of the thought to get itself accepted in the competition of the market" did not apply to the new medium of radio, as is evident from the court's *NBC* decision in 1943. It is ironic that at the very time free-expression theory appeared to be surfacing from the darkness, fears about the power of electronic communication were fueled by the events of two world wars.

Constitutional Impact

The print media First Amendment theory began to incorporate Milton's marketplace of ideas notion, despite concerns about idealism in a commercial age. By far the most common criticism was that the marketplace could be distorted by rich and powerful players, including those corporate owners who controlled the major mass media. The U.S. Supreme Court had established that corporations enjoy First Amendment rights, but one justice wondered aloud about the potential for abuse of corporate power: "In terms of 'unfair advantage in the political process' and 'corporate domination of the electoral process,'. . . it could be argued that such media conglomerates as I describe . . . pose a much more realistic threat to valid interests than do . . . similar entities not regularly concerned with shaping popular opinion on public issues" (*First National Bank of Boston v. Bellotti*, 435 U.S. 765, 1978, Justice Burger, *concurring*, at 797).

Legal scholars have grasped for different approaches to our understanding of free expression. In 1960, for example, Alexander Meiklejohn argued that not every citizen could be guaranteed the right to participate in a public debate; the important thing about the First Amendment was that "it intends only to make men free to say what, as citizens, they think, what they believe, about the general welfare" (p. 87). Eleven years later, Robert Bork turned to Justice Brandeis's view from the *Whitney* case to analyze four benefits from speech:

1. development of an individual's "faculties,"
2. happiness from the activity,
3. a safety valve for society, and
4. discovery and spread of political truth (Bork, 1971).

Bork argued that speech about "governmental behavior" should be protected—including so-called propaganda—but that scientific, educational, commercial, or literary speech should not. Likewise, speech that called for the violent overthrow of the government should not be protected, according to Bork.

Rodney Smolla's model centers on the marketplace of ideas metaphor and the suggestion that inequality requires government intervention because it is "biased in favor of those with the resources . . . ideas of the wealthy and powerful will have greater access to the market than the ideas of the poor and disenfranchised" (1992, p. 6). To Smolla, the idealism of the marketplace failed the test of everyday experience: "The marketplace does not seem to produce truth, not at least with any consistency, and so we are left with the nagging suspicion that good ideas have precious little capacity to drive out bad ones" (p. 6). Properly understood, Smolla's argument was that "truth" should be considered provisional, and the metaphor should be seen as an invitation to members of a democracy to participate. The idea is tied to self-governance and human dignity: "Even when the speaker has no realistic hope that the audience will be persuaded . . . even when no plausible case can be made that the search for truth will be advanced, freedom to speak without restraint provides the speaker with an inner satisfaction and realization of self-identity essential to individual fulfillment" (Smolla, 1992, p. 9). Such is the tradition of the soapbox street-corner speaker: "In this setting the First Amendment is conceived of as a shield, as a means of protecting the individual speaker from being silenced by the state" (Fiss, 1996, p. 12). However, technological media have ushered in a new paradigm in which corporate free-expression power is the main question:

> Capitalism just happens to be one among many social systems that distribute power unequally. I also think it wrong even in a capitalist context, to reduce social power to economic power. . . . But I think it fair to say that in a capitalist society, the protection of autonomy will on the whole produce a public debate that is dominated by those who are economically powerful. The market—even one that operates smoothly and efficiently—does not assure that all relevant views will be heard, but only those that are advocated by the rich, by those who can borrow from others, or by those who can put together a product that will attract sufficient advertisers or subscribers to sustain the enterprise (Fiss, 1996, pp. 16–17).

Although new communication technologies such as the Internet provide individuals with a street corner to shout from and although the American system of free expression provides a shield from government intervention, the present marketplace model in no way guarantees speakers a right to be heard on the main street of public debate. Individuals without the economic and other technological resources needed to push their way to the front and center are likely to be left in a slow lane or on the back road of the information highway. The failure of the marketplace metaphor is that it suggests a physical location for the exchange of ideas, and it also conceptualizes a single marketplace rather than a mosaic. Access to the media-dominated mass marketplace is influenced by economic forces, but there are less populated marketplaces with special interests, unknown speakers, and uncounted influences. The rise of hate speech on the Internet is just one example of such fringe marketplaces of ideas.

Justice William Douglas's dissent in the *Dennis v. United States* (1951) case defined a different boundary of free expression: "The freedom to speak is not absolute; the teaching of terror and other seditious conduct should be beyond the pale along with obscenity and immorality." He continued: "Yet free speech is the rule, not the exception. The restraint to be constitutional must be based on more than fear, on more than passionate opposition against the speech, on more than a revolted dislike for its contents. There must be some immediate injury to society that is likely if speech is allowed."

This is the essence of the clear-and-present-danger test outlined early in the century. But as J. H. Ely (1980) pointed out, the test failed to keep defendants out of prison the first three times the Supreme Court employed it. Words that mix with violence or other unacceptable conduct are problematic: "Words can be so vile or obnoxious that they prompt a physical response. Courts allow such words to be regulated but take care to ensure that governments don't trammel free expression in their efforts to protect other individual rights" (Hopkins, 1999, p. 43).

As will be discussed, the controversy over the antiabortion web site know as the Nuremberg Files centered on whether the identification of medical professionals amounted to creating a "hit list." In October 1998, the site drew a line through the name of Buffalo, New York, physician Barnett Slepian shortly after he was murdered by a sniper's bullet that came through a window in his home (Associated Press, January 7, 1998). The advocacy or promotion of illegal activities through speech walks the line between speech protected by the First Amendment and action deemed illegal by state and federal laws. In this case, identifying doctors as "baby butchers" or "child-killers" was an inflammatory use of the Internet (http://www.christiangallery.com/atrocity) that was challenged by the American Medical Association's Ted Lewers on the AMA web site:

"The AMA strongly condemns violence against all physicians and health-care workers involved in any aspect of the legal practice of medicine" (November 2, 1998). Freedom of expression is problematic, in part, because the freedom to speak cannot be completely separated from action. The most controversial speech in society is normally linked to an appeal for social change or action. The Nuremberg Files case centered on whether people involved in the web site should be subject to large civil penalties, whether a judge has the power to edit or close such a site, and whether a "hit list" (if the page was one) should be subject to prior restraint.

Twentieth-Century Approaches

As late as the Pentagon papers case, the issue of prior restraint was still open to interpretation by the Supreme Court. Referring to the only time government had tried to stop a newspaper from publishing what its staff had gathered, Justice Brennan stated, "The First Amendment tolerates absolutely no prior judicial restraints of the press predicated upon surmise or conjecture that untoward consequences might result" (*New York Times v. United States*, 1971).

Justice Brennan's opinion for the court in *New York Times v. Sullivan* (1964) seemed to define the modern era of free expression. In it, he spoke of "a profound national commitment to the principle that debate on public issues should be uninhibited, robust, and wide-open, and that it may well include vehement, caustic, and sometimes unpleasantly sharp attacks on government and public officials" (*New York Times v. Sullivan*, 1964). In a sentence, Brennan had constitutionalized libel law and eliminated the legal validity of future seditious libel notions. Clearly missing from this view of the law, however, was the idea of "social responsibility" espoused earlier in the century. Brennan's language also failed to address caustic attacks on private citizens or commercial enterprises.

Emergence of the Marketplace of Ideas

One way to think of the concept of the marketplace of ideas is as a metaphor for explaining a limited approach to government regulation of communication. In the marketplace of ideas, it is possible for individuals in a society to retain the power of choice over the words they speak and hear:

> In an economic free marketplace, such as a bazaar or swap meet, sellers are free to offer their products for sale at any price they choose. Buyers are free to accept the goods on the seller's terms, offer a lower price, or reject the

seller's wares. In a marketplace of ideas, the source of the message is the seller. She or he is allowed to express ideas to anyone who is willing to listen. The receiver of the message is like the buyer, and may freely decide to agree or disagree with the message (Fraleigh and Tuman, 1997, p. 13).

Justice Brandeis contended that the marketplace of ideas would reveal truth if ideas were given the chance to compete: "If there be time to expose through discussion the falsehood and fallacies, to avert the evil by the process of education, the remedy to be applied is more speech, not enforced silence" (*Whitney v. California*, 1927).

Criticisms of the Marketplace of Ideas

Herbert Marcuse's attack on the marketplace of ideas was based on the Marxist assumption that people are not free to speak because they are manipulated by government and monopolistic mass media; therefore, he suggested, free-speech rights should be suspended (Carter, Franklin, and Wright, 1996). Such a remedy, however, runs counter to the historical notion of free expression as a tool for individual liberty. The powerful mass media argument may be more useful in understanding why individuals who have legal rights of free expression do not use them. Other issues are the lack of public support for "press freedom" that would give special treatment to the institution of mass media and the need for the courts "to protect democracy from itself" (Fiss, 1996, p. 146).

However, classical Marxism may be theoretically useful in understanding the condition of a political economy founded on notions of private property:

> Political economy does not disclose the source of the division between labour and capital, and between capital and land. . . . Similarly, competition comes in everywhere. It is explained from external circumstances. As to how far these external and apparently fortuitous circumstances are but the expression of a necessary course of development, political economy teaches us nothing . . . we have to grasp the essential connection between private property, avarice, and the separation of labour, capital and landed property; between exchange and competition, value and devaluation of men, monopoly and competition, etc.; the connection between this whole estrangement and the *money*-system (Marx, 1844, reprinted in Lemert, 1999, p. 30, emphasis in source).

The Internet age poses new difficulties precisely because our conceptions of land and capital are sure to be altered by cyberspace. An online store may operate inexpensively and without land if the owner has the technological know-how and minimal capital required for start-up. Such a system offers the possibility for reordering wealth and thus power in the society. It is at that point that free-expression issues might reemerge. How would the new cyber wealthy exercise free speech? Would they protect their self-interests at the expense of the less fortunate?

Calls for Social Responsibility

A commission on freedom of the press in the 1940s, which argued for an increased sense of social responsibility and self-regulation on the part of mass media, also was concerned about corporate control of information dissemination and government promotion of free speech: "Law can perhaps remove some of the obstacles which dam a stream, but law cannot make the current flow during a drought" (p. 704), Z. Chafee theorized in 1947. Social responsibility theory is seen as a nonauthoritarian way to control speech (Graber, 1997). In purely legal terms, the theory has failed because media corporations have First Amendment rights (Kostyu, in Hopkins 1999).

Social responsibility seems to have no place in the Internet age because the doctrine of wide-open expression leaves no room for it. If each Internet user is left to access all available information, then it is left to her or him to decide what is or is not responsible. Concepts such as "equality" and "justice" have fuzzy meanings in an age in which norms fail and expression is entirely subjective, entirely in the eyes of the beholder (Stevenson, 1995, p. 208).

The failure of social responsibility on the Internet means that problematic speech is inevitable. The examples are numerous. Newhouse News Service reporter Sean Kirst told how University of South Carolina Psychology Department chair Jean Ann Linney has been dogged by a persistent chain letter she purportedly signed. The letter describes the dying wish of a girl named Jessica Mydek, and it claims the American Cancer Society will make a donation toward cancer research every time the message is sent along. The letter is a global hoax: "One expert told Linney this kind of hoax has a life of its own, and she may never see a total end of it" (Kirst, 1998). She has even been threatened by people blaming her for the scam.

Cyberhate is another element of the social responsibility problem. In California, a twenty-one-year-old self-described "Asian hater" was convicted on civil rights violations for sending threatening messages to fifty-nine Asian students. And racist World Wide Web sites and e-mail are common problems confronted by those seeking some regulation of cyberspace.

The Anti-Defamation League is marketing Internet filtering software that attempts to screen sites devoted to anti-Semistism, racism, homophobia, and bigotry: "If a user attempts to call up a site with objectionable

---

Box 2.2   The "Racist" E-mail

A University of Nebraska–Lincoln assistant professor of English, David Hibler, became embroiled in a statewide controversy in 1998 when his e-mail accidentally went to about 300 people. The e-mail discussed whether it was proper to use the "N word" (including "nigga"), and it used variations of the word ten different times in a paragraph. The white professor, who has a mixed-race son, claimed that he was using rap poetry to protest war: "The people of this country are being driven to a war in which black people of this country are being asked to carry a disproportionate share of that war, and it's high time somebody ask what is going on." Chancellor James Moeser publicly denounced Hibler, but he said the professor was protected by free-speech rights. Hibler was later confronted by about forty students. When his son attempted to rap an explanation, one student in the crowd said: "You get your little bi-racial butt outta the way and let your racist father talk." Hibler left the confrontation. He was later terminated on other grounds. Would you support Hibler's right to use the word *nigga* in antiwar rap? Why or why not?

(Source: Jena Janovy, "Uproar over NU e-mail drowns out explanation," *Omaha World-Herald*, February 6, 1998, p. 13)

---

content, the software displays a page that says 'Hate Zone. Access Restricted.'" (*Edupage*, November 12, 1998).

Hate groups have found an inexpensive means to distribute messages to a worldwide audience via the Internet. For example, there are Ku Klux Klan web pages that identify targets for their hate messages. And anti-abortion activists listed the names of doctors providing abortion services alongside a banner that dripped blood from tiny arms and legs, according to the *San Francisco Examiner* (Scripps Howard News Service, November 14, 1998). The Nuremberg Files web site's method of naming people involved in abortion services uses speech as a political tool in an arena that also includes violence as a practice: Planned Parenthood spokeswoman Therese Wilson told the *Examiner*, "They're not telling people at the web site in direct words to kill doctors. But I can't say I don't think they encourage that or that they don't believe it's justified." Eight jurors in Portland, Oregon, deliberated for five days before reaching a verdict that contributors to the site should pay $106.5 million in punitive damages and $500,000 in compensatory damages, although they vowed never to do so (Associated Press, February 3, 1999).

The Internet, then, is a place where all ideas appear to exist with equality as users find them with their search engines. But after surfing the web,

Washington Post columnist E. J. Dionne Jr. remained skeptical that the Internet would transform human nature: "Those biblical and Porn Web sites sit there, side by side, pointing to promises and temptations that long predate the information age" (Washington Post Writers Group, July 6, 1998).

Other Approaches

It is worth viewing the American brand of free-expression legal theory within a global context. Americans have enjoyed broader freedom of expression than people in societies with authoritarian governments, where prior restraint and cruel punishment are invoked. And among free societies, the constitutional protection of the First Amendment has often made a legal difference for Americans. On balance, the American model is a work in process. A central question is whether information technology, such as the Internet, will obliterate national differences of free expression.

Our understanding about free expression is instructed by the case of David Paul O'Brien. He and three others burned their draft cards on the steps of the South Boston courthouse to protest the Vietnam War. His action was not protected as symbolic free expression because the Supreme Court found a substantial government interest in an orderly selective service system.

The *O'Brien* test provided a useful legal construction that may be applicable in a wide range of settings. It proposed that regulation could be justified if

1. it is sufficiently justified within the constitutional power of a government,
2. it furthers important and substantial governmental interests,
3. those interests are unrelated to the suppression of free expression, and
4. the incidental restriction on speech is no greater than what is "essential" to further the government interest in regulating speech (*United States v. O'Brien*, 391 U.S. 367, 1968).

For example, applied to the Nuremberg Files web site, the burden would be heavy on those trying to restrict free expression. It would be difficult for people in the private sector wishing to silence the antiabortion voice to make a case that speech was not at the heart of the suppression or that censorship was an "incidental restriction"—one that would further the interest of protecting abortion doctors from violent extremists. It has already been held that it is not the speech of abortion protesters but rather their conduct that may be restricted when physical picketing at clinics impedes access (*Madsen v. Women's Health Center, Inc.*, 129 L.Ed. 2d, 1994, cited by Fraleigh and Tuman, 1997, pp. 274–275).

First Amendment Implications

Users of the Internet enjoy the same First Amendment protections interpreted by the Supreme Court. Criticisms of government and government officials on the web cannot be restrained, and they should be defensible under American laws of free expression. Because the technology seamlessly crosses national borders, though, government attempts to apply standards of conduct seem doomed to failure. And though the American model provides the highest protection for political speech and criticism of government, it is more restrictive than some when it comes to protection for sexual material. In both cases, the technology itself pushes the ideology of openness rather than restriction.

It is interesting to note that on the Internet today, one can find World Wide Web home pages for the Oneida and Seneca Nations. The Oneida page reads, "The Oneida Indian Nation, one of the original members of the Iroquois Confederacy, enjoys a unique role in America's history having supported the Colonies in the struggle for independence from England" (http://one-web.org/oneida/). The Oneida Nation has used the technology to try to educate the public about its role in the Revolutionary War, including facts often left out of American history books, historical reenactments, and tourist sites.

History shows us that our understanding of the meaning of free expression is in constant evolution. Because the power of ideas often has political implications, the desire to manipulate, control, censor, or distort free expression is a function of the circumstances at any given moment. In times of war or social strife, when the stakes are higher, the limits of free expression are tested. At other times, when free expression does not appear to mean as much to the larger society, dissent is tolerated. The technology does not change this fact, but it does create new conditions under which free expression is practiced.

In the case of the Internet, the openness of the technology increases the possibility that information will be disclosed, regardless of whether it is right or wrong. First, "anyone—or any business—can be a publisher of something that at least looks like a newspaper" (Fitzgerald, 1995, quoted by Smethers, 1998, p. 16). Second, online information is nonstandard and can be distributed anonymously (Ketterer, 1998). "When former reporter Pierre Salinger twice used Internet information to allege TWA Flight 800 had been shot down by a U.S. Navy missile after taking off from New York, it became clear that misinformation could be easily spread on the

TWA Flight 800 Disaster: Cover-up?

THE TRUTH ABOUT TWA FLIGHT 800

by Reed Irvine

Dr. Vernon Grose, a former board member of the National Transportation Safety Board and a staunch defender of the NTSB's claim that the crash of TWA Flight 800 was initiated by the explosion of the center wing fuel tank, underwent a complete change of mind while attending a briefing on the causes of the crash by Cmdr. William S. Donaldson and others on July 20. Dr. Gross, a former consultant to CNN on the TWA 800 crash, had been interviewed on television and radio nearly 200 times, defending the official position against its critics.

He came to the briefing, which was held to unveil a new 109-page report by Cmdr. William S. Donaldson on the cause of the crash, out of curiosity. When he left some three hours later, he told reporters that what he had heard and seen had caused him to completely change his mind. He said that he was deeply disturbed and felt that he had been misled by the NTSB. He could no longer believe the government's explanation of the cause of the crash. He made his next TV appearance that night with Bill Donaldson, this time criticizing the NTSB, not defending it.

If you didn't see Dr. Grose's epiphany reported on the evening news that night, or in your newspaper the next morning, it was because the reporters and news organizations that claim to be eager to bring you the latest important, exciting news either didn't bother to attend the briefing or, unlike Dr. Grose, were either unable to comprehend what they heard or too close minded to allow it to influence their thinking. There were TV cameras at the briefing, but none from ABC, CBS, NBC or CNN. They have all swallowed the NTSB line and don't want to be bothered with the facts.

CNN, of course, got into big trouble for ignoring the evidence in doing its notorious Tailwind story and allowing itself to be guided by the belief that the government had lied about what transpired in Laos in 1970. It spent eight months working on that ridiculous story, interviewing over 200 people. But when it comes to trying to find out what really caused the crash of TWA Flight 800, it allows itself to be guided by the belief that the government would never lie, and it is not willing to spend three hours listening to experienced aircraft accident investigators and eyewitnesses to the crash tell what they have found in their 15-month investigation and, in the case of the eyewitnesses, what they actually saw.

FIGURE 3.1   TWA Flight 800 Disaster: Cover-up?
SOURCE: Reed Irving, Accuracy in Media at http:/www.aim.org/special/Col98072.1.html

Net—a problem that has been called the Internet's Achilles heal" (Cohen, 1996, quoted by Ketterer, 1998, p. 7) (see Figure 3.1). A historical understanding of the notions of free expression is vital for those seeking guidance in the information age as communication technologies evolve.

Linguists study the connection between words and social conditions. In the Internet age, it is possible to track the popularity of words searched by online dictionaries. Merriam-Webster, Inc., has found that current events in the news tend to spike searches for words. For example, the Clinton scandal produced huge increases in online searching for the words *perjury, contrite,* and *salacious.* These were words pushed into the public mind by news coverage of the crisis (*New York Times,* December 27, 1998).

Chapter Summary

This chapter placed free expression in a historical context. The influence of legal thinkers from England and the United States, as well as the natural-law ideas of Native Americans, were explored. The digital age and Internet free expression were considered in the context of the historical struggle over the rights of individuals to speak out, to criticize their leaders, and to advocate for social change.

Discussion Questions

1. What would Thomas Jefferson think of the Internet? How would he use it?
2. Would Eugene Debs have been more successful if he could have used the Internet to spread his ideas?
3. Can you think of any situation in which the government would have a right to exercise prior restraint on the Internet?
4. How would opponents of someone like Elijah Lovejoy have tried to stop him and his abolitionist message if the slavery battle had been fought in the computer age?
5. Do you think Justice Brennan would agree that the Internet promotes debate on important public issues? Would he give it absolute protection?
6. Is there a right to publish false information on the Internet? What if that information harms people? Do Pierre Salinger and others like him have an absolute right to spread Internet gossip elsewhere?

3

Broadcast Versus Print Models of Free Expression

"The Federal Communications Commission is one of the most impor-
tant and least understood government agencies."
—*Erwin G. Krasnow, Lawrence D. Longley,*
and Herbert A. Terry, media law scholars (1983)

"This [public interest] is a vague standard . . . the FCC has rarely
been barred from acting on the ground that Congress did not autho-
rize the particular regulation. . . . Congress does from time to time
pass new legislation affecting the electronic media in major ways."
—*T. Barton Carter, Marc A. Franklin,*
and Jay B. Wright, textbook writers (1996)

"Its vague mandate under the Communications Act of 1934 and its
1996 counterpart to 'serve the public interest, convenience, and ne-
cessity' has made it difficult for the FCC to identify the objectives that
should guide its regulatory powers."
—*Doris A. Graber, political scientist (1997)*

"A . . . target [of deregulation] was the . . . FCC with its mandate to
oversee the vital and powerful communication sector. It too had to be
reined in, though anyone familiar with the industry-serving commis-
sion had to regard its alleged role as a protector of the public interest
and a scourge of the broadcasters as a fantasy."
—*Herbert I. Schiller, scholar (1996)*

"Broadcast regulation is one of the most complex areas of communi-
cation law."
—*Robert Trager, media law professor (1998)*

In this chapter, I will look at how historical notions of "broadcast regulation" might impact the future of digital communication. Even in the age of the Internet, notions such as public interest have been utilized as political and regulatory tools. In this sense, electronic media, including traditional broadcasting, have been held to different social and legal standards than mass media, which tend to enjoy wide free-expression rights under the historical First Amendment legal umbrella. As I will illustrate, however, corporate control of all media forms has diminished the importance of classic regulatory models.

Public Interest, Convenience, and Necessity

At the heart of prior legal thinking on regulation was the idea that broadcasters should serve a vague standard labeled "public interest, convenience, and necessity." By one account, lawmakers drafting the Communications Act of 1934 were struggling to define radio and borrowed the language they would use in the law from railroad regulations (Friendly, 1962, cited in Carter, Franklin, and Wright, 1996). To be sure, the words held meaning when the question was whether a rail line should be routed through one town or another: Town A might, for example, deserve a line more than Town B because it is a cultural center, and therefore, routing the line through A would be in the public interest; it might be more convenient to go through Town A because of geographic barriers near Town B, such as mountains; and getting to Town A might be more of a necessity for the public than getting to Town B. The public interest question therefore was which path represented a better use of public funds, given limited resources.

In the mass media context, however, funding for services is relatively unlimited in the private sector. The regulatory question for radio in the 1920s involved who should be given licenses. Regulation was demanded by existing broadcasters, who wanted to protect their stake in a new industry and did not want new players to interfere with and squelch less powerful signals. Thinking that had become clouded in the past hindered the regulatory process. Radio had been born as a public safety medium, for it was able to help save lives. Ships at sea, for instance, could radio to shore with distress signals and get help. We see the remnants of public safety thinking in this arena even today. Regulation was justified by the idea that public airwaves were a scarce natural resource (*NBC v. U.S.*, 1943).

The Wireless Ship Act of 1910 required all steamers carrying fifty or more persons to have a working radio and a skilled operator on board. Following the first international radio treaty, the Radio Act of 1912 was more specific: "This statute forbade the operation of radio apparatus without a license from the Secretary of Commerce and Labor; it also allocated certain frequencies for the use of the Government, and imposed restrictions upon the character of wave emissions, the transmission of distress signals and the like" (*NBC v. U.S.*, 1943).

World War I accelerated development of the new technology. In just the two-year period between 1921 and 1923, the number of broadcast stations in the United States grew from one to several hundred. But the government had set aside only two frequencies for private broadcast use:

> The number of stations increased so rapidly, . . . and the situation became so chaotic, that the Secretary, upon recommendation of the National Radio Conference which met in Washington in 1923 and 1924, established a policy of assigning specific frequencies to particular stations. . . . The number of stations multiplied so rapidly, . . . that by 1925, there were almost 600 stations in the country, and there were 175 applications for new stations. . . . The National Radio Conference which met in November, 1925, . . . called upon Congress to remedy the situation through legislation (*NBC v. U.S.*, 1943).

By 1926, the courts had restricted the powers of the secretary of commerce to limit the entry of new broadcasters, and existing stations refused to develop a workable system of self-regulation. So, Congress passed the Radio Act of 1927. Both that law and the Communications Act of 1934 avoided allocating the spectrum based on the marketplace or private property rights. Instead, the "public interest, convenience, or necessity" standard was interpreted by the *NBC* court to allow the FCC to regulate beyond technical and engineering questions. This led the court to limit First Amendment rights:

> Unlike other modes of expression, it [radio] is subject to government regulation. Because it cannot be used by all, some who wish to use it must be denied. But Congress did not authorize the Commission to choose among applicants upon the basis of their political, economic or social views, or up on any other capricious basis. . . . The right of free speech does not include . . . the right to use facilities of radio without a license (*NBC v. U.S.*, 1943).

Beyond attempting to sort out the chaos of radio interference, early radio regulators rejected license renewals for content reasons as well, despite language in both the 1927 and 1934 acts that read: "Nothing in this Act shall be understood or construed to give the licensing authority the power of censorship over the radio communications or signals transmitted by any radio station, and no regulation or condition shall be promulgated or fixed by the licensing authority which shall interfere with the right of free speech" (47 U.S.C.A. Sec. 326). In one case, the court held that denial of a license renewal was not a prior restraint on speech (*KFBK v. FRC*, 1931). As a practical matter over the years, the demand to control spectrum interference came to be used as a justification to restrict the free-speech rights of broadcasters: "Without government control, the medium would be of little use because of the cacophony of competing voices, none of which could be clearly and predictably heard" (*Red Lion v. FCC*, 1969).

The government control exercised over radio through licensing and the industry pressures to grow led to a dramatic definition of the field in the years ahead—a structural approach that would be dominated by corporate players and big business. We see a similar drama played out with each new technology, as businesses jockey to take hold of a new revenue stream. Newspapers participated in the radio revolution. Radio and network operations moved into television. Media corporations took control of cable. And these same players—companies with the resources and know-how to react quickly to industry change—are rapidly dominating the Internet. Unlike radio, however, the Internet is not affected as much by interference problems as by slowdowns during heavy traffic periods.

The rapid development of the Internet mirrored the radio example. However, time and space do not bind digital communication, and spectrum interference does not present an immediate problem. Internet slowdowns and logjams, however, will need to be addressed by the creation of a second-generation infrastructure. It is not clear if limits of access will be placed on later digital forms. Meanwhile, the quick rise of the Internet has produced a "cacophony of competing voices," and as a result, the main problem for the user is finding the one voice he or she wants to hear because the use of search engines may result in millions of computer "hits" for a single request.

Spectrum Scarcity

The earliest questions of radio regulation revolved around the issue of spectrum interference. If two stations broadcast on the same frequency, at the same time, and in the same general geographic location, there was sure to be a problem in hearing the broadcast. As AM radio used stronger transmitters to broadcast coast to coast, the likelihood of interference grew. The regulatory term *spectrum scarcity* became used to explain how the government would distribute available channels to only some by applying the public-interest standard (*NBC v. US*, 1943). In reality, the so-called scarcity was artificial because: (1) the government had taken most of the available spectrum for military, police, and other uses, and (2) existing broadcasters had an economic interest in limiting the number of new players. Yet Congress used scarcity in radio and television broadcasting as a justification "to assure that the public receives through this medium a balanced presentation of information on issues of public importance that otherwise might not be addressed if control of the medium were left entirely in the hands of those who own and operate broadcasting stations" (*FCC v. League of Women Voters*, 1984).

The socially constructed scarcity produced a value in a broadcast license reaching into the millions of dollars for even stations in the smallest markets. Consider, for example, the sale of WZNN-AM, in Rochester, New York, and WMYF-AM, in Exeter, New Hampshire. The big band, nostalgia, and stardust stations fetched $5.5 million for a Boston company that sold them to Thomas Hick's CapStar Broadcasting of Austin, Texas—a company with 173 FM and 79 AM stations (*Broadcasting & Cable*, December 15, 1997, p. 124). So, though the country now has more than 12,000 radio and more than 1,500 television stations, large group operations are still the order of the day (*Broadcasting & Cable*, January 5, 1998, p. 63). The Telecommunications Act of 1996 released broadcast owners from strict limits on the number of stations that they could operate overall and the number of stations they held in a single market (Shane, 1998). As a result of this "shifting paradigm," more than two-thirds of all U.S. radio stations operated in co-ownership with another station just two years after the new law went into effect. Individual stations and even groups of stations run by general managers came to account for small percentages on megacorporate ledgers. In such a profit-driven environment, the marketplace often left no room for free expression in the form of local radio news: "Consolidation trimmed the size of many radio station news departments. Some combined forces with new siblings. Others 'outsourced' news to services like Metro Networks or Shadow Broadcast services, pooling their news coverage with other local affiliates of the same networks" (Shane, 1998, p. 6).

Thus, radio deregulation under the guise of a free marketplace ethic did not produce an increase in the number of competing ideas. Instead, when and if local ideas were disseminated was decided as a matter of format. Without supervision by the Federal Communications Commission, owners were free to gut local news. One might, of course, blame the audience for not demanding ideas or for not noticing the paradigm shift, but it is fair to say that any listeners who were concerned had nowhere to turn to lodge a complaint. The problems of market concentration and control in radio under deregulation appeared to be magnified in the nation's smallest markets (W. Williams, 1998). These communities had fewer voices to begin with, and consolidation reduced the number of individual owners to five or six.

Licenses have become a commodity to be bought and sold as investments under this system. With most individuals priced out of the broadcast industry by the 1980s, it is no wonder that media entrepreneurs became excited about the potential of the Internet.

The Internet initially had none of the scarcity issues of broadcasting related to the use of physical space. Instead, a main issue was the power of individual computer servers. With the cost of computing power declining rapidly, the investment costs in an Internet site were relatively inexpensive—in the neighborhood of $3,000. The economic barriers to entry were much lower than for print or broadcast media—where even the poorest stations sold for several hundred thousand dollars. Initially, there was a scarcity of computer programmers who could design web pages, but online training courses and simple web authoring software eliminated that shortage.

From a regulatory perspective, the Internet was not well understood. Most of the attention in the 1990s focused on concerns about the availability of pornography to children. As a matter of free expression, this content was merely a slice of what would become available, although it accounted for much of the early pay-per-view revenue on the Internet.

There has been no effort by government to make scarcity arguments about the Internet, even though the existing network has seen a considerable slowdown in data transfer; the system at times reached capacity, resulting in no service for the user. The emphasis has instead been on funding and constructing a new high-speed network, which might both render individuals' web pages obsolete and create new barriers to entry. But without a second-generation Internet, the physical capacity of the existing network may become an issue. As more people get online, attempting to go to the same sites at the same time, unavailable servers produce the same effect as interference—loss of usable service.

Without a legal argument in terms of spectrum scarcity, the licensing of the Internet by government seems improbable. This does not mean that free expression will flower in an uninhibited marketplace of ideas on the Internet and its successors. As long as expression has social, political, and economic implications, powerful players will seek to control these new digital media forms. The digital media model, in effect, treats the Internet and beyond as we treat existing print media—all those with the money and know-how to enter and succeed in the economic market will be rewarded with a voice in the market of free expression.

Fiduciary Responsibilities and Licensing

Because the historical First Amendment tradition abhorred the idea of licensing printing presses, we have never attached a formal responsibility to newspaper editors to act on our behalf. There is, however, a social obligation that some editors refer to as the "newspaper of record"—particularly in the many one-newspaper towns across America. Likewise, editors often express their support for balanced coverage and diversity of viewpoints.

Broadcasters, by contrast, were licensed to serve a public interest that they were left to define. Because not everybody who wanted a license could have one, those who did have licenses were expected to consider the range of important public issues in a local community (*Red Lion v. FCC*, 1969). The licensing system meant that broadcasters had to document their coverage of issues in a public file that became part of the license-renewal process. If a broadcaster survived the license period (now five years for TV and seven years for radio), then renewal was nearly automatic; in fact, broadcast licensing and cable franchise rules speak of "renewal expectancy." If there were complaints, then a licensee might need to document and demonstrate how the station or stations had served the public-interest standard.

In the Internet and what will follow, there seems to be no fiduciary responsibility on the part of sites, and no speakers are licensed. Internet service providers (ISPs) have, however, come under the informal scrutiny of Congress, and some of the new industry's chief executive officers (CEOs) have been called to testify on Capitol Hill. If anything, corporate players such as America Online and Microsoft have exercised self-regulation in the area of Internet indecency. So-called blocking software offers users a sledgehammer approach to squelching potentially offensive expression, which ultimately may lead to a cyberspace environment where noncorporate speakers, particularly those with caustic speech, are shut out through software filters. This has been a blow to free expression on the Internet because it removes judgment from the hands of audience members. They become, instead, atomized members of a mass society to be programmed at, measured, and sold consumer goods.

Zoning Content

The result of screening software has been the creation of what some legal theorists see as a zoning system in which minors can be kept out of adult places. The real question for those interested in free expression is whether such zoning marginalizes many forms of speech by placing them in an information ghetto—a cyberworld where mainstream Internet suburbanites are afraid to venture. Computer warnings and blocking statements serve to make judgments for the majority of the public that is unwilling to exercise independent thought. The legal system seems to support the social, political, and economic pressures to reduce the breadth of thinking on computer-based channels of free expression.

Box 3.1 Friends University Professors Oppose Filtering Software

In February 1998, Friends University, a nondenominational Christian school of 2,700 students in Wichita, Kansas, installed "Net Nanny," a popular filtering program, to prevent campus computer users from seeing pornography. President Biff Green said that the university has a policy that bans porn on campus and that computer pornography falls in that category. Twice in 1997, all campus computer users had received e-mail with hyperlinks to racy sites, and some found themselves viewing sexually explicit images. The *Chronicle of Higher Education* reported: "Besides raising free speech issues, said Wayne Howdeshell, chairman of the sociology and behavioral sciences division, the software 'doesn't discriminate well between what is material for research purposes and what is X-rated.'" President Green said of the "Net Nanny" experiment, "We might find that we cannot keep this material out and can only warn students that they may come across something that is offensive."

(Source: Lisa Guernsey, "Professors at Friends University Object to Use of Filtering Software," *Chronicle of Higher Education*, February 20, 1998, p. A-30)

The Politics of Regulation

E. G. Krasnow, L. D. Longley, and H. A. Terry (1983) coined the phrase *politics of regulation* in explaining how control of electronic media is the product of many social-political forces. Legal and technical experts that dominated the commission membership (p. 42) have controlled the FCC throughout its history. The industry, as defined by the largest businesses, has also influenced the regulatory process. Industry leaders furthered their interests by financing lobbying groups, such as the National Association of Broadcasters. Special-interest citizens groups also exert some pressures on the FCC and its creator, the Congress. Add to this mix legislative oversight and review by the courts, and the result is a complex political structure—especially because the White House appoints FCC commissioners.

In the case of the Internet, the earliest politics of regulation played out in the Congress where the Communications Decency Act was passed and in the courts where it was struck down. The development of the existing Internet and the funding of its next generation is dependent on support of political people such as Al Gore, who was a key proponent of the technology while serving as vice president. The rhetoric behind this politics was grounded in the need to educate the nation's children by providing them access to educational sites in government and elsewhere. Free expression was not so much valued in this approach as was providing students with certified knowledge or the information that fit the logic of standardized, modern testing, assessment, and outcome models. In such models, entertainment may be as important as information because learning becomes defined by its pedagogy. Entertainment is acceptable and even promoted by the political and regulatory system as long as it does not go too far and become pornographic. The mainstream political conditions of the culture guide those who fashion laws and promote the new methods of free expression.

One sign that the Internet had matured in a political sense was the news that Robert Bork, a one-time Supreme Court nominee and conservative former appellate judge, was hired to represent Netscape and other computer companies in their antitrust effort against Microsoft. A group calling itself ProComp—the Project to Promote Competition in the Digital Age—also hired 1996 Republican presidential candidate Bob Dole (*Washington Post*, April 21, 1998). With the U.S. Justice Department engaged in a multiyear battle with Microsoft over its right to package the Internet Explorer browser with its dominant operating system, political players lined up to take part in the lobbying game that has long been familiar in broadcasting—efforts that tend to favor big business in the end. In such corporate battles the common citizens' concerns typically rank behind profit concerns. The politics of regulation raises fundamental public-interest issues, including fairness responsibilities.

Regulation of Fairness

For most of broadcasting's history, a key regulation was the so-called fairness doctrine. It said that in order for broadcasters to serve the public interest, they were (1) required to cover controversial issues of public importance, and (2) mandated to provide important contrasting views on those issues. Broadcasters unsuccessfully argued in the 1969 *Red Lion* case that the rule had a chilling effect on free speech and that it left them as second-class citizens with respect to the First Amendment. But by the mid-1980s, a marketplace orientation had taken hold at the FCC, and the commission decided the fairness doctrine was no longer needed. There was a legal dispute over whether the FCC or Congress controlled the law, but in the end, the courts ruled that the FCC could eliminate it, which it did in 1987. Congress made one attempt to reinstate the law through another bill, but President Reagan refused to sign the bill into law. Today, only bits of the fairness regulations remain under political rules at election time (Trager, in Hopkins, 1999). Deregulation allowed partisan radio talk, such as that produced by Rush Limbaugh, to become popular. In the new environment, it was no longer necessary to offer time to opposing points of view.

The Internet appeared to provide an open forum for one-sided messages, both on issues and on political candidates. Clearly, the responsibility for ensuring balance or fairness fell into the hands of the web user, which was not the case in broadcasting. But the advocacy style of Internet reporter Matt Drudge and others tested the regulators' resolve to leave the Internet unfettered. Without government regulation, web sites were free to operate much like the printers who published in colonial America.

Electoral Considerations

In the Communications Act of 1934, Sections 312 and 315 speak to the issue of fairness during elections. Section 312 states that

> a license or construction permit may be revoked "for willful or repeated failure to allow reasonable access to or to permit purchase of reasonable amounts of time for the use of a broadcasting station by a legally qualified candidate for Federal elective office on behalf of his candidacy," Sec. 312, (a) (7).

Similarly, Section 315 says that

> if any licensee shall permit any person who is a legally qualified candidate for any public office to use a broadcasting station, he shall afford equal opportunities to all other such candidates for that office in the use of such broadcasting station: *Provided*, That such licensee shall have no power of censorship over the material broadcast under the provisions of this section. No obligation is imposed under this subsection upon any licensee to allow use of its station by any such candidate, Sec. 315, (a).

Bona fide newscasts, news interviews, documentaries, or spot news are exempt under the provisions.

The Internet, in contrast, operates under no such political rules. An Internet World Wide Web page developer may cover a political campaign in a biased, partisan manner. In 1996, for example, all major presidential candidates had their own web pages, political commentators provided their interpretations on their web sites, and radio and TV stations with web pages were free to editorialize about the elections. At the same time, the lack of regulation allowed for one site to parody the White House's web page and poke fun at the First Family. The Whitehouse's whitehouse.gov site was imitated in a pornographic site with the domain name whitehouse.com. Critics claimed it would be too easy for children to accidentally visit the sex site while trying to go to the White House. In fact, the developers of racy sites have gone out of their way to seek accidental hits by using similar domain names. Sports giant ESPN, for instance, has its Sportszone on the web, but if one accidentally types espm.com instead of espn.com, a sexually explicit web site appears.

Pornography, Obscenity, and Indecency

As a general rule, the FCC has injected itself most forcefully into content decisions in the area of broadcast indecency. Shock jock Howard Stern and his station's parent company, for example, paid $1.7 million in indecency fines to clear the record on complaints of what he had said on his programs during the late 1980s and early 1990s. Although obscenity has no First Amendment protection—even on the Internet—indecency is considered protected speech, except in the broadcast context (Lipschultz, 1997). This is because of a federal statute that states: "Whoever utters any obscene, indecent, or profane language by means of radio communication shall be fined not more than $10,000 or imprisoned not more than two years, or both" (18 U.S.C.A. 1464). Although the U.S. Department of Justice has not made a practice of prosecuting violations under Section 1464, the FCC utilized the standard to hold licensees to its provisions at broadcast station license renewal.

The courts have defined broadcast indecency as that which is "patently offensive" (a discussion of sexual or excretory material) at times of the day when children are likely to be in the audience. A "safe harbor" was created between 10 P.M. and 6 A.M., during which indecent material could be broadcast (*Act III*, 1996).

The Internet is not radio communication, and Section 1464, therefore, does not apply to Internet operations. In fact, it would be impossible to apply such a standard to a global medium that knows no time of day. Because the Communications Decency Act failed in a court test and the Child Online Protection Act faces future challenges, the only limitation on speech on the Internet is that it cannot be obscene. The test for obscenity is found in the *Miller v. California* (1973) case:

(a) whether "the average person, applying contemporary community standards" would find the work, taken as a whole, appeals to the prurient interest; . . . (b) whether the work depicts or describes, in a patently offensive way, sexual conduct specifically defined by the applicable state law; and (c) whether the work, taken as a whole, lacks serious literary, artistic, political, or scientific value.

Internet content that meets all three standards of the *Miller* test can be prosecuted under state obscenity laws by a county attorney before a local jury—analogous to the prosecution of an adult book store. The difficulty of the test, however, has always been the subjective nature of literary, artistic, political, or scientific value. As Supreme Court justice Antonin Scalia has observed, such value is in the eyes of the beholder. The matter becomes a social question about what a local community is willing to tolerate in terms of free expression. For example, a Memphis, Tennessee, couple who operated a subscription-based sexual computer bulletin board service was convicted of distributing obscenity across state lines on the Internet. A jury found that the content violated *local* community standards, and the conviction was upheld (*United States v. Thomas*, 74 F.3d 701, 6th Cir. 1996).

Since local zoning laws do not yet apply to cyberspace and Internet pornography is not readily visible on the streets of a local community, it is nearly impossible to apply *Miller* to the World Wide Web. An interesting test case might involve a store that places in its front window a computer that is logged onto a pornographic web site. In that hypothetical case, a local prosecutor might go after the store owner and the Internet site. As a practical matter, however, the problematic nature of defining obscenity makes obscenity law a fairly limited restriction on free expression—especially in an American society that seems increasingly open about sexual matters. From prime-time television to news magazines to radio discussions by Dr. Laura to Internet sites where users pay to watch nude dancing, Americans are more and more accepting of sexual expression, even in crude form. So, as a social matter, the laws of indecency and obscenity do not apply rigidly, if at all. And, as many have commented, violent media content—in video games, movies, television, and simulation—is pervasive and unregulated in our society. A voluntary ratings system for television, as well as one for Internet sites, attempted only to label graphic and gratuitous violent images. Yet news stories, which are exempt from ratings, often portray a violent and bloodstained world, and the 1998 news coverage of the Starr Report investigating President Clinton was sexually explicit (as was the report itself) but was nonetheless available on commercial sites such as CNN and made public on the Congress's web site.

TRAC and the Criticisms of the Distinctions

This chapter began by distinguishing broadcast rules affecting free expression from nonbroadcast or print media First Amendment rights. It concludes with a look at excerpts from an often cited case known as *TRAC*, which was one of the first to compare print, broadcasting, and computer free expression. In this case, the court upheld the FCC decision that computer data broadcast on subchannels was not covered under political rules. It was a significant decision affecting future digital broadcast services.

Box 3.2   The *TRAC* Case

TELECOMMUNICATIONS RESEARCH & ACTION CTR. v. FCC

No. 85–1160

UNITED STATES COURT OF APPEALS FOR THE DISTRICT OF COLUMBIA CIRCUIT

255 U.S. App. D.C. 287; 801 F.2d 501; 1986 U.S. App. LEXIS 30680; 61 Rad. Reg. 2d (P & F) 330; 88 A.L.R. Fed. 527; 13 Media L. Rep. 1881

February 20, 1986, Argued

September 19, 1986

SUBSEQUENT HISTORY:

Petition for Rehearing En Banc Denied December 16, 1986.

JUDGES: Bork and Scalia, Circuit Judges, and MacKinnon, Senior Circuit Judge. Opinion for the Court filed by Circuit Judge Bork. Opinion concurring in part and dissenting in part filed by Senior Circuit Judge MacKinnon.

OPINION: BORK, Circuit Judge:

Petitioners challenge the Federal Communications Commission's decision not to apply three forms of political broadcast regulation to a new technology, teletext. Teletext provides a means of transmitting textual and graphic material to the television screens of home viewers.

The *Communications Act of 1934*, . . . requires broadcast licensees to "allow reasonable access . . . for the use of a broadcasting station by a legally qualified candidate for Federal elective office on behalf of his candidacy." In addition . . . if the licensee "permit[s] any person who is a legally qualified candidate for any public office to use a broadcasting station," he or she incurs the additional obligation of "afford[ing] equal opportunities to all other such candidates for that office." Complementing these statutory provisions, there exists a form of political broadcast regulation that the Commission created early in its history in the name of its mandate to ensure the use of the airwaves in the "public 'convenience, interest, or necessity.'". . .

The case before us presents the question whether the Commission erred in determining that these three political broadcast provisions do not apply to teletext. Because we find that the Commission acted reasonably with respect to section 312(a)(7) and the fairness doctrine, but erroneously held section 315 not to apply to teletext, we affirm in part and reverse in part, and remand to the Commission for further proceedings.

I. The technologically novel element of teletext service is its utilization of an otherwise unused portion of the television broadcast signal. Television signals are not continuous but are sent in pulses. The human eye retains the image from one pulse to the next so that the picture is perceived as uninterrupted. The time between the pulses of regular television broadcasting ("main signal" transmission) is known as the "vertical blanking interval," and can be used for pulses that constitute teletext transmission. As treated by the Commission in the docket now before us, "teletext" refers exclusively to such over-the-air transmissions, and not to transmission of text and graphics by way of cable or telephone. Main signal operators now control and operate teletext, though the FCC has authorized the operation of teletext "on a franchise basis" or through the "leas[ing] of space to multiple users.". . . The Commission, however, admonished licensees "that they remain responsible for all broadcast related teletext provided via the station's facilities, whether produced in-house or obtained from outside sources.". . .

To receive teletext, the viewer must have a device to decode the signal carrying the textual information and graphics. Currently, viewers may purchase teletext decoders in retail stores selling television sets. In the future, at least some television manufacturers will build decoding equipment into selected television models. Broadcasters of teletext thus have no control over who obtains the ability to decode teletext signals.

The teletext viewer begins typically . . . by watching the display of a table of contents, which indicates what information is available and at which pages it appears. A "page" is a screen of information. Viewers may then view the information they want by flipping to the page where the desired material appears. Present teletext programming includes data of general interest such as news, sports, weather, community events, and advertising, though nothing precludes broadcasters from displaying information that appeals to audiences with special interests. Main channel broadcasting may notify viewers of material available on teletext. While teletext can display text and high-resolution graphics, no sound accompanies the visual transmissions under teletext technology. Teletext is supported by advertiser fees and involves no charge to the public . . .

In its . . . *Report and Order* . . . the Commission addressed the applicability of political broadcast requirements to teletext and concluded that "as a matter of law, . . . sections [312(a)(7) and 315] need not be applied to teletext service," and that applying these provisions would be "both unnecessary and unwise as a matter of policy.". . . In contrast, the Commission found section 315 wholly inapposite to teletext. Noting that a broadcast "use" triggered section 315's substantive obligations, that a "use" required "a personal appearance by a legally qualified candidate by voice or picture," and that the textual and graphics nature of teletext made it "inherently not a medium by which a candidate [could] make a personal appearance,". . . the Commission held that teletext could not trigger the requirements of section 315 . . .

The Commission then determined that it should not apply the fairness doctrine to teletext, "primarily [because of] a recognition that teletext's unique blending of the print medium with radio technology fundamentally distinguishes it from traditional broadcast programming,". . . Noting that "scarcity" of broadcast frequencies provided the first amendment justification of the fairness doctrine's application to traditional broadcast media, the Commission posited an "implicit . . . assumption that . . . power to communicate ideas through sound and visual images . . . is significantly different from traditional avenues of communication because of the immediacy of the medium.". . . . In other words, because scarcity inheres in all provisions of goods and services, including the provision of information through print media, the lessened first amendment protection of broadcast regulation must also rely upon the powerful character of traditional broadcasting. Because teletext "more closely resembles . . . other print communication media such as newspapers and magazines," the Commission found the "scarcity" rationale, as reinterpreted, insufficient to justify regulating teletext . . .

The Commission also reasoned that teletext, as a print medium in an "arena of competition . . . includ[ing] all other sources of print material," would not encounter the same degree of scarcity, in the usual sense, as the sound and visual images of regular programming. . . . Thus, the Commission felt it constitutionally suspect to apply the fairness doctrine to teletext. And, in light of its obligation to "encourage, not frustrate, the development" of new services like teletext, the FCC decided, therefore, to heed concerns of commentators that . . . teletext services might not prove "viable if . . . burdened by Fairness Doctrine obligations" and to exempt teletext from the fairness doctrine . . .

Two motions for reconsideration of the decision not to apply content regulation to teletext were filed. Media Access Project ("MAP"), a petitioner in this appeal, argued that "teletext . . . is intended for the general public," and, therefore, falls within the definition of "broadcasting" in the Communications Act of 1934 and triggers broadcast regulation . . .

We consider teletext clearly as an ancillary service not strictly related to the traditional broadcast mode of mass communication. First, the very definition of teletext confined the service to traditional print and textual data transmission. Thus, although these data will be transmitted at some point through the use of the electromagnetic spectrum, its primary and overriding feature will be its historical and cultural connection to the print media, especially books, magazines and newspapers. Users of this medium will not be listening or viewing teletext in any traditional broadcasting sense, but instead will be reading it, and thus be able to skip, scan and select the desired material in ways that are incomparable to anything in the history of broadcasting and broadcast regulation. In this light, we believe that the content regulations created for traditional broadcast operations are simply out of place in this new print-related textual data transmission medium. We decline to attribute to Congress an intent to extend broadcast content regulation . . . to this new medium . . .

The Commission also provided further explanation of its first amendment theory and made clear that it meant this theory to cover the applicability of all forms of political broadcasting regulation to teletext. Relying upon . . . *Miami Herald Publishing Co. v. Tornillo* . . . (1974) (striking down a state's newspaper right-of-reply statute as running afoul of the first amendment's protection of editorial judgment and control), and asserting that it considered teletext a "print medium" for first amendment purposes, . . . the Commission found that "neither the letter nor the purposes of the First Amendment would be served by . . . a ruling" that would "require [the Commission] to intrude into the editorial judgments of teletext editors.". . . Given *Tornillo's* clear refusal to allow interference with editorial judgments in the print media and "the historical sensitivity of Congress to these [First Amendment] issues," the Commission would not "construe. . . the intent of Congress to apply Section 315 and similar statutory provisions, and. . . associated rules and policies, to the teletext medium." Id. (footnote omitted). Accordingly, the Commission adhered to the results of its earlier Report and Order . . .

Observing that licensees and those who can obtain no license have identical first amendment rights, the Court in *Red Lion* further concluded that there is nothing in the First Amendment which prevents the Government from requiring a licensee to share his frequency with others and to conduct himself as a proxy or fiduciary with obligations to present those views and voices which are representative of his community and which would otherwise, by necessity, . . . be barred from the airwaves . . .

[The Court then enunciated the classic formulation of the scarcity doctrine:]

Because of the scarcity of radio frequencies, the Government is permitted to put restraints on licensees in favor of others whose views should be expressed on this unique medium. But the people as a whole retain their interest in free speech by radio and their collective right to have the medium function consistently with the ends and purposes of the First Amendment. It is the right of the viewers and listeners, not the right of the broadcasters, which is paramount . . .

Second, the Commission held that the print nature of teletext "more closely resembles, and will largely compete with, other print communication media such as newspapers and magazines.". . . The Commission's second distinction—that a textual medium is not scarce insofar as it competes with other "print media"—also fails to dislodge the hold of Red Lion. The dispositive fact is that teletext is transmitted over broadcast frequencies that the Supreme Court has ruled scarce and this makes teletext's content regulable. We can understand, however, why the Commission thought it could reason in this fashion. The basic difficulty in this entire area is that the line drawn between the print media and the broadcast media, resting as it does on the physical scarcity of the latter, is a distinction without a difference. Employing the scarcity concept as an analytic tool, particularly with respect to new and unforeseen technologies, inevitably leads to . . . strained reasoning and artificial results . . .

It is certainly true that broadcast frequencies are scarce but it is unclear why that fact justifies content regulation of broadcasting in a way that would be intolerable if applied to the editorial process of the print media. All economic goods are scarce, not least the newsprint, ink, delivery trucks, computers, and other resources that go into the production and dissemination of print journalism. Not everyone who wishes to publish a newspaper, or even a pamphlet, may do so. Since scarcity is a universal fact, it can hardly explain regulation in one context and not another, . . . The attempt to use a universal fact as a distinguishing principle necessarily leads to analytical confusion . . .

There may be ways to reconcile *Red Lion* and *Tornillo* but the "scarcity" of broadcast frequencies does not appear capable of doing so. Perhaps the Supreme Court will one day revisit this area of the law and either eliminate the distinction between print and broadcast media, surely by pronouncing Tornillo applicable to both, or announce a constitutional distinction that is more usable than the present one. In the meantime, neither we nor the Commission are free to seek new rationales to remedy the inadequacy of the doctrine . . . in this area. The attempt to do that has led the Commission to find "implicit" considerations in the law that are not really there. The Supreme Court has drawn a first amendment distinction between broadcast and print media on a premise of the physical scarcity of broadcast frequencies.

The significance of the language in *TRAC* can be understood not only in terms of the teletext technology but also in light of the larger issue of free expression. The question really is this: To what extent will electronic media forms be guaranteed freedom of expression? As Ithiel de Sola Pool wrote:

For five hundred years a struggle was fought, and in a few countries won, for the right of people to speak and print freely, unlicensed, uncensored, and uncontrolled. But new technologies of electronic communication may now relegate old and freed media such as pamphlets, platforms, and periodicals to the corner of the public forum. Electronic modes of communication that enjoy lesser rights are moving to center stage. The new communication technologies have not inherited all the legal immunities that were won for the old (Pool 1983, p. 1).

We are, then, at a social, legal, and technological crossroads in the history of human communication. The questions we face are those of freedom versus control and centralized authority over communication versus the influence of a plurality of voices. Scarcity, the central justification for broadcast regulation, is not likely to be applied to the digital world, even though physical bandwidth limits have at times been an issue during the crush of online stock-market trading. Technological solutions to "gridlock" are more likely to be touted as the developers of high-speed networks attempt to keep pace with the rush of citizens to be online (*EE Times*, February 8, 1999). At the same time, the Federal Communications Commission, which once had tried to force cable companies to give smaller Internet service providers access to their high-speed networks, has now backed off in favor of the marketplace. Cable companies successfully argued against regulation by saying they would be less likely to upgrade systems if they were treated as telephone company common carriers (*Wall Street Journal*, January 29, 1999). What remains, then, is an increasingly competitive marketplace for the major players, and in this marketplace, it appears that smaller companies are left on the sidelines. At the same time, the FCC (which also regulates interstate telephone communication) has ruled that Internet dial-ups, even to local telephone numbers, are no longer local calls—they are interstate communications. The FCC decision, if upheld by the courts, could lead to per-minute long-distance rates for Internet dial-ups (Associated Press, February 26, 1999).

Chapter Summary

This chapter reviewed broadcast and telecommunication regulations to show how the Internet differs from traditional electronic mass media. The scarcity of radio and television frequencies and the resulting legal justification for regulating these media were outlined and contrasted with the Internet's lack of scarcity. Left unregulated, the Internet appears to have a greater potential as a vehicle of free expression, but it may also be subject to corporate domination.

Discussion Questions

1. Should radio and television be regulated differently than the print medium or the Internet? Is the Internet more like print or electronic mass media?

2. Is the Internet sometimes more like a common-carrier (telephone) system than a mass medium?
3. Should local community standards for obscenity apply to the transmission of content on the Internet?
4. Does government have any interest in promoting free expression on the Internet? How would it go about doing that?
5. Should the courts reject the scarcity rationale as a justification for government regulation? Are there any other valid reasons to regulate media?
6. How do you think the nature of digital free expression will change as we shift to more sophisticated, next-generation Internet systems? Will virtual reality blur the nature of free expression? Can morality on the web be regulated?

4

Normative Legal Versus Social Theory Approaches to Free Expression

"To find the boundary line of any right, we must get behind rules of law to human facts ... there are individual interests and social interests, which must be balanced."
—*Zechariah Chafee Jr., professor (1941)*

"Public opinion is always wrong ... insufficiently informed, lacking the specialized knowledge upon which lucid judgments can be based."
—*Walter Lippmann, journalist and author (1955)*

"I am not so much concerned with the right of everyone to say anything he pleases as I am about our need as a self-governing people to hear everything relevant."
—*John F. Kennedy, U.S. president (1959)*

"There are many indications that we do not want to recognize our social nature, which forces us to conform."
—*Elisabeth Noelle-Neumann, media theorist (1984)*

"What shall it profit critics if their soapboxes occupy the periphery and they speak in tongues?"
—*Todd Gitlin, sociologist (1991)*

"Computers have emptied and filled my life for over a decade ... these rearrangements of work and play, do shake up my sense of freedom, privacy, and naturalness in ways that scare me."
—*Susan Leigh Star, policy analyst (1995)*

"It will be crucial that a broad set of people—not just technologists or people who happen to be in the computer industry—participate in the debate about how this technology should be shaped."

—**Bill Gates, CEO (1995)**

"To be a technological curmudgeon (or, let's say it, a luddite) is not to reject technology a priori and in toto, but to reject the acceptance of technology a priori and in toto (without asking questions)."

—*J. Macgregor Wise, writer (1997)*

The coming of the computer age brought with it new hopes and fears about the nature of free expression. Such issues are grounded in normative legal notions of the marketplace of ideas but will be examined here from social perspectives about modern life.

Normative Versus Social Thought

Normative theory is defined for the purposes of this volume as being "concerned with examining or prescribing how media *ought* to operate if certain social values are to be observed or attained" (McQuail, 1994, p. 4): "Such theory usually stems from the broader social philosophy or ideology of a given society. This kind of theory is important because it plays a part in shaping and legitimating media institutions and has considerable influence on the expectations which are placed on the media by other social agencies and even by the media's own audiences" (pp. 4–5).

For example, the classical libertarian ideology of free expression places a normative value on individuals having the right to speak if not to be heard. Therefore, the Internet is the perfect technology to be employed. It offers nearly everyone a soapbox, but it forces competition of ideas to be considered by the public.

Norms of individuals, which may be loosely based on normative legal theories, often lead to rules that are open to legal challenge. Such was the case when a federal judge backed a student's right to use the World Wide Web to criticize his high school.

In contrast to normative theory, so-called social scientific theory is based on "systematic and objective observation" of what is actually happening in the empirical world (McQuail, 1994, p. 4). In the case of the Internet, it would not be enough to say that people are free to use it to speak their minds. The social scientist would want to understand under what conditions they do or do not take advantage of the opportunities, as well as what constraints exist on user behavior. These conditions would need

---

Box 4.1   Missouri High School Student's Internet Rights

Federal judge Rodney Sippel issued a preliminary injunction against the Woodland School District in Marbel Hill, Missouri, and ruled a student's rights were violated when he was suspended for what was on his personal web page. Brandon Beussink had used his web site to criticize the school's official pages. Judge Sippel wrote: "Dislike or being upset by the content of a student's speech is not an acceptable justification for limiting student speech." The seventeen-year-old and his sister used a home computer to write "occasionally vulgar language," according to the Associated Press. "[They] also urged visitors to send e-mail to the principal and inform a teacher that the web site is bad." The American Civil Liberties Union brought the lawsuit against the school district after the student was suspended and punished for subsequent attendance and grade problems.

(Source: Associated Press, December 29, 1998)

---

to be studied within a cultural context of social change: "We seem to be entering an age of pronounced disbelief in which the certainties and the equivalent of moral imperatives of progressive rationalism are themselves being undermined or abandoned" (p. 377).

The industrial world is "most deeply entrenched" in a modern "episteme," one that divides space from time and the internal self from external objects (Wise, 1997, pp. 3–4). "Technology arises out of a desire to confront time and is concerned with the manipulation of time" (p. 5). J. M. Wise concluded that the clock is central to capitalism because it regulates production. Issues of "efficiency" and "control" allow for technology to "progress" without fundamental criticism (p. 10). The modern assumptions about the relationship between humans and technology are difficult to avoid: "It seems self-evident as to what is human and what is not; what is hand and what is tool; and so on" (p. 16). However, the development of cyborglike robots or Internet "agents" blurs the theoretical distinction between human and technology and even "master" and "slave." Cyberspace is social space, and it is here that law and society overlap.

If law is to be seen as a social vehicle of control grounded in our understanding of communication, then laws regarding uses of the Internet as a tool of free expression need to be seen as human products. In that sense, the formal law is like the computer; both require human encoding and interpretation:

The symbols and concepts of human beings have referents. In contrast, the symbols and concepts processed by computers are senseless; they have no referents for the computers. Only disembodied symbols inform the opera-

tions of computers. All symbols, including the most abstract concepts, that
are processed by human beings rest on the foundation of external referents
(Couch, 1996, p. 212).

In the case of free expression and the Internet, normative laws restrict prior
restraint on publication but also enable subsequent punishment for speech
through libel suits. This legal condition mingles with social forces—mostly
economic—that pose the greatest risks for those with the deepest pockets.

The $11-million lawsuit against television talk-show host Oprah Win-
frey is a good example of this. Texas cattlemen were unable to get an
Amarillo jury to accept the claim that Winfrey's fears about beef safety
led to a collapse of prices in their industry in 1996. Winfrey's show had
focused on the use of processed meat in cattle feed—a practice banned in
1997—and the possibility that this could spread mad cow disease. Winfrey concluded, "It has just stopped me cold from eating another burger!"
(Associated Press, February 28, 1998). In deciding in favor of Winfrey, ju-
ror Pat Gowdy said First Amendment rights, like other rights, were erod-
ing: "Our freedom of speech may be the only one we have left to regain
what we've lost" (Associated Press, February 28, 1998). Had Winfrey devoted a World Wide Web page to the topic, it is not likely that lawyers for
the cattlemen would have made the case that, as one of the most influential people in America, she could persuade people to quit eating beef. But
television has always been viewed by the public as a powerful medium of
influence (Graber, 1997). In part, this is because the television has been
most successful at luring huge audiences to single programs. This suggests an inherent weakness of the Internet: It appears to be a fragmented
medium that draws relatively smaller audiences over longer periods of
time. What is not known is how or whether the Internet will be transformed into a mass medium and what role the convergence of the Internet with television will play. How, then, might libel laws be applied to
free expression on the Internet?

Libel Laws

In its simplest form, libel involves damage to the reputation of an individual or a company. Defamation is a false attack. Any defamatory publication on the Internet would be considered a libel. "Words alleging the commission of a crime, charges of professional incompetence, unethical
practices, or other moral failures resulting in injury to reputation and
business standing account for nearly all libel cases" (Gillmor, Barron, Simon, and Terry, 1996, p. 46).

In a libel case, the plaintiff must prove publication, identification, falsity,
fault, and damages. Proving publication on the Internet could, in some

cases, be more difficult than it would be with other mass media forms. Unless the offending pages were downloaded and saved or printed, it is possible that the defamation could vanish in cyberspace. Assuming the material was saved, identification of the plaintiff on a web page or e-mail would be fairly straightforward and not unlike that in other media forms. The plaintiff's evidence that the material in question is false is always one of the most difficult aspects of a libel suit, regardless of media form. The Internet might pose some special problems because of the ability to cut and paste images and words digitally. The standards of fault depend on whether the plaintiff in a libel suit is a public figure or not. Most people alleging libel merely must show that the Internet publisher was negligent with the facts. Because most web page content providers are not trained journalists, it would seem that standards for negligence might be lower and more difficult to prove in court. For public figures and officials, the standard is "actual malice"—defined legally as a reckless disregard for the truth and entertaining serious doubts about the information. If all of these elements can be shown, a plaintiff in a libel suit must still make the case for economic damages, determined by how much money the publication actually cost the individual or corporation. A jury may also award punitive damages—fines imposed as punishment against the offender—that go beyond actual economic harm to the victim of a libel (e.g., money lost after being fired from a job because of a defamatory news story).

Once a plaintiff has made his or her case, the defendant in a libel suit can pursue several defenses. Had someone published a libel on the Internet, the simplest defense would be that the information was the truth. "Literal truth is not required if what is published is substantially true" (Gillmor, Barron, Simon, and Terry, 1996, p. 62). Other defenses in a libel case are the opinion defense, the qualified privilege defense, and other technical defenses (neutral reporting or consent). It is legal to make fair comments, to objectively report on government actions, to report all sides in a controversy, or to report denials of charges under some situations (pp. 62–69).

The bottom line is that people who use the Internet must be aware that their speech is vulnerable to the subsequent punishment of a libel suit. This is a sobering thought because even if the plaintiff wins such a case, legal costs for the losing side can run into millions of dollars. With these legal constraints considered, I now turn to the more common social conditions affecting free expression on the Internet.

Free Expression as the Product of Human Behavior

One theory of opinion, the spiral of silence, addresses the notion that free expression is impacted by human processing: "(1) the human ability to

Box 4.2   *Cubby v. CompuServe,* 776 F. Supp. 135, 19 Media L. Rep. 1525 (1991)

On October 29, 1991, in the U.S. District Court for the Southern District of New York, one of the first important decisions in the field helped to begin defining online rights by ruling that service providers are not responsible for content posted by members.

Peter K. Leisure, United States District considered the case of "Rumorville USA" a daily newsletter about broadcast journalism and journalists, and a predecessor to Don Fitzpatrick Associates of San Francisco ("DFA") current Shoptalk Listserv.

CompuServe provided access to "Rumorville" but did no editing of it. In 1990, plaintiffs Cubby, Inc. ("Cubby") and Robert Blanchard ("Blanchard") (collectively, "plaintiffs") developed Skuttlebut, a computer database designed to publish and distribute electronically news and gossip in the television news and radio industries, and they intended to compete.

"Plaintiffs claim that, on separate occasions in April 1990, Rumorville published false and defamatory statements relating to Skuttlebut and Blanchard, and that CompuServe carried these statements as part of the Journalism Forum. The allegedly defamatory remarks included a suggestion that individuals at Skuttlebut gained access to information first published by Rumorville 'through some back door' a statement that Blanchard was 'bounced' from his previous employer, WABC; and a description of Skuttlebut as a 'new start-up scam.'"

◆   ◆   ◆

With respect to the Rumorville publication, the undisputed facts are that DFA uploads the text of Rumorville into CompuServe's data banks and makes it available to approved CIS subscribers instantaneously. . . . CompuServe has no more editorial control over such a publication than does a public library, book store, or newsstand, and it would be no more feasible for CompuServe to examine every publication it carries for potentially defamatory statements than it would be for any other distributor to do so. "First Amendment guarantees have long been recognized as protecting distributors of publications . . . Obviously, the national distributor of hundreds of periodicals has no duty to monitor each issue of every periodical it distributes. Such a rule would be an impermissible burden on the First Amendment". . . .

◆   ◆   ◆

Technology is rapidly transforming the information industry. A computerized database is the functional equivalent of a more traditional news vendor, and the inconsistent application of a lower standard of liability to an electronic news distributor such as CompuServe than that which is applied to a public library, book store, or newsstand would impose an undue burden on the free flow of information. Given the relevant First Amendment considerations, the appropriate standard of liability to be . . . applied to CompuServe is whether it knew or had reason to know of the allegedly defamatory Rumorville statements . . .

◆   ◆   ◆

CompuServe contends that it is undisputed that it had neither knowledge nor reason to know of the allegedly defamatory Rumorville statements, especially given the large number of publications it carries and the speed with which DFA uploads Rumorville into its computer banks and makes the publication available to CIS subscribers . . .

◆   ◆   ◆

Regardless of the label used, the substance of plaintiffs' "business disparagement" claim is similar to the action for defamation. . . . Under either formulation, plaintiffs would have to prove that CompuServe had knowledge or reason to know of Rumorville's publication of the allegedly disparaging statements in order to hold CompuServe liable for business disparagement. As discussed with respect to the libel claim, supra, plaintiffs have failed to meet their burden of setting forth specific facts showing that there is a genuine issue as to whether CompuServe had knowledge or reason to know of the April 1990 Rumorville statements. Summary judgment in favor of CompuServe on the business disparagement claim is therefore granted.

◆   ◆   ◆

Based on the undisputed facts, the Court concludes that neither CCI nor DFA should be considered an agent of CompuServe. CompuServe, CCI, and DFA are independent of one another. CompuServe has simply contracted with CCI for CCI to manage the Journalism Forum; under the contract, CCI "agrees to manage, review, create, delete, edit and otherwise control the contents of the [Journalism Forum], in accordance with editorial and technical standards and conventions of style as established by CompuServe.". . . As for DFA, the original publisher of Rumorville, CompuServe has no direct contractual relationship with DFA; DFA provides Rumorville to the Journalism Forum under a contract with CCI. The contract between CCI and DFA provides that "DFA accepts total responsibility for the contents of" Rumorville; that DFA "agrees to maintain the [Rumorville] files in a timely fashion including uploading and merging into availability to the members of [Rumorville]"; and that "DFA maintains total responsibility for communicating with its members, billing them for any membership fees and collecting same". . . For the reasons stated above, CompuServe's motion for summary judgment pursuant to Fed. R. Civ. P. 56 is granted on all claims asserted against it.

SO ORDERED

◆   ◆   ◆

The decision reflects the opinion that service providers are not obligated to monitor the content of individuals posting material on their services. As Jan Fernback (1997) has noted, although American law treats service providers as libraries or bookstores (not responsible for content), ISPs can now be sued in other countries for material posted on the World Wide Web.

---

recognize when public opinions grow in strength or weaken; (2) the reactions to this realization, leading either to more confident speech or to silence; and (3) the fear of isolation that makes most people willing to heed the opinions of others" (Noelle-Neumann, 1984, p. 62). For those who take advantage of the Internet, the technology can provide them with a virtual community of like-minded people. The implication of this is that such a community might be able to sustain a viable minority in the face of majority opinion. Consider, for example, the death penalty. Opponents of the death penalty know that the vast majority of people, according to public opinion polls, support it. But the Internet can provide a place for thousands or even millions of opponents to gather, communicate, and commiserate. Likewise, any movement that has been considered outside the mainstream would be open to Internet communities of people that serve as support groups. As Baym (in Jones, 1998) observed about the culture of Usenet communities:

> If language use is an important locus of cultural meaning-making in traditional cultures, it is only more so for Usenet cultures which are so heavily linguistic in nature. The resources available for Usenet participants to create distinct communities are limited to the Usenet system, shared interest in the topic of discussion, and the approaches participants take toward one another. There are few if any shared spaces, face-to-face encounters, or physical artifacts to provide cultural foundations. Thus, the discourse, shaped by the forces of the system and object of interest as well as the idiosyncrasies of the participants, carries inordinate weight in creating a group's distinct environment (p. 33).

In one sense, such isolated communities are comforting because they lack the social dangers of the outside world. But in another sense, because these groups are isolated from the larger, public sphere, they have become marginalized from the mainstream of debate. Group participants might feel less constrained about speaking in these "safe" communities, but beyond strategizing about future outside actions, their speech is likely to have less impact externally.

To this point, Internet users have been early adopters of an innovative communication technology. In a diffusion sense, adoption is a process with five major stages: awareness, interest, evaluation, trial, and adoption (Lowery and DeFleur, 1995, p. 128). Everett Rogers's model posits an empirically verified, S-shaped adoption curve common to most new products or the spread of ideas. Five groups have been identified that roughly fit a normal curve distribution:

- Innovators: the earliest people to experiment with the change (2.5 percent).
- Early adopters: those people swayed by the innovators to jump on board of what is obviously a new trend (13.5 percent).
- Early majority: those people in the first wave of mass appeal (34 percent).
- Late majority: the last wave of mass appeal (34 percent).
- Laggards: the remaining people, who either are slow to come to the change or resist it entirely (16 percent) (Lowery and DeFleur, 1995, p. 130; Rogers, 1963, p. 247).

In the case of the Internet, innovators inhabited the text-based network and its predecessors (Arpanet, Bitnet, etc.) from the 1960s until the late 1980s. By the early 1990s, early adopters were helping drive the social communication change outside of academe and into the broader culture. At the same time, purchases of business and home computers began to soar, and people were looking for something to do with them. Based on current statistics, we have reached either the late stages of the early majority phase or the early stages of the late majority. This is a pivotal time in social terms because as computer-mediated communication becomes the norm, society will attempt to impose a more rigid set of formal rules and order on the Net. Free expression, then, is likely to be less open on the Internet as more people come to use it. This is especially true as the Internet moves from being just an out-of-the-way place to a common social arena for all ages. The World Wide Web, with its ease of use and visual stimulation, has attracted a mass audience, and this tends to produce a mall-like culture in which ideas are predicted to be commercialized and watered down. In the short term, none of this matters to the laggards. However, as maturation produces *the* place for communication in the form of the technology, those left behind in a sense become like the homeless—so marginalized as to be easily ignored by mainstream culture. This is important because it is the point at which social control can be exerted. When membership in the Internet community becomes vital to social survival, the fear of being removed from the privileges of membership is a motivating force for playing by whatever rules are imposed. After all, to paraphrase an old *Saturday Night Live* skit, would any of us like to end up "living in a van down by the river"? The alternative is to be "connected," primarily through the economic and social value of employment, and to use standardized hardware, software, and communication conventions.

For E. M. Rogers, the adoption of new media depends on a "critical mass" of people—"the point at which enough individuals have adopted an innovation so that the innovation's further rate of adoption becomes self-sustaining" (Rogers, 1995, p. 313). Rogers pegged adoption to "interactivity," or individuals' control over "mutual discourse" through communication exchange (p. 314). He traced the origins of the Internet to the earlier adoption of the Arpanet and Bitnet (pp. 315–317). Although the Bitnet fit the typical S-shaped diffusion curve model, "when BITNET joined with other computer networks in INTERNET, the total number of users skyrocketed because of reciprocal interdependence" (p. 317).

Social Constraints

Free expression is not just a matter of a free marketplace of ideas. The marketplace is inhabited by individuals faced with a variety of social, economic, and even legal constraints that limit participation in the market. Free speech may come at a price. As R. M. Entman (1989) observed: "Beyond the metaphorical marketplace of ideas lie two markets that are quite real: the economic and the political" (p. 17). Even where an individual might wish to compete in the marketplace, she or he is faced with a manipulative political landscape:

> Pressures from the political, economic, and idea markets combine and collide to yield news that frustrates all sides. Elites face a ceaseless threat of oversimplification and stereotype from opponents taking advantage of the volatile combination of aggressive reporting and uninformed public opinion. Under these conditions they have no choice but to engage in news management. For their part, journalists must endure the manipulative efforts of their sources while coping with conflicting pressures to generate accountability, remain objective, and contribute to the bottom-line of their employers. As a result, journalists' sincere and energetic attempts to illuminate the powerful often yield coverage that serves the long-term interests of nobody: neither the manipulators nor the media, and certainly not the general public (p. 125).

The cultural implication of this situation is that the market is not open: "To maintain the system that is so good to them, the rich and powerful devote much attention to persuasion and propaganda" (Parenti, 1986, p. 6):

The structures of control within the U.S. media are different from the institutionalized formal censorship we might expect of a government-controlled press; they are less visible and more subtle, not monolithic yet hierarchical, transmitted to the many by those who work for the few, essentially undemocratic and narrow in perspective, tied to the rich and powerful but not totally immune to the pressures of an agitated public, propagandistic yet sometimes providing hard information that is intentionally or unintentionally revealing (p. 6).

The argument, then, is that "freedom of the press belongs to the man who owns one" (Parenti, 1986, p. 27). Historically, we have been sold a "consumer ideology" that dominates the communication landscape: "Over and above any particular product, they [mass media] sell an entire way of life, a way of experiencing social reality that is compatible with the needs of mass production, mass consumption, capitalist society" (p. 63).

Ideology and British Marxist mass communication research become important because our analysis must explain "the continuation of structures of domination within late capitalism" (Stevenson, 1995, p. 10). Drawing heavily from the ideas of Jürgen Habermas, alternative paradigms focus on reform in the milieu of money and power:

The development of a more communicative culture that seeks . . . to "enlarge thought" is only possible in modern contexts through the radical democratisation of the culture industry. The presentation of a plurality of voices, particularly of those who are not immediately present in day-to-day encounters, is especially necessary in a globalised and fragmented culture. A source of hope, I would argue, remains ordinary people's continued capacity to feel a sense of solidarity with others in contexts far removed from their own (Stevenson, 1995, pp. 68–69).

The Internet, for those who have adopted it, has become a social space where individuals can express compassion. In fact, the irony of the moment is that it is now common for people to feel more comfortable in expressing empathy for others outside their geographic communities than engaging in meaningful, face-to-face communication with neighbors, friends, fellow church members, or work colleagues. Just as television seemed to be the first phase of withdrawal from traditional community participation, computer-mediated communication seems to re-create new community forms that are less socially risky. Cocooning in our homes by the light of the new tube, we can move in and out of global communities without incurring any social cost of transition.

Of course, as in the old communities, if we say something in a chat room or post something on a board that is not respectful of the group norms, then we may be ostracized or even removed ("R-kicked"). In extreme cases, Internet service providers may intervene. This was the case with ten-year-old Derrick Wolbert of Orchard Park, New York. He was banned for life from America Online after e-mailing a fifth-grader and pretending to be an AOL agent. AOL's Tricia Primrose said, "Someone impersonating an America Online employee is an absolute violation of our terms of service, whether it's someone 10 years old or 80 years old." Wolbert's father complained to the *Buffalo News* and the state attorney general's office, and AOL ultimately reinstated the account (CNN, February 4, 1999). Still, it is significant that the problem arose only after the recipient of the e-mail complained to AOL.

Such mediated interpersonal communication, however, must be contrasted with mediated mass communication. It relies on traditional metaphor for definition. As a metaphor, the marketplace of ideas itself is open to scholarly challenge. R. Jensen (1998) called for substituting metaphors because in a "corporate-dominated, mass-mediated society," the marketplace of ideas fails:

> Although the metaphor has in many instances helped carve out protection for free expression, I argue that at this point in history, it should be scrapped. The metaphor is unhelpful not only for the oft-stated reasons—that the notion of an open marketplace for speech is romantic nonsense in contemporary mass society, and that the marketplace is too painfully accurate a metaphor in a world in which increasingly speech is money—but because the deeper entailments of the metaphor are in some ways destructive of communication and community. In other words, the metaphor is unfortunately descriptively accurate in contemporary society, but normatively insufficient (p. 564).

He instead suggested replacing the metaphor of a marketplace of ideas with the metaphor of a potluck supper, one in which all participants contribute something to the meal. For one thing, the potluck metaphor deemphasizes the importance of the individual in favor of the role of the group. Further, a renewed interest in community presumably reduces the tension to complete:

> At a potluck, everyone has a right not only to bring a dish but to expect that some people will try it. Everyone understands that to cook something that is not eaten leaves the cook feeling unnoticed and unappreciated, not a full member of the group. . . . If there is a dish that is widely unpopular, there are ways to communicate that to the cook and at some point that person will stop bringing it. But, the dish will have had a fair hearing and the group will support the cook's attempts to make it work (Jensen, 1998, p. 583).

Like any metaphor, the potluck argument is open to immediate debate. As Jensen himself noted, "Some might argue that any system of free expression that includes such collective notions will necessarily result in the imposition of orthodoxy and the thwarting of innovation and individual creativity" (Jensen, 1998, p. 586). However, from a social theory perspective, all human behaviors are at least partially collective and open to pressures of conformity. In fact, even at times when the marketplace of ideas has been the dominant metaphor, public support for free expression rights has been limited by a desire to constrain media (McLeod et al., 1998). In the end, an orientation toward free expression for the value of ideas themselves seems subordinated to more practical, materialistic consumer wants and needs.

For the individual, we must ask how the transformation of the Internet into a commercial medium will allow for further exploitation of consumer desires. Because we find ourselves submerged in the mediated culture, patterns of communication on the Internet may well reinforce the constructed social reality, rather than challenge the social order. To the extent the Internet equates with owning one's own soapbox, we must ask if that will become any more useful than owning one's own telephone. It is ironic that individual power on the Internet continues to be mediated through traditional gatekeepers—we can, for example, participate in an instant poll on the web or send e-mail to CNN's *Talk Back Live*, and if we're lucky, our views will be heard. However, we can also build a web page and face the likelihood that only a handful of friends and relatives will visit it. And if we do create a page and decide to be controversial or opinionated on it, we run the real risk that the page will be used against us by employers, enemies, or others wishing to ignite trouble. So, the odds remain against individuals utilizing the Internet as a means to communicate in ways contrary to the established order. Even in the community-minded, potluck sense, small groups of people sharing ideas on the Internet will find it difficult to move those viewpoints beyond the community and into the marketplace, where influence is leveraged.

Persuasion, Propaganda, and Public Opinion

A variety of theorists have argued that a "ruling" or "governing class" exists whose "members are all heavily invested in the current economic system" (Milburn, 1991, p. 138). What is promoted by the mass culture, then, "is the uncontested hegemony of liberal capitalism in this country that influences the underlying values" (p. 139). Mass persuasion, propaganda, and public opinion operate within this context.

Computerized individuals, rather than being freed from oppression, may face increasing isolation in cyberspace:

> This isolation may be bred by choice, technology, or democratic circum-
> stance. For example, people may choose to subscribe to information services
> tailored precisely to their needs, tastes, and interests. They may choose to go
> on-line only with others like themselves, forming virtual communities of
> people connected only by an electronic thread of hobby, political issue, reli-
> gion, or other special interest (Bennett, 1996, p. 218).

Isolation also occurs among those who do not participate in the computer revolution because they are simply left behind. In such an environment, where meaningful communication does not occur across socioeconomic classes, the socially constructed reality of mass media persists as our common understanding of the way things are. According to one report, for example, blacks are less likely than whites to use home computers and the web: Forty-four percent of white households and 29 percent of black households had a computer in 1997. However, only 13 percent of whites and 6 percent of blacks had used the web in the past week, and higher income and education were predictors of that usage. Researchers Donna Hoffman and Thomas Novak suggested "the presence of a powerful bias that could restrict Internet use to a narrow segment of African Americans" (*Chronicle of Higher Education*, April 24, 1998, p. A-38). Without a broad-based audience, the Internet cannot make the jump to becoming an arena of public opinion influence. To this point, Internet columnist Matt Drudge's influence, for example, was among elites who visited the site or followed mass mediated accounts of Drudge and his "news." Thus, cyberspace seems to be a place where elites are most likely to communicate with each other—a process that can actually widen the knowledge gap between the information poor and the information rich (Olien, Donohue, and Tichenor, 1995): "These gaps are the result of both (1) the trained capacities that accompany formal education for seeking and acquiring information from media and (2) characteristics of media reporting and distribution that are designed to appeal particularly to more affluent groups that also have higher levels of formal education" (p. 314).

In other words, people of higher income and education first have the affluence and motivation to seek out more information. The Internet is one place where they can go to gain an information advantage over competitors in the marketplace. The poor and poorly educated, however, find no utility or advantage in information-seeking behavior and tend to be left further and further behind. Even when the motivation to communicate on the Internet might exist, the gatekeeping of information exercises a measure of social, structural control. For most in society, information-seeking behavior is difficult, not worth the effort, and not very interesting.

Rarely do individuals successfully challenge this marketplace of the media powerful with opposing realities. In fact, one point of view is that public opinion is rooted in an "imagined public"—one in which "public media" seem to "constitute dispersed public spaces" (Peters, 1995, p. 15). Liberal democracy was never thought to be possible beyond the town hall without the assistance of a mass media to bring people together across space and time: "Public opinion, then, claims to be public in the first sense, as an expression of popular will, but it is often in fact public as a visible fiction before the eyes of the people" (p. 16).

> What the king's body did in the Middle Ages is not so different from what pollsters do in modern societies: both offer punctuated statements of otherwise invisible realities. The results of public opinion polls are paraded before the people in the media: today information, not the royal purple, is what makes publicness. What originates as fact can be presented only as fiction—in the sense of a constructed and condensed symbol. . . . Public opinion, as we now understand it, sees no need for the process of public discussion. The noble idea of using public opinion polls to enhance democratic participation not only backfired in practice, it confused the meanings of public and opinion. "Public opinion" in its common usage is a positively Orwellian expression (Peters, 1995, pp. 19, 21).

In this way, any meaningful discussion on the information superhighway by definition occurs outside *the* place where the public is allowed to be heard—poll results. Because public discussion is divorced from political action, the Internet further achieves the goals of the system by creating the impression of new and improved democracy. As shown in the next chapter, even the U.S. Supreme Court expresses the popular myth that our system is somehow changed by events on the World Wide Web.

Research Limitations

Because of the newness of the Internet, there is barely any research on the power of this new form of mass communication to in any way alter public opinion through persuasion and propaganda. The Internet itself has been transformed into a political symbol to be used by political elites, but we do not yet know what real or imagined effects this will have on the body politic in the years to come. As a symbol, the Internet is propagandized as a pathway to "freedom," including free expression, and as a vehicle capable of virtual transit across continents in a matter of seconds. In another sense, though, the appropriate symbol could just as well be a virtual prison. By accepting the norms of Internet culture, whatever they are or may become, one can be trapped by its rhetoric, conventions, and norms. Standardization of communication through the use of popular web page design, e-mail protocol, and the ever-increasing complexities of multimedia all serve to limit expression to accepted forms.

One research issue involves the media credibility of the World Wide Web. One study found that among politically interested web users, online publications were deemed more credible than traditional ones, but both forms were only somewhat credible in the eyes of their users:

> Previous studies of traditional media have found those who are older, male, and of high socioeconomic status tend to be the most critical of the media; this study found an identical pattern with the Internet. The young are the heaviest users of the Internet, which may contribute to their higher credibility scores. But while Internet use is highest among those who are male and have a higher income and education, such users are less likely to view the Internet as credible (Johnson and Kaye, 1998, p. 335).

Newspaper web sites have been found to be empirically distinct from their print parents. "With interconnected links, the traditional one-to-many newspaper publishing process turned into many-to-many communication centered with and facilitated by the host Internet newspapers" (Li, 1998, p. 353). Beyond the links, however, the graphics and content of online versions appear quite similar to those of their printed counterparts. In fact, research has shown that the newsroom practices of producing online versions are more similar than different from traditional methods (Martin, 1998). A limited exploratory study of two sites found that

> nearly all the online production staff members were called editors and said they believed their primary function was to select and reformat rather than write original stories, though in both groups original stories were prepared by some of these editors to supplement, for the website, the material provided by the newsprint newsroom staff. The online editors at both observational sites had traditional newsroom experience or journalism education before taking their current jobs (p. 72).

The research supports the observation that commercial publishers are moving rapidly to manage the Internet. As they compete in the economic marketplace, it seems less likely that collaborative communication models will emerge and flourish on the World Wide Web.

Political and Economic Considerations

As I will explore later in this book, it is impossible to interpret the state of free expression in the age of the Internet without placing it within current political and economic contexts. If the masses are to be controlled, largely for economic gain that can be transformed to social and political power, then the Internet as a communication tool must be managed by political elites. The job of managing the Internet is not as easy, perhaps, as the management of a relatively limited number of television, radio, or cable channels, but it can and will be managed if the current social order is to survive.

The simplest form of management is through the creation of a techni-cal-professional class of computer programmers. These employees can be rewarded when they produce products that promote the systemic goals and rejected when their work goes against cultural values. The programs themselves help control the masses—because constant change is built into the programs, the public is drained of both economic and time capi-tal that could be invested in more useful efforts. Of course, this constant change certainly fits nicely into corporate profit goals. In essence, what is being sold to the public is the belief that faster and cooler is better, and in the process, social meaning is diluted because social change comes to be defined in terms of new products. Social change that might impact on the human condition—poverty, environmental disaster, illiteracy—is lost in the propaganda of a mediated existence. The Internet, then, rather than promoting meaningful free expression and public discourse, actually marginalizes, trivializes, and buries them in a sea of bits and bytes.

The social theory of postmodernism helps explain the Internet within a context of a consumer society: "Consumer society has effectively dis-placed moral categories such as those based upon deference and thrift and replaced them with the hedonistic search for satisfaction" (Steven-son, 1995, p. 149). In Baudrillard's view, the market erects "barriers of so-cial exclusion" because goods must become object "signs" to be interest-ing to consumers: "The meaning of objects is established through the organisation of signs into codes. It is only through these codes that hu-man beings come to realise their sense of self and their needs. The codes themselves are hierarchically ordered, being used to signify distinctions of status and prestige" (Stevenson, 1995, p. 149). The capitalist beauty of such a sign-ordered system is that materialistic needs will never be fully met. Thus, media become the engine that drives consumption by display-ing the latest fads. The Internet feeds hedonism by allowing an individual to search and browse in personalized ways that encourage psychographic tendencies.

The struggle for the control of cyberspace has been joined by those who would commercialize it to the point of hedonism and those who insist it is more egalitarian than elitist:

> Cyberspace is both public and private, the communication is one-to-one, one-to-many, and many-to-many. And, because cyberspace is open-minded

space, its users will develop it in new ways regardless of what restrictions commercial service providers attempt to impose on it. . . . The collectivist ideology does not expect that freedom in cyberspace will be absolute. . . . But the sense of common good that drives the collectivity of CMC users tolerates the boundaries drawn by the desire to maintain the *whole* in the face of potentially drastic restructuring amid regulatory constraints (Fernback, in Jones, 1997, p. 50).

Some in the CMC movement are willing to justify limitations on free expression as a means to squelch that which is "clearly irrelevant or malicious"—online arguments, or flame wars, and "nonsense" are treated as disruptive. "Nonetheless, the groups that would appear to be the harshest dissenters—hackers, neo-Nazi propagandists, anarchists—are the ones who tend to benefit most from the First Amendment guarantees in cyberspace [constraints]" (Fernback, in Jones, 1997, pp. 50–51).

Chapter Summary

This chapter contrasted normative legal models such as the marketplace of ideas and potluck metaphors with social theories of conformity and empirical research on the Internet. I also raised concerns about the management of the World Wide Web by elite powers, about knowledge gaps between social classes, and about the future of free expression in a consumer-dominated communication environment—one in which technological innovation is substituted for social progress.

Discussion Questions

1. Do you think things are getting better or worse in terms of free expression?
2. Do you feel pressured to conform your speech to that which society is willing to tolerate?
3. Do you consider yourself a member of the "information elite" when it comes to the Internet? What implications does your answer have in terms of your opinions about Internet free expression?
4. Do the people who produce Internet online publications have different news values than traditional editors?
5. What do you see as the strengths and weaknesses of using the marketplace of ideas or potluck supper metaphors of free speech?
6. Does public opinion affect the boundaries of free expression in a digital age? How might the Internet act as an agent of the status quo or social change? How might the CMC movement promote or restrain free expression on the Internet?

5

Reno v. ACLU:

A Legal Test in the Age of the Internet

"As the most participatory form of mass speech yet developed, the Internet deserves the highest protection from governmental intrusion."
—*Stewart R. Dalzell, federal judge (1996)*

"The Internet allows truth to grapple with falsehood, to paraphrase Milton."
—*Charles Levendosky, journalist (1997)*

"The Internet threatens to give every child a free pass into the equivalent of every adult bookstore and every adult video store in the country."
—*Seth P. Waxman, federal government lawyer (1997)*

"The government cannot reduce the adult population to reading or viewing only what is appropriate for children."
—*Bruce J. Ennis, civil libertarian (1997)*

"The vagueness of such a regulation raises special First Amendment concerns because of its obvious chilling effect on free speech."
—*John Paul Stevens, U.S. Supreme Court justice (1997)*

"Today's opinion defines the First Amendment for the next century. . . . The court has written on a clean slate and established the fundamental principles that will govern free speech issues for the electronic age."
—*David Sobel, privacy advocate (1997)*

"The Supreme Court has made clear that we do not forfeit our First Amendment rights when we go online. This decision is a landmark in the history of the Internet and a firm foundation for its future growth."

—*Patrick Leahy, U.S. senator (1997)*

The *Reno v. ACLU* (1997) decision is a focal point for this book because the case has come to define the legal boundaries of free expression in the age of the Internet. The case was about whether the government could pass a law that restricted the types of content Internet providers, World Wide Web page developers, and even individuals sending e-mail could offer.

Because the law was written in a vague manner, it appeared to have sweeping free-speech implications—raising the possibility that the government could seek out e-mail correspondence in a search for "indecent" messages sent to children and teenagers.

The decision also set the stage for passage in 1998 of the Child Online Protection Act, which called for all commercial web sites to use credit card numbers or adult access codes as proof of age to view adult material. The law proposed six-month jail terms and fines of up to $50,000 for violators, and it was challenged by the American Civil Liberties Union (ACLU) as a violation of free speech (Associated Press, November 20, 1998). A federal judge blocked enforcement of the so-called CDA II law.

The Facts of the Case

The passage of the Communications Decency Act of 1996 by the Congress and the signing of the bill by President Clinton led to an expedited legal review of the statute by a special appeals court and the U.S. Supreme Court. Ultimately, both courts struck down portions of the legislation as an unconstitutional restriction on free speech.

The special three-judge appeals court was faced with a constitutional challenge to provisions of the CDA, which was Title V of the Telecommunications Act of 1996, signed into law by the president on February 8, 1996. Computer and communication industries were represented in the civil lawsuit against U.S. Attorney General Janet Reno, who was charged with enforcing the new law. The claim was that the measures calling some content "indecent" or "patently offensive" infringed on rights protected by the First Amendment and the Due Process Clause of the Fifth Amendment. The American Civil Liberties Union led the fight and filed its action in the U.S. District Court for the Eastern District of Pennsylvania on the day the CDA was signed and moved for a temporary restraining order to enjoin enforcement of these two provisions of the act.

The Legal Issues

I will first examine the legal issues identified by the appellate court before turning to the opinions of the Supreme Court. Both courts overwhelmingly agreed that the new law did not pass constitutional muster.

The appeals court, among other things, recognized the computer developments to protect children by categorizing Internet sites. CyberNOT software, the court reasoned, allowed parents to block access to content.

The court considered filtering software and other facts about the Internet to conclude: "Plaintiffs have established a reasonable probability of eventual success in the litigation by demonstrating that 223(a)(1)(B) and 223(a)(2) of the CDA are unconstitutional on their face to the extent that they reach indecency."

The individual opinions of the judges were as important as the actual decision. Chief Judge Dolores Sloviter highlighted Section 223(a), the "indecency" provision, which would have subjected offenders to criminal penalties of imprisonment for no more than two years or a fine or both:

1) in interstate or foreign communications . . . (B) by means of a telecommunications device knowingly—(I) makes, creates, or solicits, and (II) initiates the transmission of, any comment, request, suggestion, proposal, image, or other communication which is obscene or indecent, knowing that the recipient of the communication is under 18 years of age, regardless of whether the maker of such communication placed the call or initiated the communication; . . .

2) knowingly permits any telecommunications facility under his control to be used for any activity prohibited by paragraph (1) with the intent that it be used for such activity (929 F.Supp. 824, ED Pa 1996).

The government asserted that shielding minors from access to indecent materials was the compelling interest supporting the CDA. Judge Sloviter wrote that previous rulings should be viewed in context:

Those statements were made in cases where the potential harm to children from the material was evident. *Ferber* involved the constitutionality of a statute which prohibited persons from knowingly promoting sexual performances by children under 16 and distributing material depicting such performances. *Sable* and *Fabulous* involved the FCC's ban on "dial-a-porn" (dealing by definition with pornographic telephone messages). In contrast to

Box 5.1   CyberNOT Content Categories

Violence/Profanity: Extreme cruelty, physical or emotional acts against any animal or person which are primarily intended to hurt or inflict pain. Obscene words, phrases, and profanity defined as text that uses George Carlin's seven censored words (the *Pacifica* radio case defined these as: *shit, piss, cunt, fuck, cocksucker, motherfucker* and *tits*) more often than once every fifty messages or pages.

Partial Nudity: Full or partial exposure of the human anatomy except when exposing genitalia.

Nudity: Any exposure of the human genitalia.

Sexual Acts (graphic or text): Pictures or text exposing anyone or anything involved in explicit sexual acts and lewd and lascivious behavior, including masturbation, copulation, pedophilia, intimacy and involving nude or partially nude people in heterosexual, bisexual, lesbian or homosexual encounters. Also includes phone sex ads, dating services, adult personals, CD-ROM and videos.

Gross Depictions (graphic or text): Pictures or descriptive text of anyone or anything which are crudely vulgar, deficient in civility or behavior, or showing scatological impropriety. Includes such depictions as maiming, bloody figures, indecent depiction of bodily functions.

Racism/Ethnic Impropriety: Prejudice or discrimination against any race or ethnic culture. Ethnic or racist jokes and slurs. Any text that elevates one race over another.

Satanic/Cult: Worship of the devil; affinity for evil, wickedness. Sects or groups that potentially coerce individuals to grow, and keep, membership.

Drugs/Drug Culture: Topics dealing with the use of illegal drugs for entertainment. This would exclude current illegal drugs used for medicinal purposes (e.g., drugs used to treat victims of AIDS). Includes substances used for other than their primary purpose to alter the individual's state of mind such as glue sniffing.

Militant/Extremist: Extremely aggressive and combative behaviors, radicalism, advocacy of extreme political measures. Topics include extreme political groups that advocate violence as a means to achieve their goal.

Gambling: Of or relating to lotteries, casinos, betting, numbers games, on-line sports or financial betting including non-monetary dares.

Questionable/Illegal: Material or activities of a dubious nature which may be illegal in any or all jurisdictions, such as illegal business schemes, chain letters, software piracy, and copyright infringement.

Alcohol, Beer & Wine: Material pertaining to the sale or consumption of alcoholic beverages. Also includes sites and information relating to tobacco products.

[The CyberNOT address is http://www.learningco.com.]

(Source: http://www.cyberpatrol.com)

the material at issue in those cases, at least some of the material subject to coverage under the "indecent" and "patently offensive" provisions of the CDA may contain valuable literary, artistic or educational information of value to older minors as well as adults (p. 852).

As examples, the judge offered the "recent public interest in the female genital mutilation routinely practiced and officially condoned in some countries," as well as "photographs appearing in *National Geographic* or a travel magazine of the sculptures in India of couples copulating in numerous positions, a written description of a brutal prison rape, or Francesco Clemente's painting 'Labirinth,' . . . all might be considered to 'depict or describe, in terms patently offensive as measured by contemporary community standards, sexual or excretory activities or organs'" (p. 853). As will be addressed in the next chapter of this book, we could also add to this list the contents of the Starr Report investigating President Clinton, which contained graphic descriptions of sexual behavior but was of extreme interest to the public.

"But the government has made no showing that it has a compelling interest in preventing a seventeen-year-old minor from accessing such images," Judge Slovitar wrote in the *Reno* case (p. 853). The judge concluded: "Whatever the strength of the interest the government has demonstrated in preventing minors from accessing 'indecent' and 'patently offensive' material online, if the means it has chosen sweeps more broadly than necessary and thereby chills the expression of adults, it has overstepped onto rights protected by the First Amendment" (p. 854).

Judge Ronald Buckwalter identified the complexity of the case: "First Amendment jurisprudence has developed into a study of intertwining standards and applications, perhaps as a necessary response to our ever-evolving culture and modes of communication" (pp. 858–859).

The opinion of Judge Stewart Dalzell was applauded by Internet supporters. It was steeped in the tradition of the First Amendment marketplace approaches: "I begin with first principles: As a general rule, the Constitution forbids the Government from silencing speakers because of their particular message" (p. 865). He noted that the law provides for two exceptions—hard-core pornography and child pornography. "The Government can and does punish with criminal sanction people who engage in these forms of speech. . . . Indeed, the Government could punish these forms of speech on the Internet even without the CDA," he wrote (p. 865). Judge Dalzell also identified Internet communication as a new form of mass media:

> As such, the Supreme Court's First Amendment jurisprudence compels us to consider the special qualities of this new medium in determining whether the CDA is a constitutional exercise of governmental power. Relying on these special qualities . . . I conclude that the CDA is unconstitutional and that the First Amendment denies Congress the power to regulate protected speech on the Internet. . . . Nearly fifty years ago, Justice Jackson recognized that "the moving picture screen, the radio, the newspaper, the handbill, the sound truck and the street corner orator have differing natures, values, abuses and dangers. Each . . . is a law unto itself" (pp. 872–873).

Judge Dalzell identified four "related characteristics of Internet communication" that make a difference:

1. The Internet presents very low barriers to entry;
2. these barriers to entry are identical for both speakers and listeners;
3. as a result of these low barriers, astoundingly diverse content is available on the Internet; and
4. the Internet provides significant access to all who wish to speak in the medium and even creates a relative parity among speakers (p. 877).

Judge Dalzell then turned to Justice Holmes's dissent in the *Abrams* case and recalled "the ultimate constitutional importance of the 'free trade in ideas'" (p. 879).

> When men have realized that time has upset many fighting faiths, they may come to believe even more than they believe the very foundations of their own conduct that the ultimate good desired is better reached by free trade in ideas—that the best test of truth is the power of the thought to get itself accepted in the competition of the market . . . *Abrams v. United States*, 250 U.S. 616, 630 (1919) (Holmes, J., dissenting) (pp. 879–880).

"For nearly as long, critics have attacked this much-maligned 'marketplace' theory of First Amendment jurisprudence as inconsistent with economic and practical reality," Justice Dalzell added (p. 880). "Most marketplaces of mass speech, they charge, are dominated by a few wealthy voices. . . . These voices dominate—and to an extent, create—the national debate. . . . Individual citizens' participation is, for the most part, passive. . . . Because most people lack the money and time to buy a broadcast station or create a newspaper, they are limited to the role of listeners, i.e., as watchers of television or subscribers to newspapers" (p. 880).

> It is no exaggeration to conclude that the Internet has achieved, and continues to achieve, the most participatory marketplace of mass speech that this country—and indeed the world—has yet seen. The plaintiffs in these actions correctly describe the "democratizing" effects of Internet communication: individual citizens of limited means can speak to a worldwide audience on issues of concern to them. Federalists and Anti-Federalists may debate the structure of their government nightly, but these debates occur in newsgroups or chat rooms rather than in pamphlets. Modern-day Luthers still post their theses, but to electronic bulletin boards rather than the door of the Wittenberg Schlosskirche. More mundane (but from a constitutional perspective, equally important) dialogue occurs between aspiring artists, or French cooks, or dog lovers, or fly fishermen.
>
> Indeed, the Government's asserted "failure" of the Internet rests on the implicit premise that too much speech occurs in that medium, and that speech there is too available to the participants. This is exactly the benefit of Internet communication, however. The Government, therefore, implicitly asks this court to limit both the amount of speech on the Internet and the availability of that speech. This argument is profoundly repugnant to First Amendment principles (p. 881).

Consequently, Judge Dalzell found that the Internet was being singled out by the government:

> I therefore have no doubt that a *Newspaper Decency Act*, passed because Congress discovered that young girls had read a front page article in the *New York Times* on female genital mutilation in Africa, would be unconstitutional. . . . Nor would a *Novel Decency Act*, adopted after legislators had seen too many pot-boilers in convenience store book racks, pass constitutional muster. . . . There is no question that *a Village Green Decency Act*, the fruit of a Senator's overhearing of a ribald conversation between two adolescent boys on a park bench, would be unconstitutional (p. 882).

Judge Dalzell said that "unfiltered" speech would be expected to be sometimes vulgar, as "citizens from all walks of life have a voice" (p. 882). And though some of the content might not be fit for children, it was parents' responsibility to protect minors. The language of the three judges on the appeals court led to an interesting follow-up by the U.S. Supreme Court.

Even before a decision was handed down in 1997, oral arguments offered some insight into the views held by the justices. Some concerns surfaced after Justice Anthony M. Kennedy asked: "Doesn't the government have any interest in also protecting the kids who don't have any parent there to watch over them?. . . Does the Government have an interest in protecting children who do not have parents available?" Justice Antonin Scalia compared the CDA to laws protecting children from indecent broadcasts and dirty magazines: "We have said you can't put this material into news racks where minors can get access to it. And to the publishers we say, 'Tough luck! You have to sell it in stores.'" (*Los Angeles Times*, March 20, 1997, p. A-21).

Some of the justices pointed out that sex has long been a topic of conversation among teens: "This has been known to happen in high school," Justice Stephen G. Breyer said. "Do you suddenly make large numbers of high school students across the country guilty of a Federal offense?" Justice Breyer compared the Internet to a high school telephone conversation: "My concern is this would make large numbers of high school kids subject to a federal crime." Justice Scalia said that if he spent the time to monitor his sixteen-year-old's Internet use, "I'd know even less about this case than I know today." Justice David H. Souter worried about the parent who might allow a child to see an indecent image on a computer screen: "Could the parent go to prison?" he asked. A violation of the law would have carried penalties of up to $250,000 and two years in prison (*New York Times*, March 20, 1997, p. B-10).

The Reasoning of the Court

The Supreme Court's decision reflected both the optimism the appellate court displayed for the marketplace of ideas and the concerns lawmakers have had about a wide-open Internet. The majority of the court fashioned a case based on the legal precedent recognizing that the government must be very careful in any attempt to restrict free expression. A dissenting opinion argued that it would be legal to zone indecent materials to adult-only places.

The Decision of the Court

Key portions of the Supreme Court decision are abstracted on the following pages. They reveal the stress between legal optimism and pessimism over the marketplace metaphor. From this perspective, it can be argued that one must either have faith that an open market will ultimately lead to the public good or else support government restrictions in the name of protecting the "weakest" citizens—usually defined as the children.

Box 5.2 Key Portions of the *Reno v. ACLU* 521 U.S. 844 (1997) Decision

JANET RENO, ATTORNEY GENERAL OF THE UNITED STATES, ET AL.,
APPELLANTS v. AMERICAN CIVIL LIBERTIES UNION ET AL.
No. 96–511
SUPREME COURT OF THE UNITED STATES
117 S. Ct. 2329; 1997 U.S. LEXIS 4037; 138 L. Ed. 2d 874; 65
U.S.L.W. 4715; 25 Media L. Rep. 1833; 97 Cal. Daily Op.
Service 4998; 97 Daily Journal DAR 8133; 11 Fla. Law W. Fed.
S 211
March 19, 1997, Argued
June 26, 1997, Decided

Two provisions of the *Communications Decency Act of 1996* (CDA or Act) seek to protect minors from harmful material on the Internet, an international network of interconnected computers that enables millions of people to communicate with one another in "cyberspace" and to access vast amounts of information from around the world . . . criminalizes the "knowing" transmission of "obscene or indecent" messages to any recipient under 18 years of age. Section 223(d) prohibits the "knowing" sending or displaying to a person under 18 of any message "that, in context, depicts or describes, in terms patently offensive as measured by contemporary community . . . standards, sexual or excretory activities or organs." Affirmative defenses are provided for those who take "good faith, . . . effective . . . actions" to restrict access by minors to the prohibited communications . . . and those who restrict such access by requiring certain designated forms of age proof, such as a verified credit card or an adult identification number. . . . A number of plaintiffs filed suit challenging the constitutionality. . . . After making extensive findings of fact, a three-judge District Court convened pursuant to the Act entered a preliminary injunction against enforcement of both challenged provisions. The court's judgment enjoins the Government from enforcing . . . prohibitions insofar as they relate to "indecent" communications, but expressly preserves the Government's right to investigate and prosecute the obscenity or child pornography activities prohibited therein. The injunction against enforcement . . . is unqualified because that section contains no separate reference to obscenity or child pornography. The Government appealed to this Court under the Act's special review provisions, arguing . . . that the District Court erred in holding that the CDA violated both the First Amendment because it is overbroad and the Fifth Amendment because it is vague . . .

OPINION: JUSTICE STEVENS delivered the opinion of the Court.

At issue is the constitutionality of two statutory provisions enacted to protect minors from "indecent" and "patently offensive" communications on the Internet. Notwithstanding the legitimacy and importance of the congressional goal of protecting children from harmful materials, we agree with the three-judge District Court that the statute abridges "the freedom of speech" protected by the First Amendment . . .

The District Court made extensive findings of fact, most of which were based on a detailed stipulation prepared by the parties. . . . The findings describe the character and the dimensions of the Internet, the availability of sexually explicit material in that medium, and the problems confronting age verification for recipients of Internet communications. Because those findings provide the underpinnings for the legal issues, we begin with a summary of the undisputed facts.

The Internet

The Internet is an international network of interconnected computers. It is the outgrowth of what began in 1969 as a military program called "ARPANET". . . which was designed to enable computers operated by the military, defense contractors, and universities conducting defense-related research . . . to communicate with one another by redundant channels even if some portions of the network were damaged in a war . . .

The Internet has experienced "extraordinary growth." . . . The number of "host" computers—those that store information and relay communications—increased from about 300 in 1981 to approximately 9,400,000 by the time of the trial in 1996. Roughly 60% of these hosts are located in the United States. About 40 million people used the Internet at the time of trial, a number that is expected to mushroom to 200 million . . . by 1999 . . .

The District Court found that at any given time "tens of thousands of users are engaging in conversations on a huge range of subjects.". . . It is "no exaggeration to conclude that the content on the Internet is as diverse as human thought" . . .

The best known category of communication over the Internet is the World Wide Web, which allows users to search . . . for and retrieve information stored in remote computers, as well as, in some cases, to communicate back to designated sites. In concrete terms, the Web consists of a vast number of documents stored in different computers all over the world. Some of these documents are simply files containing information. However, more elaborate documents, commonly known as Web "pages," are also prevalent. Each has its own address—"rather like a telephone number." . . . Web pages frequently contain information and sometimes allow the viewer to communicate with the page's (or "site's") author. They generally also contain "links" to other documents created by that site's author or to other (generally) related sites. Typically, the links are either blue or underlined text—sometimes images . . .

Though such material is widely available, users seldom encounter such content accidentally. "A document's title or a description of the document will usually appear before the document itself . . . and in many cases the user will receive detailed information about a site's content before he or she need take the step to access the document. Almost all sexually explicit images are preceded by warnings as to the content." . . . For that reason, the "odds are slim" that a user would enter a sexually explicit site by accident. . . . Unlike communications received by radio or television, "the receipt of information on the Internet requires a series of affirmative steps more deliberate and directed than merely turning a dial. A child requires some sophistication and some ability to read to retrieve material and thereby to use the Internet unattended" . . .

In *Ginsberg*, we upheld the constitutionality of a New York statute that prohibited selling to minors under 17 years of age material that was considered obscene as to them even if not obscene as to adults. We rejected the defendant's broad submission that "the scope of the constitutional freedom of expression secured to a citizen to read or see material concerned with sex cannot be made to depend on whether the citizen is an adult or a minor." . . . In rejecting that contention, we relied not only on the State's independent interest in the well-being of its youth, but also on . . . our consistent recognition of the principle that "the parents' claim to authority in their own household to direct the rearing of their children is basic in the structure of our society" . . .

In *Pacifica*, we upheld a declaratory order of the Federal Communications Commission, holding that the broadcast of a recording of a 12-minute monologue entitled "Filthy Words" that had previously . . . been delivered to a live audience "could have been the subject of administrative sanctions." . . . The Commission had found that the repetitive use of certain words referring to excretory or sexual activities or organs "in an afternoon broadcast when children are in the audience was patently offensive" and concluded that the monologue was indecent "as broadcast." The respondent did not quarrel with the finding that the afternoon broadcast was patently offensive, but contended that it was not "indecent" within the meaning of the relevant statutes because it contained no prurient appeal. After rejecting respondent's statutory arguments, we confronted its two constitutional arguments: (1) that the Commission's construction of its authority to ban indecent speech was so broad that its order had to be set aside even if the broadcast at issue was unprotected; and (2) that since the recording was not obscene, the First Amendment forbade any abridgment of the right to broadcast it on the radio . . .

In *Renton*, we upheld a zoning ordinance that kept adult movie theaters out of residential neighborhoods. The ordinance was aimed, not at the content of the films shown in the theaters, but rather at the "secondary effects"—such as crime and deteriorating property values—that these theaters fostered: "It is the secondary effect which these zoning ordinances attempt to avoid, not the dissemination . . . of 'offensive speech'" . . . According to the Government, the CDA is constitutional because it constitutes a sort of "cyberzoning" on the Internet. But the CDA applies broadly to the entire universe of cyberspace. And the purpose of the CDA is to protect children from the primary effects of "indecent" and "patently offensive" speech, rather than any "secondary" effect of such speech. Thus, the CDA is a content-based blanket restriction on speech, and, as such, cannot be "properly analyzed as a form of time, place, and manner regulation" . . .

Neither before nor after the enactment of the CDA have the vast democratic fora of the Internet been subject to the type of government supervision and regulation that has attended the broadcast industry. . . . Moreover, the Internet is not as "invasive" as radio or television. The District Court specifically found that "communications over the Internet . . . do not 'invade' an individual's home or appear on one's computer screen unbidden. Users seldom encounter content 'by accident'" . . .

The Government argues that the statute is no more vague than the obscenity standard this Court established . . . in . . . *Miller v. California* (1973). But that is not so. In *Miller*, this Court reviewed a criminal conviction against a commercial vendor who mailed brochures containing pictures of sexually explicit activities to individuals who had not requested such materials. . . . Having struggled for some time to establish a definition of obscenity, we set forth in *Miller* the test for obscenity that controls to this day:

"(a) whether the average person, applying contemporary community standards would find that the work, taken as a whole, appeals to the prurient interest; (b) whether the work depicts or describes, in a patently offensive way, sexual conduct specifically defined by the applicable state law; and (c) whether the work, taken as a whole, lacks serious literary, artistic, political, or scientific value" . . .

Because the CDA's "patently offensive" standard (and, we assume arguendo, its synonymous "indecent" standard) is one part of the three-prong *Miller* test, the Government reasons, it cannot be unconstitutionally vague.

The Government's assertion is incorrect as a matter . . . of fact. The second prong of the *Miller* test—the purportedly analogous standard—contains a critical requirement that is omitted from the CDA: that the proscribed material be "specifically defined by the applicable state law." This requirement reduces the vagueness inherent in the open-ended term "patently offensive" as used in the CDA. Moreover, the Miller definition is limited to "sexual conduct," whereas the CDA extends also to include (1) "excretory activities" as well as (2) "organs" of both a sexual and excretory nature.

The Government's reasoning is also flawed. Just because a definition including three limitations is not vague, it does not follow that one of those limitations, standing by itself, is not vague. . . . Each of Miller's additional two prongs—(1) that, taken as a whole, the material appeal to the "prurient" interest, and (2) that it "lack serious literary, artistic, political, or scientific value"—critically limits the uncertain sweep of the obscenity definition. The second requirement is particularly important because, unlike the "patently offensive" and "prurient interest" criteria, it is not judged by contemporary community standards . . .

In evaluating the free speech rights of adults, we have made it perfectly clear that "sexual expression which is indecent but not obscene is protected . . . by the First Amendment" . . . ("Where obscenity is not involved, we have consistently held that the fact that protected speech may be offensive to some does not justify its suppression"). Indeed, *Pacifica* itself admonished that "the fact that society may find speech offensive is not a sufficient reason for suppressing it" . . .

The District Court was correct to conclude that the CDA effectively resembles the ban on "dial-a-porn" invalidated in . . . *Sable* . . . this Court rejected the argument that we should defer to the congressional judgment that nothing less than a total ban would be effective in preventing enterprising youngsters from gaining access to indecent communications. Sable thus made clear that the mere fact that a statutory regulation of speech was enacted for the important purpose of protecting . . . children from exposure to sexually explicit material does not foreclose inquiry into its validity. . . . As we pointed out last Term, that inquiry embodies an "over-arching commitment" to make sure that Congress has designed its statute to accomplish its purpose "without imposing an unnecessarily great restriction on speech" . . .

Under the CDA, a parent allowing her 17-year-old . . . to use the family computer to obtain information on the Internet that she, in her parental judgment, deems appropriate could face a lengthy prison term. . . . Similarly, a parent who sent his 17-year-old college freshman information on birth control via e-mail could be incarcerated even though neither he, his child, nor anyone in their home community, found the material "indecent" or "patently offensive," if the college town's community thought otherwise.

The breadth of this content-based restriction of speech imposes an especially heavy burden on the Government to explain why a less restrictive provision would not be as effective as the CDA. It has not done so. The arguments in this Court have referred to possible alternatives such as requiring that indecent material be "tagged" in a way that facilitates parental control of material coming into their homes, making exceptions for messages with artistic or educational value, providing some tolerance for parental choice, and regulating some portions of the Internet—such as commercial web sites—differently than others, such as chat rooms. Particularly in the light of the absence of any detailed. . . findings by the Congress, or even hearings addressing the special problems of the CDA, we are persuaded that the CDA is not narrowly tailored if that requirement has any meaning at all. . . .

The dramatic expansion of this new marketplace of ideas contradicts the factual basis of this contention. The record demonstrates that the growth of the Internet has been and continues to be phenomenal. As a matter of constitutional tradition, in the absence of evidence to the contrary, we presume. . . that governmental regulation of the content of speech is more likely to interfere with the free exchange of ideas than to encourage it. The interest in encouraging freedom of expression in a democratic society outweighs any theoretical but unproven benefit of censorship.

For the foregoing reasons, the judgment of the district court is affirmed.

It is so ordered.

DISSENT: JUSTICE O'CONNOR, with whom THE CHIEF JUSTICE joins, concurring in the judgment in part and dissenting in part.

I write separately to explain why I view the *Communications Decency Act of 1996* (CDA) as little more than an attempt by Congress to create "adult zones" on the Internet. Our precedent indicates that the creation of such zones can be constitutionally sound. Despite the soundness of its purpose, however, portions of the CDA are unconstitutional because they stray from the blueprint our prior cases have developed for constructing a "zoning law" that passes constitutional muster. . . .

What the Court classifies as a single "'patently offensive display'" provision . . . is in reality two separate provisions. The first of these makes it a crime to knowingly send a patently offensive message or image to a specific person under the age of 18 ("specific person" provision). . . . The second criminalizes the display of patently offensive messages or images "in any manner available" to minors ("display" provision). . . . None of these provisions purports to keep indecent (or patently offensive) material away from adults, who have a First Amendment right to obtain this speech . . .

The creation of "adult zones" is by no means a novel concept. States have long denied minors access to certain establishments frequented by adults. . . . States have also denied minors access to speech deemed to be "harmful to minors." . . . The Court has previously sustained such zoning laws, but only if they respect the First Amendment rights of adults and minors. That is to say, a zoning law is valid if (i) it does not unduly restrict adult access to the material; and (ii) minors have no First Amendment right to read or view the banned material. As applied to the Internet as it exists in 1997, the "display" provision and some applications of the "indecency transmission" and "specific person" provisions fail to adhere to the first of these limiting principles by restricting adults' access to protected materials in certain circumstances. Unlike the Court, however, I would invalidate the provisions only in those circumstances . . .

Our cases make clear that a "zoning" law is valid only if adults are still able to obtain the regulated speech. If they cannot, the law does more than simply keep children away from speech they have no right to obtain—interferes with the rights of adults to obtain constitutionally protected speech and effectively "reduces the adult population . . . to reading only what is fit for children." . . . The First Amendment does not tolerate such interference . . .

The electronic world is fundamentally different. Because it is no more than the interconnection of electronic pathways, cyberspace allows speakers and listeners to mask their identities. Cyberspace undeniably reflects some form of geography; chat rooms and Web sites, for example, exist at fixed "locations" on the Internet. Since users can transmit and receive messages on the Internet without revealing anything about their identities or ages . . . however, it is not currently possible to exclude persons from accessing certain messages on the basis of their identity.

Cyberspace differs from the physical world in another basic way: Cyberspace is malleable. Thus, it is possible to construct barriers in cyberspace and use them to screen for identity, making cyberspace more like the physical world and, consequently, more amenable to zoning laws. This transformation of cyberspace is already underway . . .

Restricting what the adult may say to the minors in no way restricts the adult's ability to communicate with other adults. He is not prevented from speaking indecently to other adults in a chat room (because there are no other adults participating in the conversation) and he remains free to send indecent e-mails to other adults. The relevant universe contains only one adult, and the adult in that universe has the power to refrain from using indecent speech and consequently to keep all such speech within the room in an "adult" zone.

The analogy to *Ginsberg* breaks down, however, when more than one adult is a party to the conversation. If a minor enters a chat room otherwise occupied by adults, the CDA effectively requires the adults in the room to stop using indecent speech. If they did not, they could be prosecuted under the . . . "indecency transmission" and "specific person" provisions for any indecent statements they make to the group, since they would be transmitting an indecent message to specific persons, one of whom is a minor. . . . The CDA is therefore akin to a law that makes it a crime for a bookstore owner to sell pornographic magazines to anyone once a minor enters his store. Even assuming such a law might be constitutional in the physical world as a reasonable alternative to excluding minors completely from the store, the absence of any means of excluding minors from chat rooms in cyberspace restricts the rights of adults to engage in indecent speech in those rooms. The "indecency transmission" and "specific person" provisions share this defect. . . .

While discussions about prison rape or nude art, see ibid., may have some redeeming education value for adults, they do not necessarily have any such value for minors, and under *Ginsberg*, minors only have a First Amendment right to obtain patently offensive material that has "redeeming social importance for minors." . . . There is also no evidence in the record to support the contention that "many [e]-mail transmissions from an adult to a minor are conversations between family members" . . . and no support for the legal proposition that such speech is absolutely immune from regulation. Accordingly, in my view, the CDA does not burden a substantial amount of minors' constitutionally protected speech. Thus, the constitutionality of the CDA as a zoning law hinges on the extent to which it substantially interferes with the First Amendment rights of adults.

Because the rights of adults are infringed only by the "display" provision and by the "indecency transmission" and "specific person" provisions as applied to communications involving more than one adult, I would invalidate the CDA only to that extent. Insofar as the "indecency transmission" and "specific person" provisions prohibit the use of indecent speech in communications between an adult and one or more minors, however, they can and should be sustained. The Court reaches a contrary conclusion, and from that holding that I respectfully dissent.

Implications for the Future of Internet Regulation

According to one interpretation, the *Reno* decision indicated that a majority of the Court had accepted the notion that the Internet was a brand-new location for the marketplace of ideas and therefore had come to champion the marketplace philosophy.

Charles Levendosky, an editorial page writer, was a member of the American Library Association's Freedom to Read Foundation board of trustees when the CDA lawsuit was filed. Box 5.3 presents a column he wrote that was published by the *Casper Star Tribune* in Wyoming and the New York Times Wire Service. In the opinion, he championed support for the marketplace of ideas philosophy. Levendosky seemed to summarize the view of many Internet supporters across the country.

Levendosky obviously preferred the marketplace of ideas over the government's attempts to regulate communication. However, he missed the point made by critics of the marketplace by lumping their criticisms with those from the people who support intrusive government regulation.

It is possible to both disdain the power of conglomerate mass media, including corporate control of the Internet, *and* recognize the flaws in the CDA. Some critical theorists are not concerned that minors will view "indecent" material; rather, they fear that the Internet, like radio and television, will come to "narcotize" the mass public into mindless consumerism, into accepting thoughtless mass politics, and into frittering away hours on ultimately useless ventures of entertainment. One can be a critic of the commercial marketplace yet still argue against *all* controls—whether they come from government or corporate boardrooms. Critical social theorists, however, find it difficult to imagine a system of communication that does not inherently contain mechanisms of social control. It is ultimately the individual, not powerful forces, that might make a difference.

The legal progression of the marketplace of ideas philosophy must be accompanied by the social understanding of the limitations of any marketplace. Thus, it is likely that as the Internet and what follows develop, the euphoria over their potential will recede as people deal with the realities of the way the technology is used.

Postcript

In 1998, the U.S. Congress made another try at containing Internet pornography. To limit online pornography and protect children navigating the Internet, the House of Representatives voted to require companies with web sites offering "obscene or indecent material" to demand that their customers prove they are at least sixteen years of age by giving credit card numbers, by using adult access codes, or by some "other reasonable measure." In what would be codified as 47 U.S.C. § 231, COPA provided that:

> (1) PROHIBITED CONDUCT: Whoever knowingly and with knowledge of the character of the material, in interstate or foreign commerce by means of the World Wide Web, makes any communication for commercial purposes that is available to any minor and that includes any material that is harmful to minors shall be fined not more than $50,000, imprisoned not more than 6 months, or both.

Box 5.3   An Opinion on the Decision

The philosophical core that Justice Oliver Wendell Holmes inserted into the freedom of speech debate over 78 years ago continues to beat like a young heart in the body of First Amendment law. His words were at the center of the U.S. Supreme Court's reasoning when on June 26 in *Reno vs. American Civil Liberties Union*, it struck down the Communications Decency Act as a violation of the Constitution.

In 1919, Justice Holmes filed a dissent in *Abrams vs. United States* in which he created the powerful and enduring "marketplace of ideas" metaphor to encapsulate the concept of freedom of speech. In the marketplace metaphor, ideas compete against one another for acceptance—with the underlying faith that truth will prevail in such a free and open encounter.

Borrowing from John Milton's *Areopagitica* (1644) and John Stuart Mill's *On Liberty* (1859), Holmes wrote in his Abrams dissent: "But when men have realized that time has upset many fighting faiths, they may come to believe even more than they believe the very foundations of their own conduct that the ultimate good desired is better reached by free trade in ideas—that the best test of truth is the power of the thought to get itself accepted in the competition of the market. . . . That at any rate is the theory of our Constitution. It is an experiment, as all life is an experiment."

Justice Holmes' pivotal concept gradually became the controlling metaphor in First Amendment jurisprudence. His voice was present in the high court's decision striking down the CDA.

In response to the ACLU and American Library Association's challenge to the Communication Decency Act, the government argued that by not controlling indecent material on the Internet, countless citizens are being driven away from the medium.

In the court's CDA opinion, Justice John Paul Stevens responds: "The dramatic expansion of this new marketplace of ideas contradicts the factual basis of this contention. The record demonstrates that the growth of the Internet has been and continues to be phenomenal."

Stevens ends the opinion: "As a matter of constitutional tradition, in the absence of evidence to the contrary, we presume that governmental regulation of the content of speech is more likely to interfere with the free exchange of ideas than to encourage it. The interests in encouraging freedom of expression in a democratic society outweighs any theoretical but unproven benefit of censorship."

In a true marketplace of ideas, the ability of the government to regulate communications is strictly limited.

And Justice Holmes' metaphor fits the Internet precisely.

The Internet is the most democratic medium of mass communication yet invented. One person sitting in front of a public library computer can e-mail tens of thousands of potential readers with a message—without spending a penny.

This reality cuts short those who argue that the marketplace of ideas concept of free speech is unfair because those who are wealthy have a greater access to communications media. The Internet and free access to it in public schools and public libraries gives even the economically disadvantaged in our communities the ability to send their messages across the world. Anyone can be a widely read pamphleteer.

While few can own a newspaper business or a radio or television station, wealth is not essential to this medium.

Corporate entities cannot even control the content of Internet speech—although they may try at local levels. The Internet is too vast, too multilayered, too interlocking, too accessible to be controlled.

The Internet has the inherent ability to overcome the social and economic monopolies of power that often control other media. It guarantees that numerous minority viewpoints in any public discussion will be expressed.

If speech is power, then the Internet disperses that power. The reality of the Internet diminishes the rational of those who argue that current First Amendment law is anti-democratic because it protects moneyed, corporate, and commercial speech which then levers greater political gains. Internet citizens are only now beginning to realize the potential political clout they can have with this new medium—without large bank accounts.

Recent critics of the First Amendment have not taken into account the impact of this revolutionary and profoundly democratic medium, the Internet. It allows ideas we respect to encounter those ideas we despise. It allows the voices of those rarely heard to mix with those who speak often. It allows racial and ethnic minorities to add their voices to the shifting electronic array.

The Internet allows truth to grapple with falsehood, to paraphrase Milton. In its CDA ruling, the U.S. Supreme Court reaffirmed the great concept of freedom of speech that the founders understood in the turmoil of revolutionary fervor: There must be room for all ideas. Pamphleteers, newspapers, broadsides, and town criers spread that debate from street corner to colonial legislatures, from homes to the Continental Congress. The flux and exchange of ideas was a flood, a tidal wave. Yet to fear an idea, any idea, meant that one was not ready for self-governance.

And that is still true.

The high court's ruling must blunt the thrust of those First Amendment critics who want the government to exercise greater control over speech—for whatever well-intentioned reason.

The marketplace of ideas represented by the Internet needs only speakers and potential audience. The government is largely superfluous.

(Source: http://w3.trib.com/FACT/lst.lev.internet.marketplace.html [reprinted by permission]; Levendosky's web site address is http://w3.trib. com/FACT/)

---

(2) INTENTIONAL VIOLATIONS: In addition to the penalties under paragraph (1), whoever intentionally violates such paragraph shall be subject to a fine of not more than $50,000 for each violation. For purposes of this paragraph, each day of violation shall constitute a separate violation.

(3) CIVIL PENALTY: In addition to the penalties under paragraphs (1) and (2), whoever violates paragraph (1) shall be subject to a civil penalty of not more than $50,000 for each violation. For purposes of this paragraph, each day of violation shall constitute a separate violation.

The law would apply "only if such person is engaged in the business of making such communication," 47 U.S.C. § 231(e)(2)(A), further defined as follows:

[a] person who makes a communication, or offers to make a communication, by means of the World Wide Web, that includes any material that is harmful to minors, devotes time, attention, or labor to such activities, as a regular course of such person's trade or business, with the objective of earning a profit as a result of such activities (although it is not necessary that the person make a profit or that the making or offering to make such communications be the person's sole or principal business or source of income). A person may be considered to be engaged in the business of making, by means of the World Wide Web, communications for commercial purposes that include material that is harmful to minors, only if the person knowingly causes the material that is harmful to minors to be posted on the World Wide Web or knowingly solicits such material to be posted on the World Wide Web.

The Congress defined material that is harmful to minors, using the *Miller v. California* (1973) test, as:

any communication, picture, image, graphic image file, article, recording, writing, or other matter of any kind that is obscene or that (A) the average person, applying contemporary community standards, would find, taking the material as a whole and with respect to minors, is designed to appeal to, or is designed to pander to, the prurient interest; (B) depicts, describes, or represents, in a manner patently offensive with respect to minors, an actual or simulated sexual act or sexual contact, an actual or simulated normal or perverted sexual act, or a lewd exhibition of the genitals or post-pubescent female breast; and (C) taken as a whole, lacks serious literary, artistic, political, or scientific value for minors.

A minor was defined as any person under seventeen years of age, and the law provided defenses for web site operators:

(c) AFFIRMATIVE DEFENSE.—(1) DEFENSE: It is an affirmative defense to prosecution under this section that the defendant, in good faith, has restricted access by minors to material that is harmful to minors—(A) by requiring use of a credit card, debit account, adult access code, or adult personal identification number; (B) by accepting a digital certificate that verifies age; or (C) by any other reasonable measures that are feasible under available technology.

Representative Michael Oxeye argued: "Unfortunately, the Web is awash in degrading smut." But Representative Barney Frank worried that "this will further erode the notion of freedom of speech." Those favoring the legislation said it would be a good test of constitutionality, even if it were struck down by the courts (Associated Press, October 8, 1998). U.S. District Judge Lowell Reed, appointed in 1987 by President Ronald Reagan, granted a temporary restraining order delaying government enforcement of the Child Online Protection Act, and he followed that action with a preliminary injunction (*Washington Post*, February 2, 1999, p. A-2). The ACLU had argued against the measure on grounds that the law would inhibit distribution of information about homosexuality, AIDS, and sexuality. *Salon* magazine editor and CEO David Talbot testified that a popular column by feminist Camille Paglia "could be deemed harmful to minors" and that readership would plummet if readers had to identify themselves (Associated Press, November 20, 1998). Plaintiffs in the lawsuit—including the American Civil Liberties Union, the Electronic Privacy Information Center, the Electronic Frontier Foundation, Time Warner, and the *New York Times*—called the law too broad to be constitutional (TechWeb [an online information service], November 20, 1998).

The Child Online Protection Act, scheduled to go into effect in November 1998, was delayed by court injunction. It would have required adult sites to move adult materials behind electronic bouncers, and the user's age could be checked by requiring a credit card for entry. Judge Reed's temporary restraining order gave opponents, including the ACLU, time to argue that the new law (which was attached to the 1998 omnibus spending budget bill) trampled the First Amendment rights of adults by raising privacy issues in regard to online identification (*Washington Post*, December 14, 1998).

"The law makes it a crime for any 'commercial' Web site to make material that is 'harmful to minors' available to anyone under 17." The injunction was extended until February 1, 1999, and the court in Philadelphia scheduled a January hearing. The press emphasized that "the new law would require sites to collect a credit card number or other proof of age. Sites that don't face fines up to $50,000 and up to six months in jail" (*USA Today*, December 2, 1998, p. 8-D). The clearest legal challenge contended that a law restricting commercial web sites does nothing to protect minors from noncommercial pornographic addresses. During oral arguments before Judge Reed, Vanderbilt University professor Donna Hoffman said: "The culture of the Internet is that everything is free" (*USA Today*, January 21, 1999, p. 1-D). Ann Beeson, of the American Civil Liberties Union, added, "On the Internet, you can't tell the difference between adults and minors" (*USA Today*, January 20, 1999, p. 7-D). It was suggested that adults would be restricted from racy material, and Dan Farber, who represented a coalition of major media plaintiffs, noted, "Almost any content provider [is] vulnerable to some pretty Draconian measures." Judge Reed blocked the new law, writing: "Indeed, perhaps we do minors of this country harm if First Amendment protections, which they will with age inherit fully, are chipped away in the name of protection" (CNN, February 2, 1999). Under the COPA law passed by Congress and signed by President Clinton in 1998, violators would face up to six months in jail and $150,000 per day in fines. "Despite the Court's personal regret that the preliminary injunction will delay once again the careful protection of our children, I without hesitation acknowledge the duty imposed on the Court and greater good such duty serves," Judge Reed wrote (*Washington Post*, February 2, 1999, p. A-2).

Judge Reed's opinion quoted the First Amendment and marketplace philosophy:

> Although there is no complete consensus on the issue, most courts and commentators theorize that the importance of protecting freedom of speech is to foster the marketplace of ideas. If speech, even unconventional speech that some find lacking in substance or offensive, is allowed to compete unrestricted in the marketplace of ideas, truth will be discovered. Indeed, the First Amendment was designed to prevent the majority, through acts of Congress, from silencing those who would express unpopular or unconventional views (*ACLU v. Reno*, 98–5591, February 1, 1999).

Judge Reed distinguished the Internet from other media forms in terms of how easy it is for individuals to publish their ideas online, and he suggested that new media create unimagined public space:

Despite the protection provided by the First Amendment, unconventional speakers are often limited in their ability to promote such speech in the marketplace by the costs or logistics of reaching the masses, hence, the adage that freedom of the press is limited to those who own one. In the medium of cyberspace, however, anyone can build a soap box out of web pages and speak her mind in the virtual village green to an audience larger and more diverse than any the Framers could have imagined. In many respects, unconventional messages compete equally with the speech of mainstream speakers in the marketplace of ideas that is the Internet, certainly more than in most other media (*ACLU v. Reno*, 98–5591, February 1, 1999).

At the same time, however, Judge Reed's opinion suggested that the marketplace should be tamed by social responsibility:

But with freedom come consequences. Many of the same characteristics which make cyberspace ideal for First Amendment expression—ease of participation and diversity of content and speakers—make it a potentially harmful media for children. A child with minimal knowledge of a computer, the ability to operate a browser, and the skill to type a few simple words may be able to access sexual images and content over the World Wide Web. For example, typing the word "dollhouse" or "toys" into a typical Web search engine will produce a page of links, some of which connect to what would be considered by many to be pornographic Web sites. These Web sites offer "teasers," free sexually explicit images and animated graphic image files designed to entice a user to pay a fee to browse the whole site (*ACLU v. Reno*, 98–5591, February 1, 1999).

The opposition to COPA was centered on three legal grounds: "(1) that it is invalid on its face and as applied to them [online communications] under the First Amendment for burdening speech that is constitutionally protected for adults, (2) that it is invalid on its face for violating the First Amendment rights of minors, and (3) that it is unconstitutionally vague under the First and Fifth Amendments (*ACLU v. Reno*, 98–5591, February 1, 1999). Judge Reed expressed First Amendment concerns about the federal statute:

The economic costs associated with compliance with COPA are relevant to the Court's determination of the burden imposed by the statute. However, even if this Court should conclude that most of the plaintiffs would be able to afford the cost of implementing and maintaining their sites if they add credit card or adult verification screens, such conclusion is not dispositive. First Amendment jurisprudence indicates that the relevant inquiry is determining the burden imposed on the *protected speech* regulated by COPA, not the pressure placed on the *pocketbooks or bottom lines* of the plaintiffs, or of other Web site operators and content providers not before the Court. The

protection provided by the First Amendment in this context is not diminished because the speakers affected by COPA may be commercial entities
who speak for a profit (*ACLU v. Reno*, 98–5591, February 1, 1999).

Judge Reed found that regulation of access to web sites has a relationship with other areas of the Internet, such as chat rooms. Therefore, the
legislation raised constitutional speech issues: "The uncontroverted evidence showed that there is no way to restrict the access of minors to
harmful materials in chat rooms and discussion groups, which the
plaintiffs assert draw traffic to their sites, without screening all users
before accessing any content, even that which is not harmful to minors,
or editing all content before it is posted to exclude material that is
harmful to minors. . . . This has the effect of burdening speech in these
fora that is not covered by the statute. . . . I conclude that based on the
evidence presented to date, the plaintiffs have established a substantial
likelihood that they will be able to show that COPA imposes a burden
on speech that is protected for adults" (*ACLU v. Reno*, 98–5591, February 1, 1999).

Republican representative James Greenwood of Pennsylvania, a sponsor of the law, called for an appeal: "I look forward to a favorable judgment at the appellate level—a day that will be celebrated by millions of
parents and grandparents across the nation." A joint statement by Greenwood and Republican representative Tom Bliley of Virginia read: "In our
view, traditional laws for minors at the state level have worked effectively
to protect children from raw pornography without limiting adults' free
expression or access to legal materials. Through COPA, we seek only to
apply the same, common-sense standard to the World Wide Web as pre-
vails in the rest of our free and democratic society."

The *Reno* litigation and its support for First Amendment Internet protection already has had an impact on other disputes. For example, a
county library system in Virginia was stopped from enacting a policy to
use filtering software on Internet terminals.

It is worth noting, too, that the ruling came at a time when pornography was considered to be the most profitable form of business on the Internet. One final point needs to be made: Moral stands against media often fail for lack of public support. South Carolina theater owner David
Crenshaw, for instance, ended a four-month ban on R-rated movies after
he lost more than $20,000 in ticket sales. As he stated in Spartanburg: "We
had vocal support, but people were just not showing up to see the
movies. . . . You can't make people want something they don't want" (Associated Press, December 29, 1998).

Box 5.4 *Mainstream Loudoun v. Board of Trustees of the Loudoun County Library*

In the United States District Court for the Eastern District of Virginia, Alexandria Division Judge Leonie M. Brinkema ruled against a library system attempting to use Internet filtering software by passing a policy that limited access. The Court held that while the library system was not required to provide Internet access, once it did so the First Amendment protected patrons against censorship.

At issue in this civil action is whether a public library may . . . enact a policy prohibiting the access of library patrons to certain content-based categories of Internet publications. Plaintiffs are a Loudoun County nonprofit organization, suing on its own behalf and on behalf of its members, and individual Loudoun County residents who claim to have had their access to Internet sites blocked by the defendant library board's Internet policy. They, along with plaintiff-intervenors ("intervenors"), individuals and other entities who claim that defendant's Internet policy has blocked their websites or other materials they placed on the Internet, allege that this policy infringes their right to free speech under the First Amendment. Defendant, the Board of Trustees of the Loudoun County Library, contends that a public library has an absolute right to limit what it provides to the public and that any restrictions on Internet access do not implicate the First Amendment . . . [D]efendant passed a "Policy on Internet Sexual Harassment" ("Policy") stating that the Loudoun County public libraries would provide Internet access to its patrons subject to the following restrictions: (1) the library would not provide e-mail, chat rooms, or pornography; (2) all library computers would be equipped with site-blocking software to block all sites displaying: (a) child pornography and obscene material; and (b) material deemed harmful to juveniles; (3) all library computers would be installed near and in full view of library staff; and (4) patrons would not be permitted to access pornography and, if they do so and refuse to stop, the police may be called to intervene . . .

◆   ◆   ◆

Plaintiffs and intervenors both allege that the Policy, as written and as implemented, violates their First Amendment rights because it impermissibly discriminates against protected speech on the basis of content and constitutes an unconstitutional prior restraint. In response, defendant contends: (1) intervenors do not have standing; (2) the Policy does not implicate the First Amendment and is reasonable; (3) the Policy is the least restrictive means to achieve two compelling government interests; and (4) the library has statutory immunity from this action . . .

◆   ◆   ◆

The extent to which free speech protection reaches links on the Internet has not been directly addressed by any court. In more traditional contexts, individuals are frequently found to have standing to challenge restrictions on speech in which they have a sufficient interest even where that speech is not originally theirs. For example, owners of adult bookstores can challenge censorship of books they intend to sell, owners of adult movie theaters have standing to protest censorship of movies they intend to show, . . . and library patrons have standing to challenge library policies restricting their exercise of the First Amendment right to receive information . . . In essence, intervenor Ockerbloom has sought to intervene in this action because he claims to have an interest in the E for Ecstasy page, material he explicitly and purposely has made available for use by others. . . . While this argument is initially appealing, its consequences would be unmanageable. Because of the ease of establishing links to any and every site on the Internet, if we find that Ockerbloom has standing in this case it would be impossible to prevent anyone from asserting standing to protest alleged Internet-related First Amendment harms wherever, whenever, and to whomever they occur.

◆   ◆   ◆

Defendant has requested that we reconsider our previous finding that it is not immune from this litigation pursuant to a provision of the 1996 Communications Decency Act granting absolute immunity to good faith users of filtering software. See 47 U.S.C. § 230(c)(2)(A). In our previous opinion, we found that § 230 provides immunity from actions for damages; it does not, however, immunize defendant from an action for declaratory and injunctive relief. We see no reason to stray from our earlier decision, which is the law of this case. If Congress had intended the statute to insulate Internet providers from both liability and declaratory and injunctive relief, it would have said so.

◆   ◆   ◆

Defendant first contends that the . . . Policy should really be construed as a library acquisition decision, to which the First Amendment does not apply . . . rather than a decision to remove library materials. Plaintiffs and intervenors contend that this issue has already been decided by this Court and is the law of the case. . . . See *Mainstream Loudoun v. Board of Trustees of the Loudoun County Library, et al.*, 2 F. Supp. 2d 783, 794–95 (E.D. Va. 1998) ("The Library Board's action is more appropriately characterized as a removal decision"; "We conclude that [Pico] stands for the proposition the First Amendment applies to, and limits, the discretion of a public library to place content-based restrictions on access to constitutionally protected materials within its collection").

◆   ◆   ◆

Next, defendant contends that even if the First Amendment does apply, we should apply a less stringent standard than strict scrutiny. Specifically, defendant argues that because the library is a non-public forum, the Policy should be reviewed by an intermediate scrutiny standard, examining whether it is reasonably related to an important governmental interest . . . defendant argues that public libraries are non-public fora and, therefore, content-based speech regulations are not subject to the strict scrutiny standard. Rather, it asserts, such regulations need only be "reasonable and viewpoint neutral" to be upheld . . . Defendant concedes that the Policy is a content-based regulation of speech and that content-based regulations of speech in a limited public forum are subject to strict scrutiny . . . The only issue before us, then, is whether the library is a limited public forum or a non-public forum. In *Perry Education Ass'n v. Perry Local Educators' Ass'n*, 460 U.S. 37, 45–46, 74 L. Ed. 2d 794, 103 S. Ct. 948 (1983), the Supreme Court identified three categories of fora for the purpose of analyzing the degree of protection afforded to speech. The first category is the traditional forum, such as a sidewalk or public park. These are "places which by long tradition or by government fiat have been devoted to assembly and debate." . . . Second is the limited or designated forum, such as a school board meeting or municipal theater. This category consists of "public property which the State has opened for use by the public as a place for expressive activity." The last category is the non-public forum, such as a government office building or a teacher's mailbox, which is not "by tradition or designation a forum for public communication." It is undisputed that the Loudoun County libraries have not traditionally been open to the public for all forms of expressive activity and, therefore, are not traditional public fora.

◆   ◆   ◆

The final consideration is whether the nature of the forum is compatible with the expressive activity at issue. While the nature of the public library would clearly not be compatible with many forms of expressive activity, such as giving speeches or holding rallies, we find that it is compatible with the expressive activity at issue here, the receipt and communication of information through the Internet. Indeed, this expressive activity is explicitly offered by the library.

◆   ◆   ◆

. . . the Supreme Court held that "regulations that focus on . . . listeners' reactions to speech are not the type of 'secondary effects' we referred to in *Renton*." More recently, in construing the *Communications Decency Act*, the Court stated that "content-based blanket restrictions on speech . . . cannot be 'properly analyzed as a form of time, place, and manner regulation'" *Reno v. ACLU*, 521 U.S. 844, 117 S. Ct. 2329, 2342, 138 L. Ed. 2d 874 (1997).

◆   ◆   ◆

Defendant argues that both of its asserted interests are compelling. Although plaintiffs and intervenors argue that these interests were not really the motivating factors behind the Policy and that they are not furthered by the Policy, they do not argue that the interests themselves are not compelling. For the purposes of this analysis, therefore, we assume that minimizing access to illegal pornography and avoidance of creation of a sexually hostile environment are compelling government interests.

◆   ◆   ◆

To satisfy strict scrutiny, defendant must do more than demonstrate that it has a compelling interest; it must also demonstrate that the Policy is necessary to further that interest. In other words, defendant must demonstrate that in the absence of the Policy, a sexually hostile environment might exist and/or there would be a problem with individuals accessing child pornography or obscenity or minors accessing materials that are illegal as to them. Defendant "must demonstrate that the recited harms are real, not merely conjectural, and that the regulation will in fact alleviate these harms in a direct and material way" . . . the defendant must show that the threat of disruption is actual, material, and substantial. The defendant bears this burden because "the interest in encouraging freedom of expression in a democratic society outweighs any theoretical but unproven benefit of censorship." *Reno v. ACLU*, 521 U.S. 844, 117 S. Ct. 2329, 2351, 138 L. Ed. 2d 874 (1997).

◆   ◆   ◆

Significantly, defendant has not pointed to a single incident in which a library employee or patron has complained that material being accessed on the Internet was harassing or created a hostile environment. As a matter of law, we find this evidence insufficient to sustain defendant's burden of showing that the Policy is reasonably necessary. No reasonable trier of fact could conclude that three isolated incidents nationally, one very minor isolated incident in Virginia, no evidence whatsoever of problems in Loudoun County, and not a single employee complaint from anywhere in the country establish that the Policy is necessary to prevent sexual harassment or access to obscenity or child pornography.

◆   ◆   ◆

Even if defendant could demonstrate that the Policy was reasonably necessary to further compelling state interests, it would still have to show that the Policy is narrowly tailored to achieve those interests. The parties disagree about several issues relating to whether the Policy is narrowly tailored: (1) whether less restrictive means are available; (2) whether the Policy is overinclusive; and (3) whether X-Stop, the filtering software used by defendant, is the least restrictive filtering software available. . . . Defendant alleges that the Policy is constitutional because it is the least restrictive means available to achieve its interests. The only alternative to filtering, defendant contends, is to have librarians directly monitor what patrons view. Defendant asserts this system would be far more intrusive than using filtering software. Plaintiffs and intervenors respond that there are many less restrictive means available, including designing an acceptable use policy, using privacy screens, using filters that can be turned off for adult use, changing the location of Internet terminals, educating patrons on Internet use, placing time limits on use, and enforcing criminal laws when violations occur.

◆　　◆　　◆

In *Sable Communications of Calif., Inc. v. FCC*, 492 U.S. 115, 126, 106 L. Ed. 2d 93, 109 S. Ct. 2829 (1989), the Supreme Court noted that "the Government may . . . regulate the content of constitutionally protected speech in order to promote a compelling interest if it chooses the least restrictive means to further the articulated interest." In *Sable* the Court declared unconstitutional a statute banning all "indecent" commercial telephone communications. The Court found that the government could not justify a total ban on communication that is harmful to minors, but not obscene, by arguing that only a total ban could completely prevent children from accessing indecent messages . . . The Court held that without evidence that less restrictive means had "been tested over time," the government had not carried its burden of proving that they would not be sufficiently effective . . . We find that the Policy is not narrowly tailored because less restrictive means are available to further defendant's interests and, as in *Sable*, there is no evidence that defendant has tested any of these means over time. First, the installation of privacy screens is a much less restrictive alternative that would further defendant's interest in preventing the development of a sexually hostile environment . . .

Second, there is undisputed evidence in the record that charging library staff with casual monitoring of Internet use is neither extremely intrusive nor a change from other library policies . . . Third, filtering software could be installed on only some Internet terminals and minors could be limited to using those terminals. Alternately, the library could install filtering software that could be turned off when an adult is using the terminal. While we find that all of these alternatives are less restrictive than the Policy, we do not find that any of them would necessarily be constitutional if implemented. That question is not before us.

◆　　◆　　◆

At issue in *Reno* was a federal statute, the *Communications Decency Act* ("CDA"), which established a criminal penalty for providing on the Internet material deemed harmful to minors although not obscene with the knowledge that such material could be accessed by minors. The Supreme Court found that because there was no way for an Internet provider to block minors from accessing such material, this statute effectively prohibited such material from being displayed at all. The Court held that in order to deny minors access to potentially harmful speech, the CDA effectively suppresses a large amount of speech that adults have a constitutional right to receive and to address to one another. That burden on adult speech is unacceptable if less restrictive alternatives would be at least as effective in achieving the legitimate purpose that the statute was enacted to serve.

Because we have found that less restrictive alternatives are available to defendant and that defendant has not sufficiently tried to employ any of them, the Policy's limitation of adult access to constitutionally protected materials cannot survive strict scrutiny.

◆   ◆   ◆

Preventing prior restraints of speech is an essential component of the First Amendment's free speech guarantee. . . ."Permitting government officials unbridled discretion in determining whether to allow protected speech presents an unacceptable risk of both indefinitely suppressing and chilling protected speech."

◆   ◆   ◆

This is insufficient because, as we noted in our previous opinion, "forcing citizens to publicly petition the Government for access to" disfavored speech has a "severe chilling effect." *Mainstream Loudoun*, 2 F. Supp. 2d at 797 (citing *Lamont v. Postmaster General*, 381 U.S. 301, 307, 14 L. Ed. 2d 398, 85 S. Ct. 1493 [1965]). . . . ("The loss of First Amendment freedoms, for even minimal periods of time, unquestionably constitutes irreparable injury"). At least one patron has stated that he failed to request access to a blocked site he believed was improperly blocked because he was "intimidated to have to go through that procedure."

◆   ◆   ◆

Although defendant is under no obligation to provide Internet access to its patrons, it has chosen to do so and is therefore restricted by the First Amendment in the limitations it is allowed to place on patron access. Defendant has asserted a broad right to censor the expressive activity of the receipt and communication of information through the Internet with a Policy that (1) is not necessary to further any compelling government interest; (2) is not narrowly tailored; (3) restricts the access of adult patrons to protected material just because the material is unfit for minors; (4) provides inadequate standards for restricting access; and (5) provides inadequate procedural safeguards to ensure prompt judicial review. Such a policy offends the guarantee of free speech in the First Amendment and is, therefore, unconstitutional.

(Source: *Mainstream Loudoun v. Board of Trustees of the Loudoun County Library*, Civil Action No. 97–2049-A, 24 F. Supp. 2d 552; 1998 U.S. Dist. LEXIS 18479 [1998])

Chapter Summary

This chapter examined the Communications Decency Act. I paid special attention to conflicting views about the application of the marketplace of ideas philosophy, drawing on the *ACLU v. Reno* case. On the one hand, the winning side in this legal dispute had an unbridled faith in the marketplace. On the other hand, there was a call to zone adult-oriented content in the name of protecting our children.

Discussion Questions

1. Given the corporate nature of communication today, do you trust those who dominate the marketplace of ideas to make decisions in the public interest?
2. If the Internet comes to be dominated by commercial interests, will that affect the ways in which it is different from conventional media?
3. Is the Internet the most democratic form of communication yet invented?
4. Is there any case in which you believe children must be protected from seeing, hearing, or reading content on the Internet?
5. Do electronic filtering software programs provide an adequate technological fix for the problem of protecting kids? What problems are associated with filtering software?
6. Might future courts see limited restrictions, such as requiring adult content users to provide their credit card numbers, as unconstitutional? What legal issues are triggered by the latest legislation?

6

The Drudge Report and the Clinton Scandal

A Case Study in Internet Content

"We aim to separate the brass tacks from the bull shine. Now if the bull shine is really interesting, then we're going to give you some of that, too."

—**Dan Rather, network TV newscaster (1997)**

"With his fedora and rumpled suits, Drudge styles himself as 'the Walter Winchell of the electronic age.'"

—**Karen Breslau, news magazine reporter (1997)**

"Whether it's catastrophic earthquakes in South America or in-fighting at ABC News, Capitol Hill hijinx or first-hand accounts from the sets of controversial films, Drudge exposes the inside scoop. . . . Drudge has no set schedule; he files when he has a story that he thinks is worth your time."

—**America Online, Internet service (1997)**

"Someone said that you [White House Press Secretary Mike Mc-Curry] or someone here has put out the word that staffers should not be allowed to log onto the Drudge Report. Is that true?"

—**Sam Donaldson,
network TV reporter (1998)**

*"No. People—it's a free country, and people can do what they want
on the internet."*
                    —Mike McCurry, former White House press secretary (1998)

*"Maybe I made some mistakes, but . . . the First Amendment protects
mistakes."*
                                   —Matt Drudge, Internet columnist (1998)

*"Whether we like it or not, he's one of us. . . . While there's a visceral
impulse to think that people of Drudge's ilk need to be punished . . .
that is a dangerous road to head down."*
                                      —Paul McMasters, media analyst (1998)

*"There is such a level of built-in irresponsibility in everything he says
and does. . . . If one were rewriting libel law today, one would try to
write it to assure that the false statements of Matt Drudge were
treated as libel."*
                            —Floyd Abrams, First Amendment lawyer (1998)

Thirty-year-old Matt Drudge styled himself as the cyberspace Walter
Winchell of the 1990s, complete with a Panama hat to cover his premature
balding. He began as a Hollywood, California, gossip columnist who
relied largely on recycled news. His Drudge Report web site (http://
www.drudgereport.com) was produced using two computers, wall-to-
wall television monitors connected to satellite dishes, and some thirty
newspapers (America Online, web page, December 11, 1997). His approach blurred the line between news and rumor:

> He began his career trolling through the trash at the CBS gift shop in search
> of movie-industry gossip that he would then post on his Web page. Soon he
> added political tidbits and became a virtual water cooler for the media elite.
> A self-described right-wing "Clinton Crazy," the 30-year-old cozied up to
> Washington's Gen-X conservative set; he was feted at a Georgetown dinner
> hosted by David Brock. When AOL hired Drudge . . . it touted his "instant,
> edgy" style. Drudge has said that his sources were "80 percent reliable"—
> and he's admitted that he sometimes gets things wrong (*Newsweek*, October
> 20, 1997, p. 63).

Drudge's freewheeling style is significant because it runs counter to
traditional beltway political reporting. It has long been known that reporters have withheld information from the public if it was difficult to

confirm or damaged political friends. As a product of ideology and culture, news is socially constrained and limited (Shoemaker, in Berkowitz, 1997, p. 59). As a matter of free expression, politics matters as a social constraint on the flow of information. So, as one might guess, the Washington journalism establishment was abuzz in June 1998 when Drudge was invited to speak to the prestigious National Press Club. Doug Harbrecht, president of the club and Washington news editor of *Business Week* magazine, quipped:

> I must confess, my first reaction to having our speaker today at the National Press Club was the same as a lot of other members: Why do we want to give a forum to that guy? Matt Drudge is the 31-year-old chronicler of "The Drudge Report," an Internet site packed daily with gossip, tidbits and information. . . . But Drudge's methods are suspect in the eyes of most journalists. He moves with the speed of cyberspace, and critics charge he has no time to know his sources or check his facts. Like a channel catfish, he mucks through the hoaxes, conspiracies and half-truths posted on-line in pursuit of fodder for his Web site. . . . So why is Matt Drudge here? He's on the cutting edge of a revolution in our business and everyone in our business knows it. And like it or not, he's a newsmaker (Federal News Service, June 2, 1998).

Drudge did not disappoint the audience. He suggested that the Internet will change journalism as we know it.

Political Considerations

One of the difficulties in the flow of political information is the cozy relationship that sometimes develops between mass media organizations and the politicians they cover. It is easy to see that a reporter who may desire a political job would not want to criticize a good source—the kind who might be in a position to make a job offer later. The cozy relationship is furthered by the desire of some in politics and government to make a lucrative career at a major network, newsmagazine, or cable channel or even to get a book deal (Graber, 1997). As a result, representatives of the mass media can become "mouthpieces for government officials or interest groups, either because of belief in their causes or in return for attractive stories and other favors" (p. 167). The result is what scholars have called a "symbiotic relationship" that favors the interests of reporters and their sources over the public they both claim to serve. (Matt Drudge, for example, may have begun his career by making a name for himself as an independent observer, but his alignment with America Online and political causes increased the likelihood that the social process would manipulate his content.) And because manipulation is an inherent part of the subjective news gathering and reporting process, virtually all information that

---

Box 6.1   Matt Drudge's Speech to the National Press Club

MR. DRUDGE: Applause for Matt Drudge in Washington at the Press Club, now there's a scandal. (Laughter.) The kind of thing I'd have a headline for. I'd like to thank the president of the Press Club, Doug Harbrecht, thank you very much, for extending the invitation to address you today, and to Kerry Gildae, the brave member of the Speakers Committee, for suggesting it. Thank you very much. You know, last time I was in town—and this is my hometown, Washington, I grew up here—I arrived to a headline in the local paper, "I was baby-sat by Matt Drudge—Exclusive!" (Laughter.)

You know, and what a place, Washington, DC, to grow up in. I used to walk these streets as an aimless teen, young adult, walk by ABC News over on DeSales, day-dream; stare up at the Washington Post newsroom over on 15th Street, look up longingly, knowing I'd never get in—didn't go to the right schools, never enjoyed any school, as a matter of fact, didn't come from a well-known family—nor was I even remotely connected to a powerful publishing dynasty.

Burning, I may have been, but I was sophisticated enough to know I would never be granted any access, obtain any credentials, get that meeting with Vernon Jordan or work with *Newsweek* magazine. There wasn't a likelihood for upward mobility in my swing-shift position at 7-11. (Laughter.) That was my last job in Washington.

So, in the famous words of another newsman, Horace Greeley, I, still a young man, went West, out to Hollywood. And I do mean Hollywood, not Beverly Hills, not the Palisades, no 90210 for this kid. It was the part of Hollywood they always promised to clean up and they never do, a part of Hollywood you see on "Cops." (Laughter.) Where you twinkle and then wrinkle and people forget about you. That's where I'm from. I swung into another clerk job, this time at CBS. I folded T-shirts in the gift shop, dusted off "60 Minutes" mugs. Occasionally after hours I had conversations with those ghost of Bill Paley. It was during one of these wee-hour chats that he reminded me the first step in good reporting is good snooping. Inspired, I went out of my way to service the executive suites. I remember I delivered sweatshirts to Jeff Sagansky, at the time president of CBS.

Overhearing, listening to careful conversations, intercepting the occasional memo, I would volunteer in the mail room from time to time, I hit pay dirt when I discovered that the trash cans in the Xerox room at Television City were stuffed each morning with overnight Neilsen ratings, information gold. I don't know what I did with it; I guess we, me and my friends, knew "Dallas" had got a 35-share over "Falcon Crest," but we thought we were plugged in. I was on the move—at least I thought so. But my father worried I was in a giant stall. And in a parental panic he overcame his fear of flying and dropped in for a visit. At the end of his stay, during the drive to the airport, sensing some action was called for, he dragged me into a blown-out strip on Sunset Boulevard and found a Circuit City store. "Come on," he said desperately, "I'm getting you a computer." "Oh, yeah, and what am I doing to do with that?" I laughed.

And as they say at CBS studies: Cut, two months later. Having found a way to post things on the Internet—it was a quick learn—Internet news groups were very good to me early on—I moved on to scoops from the sound stages I had heard, Jerry Seinfeld asking for a million dollars an episode, to scoop after scoop of political things I had heard from some friends back here.

I collected a few E-mail addresses of interest. People had suggested I start a mailing list, so I collected the E-mails and set up a list called "The Drudge Report." One reader turned into five, then turned into 100. And faster than you could say "I never had sex with that woman" it was 1,000—(laughter)—5,000, 100,000 people. The ensuing Web site practically launched itself.

Last month I had 6 million visitors, and I currently have a daily average larger than the weekly newsstand sales of *Time* magazine. Thank you, Sidney Blumenthal. (Laughter.) *What's going on here? Well, clearly there is a hunger for unedited information, absent corporate considerations.* [Emphasis added.] As the first guy who has made a name for himself on the Internet, I've been invited to more and more high-toned gatherings such as this, the last being a conference on Internet and society and some word I couldn't pronounce, up at Harvard a week ago. And I mention this not just to blow my own horn, but to make a point. Exalted minds—the panelists' and the audience's average IQ exceeds the Dow Jones—didn't appear to have a clue what this Internet's going to do; what we're going to make of it, what we're going to—what this is all going to turn into. But I have glimpses. And sometimes deep in the middle of the night I tell them to Bill Paley.

We have entered an era vibrating with the din of small voices. Every citizen can be a reporter, can take on the powers that be. The difference between the Internet, television and radio, magazines, newspapers is the two-way communication. The Net gives as much voice to a 13-year-old computer geek like me as to a CEO or speaker of the House. We all become equal. [Emphasis added.]

And you would be amazed what the ordinary guy knows. From a little corner in my Hollywood apartment, in the company of nothing more than my 486 computer and my six-toed cat, I have consistently been able to break big stories, thanks to this network of ordinary guys.

The "The Report," first to name the vice presidential nominee on the Republican ticket last election; first to announce to an American audience that Princess Diana had tragically died; first to tell the sad, sad story of Kathleen Willey; first every weekend with box-office results that even studio executives, some of them, admit they get from me . . .

And this is something new. This marks the first time that an individual has access to the news wires outside of the newsroom. . . . And time was only newsrooms had access to the full pictures of the day's events, but now any citizen does. *We get to see the kinds of cuts that are made for all kinds of reasons; endless layers of editors with endless agendas changing bits and pieces, so by the time the newspaper hits your welcome mat, it had no meaning.* [Emphasis added.]

Now, with a modem, anyone can follow the world and report on the world—no middle man, no big brother. And I guess this changes everything. It certainly changed on the night of January 17th, when *Newsweek* spiked, at the 11th hour, a well-researched, responsibly documented piece about the president of the United States and an obscure White House intern named Monica Lewinsky. After checking with multiple sources, I ran a story about the killing of the story. According to the *Los Angeles Times*, people familiar with the matter said Clinton was informed Saturday night or Sunday morning the Drudge Report had posted that Lewinsky was about to erupt.

For four days I had the story exclusively, and I took a lot of heat. Everyone was afraid of it until the water broke over at the *Washington Post* that Wednesday, and then everyone jumped on it.

Now they love it too much, and I'm still taking the heat. "He's one man out of control," a caller warned on talk radio in Los Angeles. "There is such a built-in level of irresponsibility in everything he does," cried First Amendment protector Floyd Abrams in a page one *Wall Street Journal*. "The notion of a Matt Drudge cyber gossip sitting next to William Safire on Meet the Press would have been unthinkable," smacked Watergate's Carl Bernstein in an op-ed.

I was here last night looking over the Press Club, and I noticed a room dedicated to one of—someone I can relate to, John Peter Zenger. And there's a plaque outside the room. And I think he could relate to some of the heat I've been getting. To honor members of the newspaper industry, this room commemorates the achievements of John Peter Zenger 250 years ago, whose courage in publishing political criticism helped establish the precedent of press freedom in colonial America. He was born in Germany. Zenger was a publisher in 1734 when he was imprisoned on charges of criminal libel for articles in his newspaper criticizing the royal governor. Risking his business and possibly life, Zenger stood fast and was acquitted in a jury trial after a brilliant defense of press liberty by his lawyer, at that time Andrew Hamilton.

It got me thinking that really what we're looking at here is history repeating. When radio lost out to television, there was anxiety. The people in the radio industry were absolutely anxious and demanded government stop the upcoming television wave. Television was very nervous about other mediums coming forward; cable. The movies didn't want sit-coms to be taped at movie studios for fear it would take away from the movies.

No, television saved the movies. The Internet is going to save the news business. I envision a future where there'll be 300 million reporters, where anyone from anywhere can report for any reason. It's freedom of participation absolutely realized.

The first lady of the United States recently addressed concerns about Internet during a cyberspatial Millennium Project press conference just weeks after Lewinsky broke. She said, "We're all going to have to rethink how we deal with the Internet. As exciting as these new developments are, there are a number of serious issues without any kind of editing function or gatekeeping function." I wonder who she was referring to. Mrs. Clinton continued, "Any time an individual leaps so far ahead of that balance and throws the system, whatever it might be—political, economic, technological—out of balance, you've got a problem. It can lead to all kinds of bad outcomes which we have seen historically." Would she have said the same thing about Ben Franklin or Thomas Edison or Henry Ford or Einstein? They all leapt so far ahead out that they shook the balance.

No, I say to these people, faster, not slower. Create. Let your mind flow. Let the imagination take over. And if technology has finally caught up with individual liberty, why would anyone who loves freedom want to rethink that? And that's why I'm addressing you today. It got me in the door, this new technology. You walk into the Press Club, you see a plaque dedicated to Joseph Pulitzer—someone, again, I love. Our republic and its press will rise or fall together. An able, disinterested, public-spirited press can preserve that public virtue without which popular government is a sham and a mockery. The power to mold the future of the republic will be in the hands of the journalists of the future generations. And if Pulitzer were alive today in this time, he would add using future mediums.

I was walking the streets of Washington, the streets I grew up in, last night. I found myself in front of the *Washington Post* building again, looking up, this time not longingly. This time I laughed. Let the future begin. (Applause.)

MR. HARBRECHT: Well, Matt, for our first question, let me ask you, how does it advance the cause of democracy and of social good to report unfounded allegations about individuals and the Neilsen ratings?

MR. DRUDGE: Well, that's a good question. I mean, I don't know specifically what you're referring to. You know, I have some—there's different levels of journalism; I'll concede that. One of my competitors is *Salon Magazine* On-Line, who I understand is the president's favorite Web site. And there's a reporter there,

Jonathan Broder. He was fired for plagiarism from the *Chicago Tribune*. And I read that in the *Weekly Standard*. But do I believe it? Because as much as I love the *Weekly Standard*, they have had to settle a big one with Deepak Chopra, if I recall. I heard that from CNN.

But hold on. Didn't CNN have the little problem with Richard Jewell? I think Tom Brokaw told me that, and then I think Tom Brokaw also had to settle with Richard Jewell. I read that in the *Wall Street Journal*. But didn't the *Wall Street Journal* just lose a huge libel case down in Texas, a record libel, $200 million worth of jury? I tell you, it's creative enough for an in-depth piece in the *New Republic*. But I fear people would think it was made up. (Applause.)

MR. HARBRECHT: Well, Matt, I wonder if you would define the difference between gossip and news, then, please.

MR. DRUDGE: Well, all truths begin as hearsay, as far as I'm concerned. And some of the best news stories start in gossip. Monica Lewinsky certainly was gossip in the beginning. I had heard it months before I printed it. I didn't really check it out. I knocked on Lewinsky's door. She wouldn't answer the door. At what point does it become news? This is the undefinable thing in this current atmosphere, where every reporter will be operating out of their home with Web sites for free, as I do. I don't charge. It's a question I'm not prepared to answer, because a lot of the legitimate news cycles—the Associated Press, for example, will issue news alerts, a recent one being an anthrax scare in the Nevada desert, where a group was targeting the New York subways. AP news alert. Berzerk. It went all the way to Janet Reno commenting. It turns out it wasn't true. I think that was some gossip.

MR. HARBRECHT: Let's talk a little bit about the Monica Lewinsky episode for a moment. I guess one could say you did "out" that story by reporting that *Newsweek* had reservations about reporting it. The story came out. The American people made a judgment, and Bill Clinton's approval ratings in the polls have gone up 20 points. People consistently tell pollsters they don't want to know this kind of information. They don't want to know this kind of stuff. And they blame the news media and they hate us even more. Would you comment on that?

MR. DRUDGE: Well, I disagree with the question. Ask Geraldo or Chris Matthews if the American people dislike it. Their ratings are doing quite well. I think they just expanded Matthews to two hours. I disagree with that. This is a story that's developing, that's serious. When I broke the story, I had it for four days to myself exclusively where I was reporting details, quite frankly, *Newsweek* didn't have at that point.

So I did some original reporting with that. I barricaded myself in the apartment. I was terrified, because from my Hollywood apartment a story of this magnitude was being born. I remember I teared up when I hit the "Enter" button on that one that night, because I said, "My life won't be the same after this." And it turned out to be right. I think it's—as the front page of all the newspapers say, this thing is yet to be determined. I hope the American people will not let someone who has lied potentially in office stay in office. But that's our call. You know, we've been here before and we've made these decisions before. We're letting the court do it. If you've noticed, the tapes have not been played in public, the portions of the tapes I have heard. And the people who are in possession of these tapes, I believe, are letting the courts take care of it. Some of the tapes are quite graphic in details I have heard that I ensure you will take up several news cycles once aired. So I would—I'm not convinced this thing is DOA or the American people have dismissed it as private life.

MR. HARBRECHT: Do you see your methods and your medium as controversial in and of themselves, or are they contributing to the degradation of serious or hard traditional journalism?

MR. DRUDGE: Well, you know, the editor of *Civilization* magazine . . . wrote a great op-ed in the *New York Times* talking about "Is this really something new, this type of fast reporting, this competitive, very competitive"—I'm part of the headline generation. . . . We have a great tradition of freedom of the press in this country, unpopular press. If the first lady is concerned about this Internet cycle, what would she have done during the heyday when there was 12, 13 editions of a paper in one day? What would she have done with that news cycle? That's the foundation. That's what makes this club great is the tradition. And I think we have a tradition of provocative press. And I maintain that I'm the new face on that. I'll take that for a season.

But a lot of the stuff I do is serious stuff. I was first to report that the encryption was missing from a Loral satellite, for example, a couple of weeks ago. I didn't see the main press reporting that one. So not everything I do is gossip or bedroom. To the contrary, I think that's just an easy label to dismiss me and to dismiss the new medium. But I'm excited about the launch of this Internet medium.

And again, freedom of the press belongs to anyone who owns one. (Applause.)

MR. HARBRECHT: How much do you embroider or make up in your on-line items? (Laughter.)

MR. DRUDGE: Now, which person here asked that question? (Laughter.) Well, no one's raising their hands. None. Everything I print from my apartment, everything I publish I believe to be true and accurate. I put my name on every single thing I write. No periscope here. No Washington whispers here. (Laughter.) I put my name [on] it; I'll answer to anything I write. I'll make mistakes. I'll retract them if I have to; apologize for it; try to make it right. But as I've pointed out, the main organizations in this country have let us down every once in a while and end up in trouble with editors. So I don't maintain that an editor is salvation. There won't be editors in the future with the Internet world, with citizen reporting just by the nature of it. That doesn't scare me. There's a notion that sticks and stones may break my bones, but words will kill me. I don't believe it. I get maligned every day on the news groups. I'm still standing. I still have a smile on my face. It's just the nature of this new thing. I mean, if I get defamed from Egypt, what do I do? Do I go to the World Trade Organization and ask for relief? This is the world we're going to be facing shortly, and I don't know exactly what the courts are going to do with this dynamic. I'm not too anxious about it however.

MR. HARBRECHT: Aren't you coarsening the public discourse? (Laughter.)

MR. DRUDGE: I hope not. You know, these questions are pretty tough, and I think if you directed this type of tough questioning to the White House, there'd be no need for someone like me, quite frankly. (Laughter/applause.) I have fun with what I do. A lot of it's smiles. A lot of it's "Look, Ma, I can dance." A lot of it's preempting other newspapers. I cover politicians the way the—I cover media people the way they cover politicians. I'm reporting Jeff Gerth may be breaking something in a couple of weeks, for example. That's fun stuff. That's a new paradigm. It's where the media is unchecked. It's where they're not the only game in town, where the media now is a guy with a 486 out in Hollywood. How did a story like Monica Lewinsky break out of a Hollywood apartment? What does that say about the Washington press corps? It just baffles me. I haven't come up with answers on that. (Applause.)

MR. HARBRECHT: I think Monica Lewinsky was from Hollywood, wasn't she? (Laughter.) How many sources do you require before posting an item?

MR. DRUDGE: Well, a little more than Bob Woodward's "Deep Throat" from time to time. (Laughter, scattered applause.) Sometimes I'll go with one person. The Loral worker who came forward and told me the encryption was missing from the satellite—the biggest nightmare scenario for defense types—I went with that one. I thought that was pretty solid. The guy seemed sincere. What I do is a formula where I follow my conscience—and this is upsetting to some people—but I maintain the conscience is going to be the only [thing] between us and the communication in the future, now. And I'm very happy with my conscience.

If we're—if you're looking at me and thinking about the Blumenthal case, I retracted that story within 24 hours. Even though he was demanding sources, I apologized for it in the pages of the *Washington Post*. He called the apology "drivel"—this from the White House adviser. And you know, I woke up to a very strange headline—"Clinton-Gore approved of filing libel suit." It's the first time in American history that a sitting president of the United States has approved a civil action against a reporter—in our history. Well, I guess they locked some people up before we were founded. There's a room down the hall dedicated in that spirit.

But this is a—this is something new. And as we go, I think I'll prove White House resources have been used to fight this litigation. Joe Lockhart, the deputy press secretary, admitted he called *USA Today* from the White House Press Office to complain about an op-ed that was favorable to me. Tax dollars at work. (Applause.)

MR. HARBRECHT: How many leaked stories do you get from mainstream journalists, and would you speculate on their motivation?

MR. DRUDGE: That's a good question, because what I've been doing lately is breaking news that's about to be broken, coverage of the coverage of the coverage. But that's where we are, since the media is so powerful. The media is comparable to government—probably passes government in raw power.

A lot of the stories are internal. They leak it to me wanting to get attention, wanting to get that headline. More times than not, I will not give it to them. It has to get—has to raise my whiskers. It has to be a good headline. I'm a sucker for a good story. I go where the stink is. I'm a partisan for news. If you got a story, I'll be listening outside when we're done. (Soft laughter.)

MR. HARBRECHT: All right, you've got your hat on, and you seem to emulate in your dress and advocate in your presentation the good old days of the tabloids of the '20s and '30s. But does populism equal consistently good journalism?

MR. DRUDGE: I'll have to ask Tom Brokaw that. I don't necessarily think a populism means you're out defaming people left and right. A populism press is a press that cares about the country. Most of my sources are concerned citizens, in and out of government, who don't like the direction of the White House Press Office, for example. Or quite frankly, a lot of the people on the Hill aren't quite forthcoming answering questions.

I reported a great story about a web site that had been set up, had been registered "Friends of Al Gore PAC." The billing address they used for this PAC was 1600 Pennsylvania Avenue. Someone had registered a political action committee from the White House, using it as a billing address. This is a huge story. I had it exclusively. I guess mainstream press don't know how to work the Internet and get the information.

This is an example of a populous press. It's very concerning. That, to me, was violating quite a few laws. They said someone in the office had set it up, and they were told to bring it down, and it wasn't—bring it down. They changed the address eventually. I looked up the address. It was a graveyard in Denver. That's a populous press to me.

MR. HARBRECHT: Matt, what types of stories would fall into the category that you would not publish?

MR. DRUDGE: Hmm. There's quite a few stories I don't publish that come my way. For instance, specific descriptions on these Lewinsky tapes of the presidential anatomy, I'm not reporting. I've had it, I've held it back. This, to me, composed quite an interesting dilemma on a world stage, quite frankly. That is an example that I don't think furthers the story.

That Phil Hartman may have met his wife through a prostitute doesn't necessarily interest me. I'm an advocate. I love public policy. Those are the type of stories that get me—get me typing. I also like to have fun. I like to do ratings and box office, just to show that it's not really about the product. It's more fun to talk about "Godzilla" than to watch it, for example. (Laughter.)

So I don't have one straight category of things I rule out. I tend not to do drugs, I tend not to do serious stuff that would upset people in private lives. That's probably my criterion of drawing the line, which I get a lot of it. I simply hit the "delete" and keep moving. I get 10,000 e-mails a day. There's—odds are there's another morsel at the next—the next—(inaudible).

MR. HARBRECHT: Where does your money come from? Explain the economics of the Drudge Report. How do you make a living from a free web site? (Scattered laughter.)

MR. DRUDGE: Richard Mellon Scaife is not my benefactor, if that's the question. (Scattered laughter.) I haven't made a penny off the Drudge Report. It's been free. For the four years I've been doing it now, the web site is free. There's not advertising on it. It was a labor of love, it continues to be. I sell the column, I have sold the column, first to "Wired" magazine up in South Park, San Francisco, and now to—(audio interference)—and I've just been hired to do a TV show, made some money that way.

But I didn't get into this for money. And in the early days of newspapers, no one made any money, or radio, either . . . I'm—still wear the same beat-up shoes I've had since the day I started this, still walk the same streets. So, that's—I think this is not a cash medium yet. There's probably quite a few people making money on the hype of it, but the actual application of it? Don't quite see it yet.

MR. HARBRECHT: I just have to call this to attention, because it's something that used to drive people crazy about Richard Nixon, and you just did it, which is you threw out a sort of a juicy little tidbit about Phil Hartman here, saying, "but I don't really—I don't really have any interest in that kind of thing," when in fact that's exactly what is on your web site all the time. And I call attention to it, because that's exactly the kind of thing that I think infuriates journalists about what you do. I wonder if you could comment.

MR. DRUDGE: Would you care to give me another example? I did not report the Phil Hartman thing on my web site. Another example could help me.

MR. HARBRECHT: Well, you just threw out, as you throw out things on your web site all the time. And it was—it was just put out there with no corroboration. Who—who reported that?

MR. DRUDGE: I think one of the syndicated magazines just reported that. But my question is, again, what headline on my web site would you call in that category?

MR. HARBRECHT: Okay. Fair enough. (Applause.) Could you—could you succeed as a journalist, if you worked for an organization which required an accuracy rate of 100 percent, instead of 70 or 80 percent?

MR. DRUDGE: I don't know what organization that would be. (Scattered laughter.) (Applause.) I once gave a quote—you know, I do a lot of predictions. I have "Truman Show" making $300 million. I once gave a quote that "Oh, I guess I'm 80 percent accurate, the body of my work." . . . "Eighty percent reliable." I've never talked about the reliability of my sources . . .

This is—this is mainstream press, this is—these are the—the—that bothers me. Recently, after the White House Correspondents' Dinner, I was walking down Connecticut Avenue with the top editor at one of these national magazines. And he was trying to get one of my pals to give him more information on some story that the pal has some information on.

And the pal said, "No, no. You haven't been very good on conservative things," to the editor of the magazine. "I don't think I'm going to help you. You know, you—you just take—you take, you know, stories and print them, and they hurt conservatives."

The editor of this magazine, which I won't name, says, "We just take what they give us. Now, if this is the standard—if this is the skyscraper up on Sixth Avenue that I want to dream about, I'd rather stay in my dirty Hollywood apartment. I just don't take what people give me. I tend to at least try to frame it with an angle that would consider both sides—provocative stuff."

MR. HARBRECHT: Why then don't you always call both sides when you report something?

MR. DRUDGE: I make it a point to call both sides. Unfortunately Mike Mc-Curry is not taking my calls anymore. (Laughter.) It's just absolutely amazing that he—the White House has now refused all comment on anything I'm report-ing, whether it be Betty Currie on vacation, so I have been told, on some of the days Lewinsky was checking in to see her. No comment. "We won't comment, it's based on that dirty source." They did this with the Kathleen Willey story—no comment. Anything I do. Al Gore is setting up a PAC—someone for Al Gore is setting up a PAC with a White House—no comment. Where is that coming from? George Stephanopoulos: "We've seen how discredited the Drudge Report is." That kind of stuff just rubs me the wrong way—and at their own peril—no com-ment.

MR. HARBRECHT: For someone who has been attacked by the mainstream press, your Website provides easy links to all the establishment media. Why do you do that?

MR. DRUDGE: Well, because it's—to me it's—I started it with a place where readers could keep up—links to the various columnists. The links I have on my Website I declare to be the most interesting people working in the business—all up and down—left, right and middle—I love to feature them. It's just a click away. You don't have to go through the front page—you go right to the column. A click away, you go to the AP Washington File—up to the minute.

I started it as a lark. It built itself after I started collecting these names on the Website. And it certainly has changed the way things are done—the pedestrian anyway. And I've been told quite a few people are reading it—from the top level in government down—for access—for quick access, unfiltered access—a click to Helen Thomas's latest column, reintroducing a whole new generation to wire services and columnists—I love them all. So I don't consider myself an enemy of the press whatsoever, but I do consider myself to be an untrained D student who happened to get lucky, but who happens to know a few things, and he now has the ability to shout down the street, "Extra, Extra, This Just In."

MR. HARBRECHT: What advice would you give to others, such as Jennycam, who claim—who are out to find fame through the Internet?

MR. DRUDGE: Well, you know, fame for fame's sake is—you know, always leaves a bad taste in my mouth. And you have to give them something they haven't heard. There has to be a reason they'll come to your Website. If it's just made-up fantasies, why bother? You know, if I'm so bad and if I'm so useless and I'm just a gossip hound, why was Sidney Blumenthal reading me the night before his first day at the White House? I don't quite understand that. It seems to me I'd spend my time over at the *New York Times*, who gets everything right. Advice is to follow your heart and to do what you love. And I certainly am doing what I love. Again, I wrote the Drudge Report for one reader for a while—a couple of readers—5, 10, 15 readers. I had a thousand—the first couple of months I thought, oh, that peaked that out. Again, I'm up to these millions I never thought I'd see. And with the advent of Web TV and cable modems, I don't know where this is going. Sixty million readers? What is civilization going to do with the ability of one citizen—without advertisers, without an editor—to broadcast to that wide group of people? The first lady says we need to rethink it. I say we need to embrace it. And it will take care of itself—it always has. It will get evened out.

MR. HARBRECHT: Here's a question that just came up. With all due respect, in the past half hour you have been inaccurate 8 to 10 times—about history, government, the media. You said there were no suits approved by a president, no profits in early newspaper and radio. Do you think journalists should have any minimum educational requirements?

MR. DRUDGE: Hmm, I've done—I guess I'm going to the wrong libraries, because I can't find any lawsuit—civil lawsuit approved by the president of the United States against a reporter. I can't find it. I'd like to have that information for my litigation—put it in the court papers.

Again, I don't maintain that I am licensed or have credentials. I created my own. I don't know what the problem is with that. It seems to me the more freedoms we have the better off we are. And you know I don't have a problem with chaos and new invention and confusion. I'm sure in the early days of electricity it was absolutely chaotic. The early days of cars the farmers probably said, "What are those things?"

It's not where I come from. I come from a much more of an optimistic knowing liberty and freedom is the right way to go, knowing a new invention is afoot that is going to realize things beyond anything we dreamed of. I'm not that scared of it. But then again I'm not in elected office. You know, the president, the Congress, take this personally. They're just the first to come through this Internet era. The person that sits in the Oval Office next will get my undivided attention.

MR. HARBRECHT: Are journalists obsolete who fail to include their e-mail addresses in their columns?

MR. DRUDGE: Well, you know, I'm getting so—that's a hit or miss. I mean, I would advise interaction, simply because you'll never know what you'll learn by offering an e-mail address. As I said in the speech, you'd be surprised what the average guy knows. Some of my best sources have turned out to be people who happened to be in the room that shouldn't have been in the room but who have come forward. I would provide as much contact with the public as you can. Again, I'm getting so much e-mail now I can't possibly read it. So it's a mixed blessing. But I would try to be as open as you can and offer an e-mail address—most of them do. I have correspondence with the top newspaper reporters in the business through e-mail, and it's a fun relationship—it's better than the phone. You could be doing other things at the same time.

MR. HARBRECHT: There were two recent episodes in our business where stories in the reporting of the Monica Lewinsky case, where newspapers put out prepublished stories on line that turned out to be half-baked, frankly. Do you foresee a separation of media practices where future journalists accept more your style and methods, or accept the methods of appropriate journalism?

MR. DRUDGE: Appropriate? I guess you're referring to the *Dallas Morning News* story and the *Wall Street Journal* story. Mistakes are made. Mistakes are made all the time. I am not that alarmed by these mistakes. I think they tend to correct themselves. Just because they're on the Internet doesn't mean they're less powerful, say, than if they are broadcast on CBS. I don't distinguish it.

I don't think the rush to publish is any different than the rush to get it ready for the evening news. It's the same kind of rush. It's our history. Think about the Philadelphia newspaper that had 12 editions a day. What was that rush like? Probably a lot of sloppy stuff. But this is the kind of tradition we have. It's kind of sloppy. And, again, I don't advocate being sloppy, but that is our roots. I have been doing some research on a book I'm writing—I hope to write—on populist journalism, and incredible history of reporting—quickly, fast, going up down the streets, screaming, "Extra, extra."

The problem I'm seeing immediately is if other Drudge Reports pop up—and they will—it is romantic to have one person running down the street screaming "Extra, extra," but if you have a thousand it could start looking like an insane asylum. So if indeed we start having tens of thousands of people all reporting news, hundreds of channels reporting news, all the different cable channels—click, click, click—I think people will grow disinterested. But again, they'll rally around something else. So I leave this to the free marketplace. Every reader I have comes to me. I've never placed an ad. They read me because they want to. The vice president will log on, hit my Website because he wants to, et cetera.

MR. HARBRECHT: Since when is the rationalization "We've always been sloppy" a justification for tarnishing a great institution? Does the right of every citizen to shout, "Extra, extra, this just in," outweigh maintaining a professional ethic of journalism?

MR. DRUDGE: Professional. You see, the thing is you are throwing these words at me that I can't defend, because I'm not a professional journalist. I am not paid by anyone. So you are shutting the door in my face again, and I don't quite understand what that's about, because that is not the facts. I can print something without an editor. This is where we are now. I don't know exactly why that's so scary. I again put my name on everything I write, unlike a few other columnists in this room.

If I am here to defend what I am writing, why isn't that enough? Why isn't that enough as a freedom of press, the freedom of speech, to carry water? I think it is. I just don't throw out reckless stuff at all. I do great pains. There's been plenty of stories I have killed with problems attached to them. So I just don't buy that argument. (Applause.)

MR. HARBRECHT: One more time: Where do you receive your funding? I wonder if you could address that one more time please.

MR. DRUDGE: It's not Richard Mellon Scaife. (Applause.) I had some money saved up from my gift shop days at CBS—a late bloomer. I have a small apartment, $600 a month rent. I drive a Metro Geo. I take the A Train sometimes when I'm coming out of New York to the airport. I don't need much money to do a start-up business like this. Anyone for any reason can launch a Website—little or no money—Internet connection, local phone. The modem lets you cover the world.

The modem lets you read what's happening if there is an earthquake in Alaska seconds after it happens. I think that's fun and dramatic—for free—by a medium that was built by taxpayer money. So perfectly realized. And, again, let the future begin. (Applause.)

MR. HARBRECHT: Matt, thank you for coming into the lion's den today. (Applause.) I have a certificate of appreciation for you speaking at the National Press Club; "Reliable Sources," which is our 90th anniversary history of the National Press Club—(laughter)—till the end, till the end; and our chalice, the National Press Club mug.

MR. DRUDGE: Thank you.

MR. HARBRECHT: For our final question today, what is the biggest mistake you have made so far?

MR. DRUDGE: That's a really good question. I've made a few mistakes. Ever doubting my ability was my biggest mistake, because in the beginning I didn't think much that I had the right to report things. But I was wrong. Boy, was I wrong. Whenever I tend to think, you know, "Oh, I probably shouldn't be reporting on the president of the United States, respect the office." I respect the office so much I want to cover it. And you know I maintain who is telling more truth this summer, me or the president of the United States? (Applause.) So I don't have many regrets. I don't have many regrets. I don't have many regrets in that area, except for doubting that this was my God-given right and as an American citizen, and embracing it, and saying liberty is just wonderful, thanks to the people who have come before me who have stood up for it. And thank you.

(Applause.)

(Source: Edited transcripts from the Federal News Service, June 2, 1998)

---

the public takes in has been managed. Mass media and interpersonal communication alike result from self-interests. Thus, free expression—rather than a wide-open search for truth in a pristine marketplace—is, in reality, a hike through the thicket of half-truths, missing information, and outright lies. The truth becomes less significant than what information is promoted to the top of media and public agendas through public relations, marketing, and spin control.

The Nature of the Report

The Drudge Report began as a simple World Wide Web page on the Internet. Its initial focus was on entertainment industry reporting, and that focus has remained an important element in Drudge's work. America Online has archived a select group of previous reports, and a 1998 report showed how Drudge utilized Hollywood sources and blended tabloid news with political information. Here are some excerpts of the Drudge Report from February 10, 1998:

Monica Lewinsky refers to Hillary Clinton as "Booba"—"Booba is out of town so I . . . "—in Lewinsky/Tripp tapes that have been played for the DRUDGE REPORT . . .

◆   ◆   ◆

LAWYER: NO JAIL FOR MONICA

"She is not going to jail, nobody's going to run over her constitutional rights," Lewinsky lawyer Ginsburg tells Tuesday's WASHINGTON POST.

"Nobody's going to abuse her. I'm not going to let that happen."

XXXX

◆　　◆　　◆

STARR HAS CLINTON'S VOICE MESSAGES

Exclusive

Must Credit DRUDGE REPORT

The DRUDGE REPORT has exclusively learned that Starr's office is in possession of messages left on Lewinsky's answering machine—messages that capture Clinton's own voice. Lewinsky kept Clinton's voice messages on tapes, later copied by co-worker Linda Tripp.

XXXXX

Into the Public Limelight

Drudge first entered the public limelight after his August 10, 1997, report claimed that Sidney Blumenthal, an assistant to the president, "HAS SPOUSAL ABUSE PAST." The story had been sourced through unsubstantiated claims made by Republican operatives (*Newsweek*, October 20, 1997, p. 63):

The DRUDGE REPORT has learned that top GOP operatives who feel there is a double-standard of only reporting republican shame believe they are holding an ace card: New White House recruit Sidney Blumenthal has a spousal abuse past that has been effectively covered up.

The accusations are explosive.

There are court records of Blumenthal's violence against his wife, one influential republican, who demanded anonymity, tells the DRUDGE REPORT.

If they begin to use [Don] Sipple and his problems against us, against the Republican Party . . . to show hypocrisy, Blumenthal would become fair game. Wasn't it Clinton who signed the Violence Against Women Act?

There goes the budget deal honeymoon.

One White House source, also requesting anonymity, says the Blumenthal wife-beating allegation is a pure fiction that has been created by Clinton enemies. [The First Lady] would not have brought him in if he had this in his background, assures the well-placed staffer. This story about Blumenthal has been in circulation for years.

Last month President Clinton named Sidney Blumenthal an Assistant to the President as part of the Communications Team. He's brought in to work on communications strategy, special projects themeing—a newly created position.

Every attempt to reach Blumenthal proved unsuccessful.

(*Blumenthal v. Drudge and AOL*, Civil Action No. 97–1968, D.C.Cir., 992 F. Supp. 44; 26 Media L. Rep. 1717; April 22, 1998).

After calling for a retraction, Blumenthal and his wife, also a lawyer who worked for the White House, filed a $30 million libel lawsuit against Drudge and America Online. The lawsuit alleged:

Drudge knew the information was not true, but published it anyway, the complaint alleges . . . Blumenthal says Drudge is a political conservative who harbors ill will toward the Clinton administration. . . . In addition, the Blumenthals maintain that Drudge repeated the false and misleading statements to other news organizations in the days following initial publication. . . . Although Drudge removed the story after the Blumenthals' lawyers complained, it has been copied extensively on the Internet and is impossible to remove completely, the complaint states. . . . The Blumenthals are seeking $10 million in compensatory damages, $20 million in punitive damages, and attorneys fees and costs (*Entertainment Litigation Reporter*, September 30, 1997).

The legal claim was that AOL was responsible for Drudge's reports as a "publisher" of the information, which was significant because AOL had the deep pockets. AOL's defense was that it was only a "passive carrier" of the information. AOL general counsel George Vradenburg, on a panel in late 1997, discussed the situation, as reported in *Media & the Law*:

Fortunately, said Vradenburg, the *Zeran* decision means AOL is neither a publisher nor a speaker, but merely a redistribution of information obtained from other sources. Even if the facts suggested AOL had clear notice of defamatory content on its system, if the requirement to censor the conduct of its users, an impossible task given the billions of messages that cross over its system. . . . He thought it was appropriate to say that Drudge had removed his story on his own initiative after it was challenged, retracting it and apologizing before AOL was involved (or was even aware of the problem). Matt

Drudge isn't an AOL employee, but is rather an independent contractor, Vradenburg asserts (*Media & the Law*, December 12, 1997).

The judge in the *Blumenthal v. Drudge and AOL* case ruled that AOL indeed was not responsible for Drudge's comments. Judge Paul Friedman's opinion relied on the uniqueness of the Internet:

> "The Internet is a unique and wholly new medium of worldwide human communication." *Reno v. American Civil Liberties Union*, 138 L. Ed. 2d 874, 117 S. Ct. 2329, 2334 (1997). It enables people to communicate with one another with unprecedented speed and efficiency and is rapidly revolutionizing how people share and receive information. As Congress recognized in the Communications Decency Act of 1996, "the rapidly developing array of Internet and other interactive computer services . . . represent an extraordinary advance in the availability of educational and informational resources to our citizens." 47 U.S.C. § 230(a)(1). As one court has noted: "The Internet has no territorial boundaries. To paraphrase Gertrude Stein, as far as the Internet is concerned, not only is there perhaps 'no there there,' the 'there' is everywhere where there is Internet access. When business is transacted over a computer network via a Web-site accessed by a computer in Massachusetts, it takes place as much in Massachusetts, literally or figuratively, as it does anywhere." *Digital Equipment Corp. v. Altavista Technology, Inc.*, 960 F. Supp. 456, 462 (D. Mass. 1997). It is probably safe to say that more ideas and information are shared on the Internet than in any other medium. But when we try to pin down the location of this exchange, we realize how slippery our notion of the Internet really is. Perhaps this is because "cyberspace" is not a "space" at all. At least not in the way we understand space. It's not located anywhere; it has no boundaries; you can't "go" there. At the bottom, the Internet is really more idea than entity. It is an agreement we have made to hook our computers together and communicate by way of binary impulses and digitized signals sent over telephone wires.

The judge argued that the Internet is "fundamentally different" from traditional mass communication because (1) it can maintain unlimited information, (2) there are no "gatekeepers," and (3) Internet users are also its producers:

> In other words, the Internet has shifted the focus of mass communication to the individual. . . . Never before has it been so easy to circulate speech among so many people. John Doe can now communicate with millions of people from the comfort, safety and privacy of his own home. His communication requires minimal investment and minimal time—once the word is

written, it is disseminated to a mass audience literally with the touch of a button. Moreover, Internet speakers are not restricted by the ordinary trappings of polite conversation; they tend to speak more freely online.

Internet service providers, according to Judge Friedman's interpretation of the CDA, cannot be held liable for publication:

> No provider or user of an interactive computer service shall be treated as the publisher or speaker of any information provided by another information content provider, 47 U.S.C. § 230(c)(1). The statute goes on to define the term "information content provider" as "any person or entity that is responsible, in whole or in part, for the creation or development of information provided through the Internet or any other interactive computer service," 47 U.S.C. § 230(e)(3). In view of this statutory language, plaintiffs' argument that the *Washington Post* would be liable if it had done what AOL did here— publish Drudge's story without doing anything whatsoever to edit, verify, or even read it (despite knowing what Drudge did for a living and how he did it).

Drudge was not considered an AOL employee, and the ISP could not be held responsible because Drudge alone wrote and edited the material.

> Congress recognized the threat that tort-based lawsuits pose to freedom of speech in the new and burgeoning Internet medium. The imposition of tort liability on service providers for the communications of others represented, for Congress, simply another form of intrusive government regulation of speech. Section 230 was enacted, in part, to maintain the robust nature of Internet communication and, accordingly, to keep government interference in the medium to a minimum. . . . None of this means, of course, that the original culpable party who posts defamatory messages would escape accountability. Congress made a policy choice, however, not to deter harmful online speech through the separate route of imposing tort liability on companies that serve as intermediaries for other parties' potentially injurious messages, *Zeran v. America Online*, Inc., 129 F.3d 327, 330–31 (4th Cir. 1997).

Judge Friedman, however, did cast a shadow on the wisdom of Congress providing immunity for ISPs such as AOL:

> If it were writing on a clean slate, this Court would agree with plaintiffs. AOL has certain editorial rights with respect to the content provided by Drudge and disseminated by AOL, including the right to require changes in content and to remove it; and it has affirmatively promoted Drudge as a new source of unverified instant gossip on AOL. Yet it takes no responsibility for any damage he may cause. AOL is not a passive conduit like the telephone company, a common carrier with no control and therefore no responsibility

for what is said over the telephone wires. Because it has the right to exercise editorial control over those with whom it contracts and whose words it disseminates, it would seem only fair to hold AOL to the liability standards applied to a publisher or, at least, like a book store owner or library, to the liability standards applied to a distributor. But Congress has made a different policy choice by providing immunity even where the interactive service provider has an active, even aggressive role in making available content prepared by others. In some sort of tacit quid pro quo arrangement with the service provider community, Congress has conferred immunity from tort liability as an incentive to Internet service providers to self-police the Internet for obscenity and other offensive material, even where the self-policing is unsuccessful or not even attempted. . . . While it appears to this Court that AOL in this case has taken advantage of all the benefits conferred by Congress in the Communications Decency Act, and then some, without accepting any of the burdens that Congress intended, the statutory language is clear: AOL is immune from suit, and the Court therefore must grant its motion for summary judgment.

Drudge's lawyers unsuccessfully argued to the D.C. circuit that the court did not have jurisdiction over the case because Drudge wrote his column in Los Angeles. The court reviewed the evolving case law on cyberspace and geographic issues, concluding that web interaction and nonweb activities (such as Drudge's interview on C-SPAN) afforded the Blumenthals the right to have the case heard in Washington, D.C.:

Under the analysis adopted by these courts, the exercise of personal jurisdiction is contingent upon the web site involving more than just the maintenance of a home page; it must also allow browsers to interact directly with the web site on some level. In addition, there must also be some other non-Internet related contacts between the defendant and the forum state in order for the Court to exercise personal jurisdiction. Because the Court finds that defendant Drudge has an interactive web site that is accessible to and used by District of Columbia residents and, in addition, that he has had sufficient non-Internet related contacts with the District of Columbia, the Court concludes that Drudge has engaged in a persistent course of conduct in the District. The exercise of personal jurisdiction over defendant Drudge by this Court therefore is warranted.

Also, Drudge's beltway-oriented content was more important to the court than his physical location:

Drudge may not advertise in physical locations or local newspapers in Washington, D.C., [but] the subject matter of the Drudge Report is directly related to the political world of the Nation's capital and is quintessentially "inside the Beltway" gossip and rumor. Drudge specifically targets readers in the District of Columbia by virtue of the subjects he covers and even solicits gossip from District residents and government officials who work here. . . . By targeting the Blumenthals who work in the White House and live in the District of Columbia, Drudge knew that "the primary and most devastating effects of the [statements he made] would be felt" in the District of Columbia. . . . He should have had no illusions that he was immune from suit here.

The court also refused to provide Drudge with protections as a journalist: "Drudge is not a reporter, a journalist or a newsgatherer. He is, as he himself admits, simply a purveyor of gossip. . . . His argument that he should benefit from the 'news gathering exception' to subsection (a)(4) of the long-arm statute merits no serious consideration" (*Blumenthal v. Drudge and AOL*, n. 18).

Neither defamation lawsuits nor increased attention seemed to slow Drudge in his pursuit of "the goods" on President Clinton. With rumors flying around Washington in January 1998, he broke the story of the president's alleged affair with a White House intern: "Federal investigators are now in possession of intimate taped conversations of a former White House intern, age 23, discussing details of her alleged sexual relationship with President Clinton, the DRUDGE REPORT has learned . . . 'Starr is not on the bimbo beat,' one source close to the situation told the DRUDGE REPORT late Tuesday. 'He's looking at a potential for obstruction of justice charges'" (Drudge Report, January 21, 1998).

Once Drudge published his report on the Internet, all major news organizations—from the tabloids to the television networks—decided that the allegations were lead-story material. President Clinton's interviews with PBS and National Public Radio regarding his state of the union address and coverage of the speech itself were dominated by the denials he and his wife made. Hillary Rodham Clinton followed with her own damage-control network interviews that claimed the allegations were the product of a "right-wing conspiracy." Drudge and other reporters continued to report the "leaks" of information, fueling continued coverage.

The Impact of Free Expression in a Mediated World

The case study of the Drudge Report clearly shows that the Internet has had an impact on the nature of free expression. It can, as in the case of unsubstantiated rumors about the bombing of TWA Flight 800, provide a catalyst for attention by conventional mass media. But in addition, at least for those who keep an eye on the Internet, leaks of information can produce raw material for expanded interpersonal communication—both on the Net and face to face. The difficulty, of course, is that unsubstantiated information is more likely to be a lie than information that is sourced through named people speaking on the record. The average person in society has neither the time nor the ability to sift through rumors and make a reasonable judgment. So, although such information does "increase" free expression in an absolute sense, it may do nothing to advance it in a meaningful democratic context. Information about whether or not the president had an affair with an intern and whether or not he lied about it in no way helps the average citizen participate in the democratic process or become empowered. In fact, such information can be seen as a smoke screen or a diversion from the issues that really have an impact on those same people's lives. The Internet, then, could be said to be just another cog in a mass-mediated environment in which entertainment is valued more than information; in this environment, individuals are further atomized and isolated, and gossip and rumor pass for valid knowledge.

It also has become clear that Drudge, like other journalists, works from a network of sources close to elite political power. However, he uses technology such as America Online's buddy system, which allows people to know when others are online so they can connect and chat. In March 1998, he reported about being in an AOL chat room with a member of the White House staff the previous summer:

> "Anything on Kathleen Willey?" I typed to a ranking White House staffer in an online chat last summer, "I've got the whole story."
>
> "Not familiar with her," the aide typed back.
>
> "Willey. She's the one that has been talking with NEWSWEEK about—" I typed to the White House staffer who had instigated a Buddy Chat via an Instant Message that day . . .
>
> "What's the story?"
>
> "The story is shocking."
>
> "Hmmm . . . "
>
> "I think I should just leave you with her name. Carville, Begalla, etc. would freak if they knew that she was out there and that she was talking."

Willey's allegations that the president made a sexual pass at her were released by Drudge in the first report naming her. It was not until a March 1998 *60 Minutes* interview that Kathleen Willey's name became well known to the general public. Willey claimed the president kissed her, touched her breasts, and put her hand on him. According to Drudge, "A story that was first whispered to the White House in an online chat has ended up snowballing into the ultimate political nightmare."

Epilogue to the Drudge Story

In the irony that is free expression in the context of beltway politics, the libel lawsuit against Drudge and AOL was being heard in a U.S. district court in Washington, D.C.—*Blumenthal v. Drudge* and AOL was taking place just three floors above the room where Kenneth Starr's grand jury continued to meet (*Houston Chronicle*, March 15, 1998). Sydney Blumenthal's $30-million defamation suit had all the makings of an attack on political speech, which has been at the core of free-expression law since *New York Times v. Sullivan* (1964). Meanwhile, Drudge had the backing of David Horowitz, founder of a conservative group in Los Angeles, which was significant because there is more to the story. Ten years earlier, while Blumenthal was a journalist, he wrote a story attacking Horowitz's shift away from liberalism at about the same time he "left his wife and children."

Drudge claimed to be earning $3,000 a month from AOL when the Fox TV News Channel offered him a talk show. This followed his appearance on NBC's *Meet the Press* show—one that led the Blumenthal legal team to write a letter to host Tim Russert complaining that Drudge had been treated as a reputable journalist.

Drudge posed a fundamental problem for "mainstream" journalists who themselves often walk the tightrope between reporting rumor and substantiated news. At a time when tabloid, entertainment-style news has become the norm, it would be difficult to predict whether Drudge will be mainstreamed through his Fox TV work, the mainstream will move in his direction, or both.

Following his National Press Club speech in June 1998, Drudge appeared on CNN's *Crossfire* show. Matt Drudge has raised concerns about mainstream mass media because his use of Internet technology has, in effect, short-circuited traditional power bases. Put another way, he has been able to break into the party without an invitation.

Given the social challenge that he presents and the ineffectiveness of social controls, it is no wonder that some have sought legal controls to stifle his form of free expression. The Blumenthal lawsuit against Drudge was mostly an issue for major Internet providers such as AOL because they tend to be involved in the content production, reproduction, and distribution business. As such, they are vulnerable to civil liability. However,

Box 6.2 Matt Drudge's Defense to Journalists

(BILL) PRESS: Welcome back to "Crossfire." To fans he's the founding father of a new wave of Internet journalism. To detractors, he's a gossip who plays fast and loose with the truth. To the world, he's Matt Drudge, sole author, editor and publisher of "The Drudge Report," representing himself tonight. Representing mainstream journalists, some of whom question Mr. Drudge's standards and commitment to accuracy, David Corn, Washington editor of "The Nation" magazine. Bob?

NOVAK: David Corn, you were leaning on Matt pretty hard for only using one source. A guy who only used one source, sometimes he used less than one source on most of his, on many of his stories was the, was a person I said is a role model for Matt and that's Walter Winchell. He was the most famous, most effective, highest paid journalist . . .

CORN: Journalist or gossip columnist?

NOVAK: Well, I thought we said there was no board of journalism that gives the title or not.

CORN: Well, what do you think? I mean is gossip the same thing as journalism and should it be? . . .

NOVAK: Isn't this buyer beware? I mean it's a big . . .

CORN: Well, is that how you want people to see your column, buyer beware?

NOVAK: No, not with my column.

CORN: And I say this, I'll give Matt some credit. I think the column, the site you created was wonderfully pioneering. You have links to a lot of sites. You were the first person to see that there was a role to play to sort of vet and to screen out all this stuff coming in and giving sort of short bites to people. But you go on about how this is so different from the mainstream press, most of your stuff is cribbed, though, from "The New York Times" and "Washington Post," the little items aren't . . .

DRUDGE: Before they print it . . .

CORN: It's already out here. I see it on, I see you being . . .

NOVAK: Isn't it a fact that a lot of the stuff that Matt prints is stuff that you hear in the course of, all of us hear in the course of daily life but I don't print it because I can't check out and it's pretty interesting to see it . . .

CORN: Well, why don't you print it if you can't check it out?

NOVAK: Because I can't check it out. I have a different standard than he does.

CORN: OK, so you have a different standard . . .

NOVAK: That's why I said people know what they're getting.

DRUDGE: What are you going to do when there's 300 million reporters in America, each with their own web site, each commanding audiences? What are we going to do?

CORN: If they're all reporting, who will be reading?

DRUDGE: Well, I would imagine there's enough eyeballs to go around. You laugh . . .

CORN: hundred million reporters boy . . .

DRUDGE: But what has happened is technology has caught up with individual liberty.

CORN: It's giving people the chance to get around the mainstream media, which is good, but you still need the standards and you still need to check if you care about truth.

(Source: Edited transcript from CNN *Crossfire,* June 2, 1998)

---

if Drudge is correct, there will be thousands or maybe milliions of Internet reporters who could be impacted by such lawsuits in the future.

The Drudge Report may have created a political context for the Internet release of the Starr Report and President Clinton's videotaped grand jury testimony in the fall of 1998. CNN's Charles Feldman visited the Cyberjava Internet Store in Venice, California, to watch people reading the Starr Report. Allen Manzano was one of those sipping coffee and preparing to read the allegations about the president as they were posted on the congressional web site.

FELDMAN: OK, Allen, you've been here for a while now. Are you interested in the Starr report, and if so, why?

MANZANO: Yes, I am interested. I was looking for it earlier. It wasn't posted yet, but it might be posted by now. Why?

FELDMAN: It's coming up. Yes, why?

MANZANO: Why? Because I'd like to see what's in the report, see if it warrants an impeachment, because I think the American people should see an impeachment proceeding. We have never seen one. It's good for the children to see how our Constitution cleans its own house not like Indonesia, right?

FELDMAN: Allen, let me ask you something: do you like the idea that you're going to be able to see it at pretty much the same time that everybody else is?

MANZANO: Yes, I do. That's our freedom of speech, isn't it?

(CNN, September 11, 1998)

Not everybody Feldman interviewed seemed to care. Said one customer, "I'm not that interested. It's not on the forefront of my mind. I just feel that it's going to be more of what we've already heard, and it's just not something that's real important to me. What's more important are the implications of, you know, what may happen to him for lying, not really what he did. That's really insignificant to me" (CNN, September 11, 1998).

As the Starr Report was released, the explicit sexual details it contained posed a dilemma for the mainstream media. CNN chose to have staff members read excerpts of the report live off the computer screen, and other network correspondents were obviously concerned about broadcasting "indecent" content.

CNN's congressional correspondent, Candy Crowley, told media critic Howard Kurtz that reading the Starr Report off the Internet and directly on the air was awkward:

Actually, you know, it's one of those things where you keep thinking, "Boy, I hope my mother is at the grocery store," you know. I mean, it—but once the decision was made—and it certainly was not made at my level—as to how we were going to do it—once the decision was made to read it, you know, it was a—it was the story and—you know, "Here it is, and here's what it says." Also, it helps to be reading it as opposed to describing it, you know, because you're reading along what someone else has written. It gives you just a little bit of distance instead of just looking at the camera and saying, "OK. Well, Ken Starr said the following things."

◆   ◆   ◆

Box 6.3   Television Uses the Internet to Read the Starr Report

Tom Brokaw, NBC: These are things that we never expected to hear described in the highest office of the land, but they're out there now, and the question is can we keep it all in some kind of appropriate context.

Candy Crowley, CNN: Let's issue our cautionary tale here that, if you are the least bit squeamish, you might not want to listen to this.

Dan Rather, CBS: We want to be careful here. This is daytime television, and there are children in the audience.

(Source: CNN, *Reliable Sources*, September 12, 1998)

I didn't retreat to euphemisms, and I tell you that in my head—someone said, you know, "Well, what do you think of the decision?" and I said, "Look, I think if it can be done in and around the Oval Office and it can be reported in a government report to the House Judiciary Committee that it can be" (CNN, *Reliable Sources*, September 12, 1998).

On NBC's *Today* show, journalist Seymour Hersh told anchor Matt Lauer: "Look, we live in a society where there are laws, there's a Constitution, and I'm never going to argue for silence. I'm against it. You know, I want the Matt Drudges of the world to speak as much—I think everybody has a forum in the world" (*Today*, July 21, 1998).

Matt Drudge's work certainly led to the publication of a story about a thirty-year-old affair between Republican representative Henry Hyde and a housewife, which appeared on *Salon* magazine's web site in September 1998. Hyde apparently was targeted by the online magazine as the chair of the U.S. House Judiciary Committee, the body that would consider impeachment of the president. *Salon* regularly attacked the investigation of the president and forced the seventy-four-year-old Hyde to admit to the relationship; Hyde said: "The only purpose for this being dredged up now is an obvious attempt to intimidate me, and it won't work" (*Omaha World-Herald*, September 17, 1998, p. 12). (See Figure 6.1.)

Steven Johnson, editor of *Feed*, told National Public Radio that one problem with the Web is that there are no established conventions for readers to follow as cues. Beyond this, he noted, there is the need for web publishers to get noticed: "On the web, without television, you'd really have to slowly, organically grow your audience by building their trust in

(none)

S A L O N

A L S O   T O D A Y

Loyal to the end
By Jessica Seigel
Susan McDougal,
on trial in California
on non-Whitewater
offenses, feels
vindicated
(09/18/98)

Editorial
Why we ran the
Henry Hyde story

The full text of The
Starr Report and
The White House
Rebuttal

T A B L E+T A L K

George Wallace,
R.I.P.: Mourn or
scorn the
controversial
Alabama politician
in the Politics area
of Table Talk

R E C E N T L Y

Lives of the

"This hypocrite broke up my family"

Henry Hyde and Cherie Snodgrass at a Chicago nightspot
in the late 1960s.

HENRY HYDE, THE MAN WHO WILL SIT IN
JUDGMENT ON PRESIDENT CLINTON, CONFIRMS
THAT HE CARRIED ON A SECRET AFFAIR.

BY DAVID TALBOT | Fred Snodgrass, a 76-year-
old Florida retiree, says he gets so upset when he
watches Rep. Henry Hyde on TV that "I nearly
jump out of my chair." Hyde, the Illinois
Republican who heads the House Judiciary
Committee, is on television often these days.

FIGURE 6.1   Salonmagazine.com

a way that you don't really have to do now if television decides that you're the story" (*Morning Edition,* July 20, 1998).

The role of the Internet in the Clinton scandal seemed to hit a high point at the end of September 1998, when the president's videotaped testimony was released both on the broadcast airwaves and on the Internet. RealNetworks estimated that a record 2 million personal computer users accessed the streaming video. It was a record for video, but it fell far short of the "record-setting web activity" ten days earlier when the Starr Report was released (*Broadcasting & Cable,* September 28, 1998, p. 52).

Quickly, it would seem, Internet sites of all political persuasions were being manipulated by political operatives on both sides. Missouri Democrat Richard Gephardt argued that the technological release on the Internet of the huge volume of information against the president meant that the Congress should move quickly to deal with the case:

> My point is, look, we're in a new world. Information flows freely, information has now made its way all across the world. Last week you could have read this material on the Internet in Africa or China or South America as quickly as somebody could read it in St. Louis, Missouri. It is now known to everybody. You've seen the raw videotape of the president's testimony. You've seen the facts. And all I'm saying and all we're saying is that in this new world of instant communication worldwide, the global village, we believe it is possible, sensible, rational for the Congress of the United States to deal with this on some sensible timetable (Statement, September 23, 1998).

In time, Matt Drudge himself became the target for political attacks. Numerous web sites popped up that were direct parodies of his work. One such site claimed the deliberately confusing domain name http://www.drudge.report; another, the Dredge Report, claimed http://www.dredgereport.com. It appeared that the virtual world Drudge helped pioneer was being used against him. Also at issue is whether an entertainer such as Drudge should be considered a journalist, a status that affords legal protections.

In this sense, the Internet clearly helped us see the direction of free expression at the turn of the century. Speech was being utilized as a form of political manipulation, and questions of politics remained just below the surface of the political rhetoric. Whether or not one called Matt Drudge and his prodigy journalists seemed less important than the larger phenomenon emerging—the Internet as a social space where political wars could be fought. To the extent that the political speech remained highly controlled and manipulated, one could argue, the illusion of a greater freedom of expression clouded the ability of the average citizen to be empowered by the new technologies.

Box 6.4 *In re Madden v. Turner Broadcasting Systems*

The Third Circuit of the United States Court of Appeals has addressed the issue of who is considered a journalist. The Appeals Court reversed a lower court decision that said an entertainment reporter is a journalist and guarded by state shield laws that allow him to protect news sources. However, the test employed by the court would seem to define Matt Drudge as a journalist because he intends to disseminate information to a mass audience.

Appellant Titan Sports, Inc., and its competitor, Turner Broadcasting Systems (TBS), are the most prominent professional wrestling promoters in the United States. TBS's "World Championship Wrestling" (WCW) has challenged Titan's "World Wrestling Federation" (WWF) to engage in "interpromotional events," wherein WCW wrestling personalities would compete with WWF personalities. Titan has refused to permit any of its wrestlers to engage in the activities.

Titan sued TBS in the United States District Court for the District of Connecticut alleging unfair trade practices, copyright infringement and other pendent state law claims, none of which are germane to this appeal. . . . As part of the discovery process in the Connecticut action, however, Titan issued a subpoena to take the deposition of Mark Madden, a non-party witness who is employed by WCW, and resided in the Western District of Pennsylvania. WCW employs Madden to produce tape-recorded commentaries, which are replayed to callers on WCW's 900-number hotline. These commentaries promote upcoming WCW wrestling events and pay-per-view television programs, announce the results of wrestling matches and discuss wrestlers' personal lives and careers. Madden asserts that in the course of preparing statements for the WCW hotline, he receives information from confidential sources. He admits, however, that his announcements are as much entertainment as journalism.

During a deposition, Madden refused to identify the sources of certain of his allegedly false and misleading statements recorded for the WCW's 900-number hotline. Madden, through counsel, invoked a "journalist's privilege" and the protection of the Pennsylvania Journalist's Shield Law, 42 Pa. Cons. Stat. Ann. § 5942. Titan filed a "Motion to Enforce Subpoena and Otherwise Compel Discovery by a Nonmoving Party." After Titan moved to enforce the subpoena, counsel for Madden and the WCW interposed the qualified federal common law privilege which protects journalists from revealing their confidential sources.

The district court denied Titan's motion insofar as it sought to compel Madden to identify the sources from which he got information for his commentaries. The district court concluded that Madden was a "journalist" with standing to assert the privilege because he intended to disseminate information to third parties. The district court also held that Madden's interest in protecting his sources was not outweighed by the need for disclosure. Titan now appeals.

◆ ◆ ◆

We have found few cases that discuss who, beyond those employed by the traditional media, has status to raise the journalist's privilege. Courts have previously permitted documentary film-makers to invoke the protections of the journalist's privilege. . . . Also, authors of technical publications and professional investigative books have been permitted to claim the privilege. . . . No other court, however, has considered whether the privilege may be invoked by those like Madden who are neither "pamphleteers" nor "metropolitan publishers," and certainly not engaged in investigating, publishing, reporting or broadcasting in the traditional sense. . . . To date, only one other court of appeals has fashioned a test to answer the question of who has status to invoke a journalistic privilege. In *von Bulow v. von Bulow*, the Court of Appeals for the Second Circuit identified the principles underlying the application of the journalist's privilege. . . . First, the court recognized that the process of newsgathering is a protected, albeit qualified, right under the First Amendment. This right emanates from the strong public policy supporting the unfettered communication of information by a journalist to the public. Second, the court required a true journalist, at the beginning of the news-gathering process, to have the intention of disseminating her information to the public. Third, the court stated that an individual may successfully claim the journalist's privilege if she is involved in activities traditionally associated with the gathering and dissemination of news, even though she may not ordinarily be a member of the institutionalized press. Fourth, the relationship between the putative journalist and her sources may be confidential or nonconfidential. And fifth, unpublished resource material likewise may be protected.

◆ ◆ ◆

This test does not grant status to any person with a manuscript, a web page or a film, but requires an intent at the inception of the newsgathering process to disseminate investigative news to the public. As we see it, the privilege is only available to persons whose purposes are those traditionally inherent to the press; persons gathering news for publication. It is the burden of the party claiming the privilege to establish their right to its protection . . .

Under the test employed by this court, it would appear that Matt Drudge is a "journalist" because he intends to disseminate information from his web page to a mass audience.

(Source: *In re Madden v. Turner Broadcasting Systems*, No. 97–3267, 151 F.3d 125, 26 Media L. Rep. 2014 [1997, 1998])

At the same time, the decision by the Congress to release the Starr Report with all its sexual details seemed odd in the wake of the Communications Decency Act. On the one hand, representatives claimed to be concerned about children's access to sexual content; on the other, they were responsible for creating a difficult environment for parents and teachers to manage. The defense that holds that there was a strong public interest in release of the content inevitably leads to problematic definitional issues of what is or is not in the public interest. So often, these problems bring us back to the marketplace metaphor, in which the responsibilities of free expression are left to those who read, see, or hear messages. Meanwhile, there appears to be a continuing gulf between press and public views on such matters: Although news media in 1998 ranked the Clinton scandal the most important story of the year, polling by the Pew Research Center suggested that the public cared less about impeachment than about school shootings, elections, and military actions (*New York Times*, December 23, 1998). Despite public opinion, however, the nation's television news magazines devoted nearly four times as many stories (810) to the Clinton affair as to any other coverage (Seinfeld, 241; Princess Diana, 221; the Oscars, 216; and the movie *Titanic*, 206) (*NewsTV*, December 1998).

As the Clinton scandal came to an end in early 1999, Drudge's nemesis Blumenthal was called as one of three videotaped witnesses in the president's U.S. Senate trial, along with Monica Lewinsky and Clinton's friend Vernon Jordan. In the closing days of the trial, Drudge reported that NBC was withholding interviews with other women making claims against the president. In the end, the acquittal of the president raised the issue of what leaks and rumors would be fodder for future Drudge Reports. (See Figures 6.2 through 6.7.)

Matt Drudge has continued to turn his persona into a celebrity image that translates into dollars. Despite complaints from news executives, he was hired as an ABC Radio talk show host. Drudge received "a six-figure deal" (*Washington Post*, July 8, 1999).

Chapter Summary

This chapter focused on how Internet gossip columnist Matt Drudge made a name for himself by using the technology to report news bits and rumors to an increasing number of readers. The case study raised questions about how free expression will operate in the journalism context at a time when information is so widely available. The chapter concluded with thoughts about how Drudge's use of the Internet fostered a political climate that made release of the Starr Report and President Clinton's videotaped grand jury testimony possible.

164

DRUDGE REPORT
By Matt Drudge

XXXXX DRUDGE REPORT BREAK XXXXX 20:14:14 PST WED MAR 25 1998 XXXXX

WASHINGTON POST TELLS WEBSITE TO STRIP IT!

One of the nation's premiere newspapers has warned one of the Internet's premiere
discussion groups to stop featuring its content -- a development that turned
keyboards emotional Wednesday evening.

"I say they can kiss our butts!!!" wrote one poster on the online FREE REPUBLIC.

"I can see the headlines now: WASHINGTON POST FILES LAWSUIT TO STOP FREE SPEECH,"
blasted another.

The action heated Wednesday after WASHINGTON POST Vice President and General
Counsel Caroline Little e-mail served FREE REPUBLIC's webmaster Jim Robinson a
fresh warning: "The reposting of material from the WASHINGTON POST on your
website without our permission is a copyright infringement, and is not within the
bounds of fair use... I am respectfully requesting that you remove all WASHINGTON
POST content from your sites."

In recent months the bulletin board has become the hottest spot online to monitor
instant reaction to scandal news developments. Unlike commercial outlets: TIME,
CNN and MSNBC, Robinson has developed a spot where comment flows raw. A scout
will first post an original news story, readers immediately begin to dissect in
follow-up threads. The site has captured a dedicated following among media and
political heavyweights and receives a reported 30,000 visitors a day. It is read
daily in the White House and is accessed by top congressional leaders. One
network news executive recently whispered to the DRUDGE REPORT: "That place has
more hot news on it than I find at my local newstand."

[The website's "Whitewater File" has been linked from the DRUDGE REPORT since its
inception.]

What constitutes copyright infringement, and just what is fair use in an online
world with no borders?

"FREE REPUBLIC website is a non-commercial not for profit public bulletin board
which we're operating under the 'Fair Use' exemptions of copyright laws,"
Robinson argues to the WASHINGTON POST.

FIGURE 6.2   The Drudge Report Page, March 25, 1998

165

 MATT DRUDGE

Defense Fund

brought to you by:

—**Matt Drudge Archives**

—**Matt Drudge Information Center**

WHEN THE CLINTON WHITE HOUSE slapped Internet journalist Matt Drudge with a $30 million libel suit last fall as part of its standard operations policy of deny, defy and, above all, act quickly to silence opposition by any means necessary—he was facing personal ruin and the destruction of the Drudge Report. At the time Drudge came under White House attack, the journalist had no money, no libel insurance, and no lawyer to provide him with a defense.

The Center for the Study of Popular Culture through its Individual Rights Foundation rallied to his cause. The Center and the IRF have a history of defending First Amendment issues and cases. The Center was a leading voice in the entertainment and media community opposing the V-chip and the ratings system, as well as on congressional attempts to censor the Internet. The IRF was a leading legal force in the efforts to end speech codes on American campuses. In its most famous case, the IRF compelled a Vice-Chancellor at the University of California, Riverside, to undergo 5 hours of "sensitivity-training" in the First Amendment, after the Vice Chancellor had banned a fraternity for producing a T-shirt that the Administration didn't like. The IRF provided Drudge with its own staff attorney, Patrick Manshardt, and its legal adviser Manuel Klausner to be his defense team on a pro bono basis.

The Center for the Study of Popular Culture then established the Matt Drudge Information Center and Defense Fund (800-752-6562) to provide the facts in the case and to help defray legal costs.

All donations to the Matt Drudge Defense Fund go directly toward defending Matt in both the court of law and in the court of public opinion. Trustees of the Fund are David Horowitz and Andrew Breitbart.

Join us today, by contributing online or printing out this page, completing the form below, and faxing it to (310) 843-3692. To contribute by check, print out the form and mail it in to the address below. For more information, please call (800) 752-6562.

Name	
Organization (optional)	
Work Phone	
FAX (optional)	
E-mail	

FIGURE 6.3   The Matt Drudge Defense Fund page, from the Center for the Study of Popular Culture

166

Page 1 of 2

Please Click Above To Visit Our Sponsor

DREDGE REPORT

By Mutt Dredge

Featuring
Headline News
Bogus Pages
Target Find

Plus Try
Virtual Vacation
FakeMail

**Fun With
Faces**
Build-A-Date
Celeb Blender
Face Challenge
Build-A-Dad

Cheap Thrills
Rubber Chicken
Card Shop

RubberChicken
Book Store

Feedback
Links
Awards
Comments

E-Mail feedback to
jester@aprilfools.com

© 1998 OutPost Network
All rights reserved.

XXXXX DREDGE REPORT XXXXX 8:45:31 PST 23 1998 XXXXX
Exclusive **Contains Graphic Description**
[Enter Target's First Name:]

[Enter Target's Last Name:]

to be called as a witness before Grand Jury
Prosecutors in Kenneth Starr's office have been investigating a link
between Monica Lewinsky
and [Your Target's Name] of
[Enter Target's City of Residence:]

[Enter Target's State of Residence:]

It has been alleged that [Your Target] was
connecting via private AOL Message Boards
with [Your Bimbo] over a six-week period in January and February of
1998. Each session lasted from 45 minutes to three hours and took place
late at night. [Your Target] used the alias [Make up Target's Alias:]

These conversations centered around [Your Bimbo]'s
comparisons of the Presidential member to a mature yellow squash

[Your Target] allegedly provided useful insights and suggestions for
[Your Bimbo]. During the course of these conversations [Your Bimbo]
revealed that her lawyers   would pay $120,000
to anyone who will

FIGURE 6.4   The Dredge Report, One of the Many Satires of the Drudge Report

back to Bob's Fridge Door for more satire

CLINTON RECEIVED ORAL SEX DURING GRAND JURY TESTIMONY!

SLUDGE REPORT

"Gossip roadkill on the Information Highway"
About the Sludge Report

AP NATIONAL	MAT SLUDGE	SLUDGE EXCLUSIVES:
AP WASHINGTON	THE GAP	
AP WORLD	CIGAR AFICIONADO	*HILLARY DEMANDS
AP ONLINE	ADRESS FROM THE OVAL	GORE BECOME MORMON
AP ON THE HOUR	OFFICE	AND TAKE HER AS SECOND
AP HEADLINES	RUSH	WIFE. "I'M NOT LEAVING THE
AP BREAKING	WHAT'S THE RUSH	WHITE HOUSE"
AP ALERTS	RUSH/MOLLOY	
AP FOX	CONG.BILLYBOB	*CHRISTIAN RIGHT
Search	JOURNAL X	CONSIDERS BEING A
	MITCH FINK	LIBERAL A
Headline:	RAT FINK	CURABLE DISEASE
	LIZ SMITH	
Date Range:	BLUMENTHAL BEATS HIS	*WASHINGTON POST OWNED
Within 14 Days	WIFE	BY CHINESE MILITARY
Any word(s) in article:		
		*WHITE HOUSE AIDE
	WHITEWATER FILE	SIDNEY BLUMENTHAL BEATS
AP Within 14 Days	ARIANNA	HIS WIFE DESPITE THE
	MICHAEL SNEED	RETRACTION MY LAWYERS
	BILL GERTZ	FORCED ON ME.
	PEGGY NOONAN	
	HOWARD KURTZ	CALL YOUR STORY IN TO
REUTERS WORLD	TV COLUMN	THE SLUDGE REPORT
U.K. TABLOIDS	PETER JOHNSON	(NOTE:I CAN'T USE ANY
US INFO WIRE	MICHAEL KELLY	DAMAGING GOSSIP ABOUT
SHOWBIZ PR	AL KAMEN	REPUBLICANS OR I'M TOAST)
PRESS DIGESTS	MOLLY IVINS	
WorldNetDaily	JUDE WANNISKI	
ABC NEWS	CHRIS MATTHEWS	SAVE SLUDGE'S ASS
ABC NEWS AUDIO	CARVILLE	DEFENSE FUND
CNN	LARRY NICHOLS	
CNN BREAKING	R. E. TYRRELL	
MSNBC	JOSEPH FARAH	
FRANCE-PRESSE	CAMILLE PAGLIA	

FIGURE 6.5   The Sludge Report

168

Your Trusted Source for Health Information
FREE **drkoop.com**
Your Personalized Health & Fitness Planner
Click Here to Visit our Sponsor

SUCK:

- **DAILY**
- **HIT AND RUN**
- **FILLER**
- **THE FISH**
- **PROBE**

[SEARCH]

SALON
SMUG
FEED
MCSWEENEY'S
TEEVEE
THE ONION
CTHEORY
CU DIGEST
BUD
THE SMOKING GUN
INTERTEXT
METAJOURNALS
NETFUTURE
SLASHDOT
TECHSIGHTINGS
SUCK HARDER
BRUNCHING SHUTTLECOCKS
MEDIA CULPRIT
MEDIA CULTURE REVIEW
HAIKU HEADLINES
CRUEL SITE OF THE DAY
MISANTHROPIC BITCH
KVETCH
CONK! HEADLINES

THE RETORT
» ROGERS CADENHEAD (02/12)
» JONATHAN BOURNE (03/15)
» CORRESPONDENTS (02/22)
» EXCERPTS (01/14)

JIM ROMANESKO
HANS EISENBEIS
MICHAEL SIPPEY
OWEN THOMAS
HAROLD STUSNICK
TIM CAVANAUGH
DEREK POWAZEK
DAVID HUDSON
DANNY O'BRIEN
ROBIN MILLER
REBECCA EISENBERG
CARL STEADMAN
CHRISTOPHER LOCKE
G. ALKAITIS-CARAFELLI
JUSTIN HALL
SAM PRATT
GREG KNAUSS
FARAI CHIDEYA
JOHN STYN
LANCE ARTHUR
JEFFREY ZELDMAN
JOE OTTERBEIN
KEN LAYNE
BOB HIRSCHFELD
CHARLIE BERMANT
SCOTT ROSENBERG
JOHN HARGRAVE
MICHAEL MOORE
CATTLOVRR
JOE CONASON

YOU SAID A MOUTHFUL!
MONICA EXPOSES HERSELF
ON AMAZON.COM...

DISINFORMATION:

- PROPAGANDA
- REVOLUTIONARIES
- CENSORSHIP
- COUNTERCULTURE
- COUNTERINTELLIGENCE
- NEWSPEAK

[SEARCH]

E-MAIL:
UNRELIABLE@DRUDGE.COM
DRUDGE RETORT
PO BOX 4790
CANOGA PARK, CA 91308-4790

RETORT FLASHBACK...
MAIL BONDING...

MATT DRUDGE: "I've blown it a few times. I don't want the humiliation of having my words coming back to haunt me."...

x x x x

"Barnicle's new duties in the Big Apple will

FIGURE 6.6   Drudge Retort '99: Putting the Yellow Back in Journalism

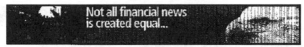

x x x x x

DRUDGE REPORT

XXXXX DRUDGE REPORT XXXXX 04/15/99 23:58:22 UTC XXXXX

MONEY MAN CHUNG SUBPOENAED, WILL BE CALLED TO TESTIFY BEFORE CONGRESS

Exclusive Details

Dan Burton bounces back. The DRUDGE REPORT learned late Thursday night that
former Democratic fund-raiser Johnny Chung will be subpoenaed to appear before a
congressional committee. The subpoena, which will be issued late Friday, calls
for Chung to appear on APRIL 27 and 28 before the House Government Reform
Committee.

With TV cameras running, Chung will be questioned in great detail about what he
knows, and Chung has indicated that he will fully cooperate with the committee,
the DRUDGE REPORT has learned.

The House Government Reform Committee wrote Attorney General Janet Reno
requesting permission to question Chung on April 7 after a story appeared in the
LOS ANGELES TIMES.

The story stunned the city: China's head of military intelligence took funds from
Beijing and secretly spent them to reelect President Clinton, Chung has told
federal investigators.

"Chung's testimony has provided investigators the first, direct link between a
senior Chinese government official and illicit foreign contributions that were
funneled into Clinton's 1996 reelection effort," the TIMES reported.

Late Thursday, AG Reno gave the green light for The Hill to subpoena Chung.

Reno put no limitations on the questioning, according to senior government
sources.

"Chung wants to tell his story, in public," one well-placed source told the
DRUDGE REPORT from Washington.

x x x x x

HOW CNN LEARNED TO LOVE THE BOMB, 'NIGHTLINE' TOO

There are reports tonight out of Yugoslavia of complete carnage and chaos in the
wake of the continued NATO bombing.

FIGURE 6.7   Drudge Report, April 15, 1999

170

News Scoops

Livingston Confesses Affairs

By Jim VandeHei

Incoming House Speaker Bob Livingston (R-La.) tonight disclosed to the Republican Conference that he has had sexual affairs in his past and had planned to resign his post, according to GOP sources.

However, at the Conference meeting Livingston received a thundering round of applause and felt that there was no reason to offer his resignation, sources said.

Livingston confirmed to Roll Call, "When I did an early interview with the media after announcing my candidacy for Speaker I told a reporter that I was running for Speaker, not SAINTHOOD. There was a good reason for those words." "I have decided to inform my colleagues and constituents that during my 33-year marriage to my wife, Bonnie, I have on occasion strayed from my marriage and doing so nearly cost me my marriage and my family," he said in the prepared statement.

"I want to assure everyone that these indiscretions were not with employees on my staff and I have never been asked to testify under oath about them," he said.

Sources said Livingston had planned to offer his resignation to the entire GOP Conference. If Livingston had offered his resignation, Majority Whip Tom DeLay (R-Texas) had planned to stand up and say Livingston should not resign his post, sources said.

Sources said the affairs occurred during Livingston's Congressional career.

Sources say Livingston was called recently and told a story about his past could be coming out soon.

Livingston first came to Congress after winning a special election in 1977. Livingston was nominated to be the next Speaker by the GOP Conference Nov. 18.

Livingston's statement went on to say, "Because these were personal

FIGURE 6.8   Roll Call Web Site Highlighting Affairs of Short-Term House Speaker Candidate Robert Livingston

Your Tour Guide through the Past, the Present and, perhaps, the Future

Current Calls
who is calling for the
president's resignation

Resignation Chat
converse with other visitors here

Historical Documents
the greatest speeches &
writings through out history

Resignation Forum
updates, articles and debate

Predict History
write the President's
resignation speech

Grass Roots
make your voice heard here

Links
websites of interest

Let's take stock. Speaker of the House Newt Gingrich has resigned. Speaker-elect Bob Livingston has resigned. Charles Bakaly, Ken Starr's high-profile spokesman, has resigned.

William Jefferson Clinton, on the other hand, chose not to take the advice of over 150 newspapers and hundreds of public officials and pundits from the right and the left and spare his country the long ordeal of the past year. Barring some cataclysmic national security debacle (and one may be in the offing), Bill Clinton will remain our president until the next millennium.

Taking a cue from our commander in chief, RESIGNATION.COM will also be here. We've been there for you, chronicling the growing chorus of pro-resignation voices, giving you a window on the history of resignations and providing a daily forum for your thoughts on the matter. We have no intention of leaving you now.

In 1945, Interior Secretary Harold L. Ickes -- father of Clinton's former deputy chief of staff -- condemned President Truman's "lack of adherence to the strict truth" and resigned from his cabinet. "I don't care to stay in an administration," he said, "where I am expected to commit perjury for the sake of the party." The distance we've traveled between Harold Ickes *pere* and Harold Ickes *fils* shows how far down we have defined presidential deviancy. RESIGNATION.COM will serve as a reminder to public servants everywhere that resignation remains an honorable option clearly placing the national interest above narrow self-interest.

To call for the president's resignation, sign up here:

Name:

E-mail Address:

City:

State:

Email submission policy

View Current List

Press Release

E-MAIL

Quote of the Day

"I really do not think he ever would resign unless Hillary gave up on him" -- Clinton biographer David Maranis

"An Arianna Online Project"
Website powered by BOLD NEW WORLD

FIGURE 6.9   Resignation.com Home Page

Discussion Questions

1. Do you think Matt Drudge should be considered a journalist? What difference does it make to be called a journalist?
2. Has journalism been changed by the Drudge Report? How might journalism be altered by the Internet in the future?
3. Is it accurate to say that everyone will have the power to be a journalist in the future? What would happen if everyone tried to use this power?
4. How is information utilized by Drudge, as well as mainstream journalists, to manipulate public opinion?
5. Do you think Congress should have released the Starr Report on the Internet? How did the release affect mainstream media?
6. Is it possible to exercise gatekeeping on the Internet and still promote free expression?

7

A Survey of the Range of Internet Content

"It is time that we give up our notion that we may find solutions to our emptiness through technology. We must now turn to our poets, playwrights, composers, theologians, and artists."

—Neil Postman, professor (1996)

"It has been suggested that this technology will fundamentally change the way we think, learn, consume, communicate, and govern our affairs in the next century."

—Douglas Fraleigh and Joseph Tuman, authors (1997)

"It is easy to get lost for hours, sampling usable and unusable intellectual growths without knowing whether one has actually reached the most important specimens."

—Doris Graber, political scientist (1997)

"Image the world, but understand nothing."

—Arthur and Marilouise Kroker, authors (1997)

"The so-called 'new media' (call-in radio shows, Internet Web pages, chat rooms and news groups) have yet to find a clear definition or task in the democratic process, and it's too early to evaluate their impact on politics."

—W. Russell Neuman, author (1998)

"Garbage in, garbage sloshing around . . . this does not mean they [the public] are either deepening their sensibilities or improving their democratic capacity to govern themselves."

—Todd Gitlin, sociologist (1998)

Arthur and Marilouise Kroker opened their book *Digital Delirium* with a brief poem that moves the reader from the "slow suicide" of the modern world to the slow media:

> *Image the world, but understand nothing.*
> *The real can no longer keep up to the speed of the image. Reality shudders and collapses and fragments into the vortex of many different realities: some cybernetic, some designer, some residual, some an out-moded stock of the vanishing real. . . .*
> *Speed economy, but slow jobs. Speed images, but slow eyes. Speed finance, but slow morality. Speed sex, but slow desire. Speed globalization, but slow localization. Speed media, but slow communication. Speed talk, but no thought (Kroker and Kroker, 1997, p. IX).*

They argued that "the faster the tech, the slower the speed of thought . . . the more accelerated the culture, the slower the rate of social change . . . the quicker the digital decomposition, the slower the political reflection" (p. X). Sociologist Todd Gitlin expressed similar concerns about what he called "a lightweight culture whose main value is marketability"—one in which "information" is valued for its own sake and piling up "higgedly-piggedly" as noise: "When a neo-Nazi creates a World-Wide Web site that maintains that Auschwitz was not a death camp, he is, technically, adding as much 'information' to the gross informational product as when someone posts an analysis of global warming" (*Chronicle of Higher Education*, May 1, 1998, pp. B-4–B-5).

Still, some scholars suggest that the new technologies offer new opportunities. Political scientist Doris Graber expressed her belief that the Internet has a huge *potential* to change mass media and American politics, and for this reason, both media and politicians have gravitated to the web. But they are not alone:

> The Web makes it possible for average individuals, who have long been ignored by the traditional news media, to make their voices heard in the public arena. . . . Their messages can be constructed to inform or deceive, to rally people for good and bad causes, or to entertain them in socially approved or condemned ways. . . . Whether audiences will choose to receive these messages remains to be seen (Graber, 1997, p. 392).

In this book, I have examined Internet World Wide Web sites as mass-mediated content. As a social construction of reality, content is not a perfect, mirrorlike reflection. Content is a social product of complex decision-making: "Mass media content—both news and entertainment—is shaped, pounded, constrained, encouraged by a multitude of forces. Sometimes the reality presented by the media matches the world as you know it, and sometimes it is very different," P. J. Shoemaker and S. D. Reese (1996, p. IX) noted. It is possible for two media organizations to tell a similar story about one event and yet offer quite a different portrayal of another, for media content can be influenced by the people who create it, by the "routines" they utilize, by social institutions and forces, and by "ideology" (pp. 6–7). Shoemaker and Reese, however, showed little interest in the Internet, seeing the information superhighway as merely an extension of traditional mass media content (p. 216).

In this chapter, Internet sites will be categorized under four headings: corporate media, education, government, and private. The focus of examination is the extent to which such cyber locations promote or preempt free expression.

Corporate Media Sites

Mass communication has been defined as a system in which "professional communicators operate the media for profit by disseminating content to large and heterogeneous audiences on a more or less continuous basis" (De-Fleur and Ball-Rokeach, 1989, p. 336). The major mass media continue to utilize this model as they develop their vision of the web. A visit to the Internet pages of CNN, *Time*, the *Los Angeles Times*, or CBS News shows that fairly traditional news models exist on the web. Early page development featured reproduction of offline versions on the stories. More recently, some news organizations have created subcultures within their offices to create original web content. Such material is targeted at younger, more highly educated, and more affluent people, who tend to use the web at higher rates.

We are told that "business is booming on the web," that traffic doubles every 100 days, and that commerce could exceed $300 billion by the year 2002: "The Internet is growing faster than all other technologies that have preceded it. Radio existed for 38 years before it had 50 million listeners, and television took 13 years to reach that mark. The Internet crossed the line in just four years" (Associated Press, April 15, 1998).

Such favorable statistics, however, do not reflect population increases during the century, and as a commercial and profitable venture, the Internet remained volatile as the twentieth century came to a close. E-commerce remained a risky venture. Few sites were turning a profit, and most initially viewed the web as low-cost advertising—a way to reach the segmented marketplace. (See Figures 7.1 through 7.6.)

From a mass media perspective, the goal of commercial sites is to attract the largest possible audience. By doing so, these Internet content providers will create value in their pages as places for advertising. As a

176

Search: Books [Go!] **Browse:** Business [Go!]

Full Search:
Books, Music, Video
Find the books
you want.
Save up to [40%]

New Guterson
Pre-order *East of the Mountains* now!

Pulitzer Prizes
See all the winners.

Star Wars: Episode I
One book. Four covers. Reserve one or get them all.

Sell books, CDs, and videos from your Web site. Join Associates

New Oprah Book!

Hardcover or paperback

Visit our Oprah® page.

Shopping Services
• Try our shopping service: Shop the Web!

• Amazon.com Delivers e-mail

Welcome! Shopping at Amazon.com is 100% secure-- guaranteed.
Already a customer? Sign in.

What We're Reading
Happy Birthday, Duke!

CD and Book

As the centenary of his birth approaches, Duke Ellington looms larger than ever over the musical landscape. Prepare yourself for a celebratory blowout on April 29 with our selection of music and books. And be sure to explore our package of Ellingtonian features, including essays and a list of essential recordings.

Check out the Amazon.com Hot List.

Browse Subjects
Heaven Sent
Annie Dillard talks about natural calamity, God's laissez-faire policy, and *For the Time Being*. (In Literature & Fiction)

Find more articles and interviews in:

Health, Mind & Body   Literature & Fiction
Science & Nature   Science Fiction & Fantasy
Religion & Spirituality   Plus many more...

ANNOUNCING

Amazon.com Auctions!
8 million Amazonians are preregistered to bid, buy & sell. Join the fun!

Check out our current charity auctions benefiting Kosovo refugees and World Wildlife Fund.
ANNOUNCING

Today in Music
Get started in international or jazz.

Chart Toppers

1. Sogno
   Andrea Bocelli
2. Echo
   Tom Petty
3. Something For Everybody: Baz Luhrmann
   Various Artists - Dance & DJ

More **Chart Toppers**

FIGURE 7.1   Amazon.com

GO Kids GO Family GO Money GO News GO Sports GO Home

INFOSEEK SEARCH ◉ ABC.com ○ WEB   · About GO Network
                    Free E-mail

"You're a bum!"

We Love TV

Friday, April 16, 1999

Tonight on TV
(Eastern Time)

Two Guys, a Girl and a Pizza Place:
Does T.G.I.F. stand for Two Guys Invade Fridays? We've got the scoop on the show's April appearances.

20/20 Friday: A look at an experimental surgical procedure used to treat stroke victims. **The Big Moment:** How far will people push themselves when it's their big moment? **Live chat with Rider Strong:** Chat with Boy Meets World's Rider Strong tonight at 7:00pm, ET!

Find out what's coming up in May with our day-to-day calendar.

8:00 pm	Sabrina, the Teenage Witch — Sabrina clones Valerie into another Sabrina.
8:30 pm	Boy Meets World — Fred Savage guests as a professor who comes on to Topanga.
9:00 pm	Two Guys, a Girl and a Pizza Place — Berg goes to England in pursuit of Ashley.
9:30 pm	Brother's Keeper — Porter & Bobby fight over Oscar's teacher.
10:00 pm	20/20 Friday — The lives of 2 gay policemen.
11:35 pm	Nightline
12:05 am	Politically Incorrect with Bill Maher

abc home
abc primetime
abc daytime
○ abc soaps
○ the view
abc tgif
one saturday morn.
abc news
Is Your star a Planning Tool?
Tactics?
abc sports
books
music
video
shopping
shows A-Z
stars A-Z
tv schedule
local stations
message boards
site map
help

Bargain Books up to 90% OFF!
barnesandnoble.com

Shows | Find Your Favorite   ABC Primetime Schedule

The View

Red Lobster presents The View Across America. Find out when they're coming. Weekdays at 11pm ET.

Brother's Keeper

Love him or hate him-- we wanted to know. See what Brother's Keeper fans think of brother Porter. Fridays at 9:30pm ET.

The Practice

Do you know the lowdown on The Practice's litigating ladies? Play our trivia! Sundays at 10pm, ET!

MUSIC BOULEVARD

FIGURE 7.2 ABC.com

178

FIGURE 7.3   Disney.com

Daviess County residents will begin locking their doors

by Shannon Samson

Washington, IN April 2– Until Wednesday, folks who live in Washington, Indiana say they didn't have to lock their doors at night. Residents say they're shocked the first murder in nine years here turns out to be three. More surprising, the two young men accused of the crimes also live here.

One of the suspects, 21-year-old Steve Hale lives near the courthouse in this house on southeast Fourth Street. Neighbors say they often saw him mowing the lawn, but Hale kept to himself. They say can't believe now he's accused of murder.

FIGURE 7.4   MSNBC.com

180

MAIN PAGE
WORLD
U.S.
U.S. LOCAL
ALLPOLITICS
TIME
CQ
analysis
community
WEATHER
BUSINESS
SPORTS
SCI-TECH
NATURE
ENTERTAINMENT
BOOKS
TRAVEL
FOOD
HEALTH
STYLE
IN-DEPTH

custom news
Headline News brief
daily almanac
CNN networks
on-air transcripts
news quiz

CNN WEB SITES:

allpolitics
EN ESPAÑOL
em português
SVENSKA
NORGE
danmark

PATHFINDER SITES:

Go To ...

President Clinton's videotaped testimony

On Monday, September 21, the House Judiciary Committee released President Bill Clinton's videotaped testimony in the Monica Lewinsky affair, along with an estimated 2,800 pages of supporting documents from Independent Counsel Ken Starr's sex-and-perjury investigation of the president.

In this story:

- The complete testimony
- Testimony highlights
- Starr Report supporting documents
- Pictures and graphics from the Starr documents

On this page you will find streaming video and links to the documents, as they become available.

A message to CNN viewers

CNN is presenting this testimony in its entirety because of the gravity of the crisis involving the presidency -- and because, through its actions, the Congress is asking you, the public, to judge this material for yourselves.

It is our understanding that some of this testimony is sexually explicit and may be inappropriate for children and offensive to some viewers. Viewer discretion is advised.

Given the constitutional process that is under way, we feel it is our journalistic responsibility to bring this material to you. We also feel it is our responsibility to caution you about its contents.

Players, Timeline, documents, transcripts, quiz. AllPolitics' in-depth look at the investigation into the president's relationship with Monica Lewinsky has it all.

DOCUMENTS

The Starr Report
The Second Clinton Rebuttal
The Clinton Rebuttal

VIDEO

Partisanship rules Judiciary Committee (9-18-98)
Real: 28K | 56K Windows Media: 28K | 56K

Internet magazine Salon drops bomb on Capitol Hill (9-18-98) Real: 28K | 56K Windows Media: 28K | 56K

MORE VIDEO

POLLS

Releasing Clinton video wrong (9-18-98)

FIGURE 7.5   CNN.com

181

FIGURE 7.6   Real.com

result of this trend, ratings companies have emerged to estimate audience size. Media Metrix claimed that the Internet audience encompassed 45 million users from home and 27 million office users near the end of 1998 (*Broadcasting & Cable*, September 28, 1998, p. 52).

At first, the Internet's leading commercial sites were search engines such as Yahoo! But as the Internet audience matured, content sites began to dominate the list. (See Table 7.1.)

A company called RelevantKnowledge tracked the top domains and Internet properties and reported that time on the web increased during the summer, which is the opposite of what happens with television: "This increased frequency and duration is being driven by the growth in the work segment and the fact that teens are out of school," said Jill Frankle, a senior analyst (RelevantKnowledge press release, August 7, 1998). The company also found:

- The gender gap on the web is narrowing. Now, 46 percent of users are women.
- Three-fourths of Internet users are between the ages of eighteen and forty-nine, a prime demographic target for advertisers.
- About one-fourth of web users have college degrees (Relevant-Knowledge press release, August 7, 1998). (See Table 7.2.)

TABLE 7.1 Media Metrix Top-Rated Internet Sites

Home Access	Rating[*]	Work Access	Rating
1. ZDNet.com	7.7	ZDNet.com	13.2
2. Disney Online	6.8	Weather.com	10.2
3. Weather.com	6.4	CNN.com	9.6
4. MSNBC.com	6.3	MSNBC.com	8.5
5. Pathfinder.com	5.2	Pathfinder.com	7.7
6. TheGlobe.com	4.7	USAToday.com	7.4
7. Sony Online	4.7	Disney Online	6.4
8. CNN.com	4.3	ABCNews.com	6.4
9. ESPN.com	4.2	CNNfn.com	6.0
10. DigitalCity.com	4.1	CBSNow.com	5.2

[*]Each rating point represents 450,000 at-home users, or 270,000 at-work users. Data for some sites include aggregate hits from local affiliate sites.
SOURCE: Tedesco, 1998

TABLE 7.2 Top Domains and Properties

July 1998 Rank and Site	12+ (in 000s)	Reach (%)
1. yahoo.com	12,011	48.8
2. aol.com	21,868	41.0
3. microsoft.com	18,575	34.8
4. netscape.com	17,625	33.0
5. excite.com	14,378	26.9
6. geocities.com	14,239	26.9
7. infoseek.com	11,469	21.5
8. lycos.com	10,678	20.0
9. msn.com	10,652	20.0
10. altavista.digital.com	8,878	16.6

Other top twenty-five .com sites were: 11, hotmail.com; 12, tripod.com; 13, angelfire.com; 14, amazon.com; 15, zdnet.com; 16, real.com; 17, xoom.com; 18, looksmart.com; 19, mapquest.com; 20, switchboard.com; 21, msnbc.com; 22, pathfinder.com; 23, webcrawler.com; 24, mirabillis.com; 25, cnn.com.
SOURCE: Michelle Beilsmith, RelevantKnowledge, Inc., July 1998

Commercial web sites ultimately stand to be dominated by major corporate players that control other mass media. The more investment that can be made in such sites, the more sophisticated and appealing these sites will be to mass audiences.

One of the most influential developments on the web was the rise of so-called Internet broadcasting. Audio and video streaming software allowed traditional broadcasters and new players to place signals on the Internet, and on the Web, commercial and noncommercial broadcasters would not be limited by spectrum scarcity of the airwaves. (See Table 7.3.)

Educational Sites

The earliest users of the Internet were people at American universities who had access to it before the general public did. Such people tend to store and harvest huge quantities of data and information. So, the Internet became a good way to catalog, maintain, and distribute common information.

In the past few years, as American universities have taken on a corporate look, the Internet has become a vehicle used in the business of public relations, admissions, and enrollment management. Distance education technologies have become important, and universities now see the Inter-

TABLE 7.3 Radio and Television Stations on the Internet

Station	Description
3ABN	Three Angels Broadcasting Network is a Christian-based satellite RealVideo service from Illinois.
America's Health Network	Health and medical news RealVideo service targeted at doctors.
Antenna 97.5	Adult contemporary music from Thessaloniki, Greece.
C-SPAN & C-SPAN 2	Simulcast of cable public affairs channels based in Washington, D.C.
CCCTV	The Chinese Communication Channel broadcasts from North America Chinese news and entertainment in RealVideo.
Canal de Belo Horizonte	CBH, Channel 25, Belo Horizonte, Brazil, features live TV broadcasts.
Fox News Channel	Live RealAudio and RealVideo broadcasts of the cable news programming.
Hydro Active Newport	Live RealVideo from the top of Goat Island, Newport Harbor, Rhode Island.
IRNA TV	Islamic Republic News Agency broadcasts from Iran.
KMEX-TV	KMEX-TV Channel 34, Los Angeles, is one of the nation's leading Spanish-language stations.
KSBT TV	African American–owned TV from Oakland, California.
M2 Europe	MTV's European Internet music television channel.
MBC TV	Live news in RealVideo from Seoul, South Korea.
MITV 36	MIT's on-campus cable station featuring "The Button," in Cambridge, Massachusetts.
Mt. Fuji	A live view of Mt. Fuji, Japan.
Regional News Network	Live news, sports, weather, and talk from the New York area cable channel.
Thai Army Television	Online entertainment, music, and news from Bangkok.
ValueVision	An online shopping channel in RealVideo.

SOURCE: The Timecast Network, http://www.timecast.com, August 1998

net as a way to deliver course materials—both to traditional on-campus and nontraditional distant students.

Universities across the globe have jumped on the Internet bandwagon. Among other things, the Net has become a way to access rare collections and museum holdings. European art, for example, may be downloaded and studied in seconds, at little or no cost to students. In the future, we are likely to see educational sites become more profit-oriented. As such, they are likely to adopt the look and feel of commercial sites.

The first major online effort came from the University of Phoenix (http://www.uophx.edu), which offered online credit courses for adult learners:

> In 1989, the University established "Online Campus" in San Francisco, California. Online computer-mediated education was an outgrowth of the technological transformation of the work place and a response to the increasing use of computers and modems for communication. The Online Campus currently enrolls degree-seeking adult students from all over the U.S. and the world. It is a group-based learning environment offering the kind of interaction and support which take place in a traditional face-to-face seminar-style classroom (http://www.uophx.edu/online/about.htm, September, 1998).

The university offers a bachelor of science in business degree program.

The Western Governors' Association currently is modeling its own online distance education programs that link major universities in the western half of the country.

Additionally, there are numerous noncredit or certification programs online, such as ZDUniversity, which offers people of all ages the opportunity to learn computer skills in virtual classrooms and chat "cafés." Students are led by an instructor, purchase a textbook online from a bookstore, and engage in communication threads that feature Internet links to various web sites. At the heart of such online exercises, beyond obtaining temporary support systems, there are loose attempts at community building.

Steven Jones (1998) centered the issues of "cybersociety" in more fundamental concerns of community, time, and space. As a mediated form of communication, CMC can create "electronic communities" in cyberspace, but the surplus of information produces a condition of disorder: "Such disorder and the attempts to control it underscore the mythical investment we have in computer technology. The chaos and confusion generated by the opening of new frontiers led us to devise means of communication and transportation as if those means were one, part and parcel of the same process" (pp. 7–8).

It is clear that these virtual worlds employ social constructions of reality defined by individual users and that significant free-expression issues surface in regard to the huge stores of data that *may* be accessed, if located. Because free expression has traditionally tended to be defined by local communities, the erosion of geography may only confuse social ordering and norms.

Government Sites

Governments across the world are keepers of vast amounts of information. In America, investigative journalists have long used public-access laws and open-meetings laws to cover the public sector. Before computers, the job of finding information in file cabinets was very difficult. Now, the job is easier, but news organizations have had to go to court to fight for the right to access electronic records. These battles have been affected by a patchwork of state laws. The Internet adds a new component to the issue of access. Government may provide personal data to a trained journalist who works with editors on the decision to use them, but it is quite another matter when the same data are readily available to anyone who can operate a search engine on the Internet. If anyone can access the data and publish them in any form, traditional standards of accuracy need not apply.

Much of the government data stored in computers during the 1980s are formatted in databases that are not compatible with Internet browsers. So, even if governments were to make the data more available, they might not be usable. However, computer scientists are working to develop interfaces between older mainframe data, the Internet, and client-side processing software. So, the issue of access involves both technical standards and social norms on the usage of the information.

As a matter of law, free expression traditionally has been defined as limiting the power of government to exercise social control. It is unclear how the world of the Internet and its computer network might empower government or further reduce its influence in the years ahead.

Government, like education, is moving to privatize work. Consequently, web sites will be influenced by the tight budgets of the future: Much of what is free now may eventually cost something. Additionally, because politicians operate government, there is a considerable amount of "public relations" on government sites, designed to fashion the image of officeholders. Politicians see great benefit in finding inexpensive ways to access the electorate in an unfiltered way, working around the journalists who sometimes alter their messages.

At times, the line between government sites, such as the White House location, and campaign sites, such as President Clinton's 1996 reelection web page, becomes fuzzy. In both cases, modern political marketing manipulated messages and images. (See Figure 7.7.)

To this point, governments have seemed to want to use the Internet as a way to give average citizens greater access to information. The Internal Revenue Service (IRS) is a good example. In April 1998, as the tax deadline neared, the IRS web site was swamped with Internet activity from people looking for government forms and information. The new technology provided a technical solution to the problem of long lines. However, such computer technology is also an excuse for government employees to avoid face-to-face encounters with the public they are hired to serve.

It is unclear how much of what makes up the .gov sites really can be classified as free expression. In fact, free expression seems to generally reside outside of the forces of governments. About all government types can do is to try to stay out of the way of private citizens wishing to exercise free expression. Although the Internet was built as a government infrastructure project, the national powers have tended to step back and allow marketplace forces to develop it. The degree to which CMC empowers individuals to *participate* in political concerns or further leaves individuals in a condition of apathy, alienation, and anomie will determine whether we are truly dealing with "technologies of freedom."

Private and Other Sites

Perhaps the best example of the type of problems engendered by the Web was the site with the address www.whitehouse.com. It featured the sale of pictures of nude women and thrived on making fun of the real White House site, www.whitehouse.gov. It even went so far as to use the e-mail address of president@whitehouse.com, although it ran the disclaimer: "I realize WhiteHouse.com is one of the most controversial and erotic websites in the world. I am at least 18 years of age or the legal age to view pornography in my area. I have a legal right to view images of naked women and other erotic materials and you have a right to transmit them to me" (April 29, 1998). (See Figure 7.8.)

Such sites have caused countless people trouble in the workplace. A Gibson County, Indiana, teacher, Larry Krohn, for example, was fired in 1998 after another teacher discovered a pornographic web site left on a school computer screen. Krohn told WFIE-TV, in Evansville, Indiana, that he accidentally called up the site and left it on the screen (April 27, 1998).

In another case, a radio news reporter in Maryland faced criminal charges after he pretended to be an online pornographer and exchanged photos of young girls. Larry Mathews claimed the First Amendment allowed him to report on the subject, but a prosecutor said he was seeking absolute immunity to break the law (*Edupage*, April 28, 1998).

Anyone with a personal computer may now create Internet pages in a matter of minutes, which may be the most fundamental difference of the web era. In effect, this ability allows an individual to own the printing press, be her own publisher, and have the potential to reach a worldwide audience at little cost. Obviously, this opens the door to a wide range of media content—as broad as human existence. One can find pages on sub-

188

[Text version]

Good Afternoon

Welcome to the
White House

U.S. Humanitarian Relief Efforts: 1-800-USAID-Relief

The President & Vice President:
Their accomplishments, their families, and how to send them electronic mail --

Interactive Citizens' Handbook: Your guide to information about
the Federal government

White House History and Tours:
Past Presidents and First Families, Art in the President's House and Tours -- **Tour Information**

The Virtual Library:
Search our site, including an extensive archive of White House documents

White House Help Desk:
Frequently asked questions and answers about our service

Commonly Requested Federal Services:
Direct access to Federal Services

What's New:
What's happening at the White House -
President Clinton's Remarks to Humanitarian Relief Organizations

Site News:
Recent additions to our site
-**The President's Trip to Central America**
-**A Visit by the First Lady to Save America's Treasures**
-**White House Millennium Council**

The Briefing Room:
Today's releases, hot topics, and the latest Federal statistics

White House for Kids:
Helping young people become more active and informed citizens

To comment on this service, send feedback to the Web Development Team.

Read our Privacy Policy

FIGURE 7.7   Whitehouse.gov

189

Page 1 of 2Page 1 of 2

White HouseWhite House

New for 1999

Free Chat | Free Cartoons | Free Daily Pics
WhiteHouse For Ladies | Gaming&AuctionZone
Get a Free @whitehouse.com Email Address!

This WhiteHouse has been featured on ABCNews, CNN,
C|Net, NBC-DateLine and Newsweek.

We are in no way endorsed by or associated with the U.S. Government. You
must be 18 years or older to enter this site!

New for 1999

Teen
Buffet

JOIN!

Get 5 Days Free!

WhiteHouse.com

Click here

Take the FREE

WhiteHouse
First Ladies

Photo Galleries

Live Video
Feeds

Free Live
Sex Chat

15
Live Shows

Teen Amateurs

Erotic Stories

Live Sex FEEDS!

WhiteHouse Intern!

WhiteHouse
FirstLadies!

Recorded Sex
Feeds

**XXXclusive
Models**

**15,000+
Recorded
Hardcore
Feeds**

**Raw, Teen
First Timers**

**Ultra Erotic
Text & Audio
Stories**

**Hilarious Sex
Cartoons!**

**Recorded
Feeds
& MovieZone
Video**

**Amateur
Photos**

JOIN NOW and
Get 5 Days for
FREE!

By entering WhiteHouse.com, you agree that you are of at least 18 years
of age and are not in violation of any laws within your community. By
clicking on the link below or clicking on our Daily Teaser Pics, you
warrant you are interested in seeing material of a pornographic nature
and that you are not supplying a minor with access to lewd, erotic, or
pornographic material

JOIN NOW and
Get 5 Days for
FREE!

ENTER WHITEHOUSE.COM

Free Daily Teaser Pics

FIGURE 7.8   Whitehouse.com

**Click here to get your own Free
@whitehouse.com Email Address!**

**Click here to go to our MyNews and
MyStocks Sections**

LewinskyGate-The Song. Note that this
will open a new browser window

StarGate-The Song. Note that this will
open a new browser window

*To contact us at WhiteHouse.com send e-
mails to webmaster@thewhitehouse.com
or Click Here to Send.*

*If you are interested in protecting Free
Speech Online and protecting Kid's rights
online check out these two sites.*

Electronic Frontier Foundation | SafeKids

FIGURE 7.8   *(continued)*

jects ranging from the lost empire of Byzantium to children's building blocks. As a result, content is difficult to categorize, and it is impossible to judge the social meaning inherent in such breadth.

Former television news people started the site Newsblues.com to give people in the business a forum to air gripes about their jobs, a function that had traditionally been handled by sharing beer and pizza with colleagues after hours (*Electronic Media*, October 5, 1998, p. 1). (See Figure 7.9.) One of the founders of the site, Mike James, responded to a series of questions I raised.

James said the staff at Newsblues.com knows of "open management hostilities" and job threats resulting from submissions to the site: "We know that station e-mail systems are being examined for indications of correspondence with our web site," he wrote. Even heavy editing of the web site has not been enough for the targets of the complaints:

> I personally have had two general managers send me threatening e-mail. In one case, I was called a "curse to the industry." Another promised to destroy me in court.
>
> Management is angry and we're quite sure it's trickling down to the troops . . . and this has really fueled the internal revolt. We know that most of the consulting firms and several major broadcasting chains have "sug-

"The TV business is a cruel and shallow money trench, a long plastic hallway where thieves and pimps run free, and good men die like dogs. There's also a negative side." Hunter S. Thompson

CLICK HERE TO TELL US ABOUT YOUR STATION

342 STATIONS LISTED

ON AIR

TV MARKETS
SALARY INFO
TV AGENTS
NEWS DIRECTORS
CONSULTANTS
BITCHING AREA
LOST & FOUND
COOL LINKS
ABOUT BLUES

SEAL
OF GOOD
PRACTICE

E-mail Us

NEW BLUES

Differing opinions emerge in Shreveport as KTBS demonstrates a ratings bounce-back after a fresh News Director joins the team. Some employees give her all the credit. Others say the old boss got the ball rolling. Read what both sides have to say.

They're stuck in no-man's land between Lawton, Oklahoma and Wichita Falls, Texas...(Market #161) and most of their viewers watch Oklahoma City on cable, but little KSWO is trying hard and seems like a good place to kickstart a career.

The lucky folks from WEWS who attended a seminar in Cleveland last week by KGO reporter Wayne Freedman came away believing they'd had a religious experience. Read about Wayne's magic in our Consultants section.

It's been called a "slave labor camp," but a recent contributor says KWTV in Oklahoma City isn't really all that bad. The News Director is demanding, but the local owner spends dough and likes to buy news toys.

WHSV in itty-bitty Harrisonburg, Virginia (Market #180) is undergoing a facelift. You wondered what tightwad Benedek Broadcasting was doing with all its cash? Looks like they're pouring it into this little market.

Cablevision's Long Island news operation, known as Neighborhood News, is accused by an insider of copying items directly from local newspapers, broadcasting pointless features and endlessly repeating insignificant local news stories. Sound familiar?.

FIGURE 7.9   Newsblues.com

Box 7.1   Newsblues.com: Internet Whining, Moaning, and Bitching

Mike James (formerly of WFTV, Orlando, and WHAS, Louisville) and Mona Scott (formerly of WBNS, Columbus, WKYC, Cleveland, and WCPX, Orlando) said they were serving as "moderators" for the open discussion about television news: "We daily must slog through hundreds of bile-filled correspondence and either edit them ruthlessly or toss them back for a rewrite (which we rarely get)," James wrote in an e-mail. "Frankly, after three weeks, we are truly in awe at the amount of pure unadulterated anger, in all forms, being expressed on a daily basis" (e-mail to the author, September 3, 1998).

James said they expected "garden variety bitching and moaning about salaries, equipment and personality conflicts," but they received much more:

(1) from the lower markets, wild-eyed, obscene, libelous ranting . . . almost drunken in their rage. Over time, after correspondence with these folks, we found that, for the most part, they were VERY young, VERY inexperienced and had difficulty expressing themselves. Most of the correspondence was filled with profanity. Punctuation was non-existent. Spelling was atrocious. In many, many cases, the letters were long, rambling diatribes in ALL CAPS. The universal complaint was (a) upper management are crooks (b) news directors don't understand news

(2) from the medium markets, so many personal attacks, sexual rumors, unsubstantiated stories of drug use and alcohol abuse, most of it directed against fellow workers . . . producers, Eps, anchors. A lot of infighting and, we gathered, a lot of career positioning and jealousy. These folks produced letters that were blatantly libelous, containing claims that ANY legitimate news reporter would instantly recognize as unprintable. Yet many of these folks persisted, resubmitting the claims again and again even after being rejected. We called this group the "ax grinders" and

(3) the upper market professionals who produced well conceived letters, carefully considered, with strong points against news judgment and management choices. Almost every letter from this group was able to be published without editing . . . clearly the work of education and experience and all especially enlightening. They seemed to have a very good understanding of where they fit into the news food chain. Their concerns were with larger issues. The handful of petty complaints came from very young members of studio crews who were really unconnected with the news operation and were obviously jealous

(E-mail to the author, September 1, 1998)

gested" to their management to keep an eye on News Blues (e-mail to the author, September 1, 1998).

The site attempts to protect the anonymity of those who post "serious, well-considered, inside information about local newsrooms" (Newsblues.com, September 3, 1998). One typical message posted on the site read: "This Fox affiliate has it all—low pay, low morale, overworked production people and underqualified reporters and producers" ("GM at the Wrong Party," newsblues.com/Stations/kptm.htm, September 3, 1998). Often, the complaints are about news judgment at local stations, such as this one: "Its assistant news director just quit recently after the GM and ND refused to allow him to interrupt an afternoon soap opera with a news bulletin to warn TV-5 viewers about an escaped prison inmate who shot and wounded two police officers and was still on the loose" ("Gasping for Air . . . and Ratings," Newsblues.com/ Stations/ kctv.htm, September 3, 1998). A series of complaints from different stations centered on broadcast consultant Larry Rickel, who operates Broadcast Image Group: "When his ideas don't work, he says the station didn't execute them correctly" ("From WTLV—Jacksonville, Florida," Newsblues.com/consultants.htm, September 3, 1998). Wrote another, "Larry, like everyone else who really understands what TV news is all about these days, knows that TV news is money and Larry is a great salesman" ("Peddling Crap for Profit," Newsblues.com/consultants. htm, September 3, 1998). James then posted a letter he sent to Rickel:

OPEN LETTER TO LARRY RICKEL, Consultant

Sent via e-mail 8/24/98—12:30 pm–c/o Broadcast Image Group

Dear Larry,

As editor of a website known as NewsBlues, I have been surprised and, frankly, quite shocked by the incredible amount of mail we've received directly challenging your methods and ideas. Nearly all of the correspondence regarding Larry Rickel has been negative.

Broadcast Image Group is a well-respected and very successful entity, so we know your concepts must have support from management. We encourage you to visit our site and read some of the letters from client newsrooms.

If you have comments, or if you would like to make use of these pages to elaborate on your beliefs, we would be glad to publish your thoughts. We encourage you to respond.

Sincerely,

Mike James

Editor's Note: Mr. Rickel has not responded to our correspondence. If you would like to contact him directly, his address is: LMRBIG@aol.com (Newsblues.com/consultants.htm, September 3, 1998).

One general manager, Lon Lee of Spokane, Washington, wrote to defend Rickel: "I am particularly sickened by the attacks. . . . Some don't like new ideas, especially if those ideas are completely different from anything they've previously faced," he said. James added this comment to the posting: *"Editor's Note: The writer of this note . . . neglected to mention that his daughter works for Larry Rickel. In fairness, we thought you should know"* (Newsblues.com/consultants.htm, September 3, 1998).

The Newsblues.com web site, therefore, is edited—unlike huge chunks of sites now available. The issue for all employees in the Internet age is the lack of safety in venting gripes online. "If you vent to your best friends and your spouse, the boss never finds out," Houston Labor lawyer Linda Wills remarked. "If you vent in the hallway or on the Internet, you're asking for trouble" (*Dallas Morning News,* February 14, 1999). Of course, Internet monitoring is just one way employers track employees. "There is a complete lack of freedom in the American workplace," the ACLU's Jeremy Gruber said. "Most people who work for private employers have their constitutional rights put in the garbage for eight to ten hours a day" (*St. Petersburg Times,* February 14, 1999).

The so-called Internet2, the next generation of digital technology, is likely to alter the range and type of content available in the future. It will be designed for faster data transfer of multimedia content. The political purpose for the upgrade is said to be threefold: (1) to improve commerce and security on the web, (2) to provide more and better access to students and scholars, and (3) to keep the United States in front as the premier information technology nation. Vice President Al Gore, in announcing a fiber-optic research network, proclaimed: "The speed of scientific discovery will be accelerated" (*Chronicle of Higher Education,* April 24, 1998, p. A-36). At least one proposal also calls for a higher-cost "express lane" for Internet traffic.

A huge component of Internet content in the future also will be commercial enterprises. The electronic marketplace on the Internet already makes it possible to shop for everything from books to dinner meats to cars. Given the ever-increasing 1-800 shopping marketplace, it is obvious that the Internet will merge over time with catalog shopping for nearly all products. Consequently, cyberspace has begun to challenge the shopping mall as the "place" in which commerce will be conducted in the twenty-first century, just as the mall replaced most downtown shopping centers in the late 1900s. Credit card security and fraud, however, seem likely to inhibit this development, as well as the hesitation of people to change their shopping patterns.

The advancement of cyber commerce will turn the computer infrastructure into an electronic marketplace, a phenomenon that advances the marketplace of ideas in the wired network. However, it remains to be seen if cyberspace is a place suitable for zoning.

CNET (http://www.cnet.com/) has argued that there should be an X-rated, adults-only zone on the net: "The biggest hurdle would be convincing porn sites to relocate. But operators of porn sites may be more amenable to the idea then you'd expect. In recent Senate hearings on ways to regulate minors' access to adult material, the only operator of an adult entertainment site called to testify actually lobbied for creating an adult zone on the Net" (p. 2).

Seth Warshavsky, described by the *Los Angeles Times* as "an Internet pornographer," proposed creating a new ".adult" site for explicit sexual content. "All of the other proposals aren't First Amendment–friendly, and we don't think they'd be effective," he said. "We're trying to create a minor-free environment where adults can see what they want." And he added, "We're trying to be proactive and create that brick wall on our own."

Yet it is unclear how creating a set of ".xxx" domain sites would guarantee that only adults will access the material. Further, some individuals will no doubt complain that such a system infringes on their right to do business. If such a scheme is to pass constitutional muster, the Supreme Court would need to accept Justice O'Connor's zoning metaphor for the Internet.

Nude sunbathers on Miami's South Beach were captured in pictures posted on the World Wide Web even though the subjects were neither paid nor aware that their images were being disseminated on the Internet. "Voyeur sites are the biggest thing on the Internet," David Bernstein, vice president of an adult publication, told the *South Florida Sun-Sentinel* (February 26, 1999). Such sites are clear violations of international copyright law, which makes it illegal to exploit a person's image. However, sex sites are the most profitable on the web, and vendors are willing to risk lawsuits.

Finally, we must turn to the fundamental question of whether communicating in cyberspace makes a true difference when it comes to the business of idea or content production. Neil Postman presented the case that technology in and of itself does not "touch" our problems:

The engineers, computer gurus, and corporate visionaries who claim to speak for the future are, in fact addressing problems that have already been solved. It is time for us to give up the notion that we may find solutions to our emptiness through technology. We must now turn to our poets, playwrights, composers, theologians, and artists, who, alone, can create or restore the narratives that will give meaningful pattern to our lives. They are the weavers who can liberate us from cyberspace and put us back in the world (Postman, in Strate, Jacobson, and Gibson, 1996, p. 382).

The idea that cyberspace can be a prison dramatically departs from the view that is a place of liberation. As a matter of legal thinking, this tension between technological trap and open space is critical in our broader understanding of free expression, the marketplace of ideas, and speech in the future. The division is plain when one ponders whether cyberspace is an easy way to interact with a broader circle of people or an illusion of communication that inhibits more meaningful, personal exchanges. It is a question of triviality. Virtual reality enthusiasts, for example, may be seen as looking for life in all the wrong places: "Finding themselves insufficiently stimulated by real reality, they seek a solution by escaping from it, exciting themselves through technologically simulated experience" (Postman, in Strate, Jacobson, and Gibson, 1996, p. 381). Such user-driven content adds one more dimension: control. Computer-programmed communication is necessarily patterned and limited by the programming that drives it. As such, once the pattern is determined, it should be easier to predict than an unpredictable human being or group of human beings.

In any event, as the content of virtual reality becomes mixed with human actors participating in it, the complexity of communication will increase. Consider the chat room environment called "The Palace." In it, people take on cyber identities (of *Star Wars* characters, for example), move about in rooms that approximate movie scenes, and interact with other players; it is possible to offer a visitor a virtual beer or to play a game of cards. In such an environment, the persona of the actor may begin to consume one's own image, and the extent to which meaningful free expression is being practiced in such places is debatable. Clearly, on the one hand, participation serves a psychological need to interact. Not so clearly, on the other hand, does this communication become framed in ways that activate individuals outside of cyberspace. I call communication of this type a personal form of free expression, and in the next chapter, I will deal with such forms and begin to relate them to notions of personal privacy.

The idea that individuals will take on personas in the form of "agents" or "alters" or that we will send out "bots" into cyberspace on our own behalf leads us to think about the physical and psychological components of free expression in a deeper way than is possible through normative free expression theories. Message content and context are open to reinterpretation in a world in which our "agents" can manage ideas.

Clearly, the Internet will continue to develop as a source of information beyond the range of traditional mass media. For example, in one Internet venture, the "Ghoulpools," people gamble on when famous people will die. Jake Maruby operates another site, known as "Dying for Dollars." He told a reporter: "We certainly don't wish for anybody to die, but nothing we do is going to change things" (*Boston Globe*, July 12, 1998). People submit lists of as many as fifty people they think might die during a calendar year. Shrewd betters who picked Princess Di made money in the 1997 death pools.

Musician Arlo Guthrie has moved "Alice's Restaurant" into cyberspace. A visitor to the online Guthrie Center, http://wwwguthriecenter. org, can learn about the nonprofit interfaith center. Guthrie said: "Our center provides help for people with AIDS, cancer, life-and-death situations. I don't believe anyone should die alone. We try to serve those people ostracized by society with normal services most others get" (*Omaha World-Herald*, August 30, 1998, p. A-4). Guthrie hopes to use the foundation and the Internet to promote deeper understanding of people worldwide. (See Figure 7.10.)

Even the Vatican has built a computer network for the church. Aside from its Internet World Wide Web site for visitors, the Vatican has created a private network that "will be a major advantage, particularly in countries where Internet connections must be made through state-controlled servers," Sister Judith Zoebelein said (Associated Press, August 22, 1998).

It is interesting to note, however, that when Pope John Paul II was visiting Saint Louis in 1999, a judge ordered that a web site featuring information about the trip along with "erotic pictures" be shut down. "The Archdiocese of St. Louis said a Web site by Internet Entertainment Group [IEG] was confusing Internet visitors seeking information. . . . The judge told Seattle-based IEG to dismantle its site immediately" (Associated Press, January 9, 1999). Although many sites on the Internet may be confused by users, lawyers for the church successfully argued that this particular one infringed on the archdiocese's trademark. The site, in fact, simply listed a schedule of the pope's visits, linked to Saint Louis attractions, and advertised IEG's "erotic adult Web site" at the bottom of the page.

Chapter Summary

This chapter focused on content issues that raise free-expression concerns. The diversity of the messages on the Internet makes it impossible to generalize about what is present. However, we can say something about those corporate players that will dominate and attract the largest audiences. The real question, in terms of free expression, is whether individuals with something to say will be able to survive and prosper in such a marketplace of ideas.

198

The Guthrie Center

Home

News & Info

Virtual Tour

Gallery

Programs

Volunteers

Membership

Wish List

Directions

Links

E-Mail

Alice's Restaurant isn't around anymore. But, as the song says, "Alice didn't live in a restaurant. She lived in the church nearby the restaurant..." And the old Trinity Church, where Alice once lived and where the saga began has become...The Guthrie Center.

The Guthrie Center was founded in 1991 by Arlo Guthrie providing a place to bring together individuals for spiritual service, as well as cultural and educational exchange. The Guthrie Center is located in the old Trinity Church of Alice's Restaurant fame. The church is also home to Arlo's recording company Rising Son Records.

Originally built as the St. James Chapel in 1829, the church served the Van Deusenville Episcopalian community for 37 years when it was destroyed by fire. The structure was rebuilt in 1866 and was renamed the Trinity Church. Ray and Alice Brock purchased the property in 1964 and made it their home. The building has had several owners since the early seventies.

The Brocks had been on the staff of a private boarding school in the area - The Stockbridge School. Ray Brock, trained as an architect, taught a shop class and Alice became the school librarian. They were wonderfully creative people and attracted a number of students with whom they shared their idealism and their creativity. Arlo Guthrie was one of them.

After four years of high school in Stockbridge, Arlo graduated in the spring of 1965 entering Rocky Mountain College in Billings, Montana the following fall. His college career was short lived, however, and he returned to the Berkshires in November of 1965. He stayed with his friends, Ray and Alice, at the church during the Thanksgiving holidays. The rest, as they say, is history.

Thirty years later, Arlo has come home to the Church. The Guthrie Center is a not-for-profit Interfaith Church Foundation. Following in the tradition of service and compassion as exemplified by Ma Jaya Sati Bhagavati, the center is flexibly designed to meet the ongoing needs of the local and universal community.

FIGURE 7.10   Guthriecenter.org

Discussion Questions

1. How would you go about launching an Internet web site today? What barriers might make it difficult for you to succeed?
2. What are the content implications of corporate domination of the Internet?
3. What will happen to educational sites if a next-generation Internet2 is developed and managed by the private sector?
4. How will technological developments alter future content on the Internet?
5. Why do the majority of Internet users gravitate to a relatively small number of popular sites?
6. The Internet was heralded as the coming of the interactive age. Do you think there is a lot of interactivity on the most popular sites?

8

E-mail, Listservs, and Other Personal Forms of Free Expression

"Today, computer time, computer space, and computer memory, notions we dimly understand, are reworking practical consciousness coordinating and controlling life in what we glibly call the postindustrial society."

—**James Carey, media theorist (1992)**

"This is arguably the most fundamental technological change in the American household over the last decade—the arrival of the personal computer."

—**Andrew Kohut, pollster (1994)**

"In a typical day, the average home computer user reads 11 minutes more and watches 20 minutes less entertainment television than the average person without a home PC."

—**The Times Mirror Center for the People and the Press,** *polling organization (1994)*

"E-mail is exploding in popularity because it is both an asynchronous and a computer-readable medium."

—**Nicholas Negroponte, futurist (1995)**

"The trend towards more technologically integrated and functionally specialized computer systems is a double-edge sword, and is not necessarily what is of most benefit."

—**Eevi Beck, researcher (1995)**

"I'm committed to a free society in which a person's right to say something that offends me is equal to my right to say something that offends him."

—**Michael Godwin, author (1996)**

"Once you are computer-literate, you must become Net-literate and understand the online marketplace, how to navigate it, and how to express yourself effectively in it."

—*Jay Levinson and Charles Rubin,*
Guerrilla Marketing Online (1997)

Choosing the proper metaphor for the Internet is difficult because the technology is fluid. Sometimes, computer-based communication approximates a letter. In other situations, it is like a business memorandum. At still other times, it is like a telephone call. It is also difficult to characterize the potential of the Internet: At home, the personal computer hooked to the Internet has the power to make and destroy marriages; at work, it has made and broken careers; and in society, it has both cultivated and caught criminals. In this chapter, I explore the social significance of personal forms of free expression.

What Is Known About E-mail as Communication

Computer-mediated communication affects organizational structures, environments, and cultures. In the business setting, e-mail has the potential to alter patterns of social interaction (Mantovani, 1994). On the one hand, it is less rich with social cues, but on the other hand, some people feel freer to speak through e-mail—particularly to their superiors in the workplace (Sproull and Kiesler, 1991). Such a change in relationships may lead to managers adapting to communication in a nontraditional workplace (Barnes and Geller, 1994).

One area of concern involves the way in which mediated realities are experienced. S. G. Jones asserted that the bias of organizational communication research is that mediated realities are less "rich" in terms of experience:

Each belief fuels the bias toward filling cyberspace with information and gives rise to two distinct ideas: First, unused space is wasteful and, second, more information is desirable and better. The trend in CMC, as in other areas of computing, has been to provide greater speed and more levels of organization to cope with that bias. . . . Regarding community most directly, though, the most readily discernible [trend] is toward the removal of boundaries. And yet . . . "it is boundary [that] encapsulates the identity of the community" (Jones, 1998, p. 26, quoting Cohen, 1985).

Two empirical questions are raised in this regard: whether computer-mediated communication attacks social boundaries or facilitates them and whether organizational hierarchies are flattened or magnified by CMC. The potential for e-mail to be both purposefully public and enabling to private communication is a fertile research arena. Jones's conclusion that boundaries are essential for the existence of communities is important. Traditional free-expression literature has implied that the elimination of boundaries is normatively good and that the creation of boundaries is normatively bad. However, to the extent that meaningful communication must happen within a community, we may argue that it will be impossible for the Internet to establish community without erecting borders.

The central question seems to be the degree of community building taking place with a particular group: "Ongoing CMC groups tend to develop behavioral norms as well as shared significance, personalities, and relationships" (Baym, in Jones, 1998, p. 60). Thus, to understand the functioning of online interaction, we must understand member and group values. These cyber relationships, then, might vary widely. In free-expression terms, some communities may be open to new ideas, but others may be openly hostile. Leadership, norms, and sanctions will regulate the social conformity of group members. There will be social regulation of perceived or agreed on boundaries, as well as punishment for those who cross the lines.

Interest Groups in Communication

Digital communication is particularly open to interest-group communication because it is placeless; residing in cyberspace corresponds with no particular geographic location:

> When you have an account with America Online, CompuServe, or Prodigy, you know your own e-mail address, but you do not know where it physically exists. In the case of America Online, your Internet address is your ID followed by @aol.com—usable anywhere in the world. Not only do you not know where @aol.com is, whosoever sends a message to that address has no idea where either it or you might be. The address becomes much more like a Social Security number than a street coordinate. It is a virtual address (Negroponte, 1995, p. 166).

This means that communicators may be anonymous if and when they choose to be so but only to the extent that others do not investigate and learn more about the person.

As a technical matter, anonymity is being lost or confused by conventions of programming within operating systems such as Windows98. Through cookies or other technological information seeking, web providers can identify the names assigned to particular computers through previous hardware and software registrations. Such automatic identification may lead to misidentification or be subverted by multiple log-on screen names.

Anonymous communication seems to encourage "spamming" or the transmission of other unwanted messages. This raises the communication-oriented free-expression issue about message receivers: Do they have a *right* to control their communication space? This question usually is treated as a matter of invasion of privacy, as will be shown later, but it can also be seen as a free-expression concern. How does one effectively engage in free expression in an environment that is awash in garbage? The problem, of course, is that one person's garbage is another person's treasure, which means that message value is a function of personal, individualized taste. Although concerned about free-speech issues, the Federal Trade Commission (FTC) has considered regulating e-mail spam, and its report on unsolicited commercial e-mail described hours of productivity lost and clogged mailboxes. Jill Lesser, director of law and public policy at America Online, noted that spammers play cat-and-mouse games to dodge AOL filters (Associated Press, July 20, 1998).

The state of Washington has attempted to crack down on illegal e-mail. It charged the owner of a company called Natural Instincts with fraud by using forged return addresses in an e-mail pitch titled, "Did I get the right e-mail address?" The company was selling 50,000 e-mail addresses for $39.95 (*ZDNet*, October 23, 1998).

In Virginia, legislation attempted to outlaw spam by making it a misdemeanor to use fake online identities or addresses. If it could be shown that the spamming was a "malicious act" that caused more than $2,500 in damage, a spammer could be charged with a felony offense. Fines could be as high as $25,000 per day (Associated Press, February 24, 1999).

America Online, the nation's largest Internet service provider, continued to wage its war against annoying spam in court. AOL filed suit in the U.S. district court in Manhattan against a group that was selling apricot seeds as a cancer cure (Associated Press, December 21, 1998).

Although much unwanted e-mail spam consists of sales pitches, some of it must be considered simple hoaxes. One such mailing suggested that by forwarding the message, the reader would be eligible for a $1,000 gift from Microsoft's Bill Gates. Still another touted a $5,000 offer from Disney (*Washington Post*, November 5, 1998). The intent of these pranks seems to be simply seeing if people will believe the phony messages and giving the authors a chance to go after the rich and powerful by attacking their credibility.

Personal Forms of Free Expression

Free expression, seen from an interpersonal communication perspective, is a matter of social exchange and closeness (Altman and Taylor, 1997). Tastes and interests may be seen as at the periphery of one's personality structure, somewhat removed from the concept of self, deeply held fears, and convictions (p. 145). The extent to which one practices "self-disclosure" depends on deeper feelings:

1. *Peripheral items* are exchanged more frequently and sooner than private information;
2. *New acquaintances* will reach roughly equal levels of openness;
3. *Social penetration* is rapid at the start but slows down quickly as the tightly wrapped inner layers are reached; and
4. *Depenetration* is a gradual process of layer-by-layer withdrawal. . . . Relationships are likely to terminate not in an explosive flash of anger but in a gradual cooling off of enjoyment and care (pp. 146–147).

The attention paid to Internet "flaming"—harsh personal attacks—is interesting because, according to communication and social-exchange theory, such behavior indicates a lack of closeness. The unique quality of Internet communication is that it has the ability to bring strangers together rapidly—perhaps too rapidly in social terms. The willingness to engage in social disclosure at an early stage of a relationship makes it more likely that a jolt will occur. The "desire to be polite" is a function of one's "wishes to adhere to socially appropriate behavior in accordance with courtesy or social norms" (Kellerman, 1987, p. 200), but when digital norms do not value "polite" communication, flaming may be inevitable. Politeness is just one outcome goal; seeking information, providing information, and anticipating future communication also must be considered. K. Kellerman (1987) outlined a set of relevant tendencies, which include one's wishes to be clear or not, personal or not, interesting or not, accurate or not, and positive or not (p. 203). Communication content in an interpersonal relationship, then, is a function of not only content but also form and value in a process of information exchange (p. 209).

Cyberspace flaming—insults, outbursts, impoliteness, heated exchanges—has been broadly defined (Thompsen, in Strate, Jacobson, and Gibson, 1996). According to one definition, flaming includes "the practice of expressing oneself more strongly on the computer than one would in other communication settings" (p. 209, Thompsen citing Kiesler, Siegel, and McGuire, 1984). Three theoretical explanations for it are

1. *Deindividuation*—People lose their sense of social identity through a kind of mob behavior.
2. *Social presence*—Computer-mediated communication has an inability to capture complex social, face-to-face type, cues.
3. *Information richness*—Information-poor media constrain messages to a limited range of expression (p. 301).

Flaming, from a social influence perspective, may be the product either of misunderstanding or of dyadic communication in which people know each other too well: "It is also clearly a social phenomenon, reflecting rational purpose, human conflict, and subjective interpretation" (p. 310).

The works of E. Goffman (1959) and J. Meyrowitz (1985) help us to understand the public and private aspects of social life and its connection to computer-mediated communication. Cyberspace is inherently interactive: "In order to use the technology of cyberspace one must be active, whether manipulating the technology or navigating through it to communicate with others" (Cutler, in Strate, Jacobson, and Gibson, 1996, p. 324). This fact drives people toward public and front stage behavior, even when they desire a private, backstage life.

In geographic space, one has historically had a physical place to retreat inward—the home—but in cyberspace, one must leave altogether in order to find peace. If one stays online, the space and the user's presence in it is electronically accessible to others. It is at this point that Negroponte's bits and atoms blur further because technology increasingly tracks and monitors physical space, as well. Police helicopters, cable television systems, computerized credit card receipts, supermarket scanning systems, and store security cameras create a physical world in which individuals are watched. The adoption of technology in the home, including computers networked through cable operators, offers the dark possibility of a further erosion of the home as a distinct environment.

Mats Edenius, a business professor in Stockholm, Sweden, has written that the new electronic networks are much like Jeremy Bentham's eighteenth-century plans for a prison based on windows, one he called the panopticon:

> The function of a panopticon is to increase control. . . . With light streaming through the glass walls of the prison cells, the guard in the tower can see everything without being seen by others. . . . With electronic networks, employees are subjected to continual oversight from their managers, and, like the prisoners in a panopticon, they discipline themselves. Interactions within

electronic networks occur within a context of moderation, correctness and efficiency (*Omaha World-Herald*, July 19, 1998, p. 25-A).

The presence of "lurkers" who read but do not participate in e-mail newsgroups creates a context of power, as does online monitoring by officials. Consider the online debate that erupted at one university over speaking out about a proposed tax-lid ballot issue in a state election. The messages were bounced to a campuswide community by a faculty-staff-student mailing list including all e-mail users. Although a majority of the community opposed the tax lid because it threatened university funding, supporters of the measure opposed people using the e-mail system to advocate against it. This led others to call foul:

Hi [university] Colleagues;

I have been lurking and reading all the interesting comments on the current ballot issues. For the record if there are any legal-types listening, I'm a consenting male, using my own computer, in my own home, through service of an ISP which I pay for myself so as far as I am concerned, the proportion of [university] facilities, equipment, and time I'm employing for my little opus in the fray is really teeny and I should be able to say what I wish. . . . I believe academic as well as speech freedom are still alive . . . aren't they?

Another faculty member responded that tax-lid supporters should read what Thomas Jefferson had to say about speech freedom and ask

if there is a more productive use of . . . time other than trying to shut up our faculty's cacophony on [the] initiative.

Clearly, the campus was struggling to define normative behavior in using the computer e-mail system.

Stable and meaningful relationships develop only after a period of orientation, exploration, and emotional exchange—a time when the two people in a dyad come to know and understand each other (Taylor and Altman, 1987, p. 259). The new technology creates a virtual environment in which social exchanges occur without the benefit of understanding. This is why so many e-mail communications may succeed as a form of personal free expression but fail as a matter of communication.

Any two people engaged in communication can be seen as a dyad selecting formal or informal channels, separated by some measure of social space (Gieber and Johnson, 1961; Gieber, 1960). Communication models focus on interactions and orientations with individual communicators varying in intensity about the relationship (Newcomb, 1953; Carter, 1965; Stamm and Pearce, 1971; McLeod and Chaffee, 1973). The idea of communication *co-orientation* asserts that agreement between two people or groups of people is a function of their accuracy about the communication and their perceptions of congruency—the degree to which they perceive similarities. The problem with the new forms of communication such as e-mail is that they often give rise to misperceptions. Belonging to a List-serv group might lead some to overestimate the similarities of group members. But gaining membership in loosely organized groups is too simple a matter—subscribe. Leaving the group is equally easy—unsub-scribe.

In cyberspace, the lack of physical closeness may contribute to social distance, as well. One can only speculate about the extent to which this condition interacts with free-expression behavior. First, it may well pro-mote caustic forms of free expression because physical retribution is diffi-cult. Second, it may promote inhibition, as is the case with so-called lurk-ers who join Internet groups but do not speak. (The right to remain silent must, however, be considered part of the right of free expression.) Third, as in any group setting, leaders emerge who are inclined to speak fre-quently, and, just as we see in terms of jury behavior, those who are com-municating may lead others to withdraw and stay silent. Fourth, free ex-pression may be episodic and dependent on expertise in a particular subarea. Fifth, group communication might serve as a catalyst for two in-dividuals to break off from the group and develop more personal social exchanges.

Personal exchanges in cyberspace may be filled with text, images, and so-called emoticons—the emotionally laden shortcuts that express gestures and feelings. Acronym shortcuts also are common in e-mail exchanges.

In the case of emoticons, text-based characters such as :-) are giving way to image-oriented smiley-face icons. In either case, the intent seems to be to quickly express gut reactions with brevity.

Cyberspace may be different from traditional social space in that it al-lows people to jump across time and space, and in doing so, it creates op-portunities for social interaction that would not have happened in prior contexts. E-mail has renewed the importance of written communication that favors some individuals over others—particularly those who string words together well. But the emergence of instant audio-video communi-cation technologies might lead to another decline in the value of the writ-ten word. The movement from a text-based, computer-mediated technol-ogy to one that is dominated by multimedia will again favor those who speak well and look good, and thus, it begins to approximate traditional social culture. Another possibility is that mediated images will dominate free expression in the future as we essentially speak at each other in sound bites and personal advertisements.

Box 8.1   Common E-mail Acronym Shorthand

AFAIK	As far as I know
BG	Big grin
BRB	Be right back
BTDT	Been there, done that
EG	Evil grin
FWIW	For what it's worth
IIRC	If I remember correctly
IMHO	In my humble opinion
IMNSHO	In my not so humble opinion
IMO	In my opinion
IOW	In other words
IRL	In real life
LOL	Laughing out loud
TTYL	Talk to you later
ROFL	Rolling on the floor laughing
ROFLBF	Rolling on the floor laughing breaking furniture
ROFLSTC	Rolling on the floor laughing scaring the cat
YMMV	Your mileage may vary
VGB	Very big grin
WG	Wide grin

Note: These shorthand devices are used in varying degrees in current e-mail exchanges, as well as on Listservs or other distribution lists. It would be impossible to know how often individual devices are employed in private or quasi-private communication.

Internet culture is also transforming the language. New phrases such as *mouse potato* (someone who spends a lot of time on the computer) are being added to dictionaries as lesser-used words are deleted. And words such as *saddo* (which describes a dull or inadequate person) were born from a culture driven by e-mail and instant messages (IMs) (Associated Press, August 13, 1998). Teens seem particularly compelled to ignore rules of language in e-mail communication, as in this IM from Gianina to Jessica: "What dId i miss in sCIENCE 2day????" (*USA Today*, December 9, 1998, p. 5-D). It is also said that busy parents are making emotional connections with their kids in office-to-home e-mail when face-to-face communication has failed. Some parenting experts claim the intimacy of e-mail lowers barriers and frees children and teens to communicate with adults as equals (*Wall Street Journal*, November 30, 1998).

Box 8.2   Emoticons, or Smileys

In e-mail communications, emoticons replace the gestures and expressiveness that typify face-to-face conversations.

:-)	Happy, smiling or just kidding
;-)	Winking
:-(	Sad
>:-<	Angry
:-p	Sticking tongue out at you
:-O	Shocked
:-*	Kissing
:^(	Nose out of joint
#-)	Drunk
B-)	I'm cool
::-)	Four eyes, eyeglasses worn
<:)	I'm a clown
+-<:-)	I'm the Pope

◆   ◆   ◆

The following emoticons also have been used and convert to smiley face images in Proxicom Forum Auto-Format:

8-)	Bug-eyed happy
8-(	Bug-eyed sad
8-o	Bug-eyed shocked
8-p	Bug-eyed disgusted, ill

(Source: ZDUniversity [http://www.zdu.com/handbook/emoticons.asp], and Andy Ihnatko, *Cyber Speak, Online Dictionary*. New York: Random House, 1997, pp. 64–65)

Personal communication such as that practiced in chat rooms exposes users to an electronic environment at the nexus of society and the law. Consider the San Francisco lawsuit against Stacey McCahan, a recruiting coordinator at the consulting firm Arthur Andersen. In small-claims court, a judge tossed out a complaint against his employer but hit him with a $5,000 penalty:

McCahan's comment was part of a discussion of Critical Mass, the bicyclist protest that fills downtown streets during the evening rush hour on the last Friday of each month.

[The complaining party] started things by criticizing the way McCahan served as an unofficial spokesperson for bicyclists after police arrested over

100 protesters in a July incident. McCahan gave several newspaper interviews and appeared next to Mayor Willie Brown Jr. at a press conference.

After seeing unfriendly postings, McCahan fired back.

"It's a very volatile forum and people call each other names all the time," says McCahan. "I'm baffled that I was sued" (*The Recorder*, March 24, 1998, p. 4).

The case showed how Internet communication happens as quickly as a telephone conversation yet is more permanent and available because of the words typed online.

Because of its form, the printed word historically has been treated as publication. Although the law limits regulation through prior restraints, it does not discourage post hoc litigation. So, while the San Francisco case was on appeal, observers speculated about what would happen if everyone who had ever been flamed on the Internet sought legal recourse.

Anecdotal evidence about e-mail suggests that it may be so quick and easy to send a message to a large mailing list that people may not stop to reflect before they hit the "submit" button. When sending a corporate memorandum in the pen-and-paper world, it often took some time to produce and duplicate the message, which meant that errors could be caught and memos could be withdrawn. In the world of e-mail, however, the message often is sent before there is time to stop it. In one sense, this might promote free expression by creating a space where people are more likely to speak out without thinking about social consequences. However, such decisions may produce "gut" responses that would be altered with further reflection. If free expression is normatively thought of as promoting social progress, then it is not clear that reflex responses are always functional.

At the same time, personal communication forms have led to new approaches to free expression, particularly among teenagers. In America Online chat rooms, teens now "brag" with encoded scrolling messages laced with profanity. The ganglike communication exists because the Internet, like the streets, is a place where people go to connect with others— particularly people left out of the mainstream. Because scrolling is against AOL's terms of service (TOS), it often leads to the communicator being disconnected; in response, hackers have devised so-called punters programs ("proggies") that threaten, annoy, and kick people offline. These forms of free expression can only be valued in the eyes of the beholders, so it would be premature to pass judgment on the significance of such fringe forms. What is clear is that for teens, typically bound by a fairly repressive speech environment during school hours, the Internet is a haven for experimenting with free expression.

There are theoretical problems with addressing such issues. First, as John Corner has suggested, we cannot even adequately define meaning, except to say that we need to make sense of the world around us. Genre and context also present difficulties. Theorizing, as Todd Gitlin has noted, is partly a function of the criticism that grows from a general sense of dissatisfaction (see Curran and Gurevitch, 1991). When we toss in the concept of cyberspace as an "essence" of something (Strate, Jacobson, and Gibson, 1996), we find that human experience and meaning end up as matters of individual perception:

> The concept of space is actually quite complex . . . perceptual space can only correspond to a portion of physical space and is always subject to error. Also, we tend to equate perceptual space with visual space, but we also experience auditory space; tactile, thermal, and kinesthetic space; and even olfactory space—generally, our perceptual space is based on the interactions of all these senses (p. 14).

We are not yet prepared to advance social theory to the point of making sense of the meanings of each individual's interactions in cyberspace. It is fair to say that people themselves do not necessarily know what they are doing there. When we say someone is "surfing the Net," the phrase implies a physical, fast-paced trip that remains at the surface. However, Internet travel can involve deep dives, side trips, and dead ends. Electronic communication, even as it becomes a part of our being, is simply not well understood. No wonder, then, that the law of cyberspace is mostly speculative.

As a "social landscape," the Internet can be thought of in cultural terms as building collectivity, affecting structural relations, experimenting with virtual communities, helping marginalized groups find identity, and even contributing to a set of social rules (Jones, 1997). As Harris Breslow reminded us, we cannot predict how society will reconceptualize itself:

> If one thing is clear it is that theory and praxis are not in sync. Contemporary political and social thought still operates according to logic more properly part of principles of density and contiguity as opposed to dispersion and isolation. For nigh the two hundred years the ideals of solidarity, community, and identity—born as much out of the satanic mills as they were the city square—have informed our sense of political ethics, our understanding of the language we speak and the identities we occupy . . . I'm not sure what we are able to say about the Net, since we all live in the shadow of civil society (Breslow, in Jones, 1997, p. 255).

The previous split between humans and technology—the one that predicted "dehumanizing" outcomes—is being replaced by something we cannot seem to grasp:

> Rather what is human is changing—or in other words, what it is to be an
> *agent* in our society is changing. Human agency always consists of both tech-
> nological and linguistic agency, the particular configuration of each and the
> relations between the two depend on the overall stratification of social space.
> That change [that] is taking place . . . is neither good nor bad in and of itself.
> What is important is that it is changing without a conceptual apparatus to
> help us negotiate within the changing conditions (Wise, 1997, p. 167).

The merging and blending of our culture and technology means that we
speak either in mediated or nonmediated spaces. When we speak in mediated, virtual worlds, we tend to conform to the structures of those worlds.
As the nonmediated world becomes increasingly dominated by the computer and increasingly dominated by electronic forms of communication, it,
too, begins to conform to a new set of norms. What is acceptable as terse e-
mail communication begins to be utilized in the face-to-face world. This is
the phenomenon that some popular philosophers such as William Bennett
refer to as a loss of "civility" in the culture. In this view, it is normatively
"better" to be conformed by socially controlling rules of politeness. Clearly,
even with moving boundaries, a lack of civility at some point defeats free
expression because it leads to a breakdown in meaningful communication
and tends to produce polarization. At the other end of the spectrum, however, in a purely "civil society," free expression gives way to deference to
the powers that be. Silence is expected of those on the lower rungs.

What is unique about the age of the Internet is that the traditional lines
of power and authority sometimes accede to dyadic or small-group communication that creates virtual spheres of power. Personal communication, as one form of free expression, inevitably clashes with the idea that
one's personal privacy should be protected from invasion by uninvited
guests. It is this thorny problem that I turn to next. The following excerpts
from a 1998 story show how the Internet can be perceived as private space,
even though it is not. It also shows that new forms of communication do
take place online.

People engaged in online, virtual communities struggle with their ability to interact with individuals they have never seen or met. On the one
hand, because we all are humans, we share a certain commonality that allows for communication. On the other hand, without truly knowing an individual, communication may be devoid of meaning.

The technology blurs that which is private or personal with the public
sphere. Such was the case when America Online provided the *Orange
County Register* with the name of one of its employees, a subscriber
named Slave4OCR who ran a site filled with office rumors, gossip,
complaints, and listings of the "idiot of the month." According to one account, "Legal experts were stunned by the trademark-infringement law-

suit ... noting the irony that a news outlet ... could set a precedent that effectively limits 1st Amendment rights on the Internet" (*Los Angeles Times*, July 18, 1998, p. 1-D). However, AOL has been found to be immune from liability for damages from messages of its members.

Box 8.3   The Illusion of Private Conversations in Cyberspace

The New York Times' Amy Harmon (April 30, 1998, p. A-1) reported on how a man confessed to a killing on an Internet support group for problem drinkers.

A member of that group, Elisa DeCarlo "lost faith in her virtual community" when she read a posting from a man she knew only as Larry. "In graphic detail, Larry described how in 1995 he killed his 5-year-old daughter, Amanda, here in the southwestern corner of North Dakota," the newspaper reported.

A bitter custody dispute, it seems, had led him to set fire to his home with his daughter trapped inside. Some group members were "appalled" by the e-mail, but others came to his defense. "It seemed to Ms. DeCarlo that the nature of on-line communication—which creates a psychological as well as physical distance between participants—was causing her friends to forget their off-line responsibilities to bring a confessed murderer to justice," the newspaper reporter wrote.

It took a flame war online before one member called police, who later arrested Larry Froistad, twenty-nine, a computer programmer in San Diego, after he allegedly confessed.

DeCarlo told the newspaper she would now attend only face-to-face meetings of the chapter she leads in New York: "Ultimately, we are alone," she said. "The closeness is for the most part illusory. If Larry walked into a room, I wouldn't know him. On line, they're just words on a screen."

Verbatim: The Steps in a Confession

The following are excerpts from e-mail between Larry Froistad and group members:

LARRY: 'AMANDA I MURDERED'

My God, there's something I haven't mentioned, but it's a very important part of the equation. The people I'm mourning the loss of, I've ejected from my life. Kitty had to endure my going to jail twice and being embarrassed in front of her parents. Amanda I murdered because her mother stood between us. . . .

ELISA: 'What DO YOU MEAN?'

Okay, Larry, what do you mean, you murdered your daughter? Is this emotional hyperbole or cold fact? And are you getting professional help? Worriedly, Elisa

LARRY: 'Listened to her scream'

OK, it seems to me that there's a great deal of risk to this; my e-mail can be traced, I've been wide open about my identity. But somehow I've unintentionally left the impression that I'm flailing myself for some sort of weird self-gratification. Maybe I do that to some extent. But when I talk about killing my daughter, there's no imaginative subcomponent.

I suffered for years trying to get custody of her after her mother divorced me. When I did, I still had to deal with her mother's constant attempts to take her back. . . . When I brought her home from her mother's, I abandoned the rules I had set and let her do whatever she wanted—in fact my mother and grandmother visited the next day and she forgot that she was supposed to get dressed before receiving visitors. :) It really was very cute when she woke up and started to walk into our living room, buck-naked. I loved her for her willingness to be fun in simple ways. I would do anything to have her back; but the conflict was tearing me apart, and the next night I let her watch the videos she loved all evening, and when she was asleep I got wickedly drunk, set our house on fire, went to bed, listened to her scream twice, climbed out the window and set about putting on a show of shock, surprise and grief to remove culpability from myself. Dammit, part of that show was climbing in her window and grabbing her pajamas, then hearing her breathe and dropping her where she was so she could die and rid me of her mother's interferences. . . . I am damaged goods, and as much as I feel I need the comfort of someone in my life that I can be good to, someone I can build a new family with—the simple fact is that I don't deserve those things and I'm meant to suffer a thousand times longer than my little girl did. I cried like a baby in the emergency room at the hospital; I was very disappointed that I couldn't see her after they pulled her out of our house (where they took her before they carted me off); I was stunned and shocked the whole time they flew me down to Rapid City for observation and such, and I've been destroyed ever since. . . .

KAY: 'What you described does not sound rational'

Whew Larry—I for one have been thinking about your post just after you wrote it and I happened to be on line. I guess I feel that I
should say something—even though I am not one that has been cor-
responding much with you recently but because I am a pediatrician
and a mother. I must admit to being a little confused in that I'm not
sure, other than numbing the situation, what role that alcohol
played in this. What you described does not sound rational—even in
drunkenness and I suspect, from what you said, you don't understand it well either.—Obviously, you should have been prosecuted
and managed not to be—I would assume your ex-wife does not know
this which makes your sharing with this group very weighty I think.
But I think you do need something very specific for what has happened—and I don't think this group is enough. What a very painful
thing, in many ways.

ELISA: 'Do the police know'

Okay, Larry, second question: do the police know you murdered
your daughter?

FREDERICK: 'Think about contacting a therapist'

Larry, Several folks have sent me private e-mails expressing genuine concern over some of the stuff that you've posted very recently.
They are concerned, that you might be contemplating suicide or
other drastic, harmful and ultimately counterproductive actions
aimed at dealing with what seems to have become for you an awful
situation. I'm writing for all of the folks who wrote me offlist, and I
believe for all of the folks on this list, to urge you to seriously think
about contacting a therapist and working things through with yourself in a safe manner. Take care of yourself, my friend. And let us all
know how things are going. The people here really care about you.

LARRY: 'I'm sorry'

I'm sorry to everyone I hurt by my post. I certainly don't want to
drive anyone away from the list, but I was hurting and continue to,
and it's a BIG part of why I drink as much as I do.

DATE: Sun, 22 Mar 1998 12:50:22

Box 8.4   *Zeran v. America Online*

The United States Supreme Court in 1998 refused to hear this Fourth Circuit 1997 case, leaving intact protection for Internet Service Providers (ISPs) against liability. The court held that ISPs could not be sued for the content of their members.

Kenneth Zeran brought this action against America Online, Inc. ("AOL"), arguing that AOL unreasonably delayed in removing defamatory messages posted by an unidentified third party, refused to post retractions of those messages, and failed to screen for similar postings thereafter. The district court granted judgment for AOL on the grounds that the *Communications Decency Act of 1996* ("CDA")—47 U.S.C. § 230—bars Zeran's claims. Zeran appeals, arguing that § 230 leaves intact liability for interactive computer service providers who possess notice of defamatory material posted through their services. He also contends that § 230 does not apply here because his claims arise from AOL's alleged negligence prior to the CDA's enactment. Section 230, however, plainly immunizes computer service providers like AOL from liability for information that originates with third parties. Furthermore, Congress clearly expressed its intent that § 230 apply to lawsuits, like *Zeran's,* instituted after the CDA's enactment. Accordingly, we affirm the judgment of the district court.

◆   ◆   ◆

On April 25, 1995, an unidentified person posted a message on an AOL bulletin board advertising "Naughty Oklahoma T-Shirts." The posting described the sale of shirts featuring offensive and tasteless slogans related to the April 19, 1995, bombing of the Alfred P. Murrah Federal Building in Oklahoma City. Those interested in purchasing the shirts were instructed to call "Ken" at Zeran's home phone number in Seattle, Washington. As a result of this anonymously perpetrated prank, Zeran received a high volume of calls, comprised primarily of angry and derogatory messages, but also including death threats. Zeran could not change his phone number because he relied on its availability to the public in running his business out of his home. Later that day, Zeran called AOL and informed a company representative of his predicament. The employee assured Zeran that the posting would be removed from AOL's bulletin board but explained that as a matter of policy AOL would not post a retraction. The parties dispute the date that AOL removed this original posting from its bulletin board. On April 26, the next day, an unknown person posted another message advertising additional shirts with new tasteless slogans related to the Oklahoma City bombing. Again, interested buyers were told to call Zeran's phone number, to ask for "Ken," and to "please call back if busy" due to high demand. The angry, threatening phone calls intensified. Over the next four days, an unidentified party continued to post messages on AOL's bulletin board, advertising additional items including bumper stickers and key chains with still more offensive slogans. During this time period, Zeran called AOL repeatedly and was told by company representatives that the individual account from which the messages were posted would soon be closed. Zeran also reported his case to Seattle FBI agents. By April 30, Zeran was receiving an abusive phone call approximately every two minutes.

Meanwhile, an announcer for Oklahoma City radio station KRXO received a copy of the first AOL posting. On May 1, the announcer related the message's contents on the air, attributed them to "Ken" at Zeran's phone number, and urged the listening audience to call the number. After this radio broadcast, Zeran was inundated with death threats and other violent calls from Oklahoma City residents. Over the next few days, Zeran talked to both KRXO and AOL representatives. He also spoke to his local police, who subsequently surveilled his home to protect his safety. By May 14, after an Oklahoma City newspaper published a story exposing the shirt advertisements as a hoax and after KRXO made an on-air apology, the number of calls to Zeran's residence finally subsided to fifteen per day.

Zeran first filed suit on January 4, 1996, against radio station KRXO in the United States District Court for the Western District of Oklahoma. On April 23, 1996, he filed this separate suit against AOL in the same court. Zeran did not bring any action against the party who posted the offensive messages. After Zeran's suit against AOL was transferred to the Eastern District of Virginia . . . AOL answered Zeran's complaint . . . AOL then moved for judgment . . . The district court granted AOL's motion, and Zeran filed this appeal.

◆   ◆   ◆

The company claimed that Congress immunized interactive computer service providers from claims based on information posted by a third party. The relevant portion of § 230 states: "No provider or user of an interactive computer service shall be treated as the publisher or speaker of any information provided by another information content provider." 47 U.S.C. § 230(c)(1). By its plain language, § 230 creates a federal immunity to any cause of action that would make service providers liable for information originating with a third-party user of the service. Specifically, § 230 precludes courts from entertaining claims that would place a computer service provider in a publisher's role. Thus, lawsuits seeking to hold a service provider liable for its exercise of a publisher's traditional editorial functions—such as deciding whether to publish, withdraw, postpone or alter content—are barred.

◆   ◆   ◆

Congress' purpose in providing the § 230 immunity was thus evident. Interactive computer services have millions of users. See *Reno v. ACLU*, 117 S. Ct. at 2334 (noting that at time of district court trial, "commercial on-line services had almost 12 million individual subscribers"). The amount of information communicated via interactive computer services is therefore staggering. The specter of tort liability in an area of such prolific speech would have an obvious chilling effect. It would be impossible for service providers to screen each of their millions of postings for possible problems. Faced with potential liability for each message republished by their services, interactive computer service providers might choose to severely restrict the number and type of messages posted. Congress considered the weight of the speech interests implicated and chose to immunize service providers to avoid any such restrictive effect.

Another important purpose of § 230 was to encourage service providers to self-regulate the dissemination of offensive material over their services. In this respect, § 230 responded to a New York state court decision, *Stratton Oakmont, Inc. v. Prodigy Servs. Co.*, 1995 N.Y. Misc. LEXIS 229, 1995 WL 323710 (N.Y. Sup. Ct. May 24, 1995). There, the plaintiffs sued Prodigy—an interactive computer service like AOL—for defamatory comments made by an unidentified party on one of Prodigy's bulletin boards. The court held Prodigy to the strict liability standard normally applied to original publishers of defamatory statements, rejecting Prodigy's claims that it should be held only to the lower "knowledge" standard usually reserved for distributors. The court reasoned that Prodigy acted more like an original publisher than a distributor both because it advertised its practice of controlling content on its service and because it actively screened and edited messages posted on its bulletin boards.

Congress enacted § 230 to remove the disincentives to self-regulation created by the *Stratton Oakmont* decision. Under that court's holding, computer service providers who regulated the dissemination of offensive material on their services risked subjecting themselves to liability, because such regulation cast the service provider in the role of a publisher. Fearing that the specter of liability would therefore deter service providers from blocking and screening offensive material, Congress enacted § 230's broad immunity "to remove disincentives for the development and utilization of blocking and filtering technologies that empower parents to restrict their children's access to objectionable or inappropriate online material," 47 U.S.C. § 230(b)(4). In line with this purpose, § 230 forbids the imposition of publisher liability on a service provider for the exercise of its editorial and self-regulatory functions.

◆   ◆   ◆

Our view that Zeran's complaint treats AOL as a publisher is reinforced because AOL is cast in the same position as the party who originally posted the offensive messages. According to Zeran's logic, AOL is legally at fault because it communicated to third parties an allegedly defamatory statement. This is precisely the theory under which the original poster of the offensive messages would be found liable. If the original party is considered a publisher of the offensive messages, Zeran certainly cannot attach liability to AOL under the same theory without conceding that AOL too must be treated as a publisher of the statements.

The opinion gives weight to the view that large Internet Service Providers cannot be responsible for the content of their members because the Internet is too large and complex. Zeran never sued the writer of the posting because he said AOL could not give him the identity of the hoaxster.

(**Source: 129 F.3d 327, 25 Media L. Rep. 2526; 10 Comm. Reg. [P & F] 456 [1997],** *cert. denied*)

Box 8.5   Trying to Stop Unwanted E-mail

Paramus Catholic School President James Vail filed suit in U.S. District Court in Newark, New Jersey, to learn who opened America Online and Hotmail (Microsoft) e-mail accounts, and used them to attack his work conduct. An e-mail sent by AngryMum@aol.com alleged Vail had attempted to cover up a sexual assault. A second round of attacks came from other AOL screen names. Vail believes the e-mail were "sour grapes" from former employees and seeks the identity of "John Doe" who school officials think is a resident of New York state. Vail's attorney has subpoenaed AOL and Hotmail records. AOL Spokeswoman Tricia Primrose said the company policy was to turn records over to law enforcement officials and give the account owner two weeks to respond to a request to be identified. Hotmail Spokesman Randy Delucchi said, "we routinely cooperate with law enforcement on such matters" (*Bergen Record*, February 23, 1999). Meantime AOL, sensitized to the concerns over spamming, has abandoned plans to create AOL Select—a direct marketing program akin to Amway and Tupperware sales. AOL has "declared itself publicly as anti-spam"—assisting customers in eliminating unsolicited e-mail (*Washington Post*, February 23, 1999, p. E–3).

The use of e-mail as an alternative to repressed speech in a work or school environment suggests that the Internet serves the venting function of free expression that Thomas Emerson suggested created a safety valve to relieve built-up social pressure.

The replacement of social relationships in cyberspace and the problem of social isolation leave us with unanswered questions about how the human condition has been changed by technology, as well as how it will be changed by future developments.

Chapter Summary

This chapter looked at e-mail, interest groups, and personal forms of expression. The degree to which the technology and human condition are involved in the alteration of cultural norms was explored, as was the question of civility on the Net. In addition, issues regarding concerns about privacy versus free expression were introduced.

Discussion Questions

1. Do you think people should have the right to be anonymous in cyberspace? Why or why not?
2. If someone confessed a crime to you as part of a Listserv support group, would you report him or her to the police?
3. Is it possible to build communities in cyberspace? How would you define a community?
4. Have you ever been involved in a flaming war on the Internet? How did it start? How did it make you feel?
5. How will multimedia technologies affect personal communications on the Internet? Will it make a difference if you can see the face of the person you are communicating with?
6. Is interest-group communication free expression or something else?

9

The Special Case of Invasion of Privacy

"The ability to compile, to transmit, and to distribute information rapidly and inexpensively qualitatively changes how personal information can be collected and used."

—Barbara S. Wellbery,
U.S. government official (1996)

"Privacy . . . considers the degree to which information traveling on the infobahn is subject to search and seizure by public authorities or private intruders."

—Henry H. Perritt Jr., author (1996)

"The defenses available to thwart a privacy claim are both broad and numerous, and as a result, successful privacy lawsuits are extremely rare."

—Donald Gillmor, Jerome Barron, Todd Simon,
and Herbert Terry, media law textbook authors (1996)

"Communications is at root based on the selective desire to communicate; the right to be let alone, free of communications, is for some as important as the affirmative right to communicate."

—Daniel Brenner, author (1996)

"Because the Internet blurs the distinction between an interpersonal and a broadcast network, it blurs the distinction between private and public speech."

—W. Russell Neuman, author (1998)

"When users don't see themselves as having privacy, they'll just lie and give totally false data, so a lot of the data that marketers get today is useless."

—Ian Goldberg, business person (1999)

*"You can't buy anything anonymously. . . . You can't get the most
personalized sites anonymously. . . . It's the computer
equivalent . . . of Social Security numbers. . . . It will follow you
through cyberspace."*

                                              —*Josh Bernoff, researcher (1999)*

*"If everybody's demanding it [identification], it's going to be hard for
a consumer to say no."*

                                        —*Deirdre Mulligan, technology advocate (1999)*

Privacy, "the right to be left alone," was a legal concern throughout the twentieth century. New information technologies such as the Internet, however, have raised previously unexplored questions about how inter-connected individuals retain personal privacy.

Barbara Wellbery told a national conference on privacy in 1996 that the National Telecommunications and Information Administration (NTIA) is concerned that there may be a loss of privacy as personal records move from traditional paper folders in government and business offices to computer files:

> In surveying privacy law, we discovered that there are minimal consumer protections. As a result, we proposed a self-regulatory framework that would apply to telecommunications companies and to on-line service providers and would require notice to consumers and an opportunity for them to consent before information was used in ways other than to provide service. Because expanding privacy protections will expand consumer de-mand for facilities and services in cyberspace, and these benefits can be pro-duced with minimal costs to business, NTIA expects that the private sector will have strong incentives to implement privacy practices voluntarily. In-deed, there are many companies that provide notice and an opportunity to consent already, such as Prodigy and America Online (11 *St. John's Journal of Legal Commentary* 659, 1996).

The central privacy problem is that computer networks store private in-formation in computer-readable forms:

> Information stored in a network computer is easy to retrieve unless affirma-tive steps have been taken to protect it from retrieval. As networks improve and as methods for storing, accessing, and transferring information on wide-spread networks become standardized, it is easier to assemble individual

profiles from bits of information obtained from many different sources (Perritt, 1996, p. 88).

In the United States, the government passed the Electronic Communications Privacy Act, or ECPA (18 USC 2510, 2710, 1986), the Computer Fraud and Abuse Act (18 USC 1030), the Privacy Act (5 USC 552a), and the Fair Credit Reporting Act (15 USC 1681). These statutes supplement the privacy law, which can be interpreted from common and constitutional law (Perritt, 1996, p. 89). In general, people who maintain computer data must protect them from unwarranted search, and people who attempt to eavesdrop on private data are subjected to penalties.

The use of cookies on the Internet—small computer files that track individuals' web surfing—has sparked the most recent privacy debates. Most often, these cookies have been used to identify visitors to web sites, which is helpful for commercial sites wanting to target consumers. However, academic researchers have also used cookies to study online behavior, and according to the *Chronicle of Higher Education*, research has been conducted without the consent of some subjects.

A cookie file is typically stored on a computer user's hard drive as the user loads a web page; warning messages about cookies are often disabled by users because so many sites have so many cookies that the warnings become a nuisance. Once a cookie is stored, it can tell the web site operator who is coming to their pages:

> One advantage to using cookies in research is the ability to track the behavior of people who gain access to the Internet by telephone. . . . Even without cookies, Web computers keep logs of which pages are transmitted to users. . . .[Researchers] are using cookies to try to develop "adaptive Web sites"—sites that reorganize themselves based on users' needs and interests (*Chronicle of Higher Education*, September 25, 1998, pp. A-31–A-32).

The researchers who have used cookies on their sites have contended that web visitors come as volunteers; some have informed visitors that they are the subjects of research, and some have not. Commercial web operators have used cookies with little or no consent.

As we use the Internet to search for library books, purchase reading and other materials, and look for interesting information, it is clear that the ability to track our behavior is now far greater than it was before the computer age. In addition, the use of a credit card online creates databases that show specific purchases. In the case of online bookstores, the information has the power to disclose what we are reading. The fact that Internet bookstores create the illusion of privacy when they tout "secure server" computers at their sites raises concerns. Consumers may believe their private information is safer than is possible on the Net.

On another front, privacy is being eroded by the development of e-mail systems in which the boundaries between office and home produce are blurred. The home, under common law, was *the* place where an individual had a reasonable expectation of personal privacy. However, technology stands to reduce the home to a place that has no special guarantees or expectations of privacy.

The free-expression component of privacy is complicated by concerns over access to information. Journalists often use their First Amendment rights to access information from government databases under freedom-of-information provisions. However, these databases hold personal information on millions of individuals, and traditionally, press access to such data has been limited to "newsworthy" situations. When the same data are available on the Internet to all who are curious, then less judgment may be exercised about its use. Some attempts have been made at the state level to limit access through so-called stalker laws, which filter requests for information from private citizens. At the same time, however, there is also a movement afoot to create a national database of driver's license pictures.

Private databases are another matter. An individual has a legal right to read her or his credit report, but such reports merely scratch the surface of what has become available as marketers use computers to scan purchases at supermarkets and drug stores. Marketers may identify purchasers by offering discounts when a customer uses a "value card" that scans their identity. Such marketing information can be merged on the computer with demographic, geodemographic, and psychographic lifestyle information to paint a portrait of the individual consumer. Companies such as SRI Research use the data to create typologies of consumer types.

Before examining the technological concerns of privacy in more detail, I will first turn to an examination of legal issues. For over a century, legal scholars have been trying to interpret the meaning of invasion of privacy.

The Law of Privacy

The concept of the invasion of privacy has been traced to a law review written by Louis Brandeis and Samuel Warren in 1890 in which it was proposed that the individual has a common-law right to be let alone—even in a case in which media reporting is truthful. Developed primarily through state statutes protecting private or intimate information, the smattering of law in this area was very confusing. Then, in 1960, a law-review article by William Prosser proposed a categorization scheme with four types of lawsuits:

- disclosing private, embarrassing facts about somebody,
- appropriating the use of a person's name, picture, or persona for commercial purposes,
- intrusion on one's solitude or seclusion, that is, trespassing, and
- placing a person in a false light, similar to a libel defamation.

It also has been argued that there is a fifth right in this regard—the right of celebrities to control and profit from their own publicity (Gillmor, Barron, Simon, and Terry, 1996, pp. 84–85).

Invasion of privacy has long been an interest of those studying new technologies, such as early aerial and ground photography, military technology, and remote-sensing satellite imagery (Lipschultz, 1988). Technology enables our mass media "to show what the human eye cannot see" (p. 509). Given its mechanization of searches, technology troubles some: "Continuous surveillance over large areas can be accomplished without the knowledge of the targets of an investigation" (p. 509).

Although satellite and aerial imagery allows for visual searches over vast geographic areas, searches in cyberspace are less limited by geography and physical obstructions. In both instances, the nature and the context of the information may be important. The law recognizes the dangers of intrusion on private space: "revelations may be so intimate and so unwarranted as to outrage the community's notions of decency" (*Restatement of Torts, 2d*, 1977). For a privacy case to be actionable, the content must be "highly offensive to a reasonable person," particularly where the information is concluded to have "no legitimate public interest" (*Dresbach v. Doubleday*, 1981).

The mere use of information, including digital images, could give rise to privacy claims in cyberspace. Imagine the publication on a web page of a photograph that had been altered by computer editing. Such images, because they have been tampered with, would be open to misinterpretation.

The use of real-time audio and video broadcasts on the Internet also pose new problems, in terms of placing people in a false light and providing live broadcasts of events that might have commercial value.

Separate from the common-law tort of invasion of privacy is the Fourth Amendment constitutional right to be "secure . . . against unreasonable searches and seizures." Typically, such actions involve police and other government searches, but the new Internet search engines now allow private individuals to access huge government databases.

Cyberspace blurs the traditional constitutional privacy distinctions between "curtilage"—the private area that extends beyond the actual walls of a home—and open fields (*Oliver v. United States*, 1984). Internet connections enter the home and become seamless. Both "push" technologies and

Internet cookies gather information from personal computers by aggressively gathering data from a user's computer hard drive. It is not clear how far the government and others may go in the search and seizure of electronic computers. Those home PCs, networked via constant cable hookups, pose particularly troubling privacy issues (*California v. Cieraolo*, 1986; *Dow Chemical v. United States*, 1986).

In computer technology, building a firewall to protect business data becomes analogous to protecting secrets with a physical roof. But because the art of computer hacking remains strong, computers continue to be fertile ground for industrial and other espionage. The U.S Supreme Court once refused to constitutionalize a general right of privacy (*Katz v. United States*, 1967), but recent developments in the new technology may force a reconsideration of the existing law.

State and local cable television ordinances vary on the degree to which companies must inform viewers "clearly and conspicuously" about the nature of their monitoring and information disclosure to others (Bittner, 1994, p. 268). Such ordinances, drafted in the 1970s and 1980s, could not anticipate the degree to which Internet access would accelerate digital interactivity in mass media technologies. Given that one common property of the technology is the digital trail left of one's traveling through cyberspace, each computer user much ask how much of this information she is willing to disclose to the world.

Access to Information

Issues regarding access to and dissemination of private information is important because the commercial marketplace is paradoxical. In that marketplace, one can argue both for openness in the name of profit and privacy in the name of a company's proprietary rights:

> As technologies create new means to access, manipulate, and disseminate information, economic opportunities will increasingly arise for individuals, firms, and government to profit. In some instances, however, other individuals or companies would rather not have this information collected, used or disseminated. Whether there should be legal means available to prevent (or prevent interference with) such collection, use or dissemination will be one of the key questions posed to citizens, Congress, and other governmental bodies (Bittner, 1994, p. 322).

Privacy can be treated as an issue related to traditional concerns over wiretapping or the illegal interception of personal communications. The Electronic Communications Privacy Act of 1986 was one attempt to see how new technologies such as wireless and cellular telephones could be protected from wiretapping when the communication was, in effect, wireless. We might expect that the U.S. Congress and other legal entities will continue to revise laws to address new problems raised by issues involving privacy in cyberspace.

Privacy as a Social Value

Neuman (1998) has concluded that although "the digital day is young," the technology has the power to be influential in terms of its social value:

> Because the Internet blurs the distinction between an interpersonal and a broadcast communications network, it blurs the distinction between private and public speech. Authoritarian nations' restrictive regulations designed to prevent speech deemed contrary to national security focus on mobilization appeals and incitement-to-riot concepts of public speech. A rabble-rouser on a street corner is, by definition, easier to locate and expurgate than, say, a thoughtful but anonymous critic at a computer terminal (Neuman, 1998, p. 247).

In such a postmodern world, there is the potential that a critical and sophisticated public audience will reemerge as the traditional mass media are bypassed:

> By most measures, the evolving media, including talk radio and especially the Internet and the Web, will enrich and empower that tradition of a vibrant public sphere. The critical literature in mass communication research argued for decades that the rhetoric of official news obscured the linkages between public policy and the daily circumstances of private life. We may expect that the dominant public language of the media will continue to interact with the private language of the street. But if, as predicted, the new media truly enhance small group communication, new forms of private speech will migrate forcefully from the street into the surviving mass media (Neuman, 1998, p. 248).

The optimistic view, however, fails to recognize that traditional mass media organizations already are transforming the new media into iterations of existing mass media. At the dawn of a new century, we face a media environment that is ever more hostile to the notion of personal privacy. For the most part, mass media have invaded the private lives of famous entertainers and politicians, and in the process, reporters and photographers have challenged the power of government to establish laws, rules, and regulations designed to protect personal privacy.

Privacy involves four competing interests: the interests of the subject; the interests of the information "custodians"; the government's interest in obtaining regulatory and prosecutorial information; and private interests in exploiting information about others (Perritt, 1996, p. 90). In general, privacy law attempts to protect people by determining expectations for privacy and by setting standards of reasonableness (p. 91). The government has intervened most aggressively in the area of credit and credit card data protection.

Some scholars contend that it is the responsibility of the public to become knowledgeable in order to raise the level of safeguards:

> It is not yet clear what activities citizens will perceive to constitute an unwarranted abuse of privacy, nor whether they will assume that reduced privacy is one of the unavoidable trade-offs to enjoy the fruits of the information age. It is essential, however, that individuals become sufficiently informed about the capabilities of telecommunications and data processing systems to make informed choices, and where necessary, to guide elected officials in legislating necessary privacy protections (Bittner, 1994, p. 325).

Unfortunately, the public is not likely to participate in the dynamics of evolving privacy law. Neither the public nor public officials have adequately conceptualized the struggle between notions of privacy and rights of free expression.

Privacy in an Electronic Age

Electronic communication laws attempt to protect people against having their transfers of data intercepted, but these protections do not apply when consent to obtain the data has been given to another person or entity or when the data are considered public (Perritt, 1996, p. 104). Most e-mail systems assume that users will protect themselves through the use of passwords and good judgment. However, certain social conditions challenge the ability of system administrators to establish workable rules—guidelines that do not encumber free expression. For example, one "model statement" included the following language: "We reserve the privilege of accessing the content of your E-mail messages if we receive a complaint or report of misuse of the E-mail system or harmful messages or messages that intrude into another's privacy or property rights" (Perritt, 1996, p. 157). This statement reflects the argument that privacy is a situational right: "When we think abstractly about privacy, we tend to order it among the most cherished values of liberty in an ordered society, alongside freedom of speech and religion. But our sensitivity to privacy interests varies with circumstances" (Brenner, 1996, p. 283).

The telephone system has come to be at the center of privacy concerns. D. L. Brenner (1996) reminded us that we have a number of expectations in this regard: "the right to own a telephone number, to keep the number from being disclosed, to control proprietary customer information, to keep secret calls between consenting parties, to operate cordless telephone, to use caller ID, and to avoid unwanted communications" (pp. 186–287). Telephones offered people the promise of universal service, but telephone service was altered in the 1980s and 1990s by use of the computer modem. It turned a very secure technology into one that provides few guarantees of privacy protection.

Cookies do not raise privacy issues, according to a federal government panel. In fact, the U.S. Department of Energy's Computer Incident Advisory Capability Office issued an advisory stating that fears that cookies can be used to obtain computer passwords and credit card numbers are false. The group said the cookies are no more dangerous than information already recorded in the log files of computer servers, and it claimed cookies just make such data collection easier. Privacy advocates, however, say that cookies are just another example of how the new technology makes it easier to track individuals' actions without consent.

Even if we do not personally use the new electronic technology, it is being used for us. Consider the example of computerized medical records. Health-care providers now use computer databases to share information, providing access to our most personal details in life and opening the door to abuses. One Colorado medical student, for example, copied patient records and sold them to medical malpractice lawyers (*Chronicle of Higher Education*, March 27, 1998). Such cases have led Congress to consider new privacy legislation, although to this point, the government has relied on state laws to protect the privacy of medical records. Health records, however, are valuable for other reasons: "Health information can be appropriately used to meet other kinds of societal needs, like the protection of public health, health oversight, and medical research" (p. A-38).

If one thinks of her or his body as the most private of all aspects of life, the marketing of online medication by overseas firms is of interest. Individuals can now use the Internet to purchase untested or risky drugs— those not approved by the U.S. Food and Drug Administration (FDA)— and if they use those drugs without being monitored by a trained physician, they could put their lives at risk. However, laws promoting the free flow of information and limits on marketplace barriers promote other national laws that are in conflict with the rules of global marketplaces (Bilby, 1997).

The technology itself may lead to the invasion of privacy in a variety of ways. Consider the example of the malicious use of JavaScript web code to, in effect, perform a virtual kidnapping.

The most obvious invasions of privacy on the Internet involve the use of a person's image, as occurred when a former boyfriend posted twenty-

---

Box 9.1   Web Sites That Won't Let Go

Brett Wright, according to the Associated Press, operated web sites that automatically route visitors to commercial sites that pay him for the "referrals." The JavaScripted sites actually capture the unwitting visitor and will not let go. When she or he tries to leave the commercial site or close the browser window, other browser windows are spawned automatically. "It can be a nearly endless, frustrating cycle to regain control of the · computer," the Associated Press wrote. Sexually oriented sites are the most frequent users of the technology, and some lure more than 250,000 visitors each day. "The whole goal is to move traffic like cattle," Wright said, "but the easiest way to send traffic somewhere is not to give them the opportunity not to go there."

(Source: Associated Press, October 11, 1998)

---

three-year-old nude photos of radio host Dr. Laura. She tried to stop the posting legally but ultimately was forced to drop her privacy and copyright infringement lawsuit against Seattle-based Internet Entertainment Group because the court could do nothing about the photos already "splattered" all over the Web (CNN, December 23, 1998).

Actress Alyssa Milano, by contrast, won a $230,000 judgment against twenty-one-year-old John Lindgren for posting nude photos at his web site, which "boasts of having 1,000 nude photos of actresses" available for purchase. The court also ordered Lindgren to pay $8,200 in legal fees. He had failed to respond to the lawsuit, and Milano won a default judgment (CNN, December 23, 1998).

Technology that impacts on privacy, though, extends well beyond the Internet. *Newsday* reported, for instance, that scientists have implanted devices in human brains that allow the individuals to move a computer cursor by just thinking about it. The electrical impulses in the motor cortex regulate movement, and such implants go one step beyond virtual-reality helmets and gloves. The direct communication interface between the human brain and the computer may be a harbinger of the potential to create, in effect, mind-monitoring or mind-controlling techniques. Certainly, such technology offers hope for disabled individuals, but it also spawns new fears about the human-technological interface. As the *Star Wars* movie trilogy first identified, there is an uneasy relationship between humans and their technology—a "dark side" through which identity may be lost to mechanization (Wise, 1997, p. 24).

In the short term, the traditional human-computer interfaces such as the keyboard remain at issue. Consider, for example, the web site known

---

Box 9.2 Privacy and the Dr. Laura Controversy

Popular radio host and best-selling author Dr. Laura Schlessinger found that the Internet can be a dangerous place when it comes to personal privacy. An eighty-year-old man who claimed to have had an affair with Dr. Laura in the 1970s while they were married to other people, posted nude photographs of her on a web site. Dr. Laura is known for her advice to callers that they live by the Ten Commandments. Dr. Laura received a court ordered injunction to shut down the page, but others had already copied the photos and were distributing them across the Internet on other pages. Then, a federal judge ruled that the twenty-three-year-old photos could continue to be seen on the Internet. Bill Ballance, the father of the so-called topless radio format, claimed to have taken the pictures during an affair the two apparently had. Dr. Laura, who admits her life has undergone "profound changes" since then, called the Internet site "morally reprehensible."

(Source: News wire reports, October 1998)

---

as Mrs. Brady's, which is devoted to tracking the investigation of the Boulder, Colorado, murder of JonBenet Ramsey. The online visitors to the site shared case leads and speculated on the guilt or innocence of various suspects. Lawyers, mental-health workers, and former police officers all joined the virtual investigation. Participants were asked for the sources of their information as the online chat operated at the same time as a grand jury probe:

Skylurk: I am a mother, and I know that affects my POV [point of view] on the case.

Weon2u: We have good intuition.

Ruthee: For me, I think it's the connection between a child and her parents.

(*Omaha World-Herald*, September 19, 1998, p. 8)

Individual sites bring virtual communities of interest together. So-called portals, such as the Microsoft Network (MSN) "free club" atmosphere, seem to produce gated online communities. But once an individual is in one of these groups, the potential that his privacy will be invaded in the name of commercial interests is obvious. After all, membership implies that the organization has access to private information about its members.

Ethical and Social Constraints

It is clear that if every citizen were to demand a right to be left alone, free expression would become a rather meaningless right. Fortunately, society is social. It demands that we interact with others in the marketplace in order to conduct everyday business. We buy and sell products and services, and in effect, we share resources to get by. The economic marketplace, then, is the primary locale where free expression is exercised.

Outside the private home, out there in the marketplace, we lose a measure of our personal privacy. The same is true when we use a computer to hop online. Through cyberspace, we psychologically leave home while actually sitting there. We express ourselves in the course of conducting a wide range of social exchanges. To the extent that we have something to gain or lose in these social exchanges, our freedom of communication may be altered in meaningful ways.

Kellerman (1987) has concluded that the concept of "information exchange" involves some set of predefined boundaries:

> In essence, information can only be defined in terms of *exchange*, for information, by itself, is an infinite set containing all past, present, and future cognition and behaviors. Information exchange, on the other hand, involves the transmission of some finite amount of the set. Information exchange focuses on what is said, done, or perceived in a given interaction regardless of whether it is detected, regardless of its accuracy, and regardless of its purpose (p. 189).

We may go out of our way to make a point, or we may gravitate to the safe social ground of the mainstream. In either case, social pressures to conform can determine what constitutes "proper" communication in a given situation. Social-exchange theory posits that relationship outcomes are equal to the perceived reward minus the perceived costs and that intimacy and self-disclosure involve reciprocity (Altman and Taylor, 1997). The Internet can both foster trusting relationships and attack them through invasions of privacy. On the one hand, the computer user has welcomed someone into his or her private life, and on the other hand, that person has become an uninvited guest. In a recent university online debate that centered on appropriate use of state-funded computer technology to advocate political causes, one reader responded:

> We academics have little room to talk about squelching freedom of speech, since universities are known for their firm adherence to "political correctness." I am more guarded in my speech on campus than in any other place, in an effort to avoid offending a multitude of groups. . . . I'm pleased to see

some opinions declared freely over email. It doesn't seem unreasonable for educators to discuss and disagree without being threatened with advisory bylaws.

The perceptions individuals hold about their ability to speak freely in any setting is a function of the setting, the individual, and the relationship of the individual to others in the setting. The difficulty about electronic communication is that it tests untested relationships. Those who speak out in such a forum do open themselves to criticisms and potential losses of a measure of privacy in response to their utterances.

Invasion of privacy may be an inevitable dark outcome of the "age of optimism" (Negroponte, 1995, p. 227), but neither the law nor society appears to be prepared for the technological evolution. The technology has fostered a level of comfort by blurring the lines between work and home, between the world "out there" and the privacy "@ home." In doing so, protection of personal privacy seems to be a difficult value to maintain. This may be good news for the free-expression absolutists who have always been in conflict with those wanting to protect personal information from the public light.

Personal data—salaries, credit information, debts, medical records, and so forth—have been available for many years to investigative journalists and private detectives. What is new in the digital age is that this information is so readily available to anyone with a personal computer and a credit card. Online businesses now sell their snooping services. And skilled computer users can locate a lot of the data without professional assistance. Some privacy experts conclude that such widely accessible information means that privacy no longer exists as a meaningful legal right.

This state of affairs might lead us to wrongly conclude that free expression will be promoted in such an open environment. In fact, the opposite may be true. People with a past may avoid speaking out on controversial issues of public importance if they fear that "dirt" will be dug up on them in a smear campaign to reduce their credibility—especially when it is now so easy to dig. The larger public good might be injured if such fear leads some not to participate in a democracy by either exercising free expression or running for elective office.

To some, what is at stake in privacy law in the electronic age is the value of personal reputation. For example, CBS-TV's *48 Hours* program has exposed the problem of people stealing identities. With a driver's license and a social security number, it is now possible to assume a person's identity and electronically steal thousands of dollars, although credit card companies and retail merchants have not yet recognized that individuals can be victimized in this way. Loss of a good credit rating is an invasion of privacy made possible because so many data are available.

The wide access to information has led to a privacy backlash of sorts in the form of legislation pending in several states and Congress, including "restrictions on credit reports and the sale of confidential medical and genetic information to marketers and other businesses" (Associated Press, April 13, 1998).

The Electronic Privacy Information Center has called for enforceable measures to give consumers control over personal information. Some industry groups have offered guidelines about how computerized membership data can be used. However, most customers remain unaware of the vast amount of personal data compiled and how it is being utilized.

This leads to the issue of how digital bits have commercial value. It is impossible to separate concerns over the social and economic issues of an electronic age. The bottom-line social value of a free marketplace, of which the marketplace of ideas is a part, is the belief in the ethic of buying and selling. By nature, then, a market orientation devalues those people who have nothing to sell or little to buy. We might assume in this scenario that those people who are not distinguished as buyers and sellers are also devalued in terms of free expression and the marketplace of ideas.

Intel's Pentium III computer chip was said to contain an identification feature that was useful in secure e-commerce transactions, but when information about that feature came to light, the Electronic Privacy Information Center complained (*New York Times*, January 29, 1999). Originally, users who wanted privacy would have been required to switch the feature off; after negotiations, Intel agreed to turn the feature off in the default mode (and users attempting to engage in e-commerce would be required to turn on the feature). Some privacy groups threatened a boycott of Intel over the rift, and the Federal Trade Commission launched an investigation. This struggle over privacy demonstrates the complex nature of the Internet problem. Nobody wants to engage in unprotected purchases over the Internet, but we also might worry about how easy it is to electronically track any individual's navigation of the information superhighway.

Chapter Summary

This chapter reviewed the law of privacy and related it to social and technological issues. The Internet and e-mail create situations in which invasion of privacy may become more commonplace. Certain technologies, such as web cookies, make protection of privacy difficult. Society seems unprepared for the social changes being driven by technology.

Discussion Questions

1. Do you worry about protecting your privacy? Why or why not?
2. Do you have the right to say anything about anyone on the Internet? Are there any limits to free expression when it comes to the issue of privacy?
3. Do researchers have the right to use cookies to track online behavior? What are the ethical concerns?
4. Should commercial web sites be able to use cookies to track visitors and personalize web sites for them?
5. Do you have any fears about the use of brain implants that can connect humans directly with computers? Is that any different from the use of computer keyboards, mouses, and monitors?
6. What is the future of invasion of privacy as a legal and social concept in a technological age that seems to bypass those concerns? Should anything be done about it?

10

Property and Commercial Rights in a Digital Age

"The National Information Infrastructure can realize its potential only if it protects private property and makes it possible to offer something for sale or license in open networks like the Internet without being misappropriated by a competitor."

—Henry Perritt Jr., legal scholar (1996)

"Economically, unauthorized use threatens the creators' livelihood. Intellectual property law gives them legal recourse."

—Donald Gillmor, Jerome Barron, Todd Simon, and Herbert Terry, media law textbook authors (1996)

"My tiny web site is not a financial threat to these Media Giants. . . . It's not because of a financial threat or unfair competition . . . truth is the enemy of government propagandists."

—Jim Robinson, web site operator (1998)

"Any further use of WASHINGTON POST content must be deemed a willful infringement of our rights, which entitles us to additional remedies."

—Caroline Little, lawyer (1998)

"With a few keystrokes, deft maneuvering of a mouse or skilled use of computerized drawing tools, a copyrighted work can be reproduced or derivative works made and displayed to literally millions of people connected by computer networks around the globe."

—Dorothy Bowles, media law professor (1998)

239

> *"The Digital Millennium Copyright Act of 1998 . . . may turn out to be profoundly important. [This will] set ground rules for traffic in information over the Internet—a business that, someday, could total hundreds of billions of dollars and control how Americans receive much of their news and entertainment."*
>
> **—Robert Samuelson, writer (1998)**

> *"The business is certainly a lot more serious now, but that to me is a good thing. The early Internet industry was fun, but it was very provincial, and tended to attract a lot of people who were kind of far-out, but not necessarily good business people."*
>
> **—Marc Andreessen, Netscape cofounder (1998)**

One of the most significant restrictions on absolute free expression on the Internet stems from the fact that the law must protect ideas as private property. Just as it is not legal to steal physical property, so, too, is theft of media content illegal: "The law protects intellectual property because intellectual creativity is stunted if creators are unable to recover their investment in inventive or creative effort before competitors appropriate their authorship or inventions and get a free ride on the creative effort" (Perritt, 1996, p. 416).

Copyright, patent, trademark, and trade secret laws create "a limited monopoly" over new information. But in the interim, digital data distribution raises concerns over "unlimited proliferation of copyrighted works through perfect digital copies"; sampling of partial works; scanning hard copy into digital forms; and immediate updating of existing works (Perritt, 1996, p. 416).

Although copyright law was not a part of the U.S. Constitution or the Bill of Rights, the first such law was passed in 1790. There have been regular revisions of the law, including the Copyright Act of 1976 and the Digital Millennium Copyright Act of 1998, by which the U.S. Congress moved to extend copyright protection to the Internet. As will be explored in this chapter, free online distribution of music and other creative works has threatened the profits of commercial media. And though international treaties have protected copyrighted works from infringement in most major nations since the 1980s, enforcement has been a problem, particularly in Asia. Copyrighted works include writings, music, plays, images, movies, and even choreography and architecture.

Common facts, ideas, and names are not subject to copyright legal protection. Government works or those in the public domain also cannot be protected. "Fair use" exemptions make copyright law very fuzzy.

Copyright Considerations

Most forms of words, pictures, sound, and images may be protected by copyright—including those produced in computer and multimedia software programs—and such protection is maintained after the death of the creator, *Copyright Act*, 17 USC 102(a), 302(a), 1988. In 1998, Congress passed the Sonny Bono Copyright Term Extension Act, extending copyright to "the life of the author plus 70 years"; in addition, the copyright terms for "works made for hire" were extended from seventy-five to ninety-five years. According to the Recording Industry Association of America (RIAA), "this should end the discrimination against U.S. works abroad, where countries applied the 'rule of shorter term' to U.S. works, thereby affording American creators less protection than their foreign counterparts" (http://www.riaa.com).

However, the Copyright Act also provides for the so-called fair use of relatively limited portions of material for educational, noncommercial purposes that do not cause economic harm to the market for copyrighted works. Copyright has become an important concern in regard to the Internet because digital word processing makes it easy to copy and paste the intellectual property of others. In 1998, the FreeRepublic web site (http://www.freerepublic.com) and its White Water page came under fire from the *Washington Post* for reprinting significant portions of stories published elsewhere. The page routinely used excerpts of media material as a catalyst for people to post raw comment on the news. (See Figure 10.1.)

Internet reporter Matt Drudge called White Water "one of the Internet's premiere discussion groups"—the product of Jim Robinson, a man who suffers from muscular dystrophy who has used $500 in donations to operate from a wheelchair in his Fresno, California, home (Drudge Report, March 26, 1998). The *Washington Post,* however, claimed that "reposting of material . . . on [the FreeRepublic] website without our permission is copyright infringement, and it is not within the bounds of fair use." According to Drudge,

> the bulletin board has become the hottest spot online to monitor instant reaction to scandal news developments. Unlike commercial outlets: TIME, CNN and MSNBC, Robinson developed a spot where comment flows raw. A scout will first post an original news story, readers immediately begin to dissect in follow-up threads. The site has captured a dedicated following among media and political heavyweights and receives a reported 30,000 visitors a day. It is read daily in the White House and is accessed by top congressional leaders. One network news executive recently whispered to the DRUDGE REPORT: "That place has more hot news than I can find at my local news stand" (http://www.drudgereport.com, March 26, 1998).

242

FreeRepublic.com *"The premier conservative news discussion forum!"*
[Home | Latest | More | Register | Login | Logoff | Post | Search | Help!]

Topic: **White Water**

Stepped up campaign will work: U.S.

- **The Hindu**
  Saturday, April 17, 1999 *Sridhar Krishnaswami*
  The Clinton administration has said it is positive that the stepped up air campaign
  against the Yugoslavian leader, Mr. Slobodan Milosevic, will work and that right now
  ground troops are not needed in the Balkans to achieve the political and military
  objectives. Law-makers here have been warned that any attempt to seriously pursue the
  idea of sending in combat units would fracture the alliance. . . .
       Web Posted: 04/16/99 13:41:29 PDT Posted by: Jai

Maureen Dowd - The sassy columnist with something to offend everyone.

- **Slate**
  Saturday, April 17, 1999 *A.O. Scott*
  Two of this year's Pulitzer Prizes were awarded for wit: one for Margaret Edson's play
  of that name, about a scholar of 17th-century English poetry facing ovarian cancer, and
  another for the quality most evident in the writing of New York Times columnist
  Maureen Dowd. Newspaper commentary, a dying art (see Jacob Weisberg's recent
  encomium on its last great), is nowadays dominated by sententiousness, not satire.
       Web Posted: 04/16/99 13:30:03 PDT Posted by: nom

Clinton and NATO are international outlaws!

- **USA TODAY and Menasha WI Register**
  4/13/99 and 4/14/99 *Rev. Tom Hutt (Ret.)*
  What the U.S. and her NATO allies are actually doing in their criminal assault upon the
  people of Yugoslavia...
       Web Posted: 04/16/99 13:26:51 PDT Posted by: Echo

Montenegro Says Yugoslav War Out of Control

- **Fox News**
  4/16/99 *Crispian Balmer*
  PODGORICA, Montenegro — The conflict between NATO and Yugoslavia is
  slipping out of control and risks sweeping through the rest of the Balkans, Montenegrin
  President Milo Djukanovic said on Friday.
       Web Posted: 04/16/99 13:17:22 PDT Posted by: marshmallow

HACK: 'Serbs Have the Best Air Defenses in the World'

- **Col. David Hackworth on George Putnam Show**
  4-16-99 *Doug from Upland*
  Col. David Hackworth, our most highly decorated living soldier, made another appearance on the George Putnam

Now on Radio Free Republic

6 am Alan Keyes
8 am Gary Aldrich
9 am Erin Hart
noon James Golden
2 pm Doug Giant
4 pm John Carlson
7 pm OnlineTonight
9 pm James Golden
(Times are Pacific)

Special Links

Alley Chat
China Spy Guide
FReeper Action
FR Media Library
Order Freep Stuff
Managers Rally
Adopt/Congressman

In the Forum

Latest 20 Posts
Latest 100 Posts
Latest Articles
Frames Version
White Water
Archives
Downside Legacy
Body Count
Clinton Convicts
Resend Password
Help & Guidelines

Main Menu

Home Page
News Media
Forum
Politics
Congress Directory
Links
Chapters
Activism
Help
TalkSpot

Daily Stats

FIGURE 10.1   Freerepublic.com

Robinson argued that because FreeRepublic was a not-for-profit bulletin board, he was exempted under the fair-use rules of American copyright law. He called the site a "grassroots effort to root out government corruption" and one that is the product of thousands of contributors. Indeed, the postings on his board are original commentaries on the reposted news articles. Robinson ran this response on the site:

> The Washington Post claims we have no right to print "their" copyrighted material . . . but most of it isn't theirs to begin with. A lot of the things from the Washington Post website are Associated Press reports. You busybodies have no authority over that material, it is not copyrighted to you. Even those stories that you write yourselves should not be posted on the internet if you do not wish them to be copied and pasted. This message board isn't the only board that Washington Post articles are posted on, so I guess you had better hire the "internet police" to search every message board on the internet [so that] none of your precious material can be "illegally" copied and pasted on these message boards. Have fun with your little games (http://www.freerepublic.com/forum/a150873.htm).

A number of contributors to Robinson's site immediately responded. Wrote one anonymous writer called Xtream1st: "Washington Post is a fat-cat maggoty faggoty liberal establishment windbag bunch of LOSERS! Who wants to read that crap anyway. I say IGNORE EM." Another contributor called Bard wrote: "Dittos! All The Post is interested in is the perpetuation of the federal 'benefit/subsidy protection racket.'" A legal analysis followed from 1L (the "name" of another person who posted a message), who said the newspaper would have to show it was harmed by the postings: "They would have to prove that the 30,000 people do not visit their website. . . . Just tell everyone to log onto the Wpost web site once a week. . . . Let the browser pick up everything and then leave" (http://www.freerepublic.com/forum/a150873.htm).

One argument holds that the bulletin board could actually enhance the *Washington Post* web site by making people more interested in it. But the profitability of pages like Robinson's and the ability to accurately count visitors for advertising purposes has been questionable thus far. Robinson himself apparently earned money from a separate company—Electronic Orchard—that worked on web design and software development. (Incidentally, the logo for that company appears to be an iteration of Microsoft's Internet Explorer logo, which could lead to a trademark infringement case.) Robinson maintained:

> FreeRepublic is designed and maintained by Jim Robinson, an individual. FreeRepublic is completely independent and is not affiliated with any group, association, political party, or news source. FreeRepublic is supported solely

by donations. We are NON commercial and [a] NOT for profit public forum and discussion group (http://www.freerepublic.com/forum/a150873.htm).

Robinson continued to post stories with a fair use disclaimer, such as this one:

Topic: White Water

Whitewater Grand Jury Recalls Ex-Loan Officer

Washington Post

Friday, March 27, 1998; Page A11 Susan Schmidt

> *Not for commercial use. Solely to be fairly used for the educational purposes of research and open discussion.*

Whitewater Grand Jury Recalls Ex-Loan Officer
By Susan Schmidt
Washington Post Staff Writer

Friday, March 27, 1998; Page A11

> A former Little Rock bank executive said yesterday he was called back to the Whitewater grand jury recently to testify about a 1986 warning he said he gave to Hillary Rodham Clinton regarding the legality of a real estate transaction . . . (http://www.freerepublic.com/forum/a150873.htm).

The problem of posting material without permission has also emerged at the university level. Consider the case of a University of Nebraska–Lincoln English professor who was sued by a student after the professor put one of her essays on the Internet. The university's general counsel Richard Wood claimed it was not responsible because the professor "was not authorized to publish anything on the internet, or anywhere, in violation of anyone's copyright" (*Chronicle of Higher Education*, February 20, 1998, p. A29). The fair-use defense in copyright is fairly narrow when it comes to unpublished works, and student works may also be protected under federal privacy law, according to the Indiana University Copyright Management Center (http://www.iupui.edu/it/copyinfo). The university, for a variety of unrelated charges, ultimately fired the professor.

Media law professor Dorothy Bowles noted that one computer bulletin board ran into a copyright infringement dilemma by posting digital copies of photographs that had appeared in *Playboy* magazine:

> A company operating such a system made digital reproductions of 170 photographs . . . and distributed the high-quality computerized images to subscribers. A [Florida] court [*Playboy v. Frena*, 1994] rejected a fair use defense,

noting that the use was clearly commercial; that the originals were for enter-tainment, not factual, purposes; and that, if widespread, such conduct would adversely affect the magazine's market (Bowles, in Hopkins, 1999, p. 158).

Of course, anyone with the means to do so may file a lawsuit against anyone else. Thus, individuals working on Internet projects in which copyright issues surface should be aware that corporations routinely uti-lize large legal staffs to protect their property against infringement. Enter-tainment and software companies regularly use copyright laws in their attempts to protect their investment in product development. Beyond this, the creative community is concerned about preserving the integrity of their ideas from parody that might weaken their value.

The music industry has been particularly concerned about the prolifer-ation of pirated sheet music and digital tracks on the Internet. The Recording Industry Association of America raised concerned about so-called MP3 digitally compressed versions of songs and even entire al-bums. The association filed a lawsuit against Diamond Multimedia of San Jose, California, over its palm-sized portable equipment that allows play-back of downloaded files: "Since it is the first major field of entertainment to face the Internet copying problem, whatever course the music indus-try's battle takes is likely to set the tone in the future of film, TV and other intellectual property that can be replicated and posted to the Net"(*USA Today*, November 4, 1998, p. 5-D). In 1999, however, the industry dropped its litigation in this matter following a federal appeals court's ruling that piracy laws are not pertinent to the MP3 Internet music player; subse-quently, the recording industry and the makers of the player began work-ing together to develop guidelines regarding music on the Internet (*New York Times*, August 5, 1999).

The music industry has favored digital systems by the American com-panies Real Networks, Liquid Audio, and a2b Music that feature copy-right encryption and so-called watermarking. But the challenge has come from Fraunhofer's German system known by the names MPEG–1, Layer 3, and MP3: "Although the format has the ability to offer copy-right protections, it has proliferated on the Net minus those standards, leading to an abundance of sites both legal and illegal" (*USA Today*, No-vember 4, 1998, p. 5-D). The global nature of the illegal copying has made it difficult and expensive for companies to find and shut down ille-gal sites.

RIAA calls protecting member companies from piracy its most impor-tant mission. "To meet these challenges, the RIAA is channeling most of its anti-piracy resources to Internet piracy, while still guarding against evolv-ing forms of CD piracy" (http://www.riaa.com/piracy/ piracy.htm). RIAA sees the Internet as a place to distribute niche music widely and reach larger audiences:

Box 10.1 Kids' *Teletubbies* Show Moves to Guard Against Internet Spoofs

In Hilversum, the Netherlands, a Dutch spoof of the *Teletubbies* children's television program was being challenged. The British Broadcasting Corporation (BBC), producer of the Teletubbies, was considering legal action against BNN, an "irreverent youth channel," which produced "Tuberculosistubbies," a takeoff depicting characters that resembled Po, Laa-Laa, Tinky-Winky, and Dipsy "simulating sex and fighting." Parents have also been shocked to find obscene messages posted on the Teletubbies Web site.

(Source: Associated Press, November 7, 1998)

Unfortunately, the Internet culture of unlicensed use means that theft of intellectual property is rampant, and the music business and its artists are the biggest victims. Unauthorized Internet music archive sites using MIDI technology or MP3 files provide illegal sound recordings online to anyone with a personal computer. They can be downloaded and played indefinitely, without authorization of or compensation to the artists (http://www.riaa.com/piracy/pirop.htm).

RIAA became embroiled in a dispute with sound-technology company Diamond Multimedia, the maker of the Rio PMP300 portable music player. RIAA's complaint alleged that the ability to download Internet music to a Walkman-like portable player violated the Audio Home Recording Act of 1992. Diamond made a counterclaim of "conspiracy between RIAA and others to restrain trade and restrict competition" (http://www.diamondmm.com, December 2, 1998). Just thirteen days later, however, Diamond announced plans to participate in the Secure Digital Music Initiative, a recording industry cooperative effort to protect music from the illegal distribution of pirated copies. "Diamond's goal is to support the digital delivery of popular music and we're pleased to see the industry working together on a solution," said spokesman Ken Wirt. "There is a huge demand for digital music. . . . It is Diamond's intention to support an industry standard that allows all musicians, independents as well as major acts, to participate on the Internet as an exciting new medium for distributing their music" (http://www.diamondmm.com, December 15, 1998). It is clear that the music and consumer-electronics industries plan to cooperate in the interest of profit.

The problem will become more of an issue as the industry-sponsored Internet2 Digital Video Network Initiative attempts to develop the software that will enable the next-generation Internet to carry broadcast- or better-quality video. The International Center for Advanced Internet Research at Northwestern University predicts that such a technology will lead to a huge increase in highly specialized programming (*Chronicle of Higher Education*, November 6, 1998, p. A-36).

Copyright infringement raises legal issues for Internet service providers and other third parties involved in network management. The law appears to be moving away from strict liability toward a new standard of "actual knowledge" (Packard, 1998). Under the Digital Millennium Copyright Act, ISPs are not liable for copyright infringement if the provider "does not have actual knowledge that the material or an activity using the material on the system or network is infringing" (Pub.L. 105–304, Sec. 512 [c]). However, "upon obtaining such knowledge or awareness," the provider must act "expeditiously to remove, or disable access to, the material" (subsection III). This provision has free-expression implications. Most end users of the Internet do not have the ability or economic stability to be on the Internet without access through ISPs. Therefore, curtailment of freedom through regulation of providers, even in the name of protecting property rights, is dangerous. Copyright law is a relatively recent phenomenon based on the assumption that creative intellectual property needs to be protected and rewarded (Packard, 1998). "By recognizing that online services cannot monitor their content for infringing material and function efficiently, Congress has given them a green light to develop to their full potential" (p. 37). The copyright extension for exclusive ownership for ninety-five years, up from twenty-eight years in the original 1790 law, has been challenged in court by Eldritch Press. Under the new law, the publisher would be required to remove work that has been in the public domain under the previous limit of seventy-five years. "You can't retroactively extend copyright protection," Harvard University law professor Lawrence Lessig said; "we should be faithful to the Framers' vision" (*Chronicle of Higher Education*, January 22, 1999, p. A-20). Hollywood, publishers, and the music industry lobbied for the extension to protect copyright on such characters as Disney's Mickey Mouse. The Berkman Center for Internet and Society is fighting the law. "The Internet is public-domain structure," Lessig said (p. A-20).

Trademark Issues

The Lanham Act protects trademarks as another form of intellectual property. Trademarks can be words or symbols that help a company to distinguish its goods from those of another, which would include media or other company logos used on Internet World Wide Web pages. The trademark has value because it is used as an advertising and commercial shortcut that may convey a series of complex meanings to consumers that have been cultivated over generations. For example, if someone grew up in a household that used Gold Medal flour, he or she might purchase the product for the home under an assumption that it has a certain standard of quality. Similarly, computer users are familiar with the Macintosh multicolored apple and the Intel microprocessor logo as more recent examples of product branding. Mass media television networks have increasingly turned to branding video as a way to distinguish their products and remind viewers of location in a multichannel world. Thus, the NBC network and its affiliates across the nation use the NBC peacock at every opportunity—both on the air and on their web sites. If a local information provider were to use a peacock as a logo, the network and local station could move to stop it from doing so on the grounds that their viewers might be confused by the logo and also because their branding has value relative to the investment placed in it. (See Figures 10.2 and 10.3).

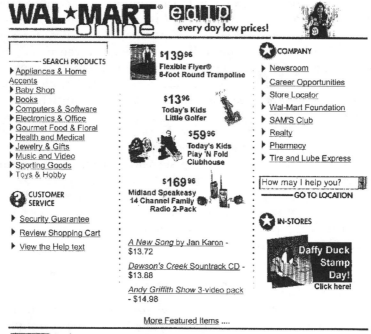

FIGURE 10.2   Wal-mart.com

Wal-Mart SUCKS

Welcome to my WalMart Sucks web site. You are probably here for one of several reasons.

#1 You have a problem with Wal-Mart. Be sure to register your complaint immediately.

#2. You stumbled upon our site. Please understand that this is a site of opinions. Not all stories can be verified for truthfullness. A considerable amount of content on this site is from other web sites from around the world.

#3. You work

Click on the picture to enter

Bangor Wal-Mart Faces Lawsuit
Read about it here

Wal-Mart in Bangor, Maine. Store #1856 207-947-5254
Please set your resolution for 800X600

P.S. Say Hi to Chowderhead Denise

Consider this your invitation / disclaimer to visit. By entering you agree not to hold us liable for the contents of our creation

Please enter through the Front Door

THIS SITE IS IN NO WAY CONNECTED WITH

THE WAL-MART CHAIN

FIGURE 10.3   Walmartsucks.com

Public television's Fred Rogers used trademark law to sue a Texas-based novelty store, Gadzooks Inc., for "hawking T-shirts that display [Mr.] Rogers with his trademark sweater and smile—and a silver handgun." The shirts read, "Welcome to my hood." Attorney Thomas Wettach stated. "It's bad for the kids. . . . It's sick humor" (Associated Press, December 27, 1998).

The Children's Television Workshop (CTW), producer of *Sesame Street*, used trademark law to challenge use of the Cookie Monster image on a computer cookie software page. The Cookie Monster "email-ware" program allowed users to delete identifying cookies stored in user computer hard drives while visiting web sites. CTW wrote nicolas@pobox.com:

> It has been brought to our attention that you have been using the name and likeness of the Sesame Street Muppet character, COOKIE MONSTER, on your web pages. . . .

◆　　◆　　◆

> We have granted you no right whatsoever to use any SESAME STREET character for any purpose. Your use thereof constitutes both copyright and trademark infringement. . . .

◆　　◆　　◆

> We hereby demand that you immediately cease any further use of the Sesame Street character, Cookie Monster, and that you, within five (5) business days, furnish to us your assurances that you will no longer use any SESAME STREET characters in any way or for any purpose. . . .

◆　　◆　　◆

> Your failure to do so shall require us to refer this matter to our outside copyright counsel for such action as it deems necessary and desirable to protect our rights. . . .

◆　　◆　　◆

> Very truly yours,
>
> Joseph Diaz, Esq.
>
> Children's Television Workshop
>
> One Lincoln Plaza
>
> New York, New York 10023
>
> > (http://www.geocities.com/Paris/1778/copyright.html).

The long-term protection of commercial images is likely to be a significant restriction on free expression in the future. Likewise, legal issues have emerged over business names. Microsoft filed a lawsuit against two Texas men for registering the domain names microsoftwindows.com and microsoftoffice.com. The pair also registered Hollywood-Video.com, AssociatedPress.com, and other business names. Microsoft called the pair "cybersquatters" and "pirates" because the names were registered without the permission on the companies (*USA Today*, December 31, 1998). It is likely that the registration of such Internet domain names by third parties is seen as an investment.

Patents

Patents protect the ownership rights of inventors. The most valuable patent ever issued went to Alexander Graham Bell in 1876, hours before a competing application was filed by Elisha Gray with the U.S. Patent Office in Washington: "The patent dispute was settled in 1979; Western Union gave up all its patent claims and its network of competing telephones in fifty-five cities in exchange for 20 percent of telephone receipts over the seventeen-year-life of the Bell patents" (Brenner, 1996, p. 1).

The Internet and its technologies have provided fertile ground for the invention of new communication technologies. Inventors working on such problems as digital compression and network data-transfer speeds require patent protection to be able to develop new products.

Information technology has also brought a variety of patent suits as inventors develop the new industry. Lucent Technologies, for example, sued Cisco Systems and accused it of violating eight digital networking patents. Cisco then charged that Lucent violated three of its patents. Lucent holds thousands of patents on former Bell Lab and AT&T research operations, and analysts feared that the aggressive action by Lucent was threatening to smaller high-tech companies (*Edupage,* June 21, 1998).

Computer-chip giant Intel called a patent infringement action by TechSearch a nuisance lawsuit. The Chicago firm claimed the Pentium II and Pro chips violated a patent on microprocessor architecture. The company was seeking royalties of $180 million, but Intel vowed to fight (*Edupage,* August 4, 1998). As computer technology continues to become more complex and interconnected, patent disputes are likely to proliferate. In general, most patent cases do not have a substantive impact on free expression.

Fair Use

Copyright is limited by so-called fair use rules. The 1976 copyright law allowed the fair use of ideas in the process of scholarship or criticism, news coverage, education, and research. In assessing fair use, a work is evaluated in terms of four factors:

1. whether it is used for purposes that are largely informational or educational,
2. the type of work in question,
3. how much of the material has been used relative to the total amount of the work, and
4. the effect the use of the material would have on the copyright owner's market to sell his or her property.

The Internet makes the fair-use exemption problematic because there are many noncommercial sites run by people who have a lot of time on their hands. These sites do not cost much to operate, and the people running them often have little in the way of money to support them. Consequently, it is unclear how to measure economic harm resulting from such sites. Commercial web sites face an uphill battle in protecting their ownership of media content.

The global nature of the Internet and the multitude of sites that pop up and fade into cyberspace on a daily basis make it very difficult to police the Net. With so-called mirror sites that reflect the content of other sites, a court order to shut down one site will do nothing to eliminate a given content from the Web if that information is posted elsewhere. Fair use of information also involves questions about what is or is not considered educational. Formal rules of law are not adequate when it comes to definitions of content, especially media content.

Commercial Speech

We must consider the degree to which free expression is impacted by the commercial nature of most communication today, particularly in the age of the Internet. Negroponte (1995) made the case that copyright law, based on analog assumptions, must be revamped to take into account the ease and perfection of digital copy-and-paste processes:

> In the digital world it is not just a matter of copying easier. . . . We will see a new kind of fraud, which may not be fraud at all. When I read something on the Internet and, like a clipping from a newspaper, wish to send a copy to somebody else or to a mailing list of people, this seems harmless. But, with less than a dozen keystrokes, I could redeliver that material to literally thousands of people all over the planet (unlike a newspaper clipping). Clipping bits is very different from clipping atoms (p. 59).

One difference is the "free" nature of electronic copying, and as Negroponte pointed out, "even if this changes in the future and some rational economic model is laid on top of the Internet, it may cost a penny or two to distribute a million bits to a million people" (Negroponte, 1995, p. 60). His point suggests that Internet digital distribution will threaten the traditional commercial advertising and direct-mail businesses, both of which, in the analog world, have a cost associated with every delivery. In fact, advertising rates are set on a cost-per-thousand basis.

The definition of intellectual property is further blurred by automated data retrieval, repackaging, and distribution because copyright law does not protect ideas per se. Instead, what is copyrighted in the traditional sense is the form of the free expression. Consequently, it is more difficult to protect electronic expression from alteration and theft (Negroponte, 1995). Further, it can be argued that World Wide Web pages are difficult to protect because the forms are often determined by technological standards and because links to pages are uses in their own right. It might make a difference if a link is a hypertext link or an icon link, and the language used within the hypertext might also be important to the content originator. The Internet norm, however, has been to accept linking as a practice that helps rather than hinders the site being utilized by drawing more hits to it.

Commercial speech is ultimately about making money in the marketplace. Merchants are currently in the business of convincing consumers that it is safe to buy online. Michael Himowitz of the *Baltimore Sun* wrote: "If you're comfortable buying something through a catalog, there's no reason not to buy it online. . . . If you're squeamish about catalogs, using a computer and the Internet won't make you feel any better" (*Baltimore Sun*, December 23, 1998). Although 1998 was a watershed year for increased online shopping, it also was a year that showed that business giants have a long way to go before cyberspace replaces main street. Likewise, governmental intervention into business practices significantly diverted the attention of corporate interests.

The Microsoft Case

Too much success in the digital world can spell trouble, as well. Despite the value inherent in standardizing computer programs to make them work effectively and efficiently, the U.S. Justice Department accused Microsoft of unfairly monopolizing competition by packaging its Internet Explorer with its Windows 95 operating system. It is an open question whether Microsoft's business strategies amounted simply to greed and profiteering or whether the software giant's monopolization could affect free expression throughout the world. Software companies stand to be gatekeepers, of sorts, in the future as push technologies and filtering software make content decisions for users. Microsoft Corporation's chairman and CEO, Bill Gates, was called to Capitol Hill in 1998 to testify, and he was met with a rather cool reception from some members of the Congress. Utah Republican Orrin Hatch chaired the hearing of the Senate Judiciary Committee. Jim Barksdale, president and CEO of Microsoft's chief Internet rival, Netscape Communications, was also there. Other witnesses included Stewart Alsop of New Enterprise Associates, Great Plains Software chairman, president, and CEO Doug Burgum, Dell Computer Corporation chairman and CEO Michael Dell, and Sun Microsystems president and CEO Scott McNealy. Said Senator Hatch in his opening remarks:

Microsoft's breathtaking growth—not just in financial terms, but also in terms of the scope and market power of its business, has for many raised serious questions about the future of competition and innovation in the software industry. One software executive, probably responding in part to bruises he may have received in the marketplace, had said that, quote, "The question of what to do about Microsoft is going to be a central public policy issue for the next 20 years," unquote. Now, whether or not this overstates the matter, many respected industry figures and observers believe that with Microsoft's tremendous success has come such a vast amount of leverage and power over the software industry and the personal computing industry generally, that Microsoft can literally dictate which markets it will control and which it will not (Federal News Service, March 3, 1998).

Vermont Democratic senator Patrick Leahy, in his opening remarks at the hearing, argued that competition may have free expression implications because the United States, in effect, is the creator of the Internet and the computer industry:

There are over 60 million users of the Internet throughout the world. When I am at my home in Vermont, in my office, or if I am vacationing or traveling or anywhere else, I can use a palm-top to get on the Internet, and I can interact with anybody in the world. This morning I had—I got up this morning, I had messages from a friend in Sri Lanka, as well as a child in California. I had—from everywhere. But today we are going to hear from the leader of competing forces in the browser war that has captured so much of our attention. Should we be concerned that even if consumers get the benefit of free browsers in the short term they are going to suffer in the long run? Giving away free browsers does not generate much revenue or financial incentive for additional investment, and for continuing innovation with this critical tool for maximizing use of the Web. In skirmishes like this there can be victims. The Web itself is suffering collateral damage. More and more I've seen popular Web sites that are only accessible using Internet Explorer. The Microsoft gaming zone is a good example. I've also seen many sites that are tagged as being better viewed with Netscape Navigator or with Internet Explorer. In fact, based on a rough search conducted just yesterday, there are 351,957 Web sites enhanced for Internet Explorer. There are 692,491 enhanced for Netscape Navigator—those are approximate numbers.

(Laughter.) Now, these notices have always disturbed me since they amount to—(inaudible)—they can end up stifling the free flow of information. So I want to hear from the leaders of this industry, the best people to speak for the implications of this partitioning of the Internet. And let me say that the Leahy Home Page will resist surrendering as long as it can (Federal News Service, March 3, 1998).

In response to concerns leveled by Congress, Microsoft's Gates said that the Internet is the best example of how freedom has led to business development in an open market:

The rapid adoption of the Internet into our everyday lives is the most exciting example of innovation and the ongoing march of progress in this industry. Overnight my company and many others reinvented themselves in order to meet customer demand. All operating systems, including IBM's, Sun's, Apple's, and many others are including Internet browsing capabilities. Microsoft is in a court battle to test its right, whether we can support these open Internet standards in its Windows system. The beauty of the Internet is its openness. It cannot be controlled or dominated or cut off, because it is simply a constantly changing series of linkages. It is such a creative, living medium that no one yet fully comprehends its opportunities. I am convinced it will be an economic boom to this industry and to our nation (Federal News Service, March 3, 1998).

The United States Department of Justice case against Microsoft, a case that went to trial in late 1998, centered on three main issues:

1. Did Microsoft illegally bundle the Internet Explorer web browser to damage rival Netscape?
2. Did Microsoft use deals with Internet providers such as America Online to further extend its reach?
3. Did Microsoft illegally prevent personal computer manufacturers from customizing their opening screens at boot-up? (*USA Today*, October 16–18, 1998, p. 1-A).

Gates was asked to explain a series of memos obtained from Microsoft's computer system. In one, an executive suggested that refusing to customize Microsoft Office software would be a "perfect club" over Apple to force use of Internet Explorer rather than Netscape. In another memo, Gates asked: "Do we have a clear plan on what we want Apple to do to undermine Sun?"(*USA Today*, October 16–18, 1998, p. 2-A). The antitrust case suggests the power that huge software giants may exercise in a digital world, and it also suggests that even the largest corporations can be victims of their own words in e-mail and the systems used to store those words.

Gates told his shareholders that the Department of Justice was using carefully edited e-mail to unfairly portray him: "The DOJ has misused e-mail snippets to create a false impression" (Associated Press, November 12, 1998). A decision by the U.S. Court of Appeals in the summer of 1998, said Gates, left the government with a weak case against Microsoft's right to bundle its browser with its operating system software.

As the case against Microsoft continued in 1999, U.S. District Judge Thomas Penfield Jackson called the $4.21 billion America Online purchase of Netscape a "significant" development (Associated Press, December 17, 1998). The AOL deal included Sun Microsystems on the business software side, and AOL was poised to control two of the top four web sites in the world (Associated Press, November 24, 1998). Meanwhile, Microsoft appeared to be moving toward a political strategy with an emphasis on lobbying and campaign contributions. Microsoft's Washington office increased its lobbying staff to seven people, and it made contributions to politicians of over $1 million (Associated Press, December 25, 1998).

Following failed negotiations, the U.S. Justice Department sought a detailed financial investigation of Microsoft to determine how the corporate giant could be broken up. Reporters Thor Valdmanis and Paul Davidson said insiders believe they can impose sanctions. Throughout 1999, a complex trial was held, and experts speculated that the case could remain in the courts for years (*USA Today*, July 29, 1999).

Other Business Issues

Because business is now an international, global affair, free-expression issues are complicated by national and international law and social systems. Musicians, for example, have found it difficult to distinguish between "teaching" one another guitar chords via Internet communications and illegally copying sheet music. According to the *Baltimore Sun*, legal threats closed a popular site known as the On-Line Guitar Archive. On the one hand, musicians around the world sought to learn new music free of charge, but the music industry refused to give away its work product without payment (*Evansville Courier Online*, September 7, 1998).

Copyright is also a thorny matter because international distribution systems make copyright laws difficult to enforce. In China, the world's largest market, there are blatant violations of intellectual property law despite a 1995 agreement. A Chinese official said the smugglers of videotapes, software, and other forms of content are like drug dealers:

> The profits are so great, they will take any risk. They're like drug dealers. It is very difficult to arrange a crackdown. You have to coordinate all these different departments, the copyright publication department, the police, the Industrial and Commercial Administration. We take copyright violations very seriously. But when it comes to copying a disk, most Chinese people don't see what's wrong (*Edupage*, March 29, 1998, citing the *New York Times*).

Social norms worldwide seem to promote large-scale illegal copying of software.

The shifting of economic distribution systems has meant that restructuring has been forced because of the Internet. For example, the use of the Internet to make long-distance telephone calls has meant a loss of revenue for long-distance telephone companies. The Federal Communications Commission determined that a system of "reciprocal compensation" from Internet service providers would be needed (Reuters News Service, October 29, 1998). Communication, whether it be over long-distance telephone lines or digital Internet connections, has a cost that must be associated with the construction and maintenance of the infrastructure. Mediated free expression uses technology, and it therefore must be considered within the context of those costs.

Ethical and Social Constraints

The commercial nature of the marketplace of ideas ultimately has the effect of making noncommercial enterprises less valuable. It is assumed in a commercial marketplace that if something has value, then people will pay for it. The same is true of Internet-mediated free expression. The most frequently visited sites are those produced by traditional commercial communicators and vendors.

This condition is a particular concern for most of the world because the United States developed the Internet and the personal computer industry. In a global sense, America has used this leverage to exercise social control over less-developed nations. And even within the United States itself, economically disadvantaged communities seem to be, at best, only along for the ride in the computer age. Even with the diversity of the Internet, the technology favors a power structure featuring few leaders and hordes of followers.

International web piracy will continue to be a problem, particularly in the back alleys of the Internet. For example, HUSKERCASINO is a web site operated from Costa Rica. For a time, the virtual casino-gambling site carried images of former Nebraska football coach Tom Osborne and Cornhusker football helmets. The images were removed after complaints by the university. But the site continued to use the Husker name and offer prizes such as tickets to football bowl games (*Omaha World-Herald*, November 11, 1998, p. 10-B).

Internet gambling was featured on about 140 web sites with $600 million in wagers as the Senate voted 90 to 10 to extend interstate prohibitions to gambling over telephones or wire (*Los Angeles Times*, July 24, 1998). The Justice Department raised questions about the government's ability to prosecute virtual casino operators based legally in other countries (Associated Press, July 23, 1998).

The virtual casinos offer card, roulette, and sports wagering. The Caribbean appeared to be a prime spot for locating the computers—especially since Caribbean governments charge casino operators as much as $100,000 each year for gambling licenses. Internet Lawyer Mark Grossman posed the key question: "If the bettor is in Florida, the computer that's hosting the Internet casino is in Antigua and the message carrying a bet travels through five states and three countries on its way to Antigua, then whose law governs the transaction?" (CNN, December 17, 1997). By the year 2000, it is predicted that online gambling will be a $10 billion industry (*New York Times*, July 27, 1997). The potential for computer-programmed fraud is huge.

There remain many unanswered questions about legal liability on the Internet. One issue is whether copyright law could be extended to web page links. Such lawsuits have failed, so far, but law professor Mark Lemley told the *New York Times* that legal action was dangerous: "It might deter surfing. . . . It might also give some unscrupulous groups the power to suppress speech or critics" (*New York Times*, September 25, 1998).

The commercial aspects of the Internet will be impacted, in part, by the viability of advertising. Former Sun Microsystems engineer Jakob Nielsen told *InfoWorld Electric* that advertisers have not learned to use interactive media and that web banner advertisements often lead to poor sites: "People are learning they can't trust these things. . . . Users are completely ignoring banner ads. Click rates are falling through the floor" (*Edupage*, August 23, 1998). Tracking the users of advertisements and web sites is an important development in the commercialization of the World Wide Web.

Other problems associated with the future development of the Internet as a commercial mass medium include security problems related to applet code that causes PC damage, sex sites that appropriate names and

---

Box 10.2   Dorm Cam Sex Site

New York University filed a lawsuit against an Internet web site that claimed to show female students "romping" in a NYU dorm room. The women wore few clothes. Free images showed women wearing tank tops in a room decorated with NYU logos. The site offered pay viewing and promised "uncensored action." The university said the site damaged its reputation. NYU's John Beckman said, "It's about somebody hijacking our name to make money under false pretenses."

(Source: *Chronicle of Higher Education*, July 31, 1998, p. A-20)

TABLE 10.1 Media "Portals"
Influence the Future of the Internet

Company	Portal	Merger Value

Major U.S. television networks have made deals with Internet gateways, called "portals" because they provide access to the web, as they attempt to dominate the Internet media market as they now dominate broadcasting.

Company	Portal	Merger Value
USA Networks	Lycos	$18 billion
@ Home	Excite	$6.7 billion
Disney/ABC TV	Infoseek/Go	$209 million
NBC TV	Cnet/Snap	$38 million
Fox TV	Yahoo	$15 million
CBS TV	AOL	unknown

SOURCE: Tedesco, 1999

images of legal businesses, the overall worldwide development rates of information technology, the ability of accountants to guarantee the security of computer transactions, and the merger of corporate powers that might hinder entrepreneurs. Online sales have been most successful in certain categories, such as books and music (Media Metrix, December 15, 1998), but it remains to be seen whether shoppers will gravitate to the Web for a wider range of purchases.

The Internet Tax Freedom Act of 1998 was a boost to the development of such online ventures. The Congress approved a three-year moratorium on the imposition of state and local sales taxes for Internet transactions. According to RIAA, the measure gives "Internet-based companies, including record companies doing business online, a boost in efforts to establish online business" (http://www.riaa.com). However, Indiana Republican senator Dan Coats attached provisions to the government's 1998–1999 spending bill that would lift tax breaks for companies found guilty of violating the Child Online Protection Act. In other words, if a company selling adult material failed to screen the ages of web site users, civil and criminal penalties would be augmented with a loss of tax advantages.

Commercial control over free expression has been magnified by the partnership of huge corporate players. (See Table 10.1.)

The free-expression implications of economically based regulation are substantial. At the same time, people with financial empires stand to lose the most if the Internet opens the floodgates to wide-open competition in the marketplace. And it can be argued that the marketplace of ideas is open to "pollution" by many who now inhabit cyberspace. Best-selling author Stephen King, for example, said he was fed up with misinformation spread about him on the web. King and the characters in his horror novels are a popular online topic. So, he has created his own web site (http://www/stephenking.com). He hopes to correct several incorrect rumors—among them, those that say he is retiring and that he offers tours of his house on Halloween (Associated Press, January 5, 1999).

Chapter Summary

This chapter examined the issue of property rights. Internet content is protected by a series of laws, but fair-use rules create loopholes that allow people to use material without compensation to authors or creators. The commercial nature of free expression has an impact on the perceived value of ideas.

Discussion Questions

1. Should music companies have the right to close sites that deal in illegal, pirated music on the Internet?
2. Do copyright laws limit free expression?
3. What would happen if none of the traditional copyright, trademark, and property ownership laws were held to pertain to cyberspace?
4. Does Microsoft's command of the computer marketplace represent a threat to free expression?
5. Do the economic strength of Microsoft's competitors such as Sun, Intel, and Netscape in any way threaten free expression?
6. How does the globalized business marketplace have an impact on the marketplace of ideas?

11

Comparative International Issues

"The first-tier global media giants are using all of these methods to see themselves among those privileged Internet content providers who are being 'pushed' into people's attention and not getting left in obscurity."
  —Edward Herman and Robert McChesney, media scholars (1997)

"There is a significant cultural component to all technological issues, particularly the component of 'self-colonization' or the acceptance of the superiority of Western values and practices."
  —Annabelle Sreberny-Mohammadi, mass media scholar (1997)

The latest settlers have little interest in the cyberstate of nature or the utopian manifestoes of pioneers, like John Perry Barlow's oft-cited "A Declaration of the Independence of Cyberspace," which defied any state's assertion of control over the Internet.
  —New York Times opinion (1998)

"It's like when you start a colony. . . . The first thing you do is you find out where the water is. The next thing you do is form couples, start families. The notion of having law, which is a way to order social interactions, only happens after you have a lot of social interactions such that they become problematic."

  —Mike Godwin, legal thinker (1998)

"It's a chance to think about first-level questions. . . . With nine-tenths of my other cases, the same issue has already been decided. With this, you can say maybe you need to think in a new way about it."

  —Cindy Cohn, lawyer (1998)

"There is a division between the incrementalists and the radicals. To me it makes more sense to think of this as a separate domain of inter-action that's going to have its own rules."
                                                            —**David Post, law professor (1998)**

"If data get interrupted [because of a European privacy law], this isn't just going to harm American companies or the United States. This is going to have an adverse impact on the operation of the economies on both sides of the Atlantic."
                                                            —**David Aaron, U.S. government official (1999)**

The Internet is global, although a handful of nations control its development (Herman and McChesney, 1997), and interest in this technology has risen rapidly: "Perhaps the extent of the boom is magnified in the culture since Internet access is so widespread among journalists, academics, executives, and others of the opinion-making classes" (p. 118). Yet the vast majority of the world and its poor people have no access to the Internet.

The Internet has not yet become a profit center, and competition is fierce for the limited advertising dollars targeted at it. By its nature, the Internet is not tightly controlled by the global mass media giants, but they are the players with money to invest:

> The nature of the Internet is that anyone can produce a website—there is no physical scarcity as in broadcasting—and the costs of launching a traditional publication. . . . What seems probable, then, is a "web within the web," where the media firm websites and some other fortunate content providers are assured recognition and audiences, and the less well-endowed websites drift off to the margins (Herman and McChesney, 1997, pp. 123–124).

For these reasons, Herman and McChesney argued that publishing on the Internet will be most like book or magazine publishing: "Assuming no explicit state censorship, anyone can produce a publication, but the right to do so means little without distribution, resources, and publicity" (Herman and McChesney, 1997, p. 125).

Some groups have attempted to use the Internet as a tool of empowerment. Aliza Sherman and her alter ego, "Cybergrrl" (http://www.cybergrrl.com), proposed that women use the web to gain unfiltered access to each other:

> By building my own web site, I could self-publish on the Internet and make my writing available to anyone anywhere in the world who went online. I didn't have to ask anyone's permission or follow anyone's rules. This was an exciting idea.
>
> In January 1995, I debuted my first website, The Web According to Cybergrrl. Instead of putting a photograph of myself on the site, which many people were doing, I drew a cartoon character instead and called her Cybergrrl. Her name combined "cyber" referring to "cyberspace,"... and "grrl" to represent the "strong version of "girl" or "girl with an attitude," or as I like to say since "girl" sounded too young (Sherman, 1998, p. 8).

What will become of the marginal web sites as corporate powers struggle to control the once wide-open Web? That may well be the critical question. One scenario is that noncommercial or less-commercial sites will be pushed to the margins and remain there for those seeking alternative views. A second scenario is that these sites will wither on the vine. Because competition for advertising has already emerged on the web, it is quite likely that the Internet will parallel radio and TV development in terms of advertiser influence over content (Herman and McChesney, 1997, p. 128).

The marketplace of ideas, from a functionalist point of view, is impacted by the economic marketplace:

> The market economy is guided by supply and demand interacting throughout the market to maintain equilibrium. In a market-based economy, supply and demand interact to make the economy function. The mass media are continually engaged in supply and demand in our country, obtaining resources on a daily basis in order to supply consumers with the media content/products they desire (Albarran, 1996, p. 23).

In the case of the Internet, the marketing approach means that content providers will increasingly search for audiences. Traditionally, media markets have been defined *geographically*—by the 211 television markets in the United States, for example. But cyberspace is defined globally as one huge market, one that could become dominated by traditional publishers of magazines, broadcasters, and cable channel operators.

National Limitations of Law

Although U.S. broadcasters have been regulated throughout their history by the Federal Communications Commission, the global media conglomerate made this obsolete even before the arrival of the Internet. R. G. Picard (1998) has shown how media mergers have been among the largest mergers since the 1980s. The $18.8-billion Disney acquisition of

ABC/Capital Cities television in 1995 ranked as the fifteenth largest merger ever (p. 196). And though the FCC has reviewed the domestic implications of mergers, the Telecommunications Act of 1996 further opened the door to acquisition in the name of an open marketplace.

Beyond the development of an international media marketplace, there is the phenomenon of open cross-border communication. Traditionally, national governments in countries without a history of free expression were able to tightly control the transmission of printed materials by filtering mail. Additionally, they controlled national broadcast systems and resorted to "jamming" international and cross-border signals. But the development of satellite broadcasting, fax telephone technology, and global Internet communication has made it extremely difficult for totalitarian governments to control all mass media content.

International Legal Concerns

To date, international media giants have been free to take their chances with foreign governments as new media markets are developed:

> After it was purchased by Rupert Murdoch's News Corp., the Star TV North satellite broadcast dropped BBC World Television because of complaints by China concerning a documentary the British service had produced about Mao Tse Tung. China was also displeased with BBC coverage of Hong Kong and other issues related to China. The Walt Disney Co. ran into difficulties as well. In 1996 the Chinese government threatened Disney's business operations in China if it released Martin Scorses's film *Kundun* about the life of the Dalai Lama (Picard, 1998, p. 207).

The control of mass media messages in countries is directly related to more obscure policies that attempt to limit free and open communication on the Internet. The fact that corporations such as News Corp. and Disney are major Internet players raises concerns about how international business issues in the broad sense might interfere with communication decisions in the narrow sense.

From a legal perspective, the United Nations and international law are unprepared to deal with the power and reach of the media giants. Their economic strength allows corporations to define the international media market. The size and reach of global media corporations translate into market control and subvert what legal philosophers treat as "the marketplace of ideas." Information is carefully managed and marketed. Robust debate on important issues is discouraged. This competitive advantage already extends to the new technologies, such as the Internet:

As the media and other business giants have invaded, colonized, and commercialized cyberspace, they have found that it is through announcements and advertisements on their already existing channels which reach millions that they can make substantial numbers of people aware of and interested in their websites. Which is another way of saying that existing command of audiences is the means of getting cyberspace audiences—or that money and power outside of the Internet is the basis for power within it (Herman and McChesney, 1997, p. 196).

Because the postindustrialized world commands the most wealth through its media conglomerates, it also dominates the international communication landscape. In this sense, again, it is the power of private corporations rather than the traditional power of governments that reflects the shift under way in the age of the Internet. Both free-expression philosophy and law, however, are more prepared to deal with limiting the government's censorship power than to respond to the manipulated media marketplace.

Cross-Cultural Considerations of Social Constraints

The merging of law and technology is creating stress within the traditional structure of national and international law. Judge Stewart Dalzell, who played a role in overturning the Communications Decency Act, said: "There is anxiety, yes. . . . I know going in that when I started to hear the testimony I went, 'Oh my God! Oh my God! I have to learn about packet switching?' And had we gone down the wrong path, it could have done immense mischief to the medium" (*Minneapolis Star Tribune*, March 22, 1998, p. 7-D).

Just as the technology has altered our culture in general, it is also transforming our notions of law. Law student Brian Dally told a group: "Maybe dividing the world up into real space and cyberspace is artificial. . . . What really came rushing to the fore for me . . . is that this should give us pause to examine some of our basic understandings about the purpose of government and the purpose of law" (*Minneapolis Star Tribune*, March 22, 1998, p. 7-D). If the twenty-six-year-old was correct, then the entire world of law has changed. National boundaries might no longer have meaning in a world where cyberspace and physical space mingle.

Some see the development of international media as a "global struggle for democratic communications," one in which media corporations hold a huge advantage (Herman and McChesney, 1997, p. 197): "The increasing hegemony of the market is especially important today because the digital revolution and convergence are forcing a rethinking of media and communications regulations and policies everywhere" (p. 198). They add: "The global market system has not ushered in a liberal democratic utopia and history is not at an end; quite the reverse, as economic polarization, ethnic strife, and a market-based paralysis of democracy hold forth possibilities of rapid and substantial social, political, and economic upheaval" (p. 205). In China, arrest and trial of political activists continued to revolve around the notion that free expression may "endanger national security," and such speech has led to prison terms of more than ten years (*Los Angeles Times*, December 28, 1998).

In the United States, by contrast, broader freedom to disseminate ideas has led to the use of traditional and nontraditional media to spread the message of hate. Two California businessmen, for example, used their profits from the computer industry to mail anti-Semitic posters and videos to 3,000 homes. Vincent Bertollini and Carl Story, according to the Associated Press in Idaho, used "quasi-biblical prose" to attack Jews and nonwhites (Associated Press, December 27, 1998). Messages of hate are disseminated through a worldwide network, and the Internet has made distribution simple and easy.

What, then, are the implications for the meaning of free expression in such an age? First, if the Internet becomes a tool of special interests through which everyone has an online group, then it could further promote a kind of narrowly based speech that fragments society. If media giants control mass-mediated messages, then free speech is destined to be filtered through gatekeepers who do not value the speech for its own sake. The profit orientation of such gatekeepers will certainly affect the social construction of the reality produced, the framing of ideas, and the meaning-making attached to such symbolic exercises.

Grassroots communication offers one alternative to the dominant model. But small-scale efforts seem to pale in the shadows of the mammoth media conglomerates. The free communication market is so tied to the free economic market and its consumer-focused goals that global democratic communication must fit the commercial model if it is to have any hope of being carried by mass communication systems.

So, the important issue is whether those who dominate the Internet and what follows can resist the economic temptation to become just another mass media form. The economic rewards suggest they may not.

There is one hopeful possibility in all of this—the fact that cyberspace will become the place where traditional cultures are preserved and maintained as physical space becomes increasingly valuable and exploited by shopping mall, theme park, and subdivision developers. Because the cost of cyberspace "land" is cheap, it is the one place where those without much economic wealth can "develop" alternative places from which to send a message different from that delivered by the consumer-driven global market economy. It is not clear how those in charge of the market economy might react to thwart such efforts. It is also not clear how such "virtual real estate" might be devalued or valued, depending on the interests at stake. Just as inner-city land may be first devalued and then repurchased by developers at bargain prices in the interests of growth, so, too, might cyberspace be open to speculation by investors.

The "electronic colonialism" metaphor is a powerful one because it addresses what so much of the communication technology literature does not—social control. Questions of social class and power must be considered: "Class power remains a central element in the political economy of communication, even if it gives up the essentialist view that would make it the position to which all others can be reduced" (Mosco, 1996, p. 271). Consequently, future examinations must not ignore the working class and the struggle of laborers in the technology age. Space, including cyberspace, can be seen as an extension of institutional power, namely, that which flows from corporate organizations:

One would also contribute to the mythology of globalization by suggesting that this is a fundamentally new process. The mythology grows out of a deeper resistance, beyond the level of surface acceptance, to the view that space, and not just time, is dynamic, that what we map, whether physical or political space, or the space of human communication flows, is constantly changing (Mosco, 1996, p. 206).

As problematic as it may be, we need to attempt to apply a human rights perspective to world communication. We need to consider the ordering of the world: "A world communication politics that would be guided by a human rights perspective would require—as a cornerstone—a robust multilateral accord on the right to communicate" (Hamelink, 1994, p. 313). But the information technology "revolution" has yet to harness the grassroots power of individuals to affect international concerns: "This means that ordinary people will have to intervene in world affairs, which are typically perceived as an arena outside citizens' intervention and not in need of democratic control. This means that people have to confront the common fear that they would really mess up if they were allowed to run the world" (pp. 313–314).

Communication and information are "strategic resources" in the battle over world order, but traditionally this has been the business of diplomats and functioned as an alternative to brute strength: "There is yet no evidence that they have been able to completely transform world order. The power of communication and the power of information can be harnessed and used, through cultural diplomacy and other means, to manage short-term crises. . . . But there is no indication that they can completely change world order" (Alleyne, 1995, p. 169).

New information technologies that cross borders so seamlessly threaten traditional international law perspectives on issues of "sovereignty" and "national law." But they do so only within the narrow legal sense. The European Union Data Protection Directive, for example, bars export of data without prior permission from the individual and his or her country. Europeans have argued that the United States has inadequate safeguards to protect individual privacy, but U.S. commerce officials worry that privacy laws will restrict international business and marketing (Associated Press, January 23, 1999). At the same time, there are international concerns over the worldwide distribution of child pornography. The patchwork of national law and the lack of international law make it possible for child pornographers to exploit children by creating kiddie porn in developing countries.

The FreeBurma.org site is a good example of how the Internet can be used to challenge an existing government. In 1998, visitors to the site were told: "Tension in Burma is rising during the observance of the 10-year anniversary of the death of 1000s of unarmed civilians at the hand of the military in August 1988" (http://www.FreeBurma.org, August 1998). The site featured live chat, U.S. government communication on the topic through the Voice of America, and newsgroups hosted in the United States.

Box 11.1   International Concerns About Online Pornography

Participants from forty countries gathered in Paris in early 1999 for a United Nations conference aimed at combating child pornography on the Internet. French lawyer Daniel Kahn told the Associated Press that the problem with international law is that it is possible for porn to be created in countries where it is legal to do so, but the content may be distributed worldwide via the Internet. He said in India and Nepal, children are being exploited on screen. The United Nations Educational, Scientific and Cultural Organization (UNESCO) sponsored the meeting to try to educate people about the problem. The international police organization INTERPOL is unable to estimate the number of web sites using child porn. In the United States alone, INTERPOL's Agnes Fournier-Saint Maur said, "We confiscated 500,000 photos showing sexual acts involving minors."

(Source: Associated Press, January 14, 1999)

Box 11.2 A Cyber Rebel

Htun Aung Gyaw is using the Internet, funded by the salary he receives as a Cornell University librarian, to battle the military regime in Burma from his apartment in Ithaca, New York. The forty-four-year-old has been doing this for thirteen of the twenty-three years that the government has held power. He has developed a web site and a mailing list of concerned people who read about the daily challenges to the military regime

He says he organizes Internet conferences: "We have a chat room where we meet and discuss strategy" (Parade, August 23, 1998, p. 12).

The government calls the country Myanmar, which means "the Golden-land." On its home page, it promotes tourism, business opportunities, culture, and media.

At the social level, the power of the economic market forges ahead, as the wares of capitalism are sold. Freedom becomes defined as much by the products consumers can lay their hands on as by anything else. The power to act democratically—to participate in politics, to speak freely, and to exercise a full range of human rights—is lost in a cultural sea of entertainment-oriented information. We float adrift eating *our* hamburgers, watching *our* videos, and surfing web sites in search of an emotional charge.

The Internet, then, contributes to sending the cultural message of mass ignorance abroad. It allows people to complain, for example, about the poor quality of television programming without ever attaching that complaint to the people in the corporate boardroom who should be responsible. It is as if the board of directors does not exist. Rather, what exists in *our* minds is the branding of a network icon. On the web, we see the imagery of the faceless media giants, and we fail to grasp that there are powerful people who do exercise social control over us.

The recent online chats with celebrities, known faces to the public, help ensure that our attention is focused away from those who hold real economic power. In the end, such wealth translates to political and social power—and accountability only to stockholders and other leaders. Thus, the global manipulation of events is advanced rather than hindered by the new communication technologies.

On the one hand, we see the Internet as the place where "homesteaders" organize "neighborhoods" on such sites as the GeoCities.com and Tripod.com; theglobe.com even offers the town *square (Hartford [Connecticut] Courant*, September 14, 1998). On the other hand, the Internet can be seen as the economic hub for a huge concentration of personal wealth.

Steve Case, the CEO of America Online, had his riches grow to more than $137 million (*Time*, September 22, 1997, p. 49), but his wealth pales in comparison to that of the major players.

The list of major players in computing continues to be dominated by white, American males. But the larger media environment shows some signs of diversity, including, among others: Oprah Winfrey, the media mogul worth hundreds of millions; Microsoft's Patti Stonesifer, who headed the company's Interactive Media Division; and Jerry Yang, who cofounded Yahoo! and made a quick $191 million.

At the opposite extreme are the individuals with little means who seek to compete in the marketplace of ideas. In once sense, the Internet has enabled them to do this. However, the distribution of messages continues to be limited by the market-driven nature of media space, which tends to favor commercial interests over public-interest obligations.

At the global level, governments continue to do the best they can to stop unwanted messages. In China, for example, the Starr Report of the President Clinton–Monica Lewinsky affair was censored, just as the government restricts "soft porn and subversive novels" (Associated Press, October 6, 1998). And a thirty-year-old software manager was arrested on charges of "inciting the overthrow of state power" for providing 30,000 e-mail addresses to a U.S. magazine (Associated Press, July 29, 1998).

The battle for free expression in cyberspace has become a matter of citizen activism (Hill and Hughs, 1998). As author Kevin Hill told amazon.com:

Box 11.3   Computer-Related Wealth

The top 10 richest people in technology are

1. Bill Gates, Microsoft	$38.66 billion
2. Paul Allen, Microsoft	14.77 billion
3. Steve Ballmer, Microsoft	8.21 billion
4. Larry Ellison, Oracle	8.20 billion
5. Gordon Moore, Intel	7.97 billion
6. Michael Dell, Dell	4.66 billion
7. William Hewlett, Hewlett-Packard	4.20 billion
8. Ted Waitt, Gateway	2.83 billion
9. David Duffield, PeopleSoft	1.73 billion
10. Charles Wang, Computer Assoc.	1.20 billion

(Source: *Forbes*, October 6, 1997)

We find that even though Internet users who engage in politics on the Net are more liberal, educated, and male than the public at large, the CONTENT of political Usenet groups, Web sites, and AOL chat rooms is overwhelmingly conservative. . . . We also find that conservative and even right-wing extremist Web pages are far more high profile and sophisticated than their left-wing and liberal counterparts (khill@fiu.edu, as posted on http://www.amazon.com).

John Perry Barlow has called for a "cyberspace declaration of independence" that would advocate freedom from sovereignty in global space.

The utopian message of A Declaration of the Independence of Cyberspace seems to acknowledge that humans must reside in the physical world of their bodies, even as it appears to urge separation of mind and body. The rhetoric of the treatise fails to deal with the physical nature of the hardware and connections that currently link us to cyberspace. Not only our bodies exist in the physical world; so, too, do our computers. Without electric power and processors and network hubs, we are disconnected from cyberspace. Further, as has been shown throughout this book, the social nature of communication challenges the view that "we are creating a world where anyone, anywhere may express his or her beliefs, no matter how singular, without fear of being coerced into silence or conformity," as Barlow contended. In contrast, the social world demands fear, silence, and conformity—whether or not the communication is mediated through computers, and the physical world demands payment for food and other life resources. Therefore, cyberspace cannot detach itself from political and economic realities.

What is certain, however, is that cyberspace is a global communication network that will inevitably alter social, political, and economic relationships. Therefore, it is fair to say that power will shift and be altered by the technological nature of evolving free expression. Iraqi officials, for example, worried about offering e-mail access in government offices. They wanted a way to be sure that workers would not be "affected by negative Western thoughts." An Iraqi government newspaper has said that the Internet is "the end of civilizations, cultures, interests and ethics" (Associated Press, February 4, 1999).

To this point, an upscale, educated population mainly interested in research, e-mail, and news has inhabited cyberspace. But, as the history of the written word has shown, "writing was invented for the exploitation of man by man" (Crowley and Heyer, 1999, p. 21) and standardization through printing and other means has led to judgments about "correctness" (p. 104). The processing of digital information is leading to an era where types of information are blurred: "In this way digitalization promises to transform currently diverse forms of information into a generalized medium for processing and exchange by the social system, much

Box 11.4   A Declaration of the Independence of Cyberspace

Governments of the Industrial World, you weary giants of flesh and steel, I come from Cyberspace, the new home of the Mind. On behalf of the future, I ask you of the past to leave us alone. You are not welcome among us. You have no sovereignty where we gather.

◆ ◆ ◆

We have no elected government, nor are we likely to have one, so I address you with no greater authority than that with which liberty itself always speaks. I declare the global social space we are building to be naturally independent of the tyrannies you seek to impose on us. You have no moral right to rule us nor do you possess any methods of enforcement we have true reason to fear. Governments derive their just powers from the consent of the governed. You have neither solicited nor received ours. We did not invite you. You do not know us, nor do you know our world. Cyberspace does not lie within your borders. Do not think that you can build it, as though it were a public construction project. You cannot. It is an act of nature and it grows itself through our collective actions.

◆ ◆ ◆

You have not engaged in our great and gathering conversation, nor did you create the wealth of our marketplaces. You do not know our culture, our ethics, or the unwritten codes that already provide our society more order than could be obtained by any of your impositions.

◆ ◆ ◆

You claim there are problems among us that you need to solve. You use this claim as an excuse to invade our precincts. Many of these problems don't exist. Where there are real conflicts, where there are real wrongs, we will identify them and address them by our means. We are forming a new Social Contract. This governance will arise according to the conditions of our world, not yours. Our world is different.

◆ ◆ ◆

Cyberspace consists of transactions, relationships, and thought itself, arrayed like a standing wave in the web of our communications. Ours is a world that is both everywhere and nowhere, but it is not where bodies live.

◆ ◆ ◆

We are creating a world that all may enter without privilege or prejudice accorded by race, economic power, military force, or station of birth.

◆ ◆ ◆

We are creating a world where anyone, anywhere may express his or her beliefs, no matter how singular, without fear of being coerced into silence or conformity.

◆ ◆ ◆

Your legal concepts of property, expression, identity, movement, and context do not apply to us. They are based on matter. There is no matter here.

◆ ◆ ◆

Our identities have no bodies, so, unlike you, we cannot obtain order by physical coercion. We believe that from ethics, enlightened self-interest, and the commonweal, our governance will emerge. Our identities may be distributed across many of your jurisdictions. The only law that all our constituent cultures would generally recognize is the Golden Rule. We hope we will be able to build our particular solutions on that basis. But we cannot accept the solutions you are attempting to impose.

◆ ◆ ◆

In the United States, you have today created a law, the Telecommunications Reform Act, which repudiates your own Constitution and insults the dreams of Jefferson, Washington, Mill, Madison, DeToqueville, and Brandeis. These dreams must now be born anew in us.

◆ ◆ ◆

You are terrified of your own children, since they are natives in a world where you will always be immigrants. Because you fear them, you entrust your bureaucracies with the parental responsibilities you are too cowardly to confront yourselves. In our world, all the sentiments and expressions of humanity, from the debasing to the angelic, are parts of a seamless whole, the global conversation of bits. We cannot separate the air that chokes from the air upon which wings beat.

◆ ◆ ◆

In China, Germany, France, Russia, Singapore, Italy and the United States, you are trying to ward off the virus of liberty by erecting guard posts at the frontiers of Cyberspace. These may keep out the contagion for a small time, but they will not work in a world that will soon be blanketed in bit-bearing media.

◆ ◆ ◆

Your increasingly obsolete information industries would perpetuate themselves by proposing laws, in America and elsewhere, that claim to own speech itself throughout the world. These laws would declare ideas to be another industrial product, no more noble than pig iron. In our world, whatever the human mind may create can be reproduced and distributed infinitely at no cost. The global conveyance of thought no longer requires your factories to accomplish.

◆ ◆ ◆

These increasingly hostile and colonial measures place us in the same position as those previous lovers of freedom and self-determination who had to reject the authorities of distant, uninformed powers. We must declare our virtual selves immune to your sovereignty, even as we continue to consent to your rule over our bodies. We will spread ourselves across the Planet so that no one can arrest our thoughts.

◆   ◆   ◆

We will create a civilization of the Mind in Cyberspace. May it be more humane and fair than the world your governments have made before.

(Source: John Perry Barlow, barlow@ eff.org, Davos, Switzerland, February 8, 1996, available at http://hobbes. ncsa.uiuc.edu/sean/declaration.html. Barlow cofounded the Electronic Frontier Foundation, and he writes for *Wired* magazine.)

---

as, centuries ago, the institution of common currencies and exchange rates began to transform local markets into a single world economy" (p. 314).

The generalization of communication coincides with the specialization or narrowcasting or targeting of ideas to interest groups. The danger is what Benjamin Barber has called "a Tower of Babel: a hundred chattering mouths bereft of any common language" (Hiebert, 1999, p. 429). There seems to be a contradiction on this point as we seek direction from the cyberspace culture.

Cyberwar is another international issue. The *Washington Post* has reported that U.S. military authorities are studying attack and defense strategies designed to deal with enemy computer networks. Computer viruses named "logic bombs" create enormous warfare scenarios, such as the feeding of false information about enemy positions, the morphing of foreign television broadcast video images, and the shutting down of telephone and other utility services (*Washington Post,* July 16, 1998). In Yugoslavia, for example, Serbian computer hackers led by someone named "Black Hand," according to a Belgrade newspaper, attacked anti-Serb web sites, such as the Albanian and NATO pages. "We shall continue to remove Albanian lies from the Internet," a caller to the newspaper *Blic* said in claiming responsibility (*Omaha World-Herald,* October 23, 1998, p. 4). The cyber rebels at war with ethnic Albanians in Kosovo also made reference to a group of Serbian officers known collectively as Black Hand a century ago who planned a coup and were believed to have executed a crown prince. In the recent fighting, both Albanians and the Serbian government utilized the Internet to plead their cases to a worldwide audience.

Cybercrimes and cyber terrorism are national security problems according to the Center for Strategic and International Studies. The Global Organized Crime Project, headed by former FBI and CIA head William

Webster, demonstrated the ability of hackers to disable most of the U.S. power grid. Governments, to this point, have tried to grapple with the implications of the information age on national security issues. Historically, attempts to protect national security have come at the expense of free-expression rights. To "protect" computer systems in the future, governments might require that the Internet be less anonymous and that access be more limited to "safe" users.

Still, the most immediate dangers to open use of the Internet come from attempts to regulate the previously discussed cyberporn or content that challenges the authority of official governments. In Germany, for example, the conviction of a former CompuServe manager, Felix Somm, for allowing pornography to be distributed on his network produced a chilling effect on free speech. "There's a significant precedent being set here," said Jerry Berman, executive director of the Center for Democracy and Technology. "It is a great setback for a decentralized, open communications medium" (Reuters, May 29, 1998).

Most of the undeveloped or underdeveloped world has not yet connected to cyberspace. For people in these areas, the gap between the first and third worlds must seem to be widening further. And even in developing Singapore, attempts to be the world's first entirely wired nation have not progressed as quickly as expected. Only about 1 percent of the island's computer-literate population was using Singapore One in 1998, "One Network for Everyone," despite $86 million in government and $114 million in private-sector expenditures. The cheaper traditional Internet access has been more popular than the fiber-optic multimedia cable network because of cost and availability of content (Associated Press, September 24, 1998). Still, computer-software development, thousands of computer-related jobs, and the associated tax revenues have resulted from the growth in such nations as China, where software piracy is said to be rampant. The creation of computer and Internet industries occurs side by side with the use of the technology for freedom of expression. University students using computer bulletin boards to call for political demonstrations in the 1990s led the government to crack down on free speech. And though Chinese press censors banned Chinese-language versions of the Starr Report, the search engine Sohoo recorded thousands of hits a day to its Clinton sex scandal site (Associated Press, October 8, 1998).

Free-speech efforts must become global in the age of the Internet. However, global efforts to establish standardized rules over such matters as what constitutes privacy have failed. The computer technology has interconnected chunks of the globe, but we appear to have neither the social nor the legal means to be prepared for the consequences of the development.

Chapter Summary

This chapter explored the implications of global communities in cyber-space. Some have called for the development of a new, idealistic world in cyberspace, while others acknowledge its presence in the physical world. It has been noted that the global nature of cyberspace will alter the social, political, and economic world, but no one can predict what the effects will be.

Discussion Questions

1. What are the strengths and weaknesses of A Declaration of the Independence of Cyberspace? Is cyberspace truly different from the physical world?
2. How are global media giants pushing themselves and their products on the international community? What are the implications of this in terms of political power?
3. Is it correct to think of the proliferation of media around the globe as electronic colonialism? Why or why not?
4. Is the globalization of communication through the Internet likely to produce more or less freedom of expression?
5. How will countries be able to square differing standards for such content as sexually indecent material in an age in which there are no borders?
6. Will the globalization of communication widen or narrow the gaps between rich and poor?

12

Toward Thinking About Free Expression in a Digital Age

"Freedom of the press is guaranteed only to those who own one."
—A. J. Liebling, journalist (1960)

"New technology has replaced scarcity with abundance and cartels with competition."
—Peter Huber, cyberspace lawyer (1997)

"When the rich, the influential and the powerful all wrap themselves in the First Amendment, it's time to wonder what that amendment is really supposed to protect these days—speech or profits."
—Lawrence Grossman, former network news president (1997)

"By operating e-mail systems, does the university become responsible for what gets posted there? We'd rather you speak good ideas so everyone is happy?"
—Peter Burke, attorney (1998)

"Computers continue to get faster, cheaper and smaller, and they're beginning to morph into new forms designed to meet specific needs."
—Bill Gates, software CEO (1998)

"The so-called 'new media'. . . have yet to find a clear definition or task. . . . The shape of political communication in an information society is still very hazy."
—Denis McQuail, Doris Graber, and Pippa Norris, media scholars (1998)

"There is substantially less freedom of speech in America today than there was at the time of the founding."
                                              —**Thomas G. West, legal philosopher (1998)**

"The very success of corporate globalism in subjugating everyone to its agenda has created the potential for a massive counter-movement, a peaceful democratic counter-revolution on a global scale."
                                              —**Manifesto for a Democratic Renaissance,**
                                                           Internet treatise (1998)

"As a society, as a country, as a national family, we don't have to put up with this kind of abuse, and we will not."
                                              —**Al Gore, U.S. vice president (1999)**

The Internet is a metaphor for both our optimism and our pessimism about the future of free expression in an electronic age. In part, this is because the notion of an information superhighway is symbolic of our search for identity through time and space, having to do with "transportation, communication, storage" in a global sense (Jones, 1997, p. 5). On the one hand, we have access and possibilities—cyberspace seems a place where anything is possible. On the other hand, traditional thinking about power and the control of speech by dominant power brokers remains a prevalent theme. As James Carey (1992) has noted, the conceptualization of communication as printing press or mode of transport contradicts the ancient notion of speech. The transmission view is too linear, and it fails to see communication as vital—that is, as complex, symbolic, and carrying with it political significance. "The contradiction is symbolized, though hardly resolved, by the uneasy juxtaposition of assembly, speech, and the press in the First Amendment" (p. 6). The Internet, by further blurring the distinction between vocal speech and publishing, may dismantle the meaning of free expression by creating a nongeographic environment where no rules can be applied.

The Internet is seen as a means to nostalgically "re-create community" and "overcome time and space" problems (Jones, 1997, p. 9). The assumption is that it is possible to produce online communities of interest and to sustain them through regular communication. Thus, even though we might be a fragmented culture, *within* our groups there is potential for understanding and empathy. Jones treated the Internet not as cyberspace but as "a discontinuous narrative space" (p. 15). When applied to law and regulation, the temptation to apply offline, geographically based controls leads to conceptual difficulties:

Box 12.1   Utopia or Apocalypse?

At a 1998 conference, "Technological visions: Utopian and dysutopian perspectives," the University of Southern California's Annenberg Center for Communication hosted a discussion about the future of the technological age. Media scholar Sandra Ball-Rokeach argued that the current debate about technology swings between extreme visions of utopia and disaster: "The current debate is flawed, and what's flawed is the ahistorical debate we're having." MIT Sociologist Sherry Turkle, author of *Life on the Screen: Identity in the Age of the Internet* (1995), said the Internet and the computer should not be spelled with capital letters: "If I asked you, 'What was the sociological impact of Conversation?'—with a capital C— you might say that some conversation is toxic and some is benign." Panelists called for more research to better understand the Internet. The cybercast of the conference can be seen at http://www.metamorph.org.

(Source: Lisa Guernsey, "Scholars at Meeting Debunk Technology's Potential to Foster Utopia—or Apocalypse," *Chronicle of Higher Education*, November 20, 1998, p. A-23)

Is the Internet subject to rules and regulations and, if so, what is the domain of jurisdiction *vis-à-vis* the Internet's lack of geographic existence? If it is a community, or a set of communities, what are its power structures and how are they articulated to ones offline? Or is it a communications medium, equally subject to rules and regulations as other media of mass communication? (Jones, 1997, p. 19).

There is a temptation to believe that our world has been altered dramatically by the Internet. In fundamental ways, however, the struggle over free expression is grounded in history. British sociologist Harriet Martineau, who had traveled the United States for two years, wrote *Society in America* (1837), in which she noted: "It is hard to tell which is worse; the wide diffusion of things that are not true, or the suppression of things that are true (http://www.runet.edu)." We live an era in which the Internet assists in the diffusion of ideas even as it allows individuals and corporations to manipulate and control information bits. The central marketplace of ideas issue is whether the massive dumping of ideas into a computer memory, interlinked worldwide, can actually produce conditions that are any more favorable to democratic communication. Jones (1997) apparently doubted this: "Perhaps it is the case that the Internet allows us to shout more loudly, but whether our fellow citizens listen, beyond the few individuals who may reply, or the occasional lurker, is questionable, and whether our words will make a difference is even more in doubt" (p. 30). The Internet is seen as interconnected with the offline world, associated with limitations on free expression.

Legal scholar Thomas West made what, at first, seems a startling proposition: "Against today's conventional wisdom, I will demonstrate that there is substantially *less* freedom of speech than at the time of the founding; and that today's liberalism, far from favoring expansion of free speech (as many commonly believed), is hostile to free speech" (West, 1998, p. 157). West also argued that we have flipped the intent of the Founders: "They protected liberty but not licentiousness. We protect licentiousness but not liberty" (pp. 157–158). He contended that government today routinely violates the prior-restraint doctrine, often punishes or prohibits speech not proven injurious in court, and avoids the role of juries. He cited federal election law, labor and harassment law, and broadcast licensing as examples. And the decline of libel law, he argued, does not favor liberty: "Publishers have broad latitude in malicious and inaccurate attacks on the reputations of public officials and private citizens. This is certainly an expansion of what is permitted. But is it an increase of freedom? The Founders did not believe a person's right to freedom went beyond its noninjurious use" (p. 173).

West also made the case that freedom of speech is not infringed in a libel punishment when the reputation of an innocent person is harmed. Such an economic approach to free speech holds that private control of wealth and resources, not government control, is the only way to protect liberty. From this perspective, the critical question might be: How do we privatize cyberspace? West failed to recognize critical perspectives that show private power to be no less offensive than government power when it comes to the social control of individuals. If, as J. Fernback contended, "virtual space is socially constructed and re-constructed space" (Fernback, in Jones, 1997, p. 37), it is "an arena of power" and one that cannot be divorced from geography: "Cyberspace is essentially a reconceived public sphere for social, political, economic and cultural interaction" (p. 37). There are *boundaries* in cyberspace because we use social and cultural rules to construct them. The rhetoric of law and regulation serves to formalize otherwise chaotic conditions in the computer-mediated communication environment:

> Questions of access to CMC technology by those other than the technological elite as well as questions of censorship, libel, copyright infringement, and other legal quandries still plague the development of cyberspace. Nonetheless, the ideals of openness, freedom, and tolerance pervade the collective consciousness of the community of CMC users. . . . The development of First Amendment law as applied to cyberspace is much more precarious than imagined (Fernback, in Jones, 1997, pp. 47–48).

The value of freedom, it would seem, must be tempered by problems associated with the unequal distribution of power, wealth, and resources—problems that create conditions favorable for the exploitation of the disadvantaged. Harris Breslow isolated a central economic concern that will challenge the marketplace of ideas by exposing "the guise of the free market" and the myth of rationality: "In the marketplace, it is often argued, the mechanism by which people remain civil with one another is the invisible hand, the rationalized relationships of supply, demand, and price which govern the actions of those engaged in economic activities within a framework of reasonable conduct" (Breslow, in Jones, 1997, p. 239). The Internet, then, serves the interests of multinational corporations and their vertical and horizontal integration by providing the needed communication infrastructure: "Thus industrial corporations of scale have the ability to dictate the terms required of their continued economic presence" (p. 251).

Such technology giants as Microsoft wield private control. By dominating the marketplace, a select group of software corporations are able to manipulate pricing. The Associated Press has reported that technology managers at large U.S. companies have complained that Microsoft is using tighter contract language to raise prices and profits. Some prices were rising as much as 50 percent each year, and these increases were expected to continue for the next few years (Associated Press, November 15, 1998). To ignore corporate power as irrelevant to free expression is to miss the point: Power is in the hands of those who control communication technologies. The rest of us must communicate within the structural boundaries of software and hardware.

Our legal structure, however, has ignored the issue of control by defining free speech around the largely mythical narrative of the "street corner speaker"—a rhetorical device that has little real meaning but has been exported to the presumed power of the Internet: "An individual mounts a soapbox on a corner in some large city, starts to criticize governmental policy, and then is arrested for breach of the peace. In this setting the First Amendment is conceived of as a shield, as a means of protecting the individual speaker from becoming silenced by the state" (Fiss, 1996, p. 12).

If an individual were to shout from the tallest soapbox today, the more likely reaction would be to ignore the poor fool, unless the local television station arrived on the scene to go "live at five." And then the story angle would have nothing to do with the content of his or her speech. The irrelevance of much that is called "government" to real power begs the question: What would happen to our soapbox speaker if she or he were at the gates of the town's main employer—a company that was a big polluter—just as a shift change was taking place? How would the company and its well-paid workers react to an "in your face" environmental attack on their pocketbooks? How would free speech rules shield our speaker from community reaction?

Some contend that the state is responsible only for providing a forum for meaningful democratic debate on controversial public issues: "The person on the soapbox should be given a *real* chance to speak" (Fiss, 1996, p. 21). Perhaps the Internet, then, is a public forum not unlike the modern shopping mall—a place where some have said speaker and owner rights must be balanced: "To assess the validity of the state intervention the reviewing court must ask, directly and unequivocally, whether the intervention in fact enriches rather than impoverishes public debate" (p. 26). The marketplace in which ideas reside favors select groups of *consumers* and markets to them, rather than providing "the kind of debate that constantly renews the capacity of a people for self-determination" (p. 40).

The Internet, however, has been a catalyst for bringing together like minds for the purposes of good and evil. Research conducted by the Southern Poverty Law Center (SPLC) has revealed that white supremacists and hate groups are using the Internet to recruit members. In its 1998 Intelligence Report, the nonprofit organization charted a 13 percent increase in the number of organized hate groups in the United States—up from 474 in 1997 to 537 at the end of 1998. "The Internet has, in a sense, empowered the white supremacy community. . . . Very often, a 'hater' was an isolated person, standing in their living room and shaking their fist in the sky," researcher Mark Potok told the Associated Press. "That same person, instead of feeling like an isolated retrograde, wakes up in the morning, turns on the computer and he's got 25 messages. . . . He feels like he is part of a movement that is happening" (Associated Press, February 25, 1999). "On the Internet, hate sites rose from 163 in 1997 to 254 last year, reflecting an alarming increase in racist propaganda," the SPLC wrote on its web site (http://www.splcenter.org).

It is clear that the marketplace is open to control and manipulation from a variety of broad cultural forces. Consider what happened at Princeton University. One day in 1998, the school's home page featured pictures of flying saucers and screaming professors, which led many people, including those at the student newspaper, to suspect hackers had vandalized the site. In reality, "the manager of the university's home page had added new images to a rotating set of postcard-like views that users see when they load the page" (*Chronicle of Higher Education*, March 13, 1998, p. A-31). What looked like an alien spacecraft was actually an experimental vehicle that once had been displayed at Princeton, and the screaming professor was Harold Dodds, a humorous university president who served from 1933 to 1957. Campus officials quickly moved to replace the images with traditional scenes. Said one university official, "If pictures look like the work of hackers, we should remove them" (p. A-31).

The incident highlights the fact that what is acceptable public-relations imagery really falls within a narrow band defined by our corporate-dominated culture. The "professional" look of web pages serves as a normative model defined by corporate rules and web authoring software rather than the earlier freewheeling code that was written without any assumptions.

Perhaps the response of the Princeton officials was related to the sensitivity that exists over the problems raised by computer hackers. One hacking incident in 1998 affected computers at twenty-five U.S. universities. The hacker-transmitted virus, which affected Microsoft Windows 95 and NT machines, led to "the blue screen of death" at lab computers used during a four-hour period on March 2. The damage was temporary because machines could be rebooted, but unsaved data were lost (*Chronicle of Higher Education*, March 13, 1998, p. A-33). Hacking has been demonized by the corporate world in television advertisements and news stories as a narrative of lawlessness. And because it involves breaking into another person's files, hacking has been normatively placed outside the boundaries of law.

Corporate America is particularly concerned about Internet security. Despite increased funding for security in businesses across the country, a survey of Fortune 1000 firms, conducted by the Computer Security Institute and the FBI, found that 1997 computer crime losses were in excess of $136 million—a 36 percent jump over the previous year (*Internet Week*, March 23, 1998). The fear is that a lot of the crime goes undetected and that computer "crackers" with only limited skills may steal huge sums of money. Such computer crime is likely to lead to more attempts by the business community to erect what essentially are police roadblocks or checkpoints in cyberspace. The control of "movement" in cyberspace is clearly restrictive in terms of freedom, but it is justified through law that applies a geographically based model. In effect, residents of cyberspace are not free to trespass on the property of others. As a practical matter, computer users may face more regular denial of service in the future because of traffic jams on the information highway or because the Internet itself is experiencing the evolutionary change of commercialization. Increasingly, there will be many tollbooths where access once was free.

One of the up-and-coming phenomena on the Web is the advent of so-called Internet broadcasting. AudioNet is a service that uses the Internet bandwidth to carry "continuous live programming from more than 260 radio stations around the world" (Associated Press, March 16, 1998); the Timecast network offers 500 radio stations and video services. The change has come because of Progressive Network's Real Player, which allows computer users to receive real-time audio and video on conventional computers hooked to the Net with just a telephone modem. Microsoft, meantime, has its Media Player program, which also allows for Internet rebroadcasts of radio signals. Likewise, long-distance telephone services now promise to exploit the Internet. Federal regulators have considered rules to charge Internet service providers and thereby level the playing field.

Commercial standards on the Internet also are emerging from dominant mass media providers—CNN, MSNBC, *Time*, the *Washington Post*, and so forth. These news services, as well as entertainment sites such as Disney, Nickelodeon, and the Cartoon Network, come to define what World Wide Web pages should look like in order to be taken seriously by the general public. The standards may involve professional production techniques that require large budgets and specialized training—in other words, the same access issues that were identified in the 1960s and limited the ability of the public to influence television.

Although some scholars argue that "the Internet will transform broadcasting into narrowcasting" (Neuman, 1998, p. 238), it also is possible that the web will transform the new forms of *narrowcasted* information into mass-oriented broadcasting. Without a mass audience, some of the original euphoria over Internet communication may falter, and many of the nontraditional services may die on the vine. As we seek to re-create a sense of community, it is clear that new technologies have a limited capacity to be a catalyst for social change. In Lynch, Nebraska, a town of just 296 people, for example, the movie theater is once again a favorite spot on Friday and Saturday nights. "It's a revival based not on new-found prosperity, but old-fashioned community," wrote the *Omaha World-Herald* (February 28, 1999, p. 1-A). But why would half the town fill a movie theater? It just may be that small-town America has learned that the movie theater offers a needed common experience: "To share that look with friends and neighbors after you've seen a good movie was important to the sense of community," said Ron Schermer of Scottsbluff (p. 9-A).

What has not emerged in philosopher Howard Rheingold's (1994) idealistic hopes for cyberspace is the development of volunteer efforts of citizens willing to participate in community projects. The commitment is just not there. The intimacy of community is less likely to be present on the Internet; more likely, the Internet will foster a distant, "anonymous" CMC *society* (Jones, 1998, p. 13). Free expression as a form of citizenship, however, may range on the Internet from mythical town hall democracy to anonymous public opinion. Meanwhile, our nagging sense of disappointment over the limits of citizen participation in the developing global village feeds our collective desire to somehow harness the technology to foster social cohesion. Cyberspace is not a place, and it lacks the physical roots needed to grow stable relationships:

It seems that with the loss of the traditional nexus of place and power, we are left with the necessity of crafting an alternate way of viewing rhetorical relationships. Discursive resistance needs a place to act on, whether that place is a body or a space. The mediation of the one and the blurring of the other within virtual communities stands as an unmet challenge in crafting cyber-places into viable public forums (Kolko and Reid, in Jones, 1998, p. 226).

Without viable forums in cyberspace, free expression on the Internet is problematic. The venting of steam, which Emerson so valued as a safety valve for democracy, inevitably turns free speech into an intrapersonal exercise in identity. But the cacophony of voices trying to be heard in the marketplace does not promote the democratic process. The problem is that a web page produces a message that is easily lost in a city rather than found in a community.

Neuman (1998) acknowledged the scholarly, "schizophrenic" nature of the current euphoria and criticism over new technologies (p. 239). He ultimately sided with those pushing new technology as a metaphor for social change: "Although there is no shortage of hyperbole, the basic argument that the Internet is radically different from all its analog ancestors is fundamentally correct" (p. 239). He argued that the media marketplace is no longer static:

Thus far in the history of media evolution, we witness a consistent pattern. New media emerge with different technical properties that are optimized to meet human needs. For the most part, the old media [such as radio] adjust, taking advantage of their technical character to survive by providing a unique format.

But everything changes with the Internet. As all specialized media begin to migrate to an interconnected digital network, audio, video, and text-with-graphics become interchangeable. The electronically delivered morning "newspaper" can be printed out on a high-speed, high-resolution home-printer, or it can be recorded as audio and played on a Walkman or car stereo, or it can be viewed on a computer monitor (Neuman, 1998, p. 240).

What such arguments ignore is the social pressure to conform communication to acceptable patterns. It might not matter, for example, that the Internet initially did not demand "special lighting, a sound crew, and a film camera person backed up by a high-speed film lab with film-editing specialist" (Neuman, 1998, p. 241) if professional culture demands emerge with the maturation of the media. It is unlikely that people, over time, will not insist on the highest technical quality and standards of the new media, and with raised standards comes a need for paid professionals with the expertise to do the media work. So, it is not at all clear that the web video model will turn out to be "more like present-day talk-radio than mainstream newspaper and television reportage" (p. 243). The multitude of options or "channels" must be weighed against issues involving who owns and operates those channels, what the values of those owners and operators are, and to what extent the content ultimately contributes to free expression. Moreover, attempts to produce communities of interest will yield the desire for safety by enforcing behavioral norms (Baym, in Jones, 1998, pp. 52–54). Expression in these contexts follows face-to-face models of needing to "generate group-specific meanings" (p. 52). Conformity of expression rather than free expression results from the social nature of discussion. And fragmenting thought into segregated groups, reflecting like-minded thinking, is very productive if the goal is to affect wide social change.

It is just as likely that activation of the public through the new digital communication networks will wither into meaningless participation about trivial matters. Consider the experiment in which visitors to the Excite web site voted on a live ice-skating competition broadcast on the CBS television network. A live audience was given handheld computers so they could vote along with the web audience. "Excite is about personalization and giving people experiences on the Web," said a company executive. "For the first time ever on the Internet, we are giving the online community a voice to affect the outcome of a live television show" (http://www.excite.com). In an age when less than half of all registered U.S. voters participate in national presidential elections, it is sad that people would be excited about participation in a meaningless figure-skating competition.

Not only has the debate over the Internet ignored history, it is argued here, it also has been atheoretical. Therefore, the generalizations about the new medium lack a framework to help us understand it beyond the immediate moment.

Social Communication Theory Revisited

Social theory might be viewed as a survival skill or as a composite of "those hidden aspects of social life we sometimes encounter in the ordinary course of daily life" (Lemert, 1999, pp. 1–2). Social theory is foundationally about power, and it is intimately related to the origins of free expression: "The development of civil society in the eighteenth century . . . permitted enough freedom of expression to encourage independent thinking" (p. 3).

At the outset of this book, it was proposed that:

1. *Free expression is not the product of an idealistic search for "truth" or objective reality but rather is subjective by its very nature. Individuals inter-*

pret *(encode and decode) speech, which must be studied in a social context.* The Internet has proven to be embedded within a social fabric, subjective to content providers and viewers.

2. *Free expression is not only understood in terms of its presumed psychological value to individuals but also is a component in a social, political, and economic system.* We have seen that the World Wide Web has come to be utilized as a political symbol in the educational reform movement.

3. *That which passes for "free expression" in no way resembles what might be at the fringes because all speech is limited by a variety of social constraints, both real and imagined.* The power of entertainment and the practical social, legal, and economic fears of communicators limit the Internet's social and ideological value.

4. *Popular concepts such as "social responsibility" and "the marketplace of ideas" have no utility in learning about free expression, except to the extent that individuals adopt and use these notions as tools of political power.* It has not been proven that free expression has been advanced in a meaningful way by merely expanding the number of messages available. In fact, the multitude of voices and the lack of coherent thought might well restrict a useful social dialogue.

One of the shortcomings of mass-communication theory building today is its lack of generalizations that can be applied to the Internet. At the core of many of our concerns about the new media is the question of media power:

> It is almost impossible to give any useful assessment of the degree to which the effects posited by this body of theory and research actually occur . . .
>
> Nevertheless, it would be difficult to argue that the media are, on balance, a force for major change in society, or to deny that a large part of popular content is generally conformist in tendency. It is also difficult to avoid the conclusion that, in so far as media capture attention, occupy time and disseminate images of reality and of potential alternatives, they fail to provide favourable conditions for the formation of a consciousness and identity among the less advantaged sectors of society and for the organization of opposition, both of which have been found necessary in the past for radical social reform (McQuail, 1994, p. 369).

The control of media by large business interests and state bureaucracies has led, McQuail contended, to an increasing concentration of power under a system in which the owners seek market stability as a long-term interest. Changing technology simply "alters what is both possible and profitable" (p. 384). McQuail saw this as change rather than a revolution, with fairly predictable consequences for audience members.

Box 12.2　McQuail's New Media Generalizations

·　Audience segmentation and fragmentation
·　Increased differentiation by source, medium, content, time, and place
·　Greater consumer choice
·　More interactive audience behavior
·　Further development of an international media marketplace
·　Further retreat of an invisible audience, albeit an interconnected audience

(Source: Adapted from McQuail, 1994, p. 294)

The fragmentation of communication created by new technological structures implies that there will be new forms of communication emerging from the complex environment. The marketplace metaphor fails to capture the complexity of the process that is unfolding. Further, it is impossible to predict how traditional social conformity might operate under such conditions and whether individual differences suggest a multitude of models. The metaphor of the "web" attempts to describe the potential complexity of communication structures, but the mere depiction of communication strands says nothing about the nature of those connections. Further, webs in the physical world can be fairly permanent or temporary, depending on their proximity to dangerous cohabitants. The implication is that radical free-expression webs must hide in the dark corners of the Internet to survive. Likewise, the superhighway metaphor fails to advance us because movement is a shallow concern when it comes to the spread of ideas. Diffusion of ideas must be accompanied by meaningful calls to action if there is to be any hope of social reform.

Social, Political, and Economic Boundaries

L. Strate, R. Jacobson, and S. B. Gibson (1996) asserted that communication should be at the center of our concern. Communication is how we transfer information, make meanings, form relationships, create communities, and construct identities: "We take the position that computer media—in fact, all media—are best understood not just as means or agencies *through* which communication takes place, but as environment or scenes in which communication occurs" (p. 1). In cyberspace, a place first envisioned by science fiction writer William Gibson as a "virtual dimension," we find technology being a part player in the redefinition of society

(Gumpert and Drucker, in Strate, Jacobson, and Gibson, 1996). Cyberlaw has its shortcomings because

> from a legal perspective real property, or physical space, is distinguished by possession and use and enjoyment. . . . Although title to real property is easily identifiable, who owns cyberspace? Bulletin boards have been called the computer-age equivalent of a public forum. . . . But there is something seductive about electronic communication with others, and we in the United States have begun to rely on mediated communication and even prefer that to the old, particularly because it is safe, forgetting that there are qualitative differences between the two. The mediated functional alternatives that we choose generally occur inside controlled private space (pp. 33, 36).

Thus, the technology can be seen as a means to "retreat inward" and replace our physical world with the cyber alternative. In one view, this is not for the better: "Cyberspace is a humanizing device for creating a kind of ersatz office/pub/common room/public square area for those deprived, rather cruelly, of one or more versions of the real thing" (Phelan, in Strate, Jacobson, and Gibson, 1996, pp. 43–44). Sold as a way to break from mass social control, cyberspace is likely to fall, as all other decentralized attempts have, to "mass persuasion and control" (Beniger, in Strate, Jacobson, and Gibson, 1996, p. 52). The addition of multimedia techniques to cyberspace only confuses notions of choice, especially in virtual-reality simulations:

> There are potential problems when we see virtual reality in a postmodern existentialist context. One is the matter of the extent, rather than the consequences, of free choice. Even if the various electronic sensors that extend our nervous system respond to our choices and make the environment change according to where we look and how we gesture, our choices are not free but essentially deterministic. They are, after all, decisively limited by the parameters and algorithms of the computer program, very much like the number and kind of objects that were used to create shadows in Plato's cave. As such, our decisions will inevitably be based on pseudochoices (Zettl, in Strate, Jacobson, and Gibson, 1996, p. 92).

Beyond the optimist and pessimist positions about information technology, at least one other alternative exists: "Pure technology in this case would not be an active agent that benefits or hurts mankind: it could not be, as it has no function . . . it just sits, existing in and of itself" (Kroker and Kroker, 1997, p. 308).

The best prediction about the future of cyberspace might be that its initial free environment will be suffocated by traditional legal structures. Social behavioral norms and the law will tend to conspire to favor rules and order over chaos and confusion. At the University of Maryland, for example, administrators have agreed to be publishers of Romantic Circles, a popular literature site. The originators felt they needed a sponsor because they feared the potential for lawsuits over copyright and other issues. As the sponsor of the web pages, the university assumed responsibility for any liability claim in order to gain "a measure of control." University lawyer Diane Krejsa said, "We're attempting to control this when the law isn't even defined" (*Chronicle of Higher Education*, March 5, 1999, p. A-25). Similarly, Southern Utah University was seeking control when a student was kicked out of a user lab for looking at pornographic and Nazi sites, ironically while doing a class project on the school's "acceptable-use" policy. Spokesman Neal Cox said: "We're not running a game room or a peepshow" (p. A-27). Control, it would seem, is the central concern, rather than teaching critical thinking skills. The tug and pull of the Internet in the 1990s might really be cultural tension as seen through the bias of the communication technology available at present:

> We can do little more than urge that we must be continually alert to the implications of this bias and perhaps hope that consideration of other media to various civilizations may enable us to see more clearly the bias in our own. . . . We can perhaps assume that the use of a medium of communication over a long period will to some extent determine the character of knowledge to be communicated and suggest that its pervasive influence will eventually create a civilization in which life and flexibility will become exceedingly difficult to maintain and that the advantages of a new medium will become such as to lead to the emergence of new civilization (Innis, 1964, p. 34).

If Innis is correct, the Internet is likely to play an important role in restructuring society and culture. Because the Internet brings with it new conventions that challenge existing norms, we will be required to change or be lost in the change. All technology, and especially the computer, is perhaps best defined by the degree to which it is outmoded by the next generation—which is faster, slicker, clearer, and better. The technology promotes a consumer ideology to buy products—especially the newest items. But this ideology has no meaningful free expression because it has no real empowerment attached to it.

Beyond the Internet

What is known today as the Internet will be technologically eclipsed by faster and more flexible technologies in the not-to-distant future. However, our lack of thinking about the communication employed to utilize breakthrough technologies will lead to shortsightedness. We will continue to pin our hopes on "better" technologies to solve our deepening social inadequacies. Without better communication theories and practices, however, the promise of the new technology will be empty.

Internet2 promises to transform the World Wide Web by using so-called supercomputers to speed up data processing, and as a result, the web will evolve into a virtual-reality environment where individuals "experience" other real and imagined worlds. As such, reality itself will not only be redefined, it will also be controlled by programming entities—not elected, but unseen, and unaccountable representatives who, in effect, make zoning decisions about the use of cyberspace. The tragedy of the development of communication technology is that it is created to serve marketing goals. The business paradigm is shortsighted because it fails to consider the long-term implications of the changes brought about by the technology. Technology is developed by technocrats working in laboratories where the focus is on innovation and profit. Given this isolation, society does not benefit from meaningful dialogue between inventors and philosophers. Moreover, the fact that we *can* do something does not always mean that we *should*. There are also political questions revolving around ecological concerns about interdependence, partnership, flexibility, diversity, and sustainability (Woolpert, Slaton, and Schwerin, 1998, pp. XXI-XXII). The value of "a new paradigm that incorporates change as a major variable" (p. 9) must be considered in both theory and practice. The evolution of free expression will not happen in static models. Instead, free expression will need to be viewed as a dynamic force central to cultural change.

The Future of Digital Communication

By some accounts, we are experiencing the most dramatic changes in electronic communication since their development three-quarters of a century ago. The change that the Internet has brought to the arena of personal free expression rivals and perhaps outdistances that of the printing press hundreds of years ago: "The electronic web of connection that is now being woven amongst us all is a catalyst for change more powerful than Gutenberg's press or Goebbels's radio. Every constraint of the old order is crumbling. The limitless, anarchic possibilities of the telecosm contrast sharply with the limits of growth we now encounter at every turn of the physical world" (Huber, 1997, p. 3).

Still, while the battle for control of cyberspace is waged, we must recognize that the people who populate that space carry old social values, norms, and behaviors. Their communication behaviors are and will be limited by convention. At the turn of the century, free expression resides within a cultural framework that values information technology. As our youngest citizens are socialized to live with technological communication, it will become increasingly difficult to participate in critical examinations of its shortcomings.

In 1998, an estimated 45 percent of U.S. homes had a personal computer, although not all of those were connected to the Internet, had high-speed connections, or were capable of full access to the World Wide Web. In America's wealthiest households, with incomes over $100,000, PC ownership was over 80 percent; in the poorest households, it was less than 25 percent. Families with children were the most highly motivated to join the computer revolution (*Edupage*, March 10, 1998).

Creators of information technology seem to be pushing cultural change by promoting new forms of socialization. Consider software maker Knowledge Adventure's *JumpStart Babyital* program, which features animated hide-and-seek teddy bears who teach words to infants and toddlers under two years of age. Although the research is unclear about the positive or negative effects of such early stimulation, one executive said: "Parents think computers will help their kids get into Harvard" (*Edupage*, April 2, 1998). Increasingly, too, people expect computers and software to solve their problems. As a result, they might be increasingly dissatisfied to find that computers may actually add to their woes. Getting into Harvard will continue to be more about social class than technological know-how. In essence, the technology becomes a diversion that leads us to believe divisions between the classes and the races have miraculously dissolved in cyberspace.

The development of cyberspace as a commercial place is on a fast track. By early 1999, the most popular commercial stops on the web were: (1) greeting-card company Bluemountainarts.com, (2) bookseller Amazon.com, (3) auctioneer Ebay.com, (4) bookseller Barnes & Noble, and (5) toystore Etoys.com (Media Metrix, January 26, 1999). Clearly, certain purchasing behaviors were better fits for the Internet than others. Consumerism, as has been discussed in this book, may involve the creation of identity and social differentiation. The social behaviors on the web are evolving so quickly that legal propositions are left behind. As the online world took hold, the United States appeared to be operating with a "Two-Tier First Amendment"—defining "high-value speech" and regulating "low-value speech" in a content-neutral way (Sunstein, 1993, p. 8). In such a manner, courts may attempt to treat "advocacy of a crime, commercial speech, hate speech, obscenity, and libel" as "outside of the First Amendment altogether" in order to "maintain a civilized society" (p. 7). However, the determination of "low value" ultimately is a normative judgment that cannot be made objectively, as is implied by legal theory.

The rapid changes in information technology bring new legal problems, as well. Sophisticated computer-graphics programs, for example, now make it possible to alter images of children to make family photos look like child pornography. A federal judge in Maine ruled that a 1996 antiporn law that defined child pornography as an image that appears to be a minor participating in sexual behavior was unconstitutionally vague (Associated Press, April 2, 1998). Though we may marvel at the ability of low-priced scanners and color printers to bring professional publishing tools into our homes, we must also worry about the possibility that these tools can be misused—especially when the Internet provides a way for content to be easily sold worldwide.

The commercial problems of the Internet extend to the issue of copyright theft. The computer-using public generally does not take the ownership of intellectual property seriously. One Canadian survey found that only 20 percent of respondents would report someone for illegally copying software, and twice as many saw stealing a chocolate bar as a more serious offense. Nearly all respondents said they rarely pirate software, but one in five admitted they had done so (*Edupage*, March 15, 1998).

A group of twelve writers, calling themselves "technorealists," has distributed a set of principles for an Internet site (*Chronicle of Higher Education*, April 3, 1998, pp. A-23–A-24). The group argued that the technology both makes life more convenient and poses new problems:

> Integral to this perspective is our understanding that the current tide of technological transformation, while important and powerful, is actually a continuation of waves of change that have taken place throughout history. Looking, for example, at the history of the automobile, television, or the telephone—not just the devices but the institutions they became—we see profound benefits as well as substantial costs. Similarly, we anticipate mixed blessings from today's emerging technologies, and expect to forever be on guard for unexpected consequences—which must be addressed by thoughtful design and appropriate use (http://www.technorealism.org).

The technorealists sought "to expand the fertile middle ground between techno-utopianism and neo-Luddism" (*Chronicle of Higher Education*, April 3, 1998, p. A-24).

As the field of telecommunication experiences both fragmentation and convergence, one author has argued for more dramatic deregulation. Proposals include abolishing the Federal Communications Commission and returning to a common-law approach in which private players, markets, and the courts, not the FCC, maintain order:

> We still need laws to defend the property rights of people who lay wires and build transmitters, to enforce contracts and carriage agreements, to defend freedom to speak and listen, and to protect copyright and privacy. Anarchy works no better in virtuality than in actuality. The question is not whether there will be rules of law, but where they will come from (Huber, 1997, pp. 7–8).

This perspective sees digital space as so vast that free speech itself has become *the* problem:

Box 12.3   Technorealism Principles

The principles of technorealism included

1. Technologies are not neutral. . . . Every tool provides its users with a particular manner of seeing the world and specific ways of interacting with others. It is important for each of us to consider the biases of various technologies and to seek out those that reflect our values and aspirations.

2. The Internet is revolutionary, but not Utopian . . . as cyberspace becomes more populated, it increasingly resembles society at large, in all its complexity. For every empowering or enlightening aspect of the wired life, there will also be dimensions that are malicious, perverse, or rather ordinary.

3. Government has an important role to play on the electronic frontier. Contrary to some claims, cyberspace is not formally a place or jurisdiction separate from Earth. While governments should respect the rules and customs that have arisen in cyberspace, and should not stifle this new world with inefficient regulation or censorship, it is foolish to say that the public has no sovereignty over what an errant citizen or fraudulent corporation does online . . .

4. Information is not knowledge. . . . We must not confuse the thrill of acquiring or distributing information quickly with the more daunting task of converting it into knowledge and wisdom. Regardless of how advanced our computers become, we should never use them as a substitute for our own basic cognitive skills of awareness, perception, reasoning, and judgment.

5. Wiring the schools will not save them. . . . These tools can, of course, augment an already high-quality educational experience. But to rely on them as any sort of panacea would be a costly mistake.

6. Information wants to be protected . . . we must update old laws and interpretations so that information receives roughly the same protection it did in the context of old media. The goal is the same: to give authors sufficient control over their work so that they have an incentive to create, while maintaining the right of the public to make fair use of that information . . .

7. The public owns the airwaves; the public should benefit from their use. The recent digital spectrum giveaway to broadcasters underscores the corrupt and inefficient misuse of public resources in the arena of technology . . .

8. Understanding technology should be an essential component of global citizenship. In a world driven by the flow of information, the interfaces—

and the underlying code—that make information visible are becoming enormously powerful social forces . . .

The fairly general, middle-ground principles were defended by the technorealists at a Harvard Law School symposium. They argued for the need to control cyberspace through government regulation. David Shenk said technorealism describes the balanced position of interest in technology: "There isn't a word for someone who is very enthusiastic about technology but is also very concerned."

(Source: *Chronicle of Higher Education*, April 3, 1998, p. A-24)

The telecosm contains extortion, fraud, libel, debauchery, and on-line clubs of individuals who molest children. Pushed to pathological limits, free speech ruins reputations, corrupts youth, incites violence, and coarsens the populace.
So we need censorship more than ever before. The challenge is to find censorship that works (Huber, 1997, p. 165).

That assertion seems to be about as far away as possible from Milton or Holmes or Brandeis and the concept of the marketplace of ideas. To say that "the problem now is free speech itself and the right of each citizen to enjoy some shelter from assaults that masquerade as discourse" (Huber, 1997, p. 177) would seem to (1) oversimplify the issues embedded in cyberlaw, and (2) ignore the problematic issue arising from opinions about communication. Huber's faith in the ability of common-law courts to protect free expression seems misguided and confused because it also ignores the constitutional protections now grounded in American law. And blind faith in the private market ignores the problems associated with monopoly control of communication systems. The transnational media corporation, for example, has been called "one of the major power brokers of our time" (Gershon, 1997, p. XI). It is unrealistic to expect that these power brokers will not jockey to also dominate the new digital channels of communication.

This book has argued that the Internet and digital communication are useful in helping us to understand free expression as it exists today. Unlike print or broadcast mass media, cyberspace has become a more open space for free expression to compete in the marketplace of ideas. As a result, there have been attempts by the government to regulate it—particularly in the areas of indecency and obscenity.

Historical legal thought shows us that ideas matter. They have political importance. So, those in power compete to control the arenas where public ideas dwell. The marketplace of ideas is an imperfect place, where "social responsibility" is often abandoned because it cannot be defined and because it may contradict with the economic self-interest of media providers—namely, their need to attract and retain large audiences. Broadcast notions of public interest and scarcity also do not fit well in the new digital world. The metaphor of zoning Internet content is a prescription for control by paternalistic censors.

Our understanding of social theory helps see free expression as it relates to human behavior. Beyond social constraints, individuals in society are moved by mass persuasion and public opinion. Free expression, then, is not an unbridled human passion. It is held in check by social pressures to conform.

The *Reno v. ACLU* case was examined to show that future attempts to regulate cyberspace are likely doomed to failure. The work of Internet gossip columnist Matt Drudge is just one example of how free expression is being transformed by an ever-expanding marketplace of ideas—one that may be slowed but not halted by private legal actions. A survey of Internet content revealed that the new digital infrastructure has created a leaky strainer; plugging one hole does nothing to stop the outpouring of ideas.

Personal forms of free expression, particularly e-mail, show us that free expression should not be thought of as simply expression that occurs in mass media. The return of private, written communications shows us what might not have been apparent during the time when a telephone call was more common: Free expression lives and breathes in the mouths and ears of all citizens—not just the media moguls. The extent to which people are willing to speak out and the extent to which social norms promote free expression are important considerations. But individual speech must be followed by collective action to produce meaningful power shifts.

It is difficult to imagine the legal notion of invasion of privacy surviving in the twenty-first century. The digital age carries with it a bias for private data being public, for access to information being universal, and for ethical issues being lost in a sea of information exchange. Likewise, copyright law seems headed for a digital showdown. Cyberspace is not a place where private property is well protected. It will be a place for conventional business norms, but those might well evolve as applied to digital transactions. If cyberspace is truly revolutionary, then the electronic marketplace may become like the street vendor's stand—open to barter and negotiation. If communication fragmentation means anything, it might be that it will usher in an era in which consumers become empowered in new ways.

A critical but unresolved issue is whether Western nations will continue to dominate cyberspace as they have from its inception. From a cross-cultural perspective, such a condition is likely to be seen as cultural imperialism. The view that cyberspace is an empowering place would be meaningful only if all peoples had access to the source of power.

The empirical question raised by this book involved the role that geographic proximity plays in exercising social control when the technology of choice has no geographic boundaries. It was suggested that social controls on free expression may be a function of spheres of influence, as well as message content. The fear of isolation appears to relate to one's local community rather than one's virtual community, although some virtual communities are so small and strong that such pressures might emerge. In the one case, loss of social connections leave few options: One can leave the community or face living in an isolated condition. In the other case, one usually has many more options afforded by cyberspace's worldwide population. If communication degrades into flaming, leaving involves only the click of a mouse. If the cyberspace community is unique, however, the sense of loss and isolation could be quite high. Still, moving from one geographic home or leaving one's job can be time-consuming, costly, and complex. Therefore, it is proposed that the pressure to conform to local norms of behavior will usually outweigh such pressures in cyberspace. In free-expression terms, we would expect individuals to exercise a greater degree of latitude in cyberspace than in their neighborhoods, workplaces, and communities.

This book has suggested that the Internet forces us to respond to the potential issues of power raised by changes in social control that are brought about by the information and consumer ages. Cities brought unlike peoples together, but subcultures emerging in cyberspace bring like or perceived like peoples together in loosely knit social networks. Under such conditions, we would expect free expression to be more open because the threat of retaliation is limited by the homogeneity of the group, as well as by the geographic distance between its members and conditions of anonymity. (See Figures 12.2, 12.3. and 12.4)

If such pronouncements as those on the MafiaCrip.Com web site were occurring in a local community rather than in cyberspace, they might be viewed as a clear-and-present danger, a threat of violence, or a conspiracy to commit murder. But in cyberspace, such words may be seen as free expression. In the end, the digital age will help us to understand free expression in new ways, but it does not solve the fundamental problems associated with the marketplace of ideas, social responsibility, and public interest. In a free society, free expression is at the core. At the same time, however, beliefs about free expression are fairly diverse and, like all other issues, open to debate. So, the true meaning of free expression cannot be found in well-defined answers. No, the true meaning of free expression must be found in an environment of openness, plurality, and diversity where all are free to speak and listen. Nonetheless, diversity of communication will ultimately lead to conflicts between those groups expressing

298

Free Hosting
Free E-Mail Address
Contact Crips.com

Full Site Disclosure
Our Purpose and Goals
Banner Section
Crips Staff Meeting
Crips World Wide
Gangsta Gals Dirkster Prod.
Vic's Gun Collection
Joke of the Day
Graffiti
Want Crip Pens?
Showcase of Artists
Tookie's Corner
Reality Check
Crip Articles
Crips Romance Room
Crip Pics
Surprise!
Member Entrance

Dirkster Productions
Hackers Canyon
CyberGangs.com
Guns-Knives-Ammo.com
Mafia Crips
Folks

1Luv
Boyz In Blue
Fly Playa
Krayzie
Lissa's Bomb Ass Site
Nikkita
Set Trippin
TRU
LA Street Gangs
United Nations
Tookie
Jamie Adams
Rap Music Online
Smithson Valley Crips
Nikon16

FIGURE 12.1　Crips.com

Tupac Shakur Autopsy Photo
rotten.com

In late 1997 Cathy Scott published "The Killing of Tupac Shakur", which
contained an autopsy photo of Shakur that had been leaked by a source
within the Las Vegas police department.

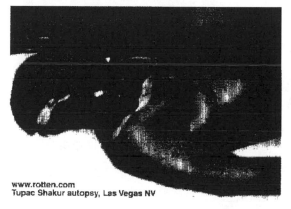

www.rotten.com
Tupac Shakur autopsy, Las Vegas NV

Tabloid offers as high as $100K were turned down for the photo, which we
reproduce above. LVMPD was not happy about the photo being leaked, but
being property of the people of the United States, it is in the public domain.
We reproduce it here. [Additionally, Cathy Scott has given explicit
permission to republish the photo here.]

Reality Check
You can sing about guns and gang life all ya want.
Tupac had some great music.
But Songs and Real life look a little different.

FIGURE 12.2   Bloods.com

300

Nice try but it aint that easy.
If
you
get
in.
We offer you
Free e-mail
yourname@HackersCanyon.com
Free Members sites
HackersCanyon.com/yoursite
ftp access
password protected.

.
..
If ya want in this canyon you will have to find the way in.
It changes and we only tell the ones who
have set up camp where the entrance is.
So go on back and look for a way in this place.
Be careful!
The best Hackers in the world have set up camp here.
You will have to earn their respect before they even
show themselves.

CyberGangs
Run these canyons
Cyber Gangs party at
Cyber City.
You most likely don't want to be here if you are
new at computers.
All you will leave with is a smoking computer.

.

.We can't tell
you how many gangs are here.
Don't ask either.
Hackers Canyon has become the place

Cyber Gangs
Eat, sleep,work, Fight and
Die here.

If you don't
know what a
Cyber Gang is then click on the # 1 bellow

FIGURE 12.3   Cyber Gangs

deep disagreement on social issues and those who maintain true ideological differences. This freedom, however, also carries with it a right to remain quiet, to ignore, and even to avoid democratic participation. The digital age does not alter this. It simply provides new avenues for the freedom to be exercised. Social rules may evolve, but they still apply. Free expression is mediated both by the power system in which it resides and by the norms of those who choose to practice it, whether the speech is face-to-face or computer-mediated.

This book would not be the first to argue that "the digital day is young" and that evolution of the media forms and regulations are inevitable. By 1999, more than 60 million visitors viewed more than 28 billion web pages each month; major players such as AOL, Microsoft, and the Go Network (Go.com) continued to dominate the landscape. Internet interest continues to expand rapidly (Media Metrix, June 22, 1999).

Regulatory flashpoints include the Federal Communication Commission's attempts to subsidize school and library connections through the imposition of fees; the development of new software programs that restrict illegal copying; and successful litigation by celebrities such as figure skater Nancy Kerrigan, who sought to halt use of her name or image on Internet porn sites (Associated Press, August 2, 1999). Likewise, the continuing struggle between the U.S. government and Microsoft over what constitutes a reasonable market share shows that the battle over the control of cyberspace is under way. Meantime, groups such as the ACLU continue to fight legal battles at the state and federal levels over legislative attempts to restrict a wide-open Internet. Although online providers have been found to be not responsible for the content of others, the courts also continue to be places where individuals creating controversial web sites may find themselves engaged in costly legal battles. And content providers such as AOL function as regulators as they crack down on pornographic and other spamming by filing lawsuits and restricting access. Not everyone sees the value of free expression as stated by author David D. Z. Mindich: "The Internet is one big stewpot of perspectives, unbalanced yet all-inclusive" (*Ottawa Citizen*, July 23, 1999). Attempts to impose journalistic or other business norms on the Internet will inevitably limit free expression. It may be generations before the full cultural impact of the Internet is measured accurately.

As the century comes to a close, the potential of the Internet to create new legal and political questions is indisputable. In 1999, U.S. Vice President Al Gore targeted cyber stalking, and asking Attorney General Janet Reno to solve the problem in a way that would not infringe on free expression rights under the First Amendment. Gore said that in some cases, American women have been bothered by people lurking in cyberspace:

Box 12.4   Crips and Bloods in Cyberspace

The Los Angeles street-gang culture of the 1960s emerged on the Internet in the 1990s. Crips.com and Bloods.com feature photographs and "rants" about gang life. "Despite the dripping-blood graphics, the gun icons one must click in order to proceed and a warning that all non-gang members should exit the premises immediately, these sites could be an indication of a kinder, gentler gang era." MafiaCrip.com webmaster Fource Warrant Mason of Philadelphia said the sites show gangs as more intelligent and "coming up from the ghettos" into society: "The Internet is the best way to show the outside world that we are coming up." Los Angeles Police Detective Chuck Zeglin convinced the KillerCop.Com site to shut down by threatening charges for offering rewards to those who would kill police officers.

(Source: *Salon*, February 26, 1999)

"And make no mistake—this kind of harassment can be as frightening and as real as being followed and watched in your neighborhood or in your home." One California man, for example, posted personal information about a woman he no longer dated in a sex chat room. Within days, people were at her doorstep. "She could have been sexually assaulted or even worse," Gore said. "As a society, as a country, as a national family, we don't have to put up with this, and we will not" (Associated Press, February 27, 1999). How politicians react to the challenges of the Internet will, in large part, determine what our norms of free expression will be in the years ahead. As Postman has observed, new technology cannot be seen as separate from cultural change: "A new technology does not add or subtract something. It changes everything. In the year 1500, fifty years after the printing press was invented, we did not have old Europe plus the printing press. We had a different Europe" (Postman, 1992, p. 18). Technology is surrounded, Postman wrote, by institutions reflecting "the world-view promoted by the technology" (p. 18). The challenge of a new technology such as the Internet is to existing power structures and organizations. Postman said the United States has entered into a "Technopoly" in which the power structure "strives furiously to control information" (p. 87). The Technopoly abuses language by refocusing the problems and solutions:

The computer argues, to put it baldly, that the most serious problems confronting us at both personal and public levels require technical solutions through fast access to information otherwise unavailable. I would argue that this is, on the face of it, nonsense. . . . If families break up, children are mistreated, crime terrorizes a city, education is impotent, it does not happen because of inadequate information. Mathematical equations, instantaneous communication, and vast quantities of information have nothing whatever to do with any of these problems. And the computer is useless in addressing them (p. 119).

Likewise, free expression in and of itself does not solve social problems. Only when free speech is persuasive in a democratic sense and can foster social change is there a possibility for the reallocation of resources in a way that benefits those suffering under current conditions. So, the marriage of free expression and the Internet should not be seen as a panacea in whatever new world emerges through the cultural changes unfolding before our eyes and ears.

Finally, the nature of law itself in cyberspace is a problem because though the new technologies reside in physical space, the information flows rapidly to all corners of the globe. Societal interconnections do not guarantee construction of new forms of community (Jones, 1997). The social construction of reality in cyberspace appears to be easier to achieve, and those most able to manipulate information have a distinct advantage. The "desire to control virtual space," as Jan Fernback put it, is real (Fernback, in Jones, 1997, pp. 36–53). It is also at the core of our questions about free expression today. Metaphors such as the marketplace of ideas are historically bound in physical places and static, linear times. To the extent that the Internet fails to be limited in traditional ways, the struggle over its control is political, as existing power structures seek to maintain their advantages. Lawyers and courts devising legal constructions should beware of classical transmission views of communication, as well as blind optimism for the potential of communication technology to alter human behavior. If communication is symbolic and if it is the background for human existence (Carey, 1992, p. 24), then legal communication is the way that humans form the rules of our social control over free expression. The picture, then, is much more complex than legal metaphors of marketplaces and balancing suggest. In fact, the critical conclusion must be that such language serves to obscure the significant exercise of power over our free expression—especially in the age of the Internet. The observations in this book lead to three recommendations:

1. Society must resist the social temptation to fear free expression. Although it appears natural to be afraid to speak under circumstances of stress, it is vital to democracy that people utilize free speech.
2. The law needs to distinguish between massive, multinational corporations and individuals when it comes to free-speech rights. To treat individuals as mere equals blatantly tilts the legal scales of justice.

3. Media literacy for adults and children is central to the development of critical reasoning skills. Free expression in the age of the Internet might be promoted by teaching people to make individual judgments about media content. We cannot bury our heads in the sand about messages we dislike. In fact, to do so is to miss the opportunity to know and understand all types of communication.

Chapter Summary

This chapter addressed the theoretical limitations in understanding free expression as a social phenomenon, as well as the problems associated with the technological overlay. It returned to the generalizations advanced at the beginning of this book, and it extended those to the most immediate concerns of the social sphere.

Discussion Questions

1. Are you generally optimistic or pessimistic about the role that communication technology will play in the future?
2. Is your optimism or pessimism really a function of deeper social concerns?
3. How should the laws of free expression be altered, if at all, to meet the challenges of cyberspace?
4. Which is more damaging, corporate or government regulation of cyberspace, in terms of free expression?
5. How will economic power play a role in the future development and zoning of cyberspace?
6. In the end, how would you define free expression in the age of the Internet?

Glossary

Active X   Microsoft interactive web page technology that is used in animated, interactive, and responsive Internet content.

Agenda setting   a theory that focuses on the power of mass media to influence public opinion through consonant coverage of major stories.

Artificial intelligence   computer science of systems that imitate human behavior.

Bandwidth   characteristic of a communications channel and the range of frequencies accurately transmitted.

Broadband channels   those communications channels capable of moving multimedia at high speeds.

Browse   searching the Internet, usually with a computer web browser software program that reads HTML code.

Cache   a computer folder that stores temporary files.

CD-ROM   compact disc read-only memory disks, which store more than 500 megabytes of data.

Channel   A web site that automatically copies Internet content to a computer.

Commercial speech   an area of law defined by purely commercial transactions and the economic interests of buyers and sellers.

Common carriers   licensed and regulated companies that move computer data at approved rates and telephone companies that must transmit all messages.

Common law   law influenced by the English practice of making decisions based on the precedents of previous laws determined by judges' rulings.

Content providers   Internet businesses that supply news, sports, financial, weather, or other content.

Copyright   ownership of the rights to sell and distribute materials by the creators of the media content.

Data   raw input for computer processing.

Data communications   transmission of data between computers separated by geographic distance.

Defamation   damage to an individual's reputation through statements that are false or negligent; defamation is punishable under libel laws.

Desktop   the workspace on a computer screen.

Diffusion   a mass-communication theory based on the spread of new ideas or innovations and visually described by S-shaped curves in which early and late adopters are distinguished from each other.

Digital data   computer information defined by discrete and predefined values, such as the numbers 0 and 1.

Download   To copy files from a computer on the Internet or elsewhere to a PC.

E-mail   data communications that typically use telephone lines or dedicated networks to send and store messages otherwise found in forms such as memos, telephone calls, and letters.

Fairness doctrine   Federal Communications Commission rules imposed upon U.S. broadcasters until 1987, requiring (1) coverage of controversial issues of public importance, and (2) presentation of opposing viewpoints in such controversies.

Fax   short for *facsimile transmission*, it is a process of sending and receiving pages of text electronically.

Federal Communications Commission (FCC)   an administrative agency charged with regulating communication over the air or by wire across state lines; broadcasters, cable operators, and telephone companies are supervised by the FCC.

Fiber optics   communications lines that transmit light through thin filaments and have properties capable of efficient video transfer.

Fighting words   those expressions likely to cause immediate violence; they are unprotected by the First Amendment.

Files   data records stored outside of a computer's temporary memory.

Folder   a computer location where files and other folders are stored.

Fox Libel Act (1792)   act by which Parliament made truth a defense in seditious libel cases and empowered juries to rule on such matters.

Hate speech   expression that attacks racial, ethnic, religious, or other minority groups; it is protected under current American law.

Home page   the first page of a web site, which may have links to other pages.

Host computer   the central computer in a network system.

HTML   hypertext markup language used to create web pages.

Indecency   refers to speech that is sexual or excretory and "patently offensive," broadcast at times of the day when children are likely to be in the audience.

Intellectual property law   a legal concept that encourages creative works by protecting the creators' ownership rights.

Internet   a worldwide network of computers linked together to facilitate communication between distant sites.

Internet service provider (ISP)   a company offering access to the Internet; AOL is currently the largest ISP in the United States.

Intranet   closed networks of computers, normally operated by proprietary businesses concerned with keeping trade secrets.

Invasion of privacy   an undeveloped area of legal thought that is similar to trespass restrictions on the access to private information, usually from one's home.

Link   a text or image hyperlink that, when clicked, takes the web browser to another site.

Local area network (LAN)   two or more computers connected by wire and designed to communicate as a defined group.

Marketplace of ideas   legal theory promoted by John Milton and twentieth-century supporters; it argues that truth will ultimately survive falsehoods in the competition fostered by the free trade of ideas.

Modem   a *modulator/demodulator* that connects a personal computer to telephone lines for internet, e-mail, and other communication.

Multimedia   digital mass media that use text, images, sound, and video to create an individualized experience for the user.

Negligence   a legal standard in libel cases whereby private plaintiffs argue that the publisher of information was careless and caused economic or other harm.

Obscenity   explicit sexual content that has no social, political, or scientific value and is unprotected by the First Amendment.

Password   a specific combination of letters and/or numbers that allows a computer user access to an e-mail account, an intranet or local area network system, or other computer services.

Plain view   a defense used in invasion of privacy cases that states that the material at issue could be seen by any person visiting a given public place.

Prior restraint   a doctrine rejected by common law in favor of subsequent punishment for the violation of free-speech restrictions.

Scarcity   the rationale for broadcast regulation based on the notion that not all people who want a license can have one because of limits in physical spectrum space.

Search engine   a computer software tool that helps the user find information on the Internet.

Server   a main computer that controls computers connected to a network and allows for the sharing of programs and access.

Social construction of reality   a theory that emphasizes the influence of the mass-mediated message in defining perceptions.

Software   computer programs that allow computer equipment to function.

Spiral of silence   a theoretical perspective that focuses on the social norms of conformity that lead people to be timid in their expression of ideas perceived to be controversial.

System crash   failure of a computer system because of a hardware or software problem.

Telecommuting   the phenomenon of working from home by utilizing computer technology as a replacement for physically being in the traditional workplace.

Teleconferencing   conducting business using computer systems equipped with Microsoft's Netmeeting, CU-See-Me, or other such software.

Time bomb   a computer virus that is set to "explode" at a later date.

Trademark   symbols, logos, or names that businesses use to create identification with customers.

Trojan horse   a computer hacker's way of sneaking past fire walls or other computer protection by riding on a disguised path.

Voice mail   digitally stored audio messages, usually transmitted over telephone lines.

World Wide Web   Internet content stored in a multimedia format.

References

Books, Articles, Legal Cases, and Theses

ACLU v. Reno, 929 F. Supp. 824 (D. Pa 1996), *affirmed.*

Action for Children's Television v. FCC, 852 F. 2d 1332 (D.C. Cir. 1988).

Albarran, A. B. (1996). *Media economics: Understanding markets, industries and concepts.* Ames: Iowa State University Press.

Alexander, A., J. Owers, and R. Carveth. (1998). *Media economics: Theory and practice*, 2nd ed. Mahwah, NJ: Lawrence Erlbaum.

Alleyne, M. D. (1995). *International power and international communication.* New York: St. Martin's Press.

Altman, I., and D. Taylor. (1997)."Social penetration theory," in E. Griffin, ed., *A first look at communication theory*, 3rd ed. New York: McGraw-Hill.

Bagdikian, B. H. (1997). *The media monopoly*, 5th ed. Boston: Beacon Press.

Baran, S. J. (1999). *Introduction to mass communication: Media literacy and culture.* Mountain View, CA: Mayfield.

Barnes, S., and L. M. Geller. (1994). "Computer-mediated communication in the organization," *Communication Monographs*, 43(2):1–12.

Barrett, N. (1997). *The state of the cybernation.* London: Kogan Page.

Bennett, W. L. (1996). *The politics of illusion*, 3rd ed. White Plains, NY: Longman.

Berkowitz, D. (1997). *Social meanings of news: A text-reader.* Thousand Oaks, CA: Sage.

Bilby, B. (1997). "Pharmaceutical advertising: A qualitative comparison of the Internet and national magazines." M.A. thesis, University of Nebraska–Omaha.

Bittner, J. R. (1994). *Law and regulation of electronic media*, 2nd ed. Englewood Cliffs, NJ: Prentice-Hall.

Blackstone, W. (1962). *Commentaries on the Laws of England.* Boston: Beacon Press. (Also see four-volume reprint of original version, Philadelphia, 1771–1772, New York: Oceana Publications.)

Block, F. (1990). *Postindustrial possibilities: A critique of economic discourse.* Berkeley: University of California Press.

Bork, R. (1971). "Neutral principles and some First Amendment problems," *Indiana Law Journal*, 47:1–35, at p. 25.

Bourdieu, P., and J. S. Coleman. (1991). *Social theory for a changing society.* Boulder: Westview Press.

Branscomb, A. W. (1995). "Emerging media technology and the First Amendment—Anonymity, autonomy, and accountability: Challenges to the First Amendment in cyberspaces," *Yale Law Journal*, 104 (May):1639–1769.

Brenner, D. L. (1996). *Law and regulation of common carriers in the communication industry*. Oxford: Westview Press.

Calvert, C. (1998). "The First Amendment and the third person: Perceptual biases of media harms and cries for government censorship," *CommLaw Conspectus* 6 (Summer):165–171.

———. (1997). "Free speech and content-neutrality: Inconsistent applications of an increasingly malleable doctrine, *McGeorge Law Review*, 29 (Fall):69–110.

Carey, J. W. (1992). *Communication as culture: Essays on media and society*. New York: Routledge.

Carey, J. W., ed. (1988). *Media, myths, and narratives: Television and the press*. Newbury Park, CA: Sage.

Carter, R. F. (1965). "Communication and affective relations," *Journalism Quarterly*, 42:203–212.

Carter, T. B., M. A. Franklin, and J. B. Wright. (1996). *The First Amendment and the fifth estate: Regulation of electronic mass media*, 4th ed. New York: Foundation Press.

Ceruzzi, P. E. (1998). *A history of modern computing*. Cambridge, MA: MIT Press.

Chafee Jr., Z. (1969). *Free speech in the United States*. New York: Atheneum.

———. (1947). *Government and mass communications*. Chicago: University of Chicago Press.

———. (1941). *Free speech in the United States*. Cambridge, MA: Harvard University Press.

Cohen, J. (1989). *Congress shall make no law: Oliver Wendell Holmes, the First Amendment, and judicial decision-making*. Ames: Iowa State University Press.

Cohen, J., and T. Gleason. (1990). *Social research in communication and law*. Newbury Park, CA: Sage.

Couch, C. J. (1996). *Information technologies and social orders*. New York: Aldine De Gruyter.

Crawford, H. E. (1997). "Internet calling: FCC jurisdiction over Internet telephony," *CommLaw Conspectus*, 5 (Winter):43.

Crowley, D., and P. Heyer. (1999). *Communication in history: Technology, culture society*, 3rd ed. New York: Addison Wesley Longman.

Curran, J., and M. Gurevitch, eds. (1991). *Mass media and society*. London: Edward Arnold.

DeFleur, M. L., and S. Ball-Rokeach. (1989). *Theories of mass communication*, 5th ed. New York: Longman.

Denniston, L. (1998). "From George Carlin to Matt Drudge: The constitutional implications of bringing the paparazzi to America," *American University Law Review*, 47 (June):1255–1271.

Dertouzos, M. L. (1997). *What will be: How the new world of information will change our lives*. New York: HarperEdge.

Dublinske, B. A. (1997). "Free speech, the Internet, and the CDA: Is a "decent" opinion just a dream?" *Creighton Law Review*, 30 (June):1229–1254.

Ely, J. H. (1980). *Democracy and distrust: A theory of judicial review*. Cambridge, MA: Harvard University Press.

Emerson, T. I. (1970). *The system of freedom of expression*. New York: Random House.

_____. (1966). *Toward a general theory of the First Amendment.* New York: Random House.

Emery, M., E. Emery, and N. L. Roberts. (1996). *The press and America: An interpretive history of mass media,* 8th ed. Boston: Allyn and Bacon.

Emord, J. W. (1991). *Freedom, technology and the First Amendment.* San Francisco: Pacific Research Institute for Public Policy.

Entman, R. M. (1989). *Democracy without citizens: Media and the decay of American politics.* New York: Oxford University Press.

Ernst, M. L., A. G. Oettinger, A. W. Branscomb, J. S. Rubin, and J. Wikler. (1993). *Mastering the changing information world.* Norwood, NJ: Ablex.

FCC v. Pacifica Foundation, 438 U.S. 726 (1978).

Field, R. L. (1997). "The electronic future of cash, survey 1996: Survey of the year's developments in electronic cash law and the laws affecting electronic banking in the United States," *American University Law Review,* 46 (April):967, 972.

Fiss, O. M. (1996). *Liberalism divided.* Boulder: Westview Press.

Flink, S. E. (1997). *Sentinel under siege: The triumphs and troubles of America's free press.* Boulder: Westview Press.

Foerstel, H. N. (1998). *Banned in the media: A reference guide to censorship in the press, motion pictures, broadcasting, and the Internet.* Westport, CT: Greenwood Press.

Folkerts, J., and D. L. Teeter Jr. (1994). *Voices of a nation: A history of mass media in the United States,* 2nd ed. New York: Macmillan.

Fraleigh, D. M., and J. S. Tuman. (1997). *Freedom of speech in the marketplace of ideas.* New York: St. Martin's Press.

Gates, B. (1995). *The road ahead.* New York: Viking.

Gerbner, G., H. Mowlana, and H. Schiller. (1996). *Invisible crisis: What conglomerate control of media means for America and the world.* Boulder: Westview Press.

Gershon, R. A. (1997). *The transnational media corporation: Global messages and free market competition.* Mahwah, NJ: Lawrence Erlbaum.

Gieber, W. (1960). "Two communicators of the news: A study of the roles of sources and reporters," *Social Forces,* 39:76–83.

Gieber, W, and W. Johnson. (1961). "The city hall 'beat': A study of reporter and source roles," *Journalism Quarterly,* 38(3):289–297.

Gilder, G. (1992). *Recapturing the spirit of enterprise: Updated for the 1990s.* San Francisco: ICS Press.

Gillmor, D. M., J. A. Barron, T. F. Simon, and H. A. Terry. (1996). *Fundamentals of mass communication law.* Minneapolis: West.

Glasser, T. L., and C. T. Salmon. (1995). *Public opinion and the communication of consent.* New York: Guilford Press.

Godwin, M. (1998). *Cyber rights: Defending free speech in the digital age.* New York: Times Books.

Goffman, E. (1959). *The presentation of self in everyday life.* Garden City, NY: Doubleday.

Graber, D. A. (1997). *Mass media and American politics,* 5th ed. Washington, DC: CQ Press.

Graber, D., D. McQuail, and P. Norris, eds. (1998). *The politics of news, the news of politics.* Washington, DC: CQ Press.

Grinde Jr., D. A., and B. E. Johansen. (1991). *Exemplar of liberty: Native America and the evolution of democracy.* Los Angeles: American Indian Studies Center.

Hamelink, C. J. (1994). *The politics of world communication.* London: Sage.

Hauben, M., and R. Hauben. (1997). *Netizens: On the history and impact of Usenet and the Internet.* Washington, DC: IEEE Computer Society Press.

Head, S. W., and C. H. Sterling. (1987). *Broadcasting in America: A survey of electronic media,* 5th ed. Boston: Houghton Mifflin.

Hentoff, N. (1992). *Free Speech for me—But not for thee.* New York: HarperCollins.

Herman, E. S., and R. W. McChesney. (1997). *The global media: The new missionaries of global capitalism.* London: Cassell.

Hiebert, R. E., ed. (1999). *Impact of mass media: Current issues,* 4th ed. New York: Addison Wesley Longman.

Hill, K. A., and J. E. Hughs. (1998). *Cyberpolitics: Citizen activism in the age of the Internet.* New York: Rowman & Littlefield.

Hopkins, W. W. (1999). "Conduct and speech," in his *Communication and the Law.* Northport, AL: Vision Press.

Huber, P. (1997). *Law and disorder in cyberspace: Abolish the FCC and let common law rule the telecosm.* Oxford: Oxford University Press.

Ihnatko, A. (1997). *Cyberspeak: Online dictionary.* New York: Random House.

Innis, H. A. (1972). *Empire and communications.* Toronto: University of Toronto Press.

_____. (1964). *The bias of communication.* Toronto: University of Toronto Press.

Jensen, R. (1998). "First Amendment potluck," *Communication Law and Policy,* 3, no. 4 (Autumn):563–588.

Johansen, B. E. (1982). *Forgotten founders: How the American Indian helped shape democracy.* Boston: Harvard Common Press.

Johnson, T. J., and B. K. Kaye. (1998). "Cruising is believing? Comparing Internet and traditional sources on media credibility measures," *Journalism & Mass Communication Quarterly,* 75, no. 2 (Summer):325–340.

Jones, S. G. (1998). *Cybersociety 2.0: Revisiting computer-mediated communication and community.* Thousand Oaks, CA: Sage.

_____. (1997). *Virtual culture: Identity & communication in cybersociety.* London: Sage.

Kaniss, P. (1991). *Making local news.* Chicago: University of Chicago Press.

Kellerman, K. (1987)."Information exchange in social interaction," in M. E. Roloff and G. R. Miller, eds., *Interpersonal processes: New directions in communication research.* Newbury Park, CA: Sage.

Ketterer, S. (1998). "Teaching students how to evaluate and use online resources," *Journalism & Mass Communication Educator* 52, no. 4 (Winter):4–14.

Kohut, A. (1994). *The role of technology in American life.* The Times Mirror Center for the People and the Press.

Krasnow, E. G., L. D. Longley, and H. Terry. (1983). *The politics of broadcast regulation,* 3rd ed. New York: St. Martin's Press.

Krattenmaker, T. G, and L. A. Powe Jr. (1995). "Emerging media technology and the First Amendment: Converging First Amendment principles for converging communications media," *Yale Law Journal,* 104 (May):1719–1741.

Kroker, A., and M. Kroker, eds. (1997). *Digital delirium.* New York: St. Martin's Press.

Lamberton, D. M., ed. (1997). *The new research frontiers of communication policy.* Amsterdam: Elsevier.

Lawrence, F. (1997). "Symposium: Pornography—Free speech or censorship in cyberspace?" *Boston University Journal of Science and Technology Law* (June 10):3.

Leahy, P. (1997). "The state of the First Amendment at the approach of the millennium," *Commlaw Conspectus,* 5 (Summer):169.

Lemert, C., ed. (1999). *Social theory: The multicultural and classical readings,* 2nd ed. Boulder: Westview Press.

Lerner, D. (1996). "Modernizing styles of life: A theory," in J. Hanson and D. J. Maxcy, eds., *Sources: Notable selections in mass media.* Guilford, CT: Dushkin Publishing/Brown & Benchmark.

Lessig, L. (1996). "Surveying law and borders: The zones of cyberspace," *Stanford Law Review,* 48 (May):1403–1411.

Levinson, J. C. and C. Rubin. (1997). *Guerrilla marketing online,* 2nd ed. Boston: Houghton Mifflin.

Levy, L. W. (1985). *Emergence of a free press.* New York: Oxford University Press.

Lewis, A. (1991). *Make no law: The Sullivan case and the First Amendment.* New York: Random House.

Li, Xigen. (1998). "Web page design and graphic use of three U.S. newspapers," *Journalism & Mass Communication Quarterly,* 75, no. 2 (Summer):353–365.

Lipschultz, J. H. (1997). *Broadcast indecency: FCC regulation and the First Amendment.* Boston: Focal Press.

_____. (1988). "Mediasat and the tort of invasion of privacy," *Journalism Quarterly,* 65, no. 2 (Summer):507–510.

Lowery, S. A., and M. L. DeFleur. (1995). *Milestones in mass communication research: Media effects,* 3rd ed. White Plains, NY: Longman.

Mantovani, G. (1994). "Is computer-mediated communication intrinsically apt to enhance democracy in organizations?" *Human Relations,* 47(1):45–61.

Martin, S. E. (1998). "How news gets from paper to its online counterpart," *Newspaper Research Journal,* 19, no. 2 (Spring):64–73.

_____. (1995). *Bits, bytes, and big brother: Federal information control in the technological age.* Westport, CT: Praeger.

McKay, L. J. (1996). "The Communications Decency Act: Protecting children from on-line indecency," *Seton Hall Legislative Journal,* 20:463, 502.

McLeod, J. M., and S. H. Chaffee. (1973). "Interpersonal approaches to communication research," *American Behavioral Scientist,* 16:469–499.

McLeod, J. M., M. Sitrovic, P. S. Voakes, Z. Guo, and K. Huang. (1998). "A model of public support for First Amendment rights," *Communication Law and Policy,* 3, no. 4 (Autumn):479–514.

McLuhan, M., and B. R. Powers. (1989). *The global village: Transformations in world life and media in the 21st century.* New York: Oxford University Press.

McManus, J. H. (1994). *Market-driven journalism.* Thousand Oaks, CA: Sage.

McPhail, T. L.(1981). *Electronic colonialism: The future of international broadcasting and communication.* Beverly Hills, CA: Sage.

McQuail, D. (1994). *Mass communication theory: An introduction*, 3rd ed. London: Sage.

Meiklejohn, A. (1960). *Political freedom: The constitutional powers of the people*. New York: Harper.

Meyrowitz, J. (1985). *No sense of place: The impact of electronic media on social behavior*. New York: Oxford University Press.

Middleton, K. R., and B. F. Chamberlain. (1995). *Key cases in the law of public communication*. White Plains, NY: Longman.

Milburn, M. A. (1991). *Persuasion and politics: The social psychology of public opinion*. Pacific Grove, CA: Brooks/Cole Publishing.

Mills, C. W. (1963). *Power, politics and people: The collected essays of C. Wright Mills*. New York: Oxford University Press.

Mosco, V. (1996). *The political economy of communication*. London: Sage.

National Broadcasting Co. v. United States, 319 U.S. 190 (1943).

Negroponte, N. (1995). *Being digital*. New York: Alfred A. Knopf.

Neuman, W. R. (1998). "The global impact of new technologies," in D. Graber, D. McQuail, and P. Norris, eds., *The politics of news, the news of politics*. Washington, DC: CQ Press.

Newcomb, T. (1953). "An approach to the study of communicative acts," *Psychological Review*, 60:393–404.

Noelle-Neumann, E. (1995)."Public opinion and rationality," in T. L. Glasser and C. T. Salmon, eds., *Public opinion and the communication of consent*. New York: Guilford Press.

————. (1984). *The spiral of silence: Public opinion—Our social skin*. Chicago: University of Chicago Press.

Olien, C. N., G. A. Donohue, and P. J. Tichenor. (1995). "Conflict, consensus and public opinion," in T. L. Glasser and C. T. Salmon, eds., *Public opinion and the communication of consent*. New York: Guilford Press, 1995.

Packard, A. (1998). "Infringement or impingement: Carving out an actual knowledge defense for sysops facing strict liability," *Journalism & Mass Communication Monographs*, no. 168 (December).

Parenti, M. (1996). *Dirty truths*. San Francisco: City Lights Books.

————. (1986). *Inventing reality: The politics of the mass media*. New York: St. Martin's Press.

Perritt Jr., H. H. (1996). *Law and the information superhighway*. New York: John Wiley & Sons.

Peters, S. L. (1995). *Emergent materialism: A proposed solution to the mind/body problem*. Lanham, MD: University Press of America.

Picard, R. G. (1998). "Media concentration, economics, and regulation," in D. Graber, D. McQuail, and P. Norris, eds., *The politics of news, the news of politics*, Washington, DC: CQ Press.

Pool, I. S. (1990). *Technologies without boundaries*, ed. E. M. Noam. Cambridge, MA: Harvard University Press.

————. (1983). *Technologies of freedom*. Cambridge, MA: Harvard University Press.

Postman, N. (1992). *Technopoly: The surrender of culture to technology*. New York: Alfred A. Knopf.

Rappaport, K. L. (1998). "In the wake of *Reno v. ACLU*: The continued struggle in Western constitutional democracies with Internet censorship and freedom of speech online," *American University International Law Review,* 13:765–814.

Red Lion Broadcasting Company v. FCC, 395 U.S. 367 (1969).

Redmond, J., and R. Trager (1998). *Balancing on the wire: The art of managing media organizations.* Boulder: Coursewise Publishing.

Reno v. ACLU, 521 U.S. 844, 117 S.Ct. 2329, 138 L.Ed. 2d 874 (1997).

Rescher, N. (1995). *Public concerns: Philosophical studies of social issues.* Lanham, MD: Rowman & Littlefield.

Rheingold, H. (1994). *The virtual community: Homesteading on the electronic frontier.* New York: HarperPerennial.

Robinson, G. O. (1996). "The 'new' communications act: A second opinion," *Connecticut Law Review,* 29 (Fall):289, 309.

Rogers, E. M. (1995). *Diffusion of innovations,* 4th ed. New York: Free Press.

––––––. (1963). *Diffusion of innovations.* New York: Free Press.

Rowland Jr., W. D. (1997). "The meaning of 'the public interest' in communications policy—Part II: Its implementation in early broadcast law and regulation," *Communication Law and Policy,* 2, no. 4 (Autumn):363–396.

Sable Communications Inc. v. FCC, 492 U.S. 115 (1989).

Schudson, M. (1998). "The public journalism movement and its problems," in D. Graber, D. McQuail, and P. Norris, eds., *The politics of news, the news of politics.* Washington, DC: CQ Press.

Schwartz, B. (1971). *The Bill of Rights: A documentary history.* New York: Chelsea House.

Shane, E. (1998). "The state of the industry: Radio's shifting paradigm," *Journal of Radio Studies,* 5, no. 2 (Summer):1–7.

Sheridan, D. R. (1997). "*Zeran v. AOL* and the effect of Section 230 of the *Communications Decency Act* upon liability for defamation on the Internet," *Albany Law Review,* 61:147–179.

Sherman, A. (1998). *Cybergrrl! A woman's guide to the world wide web.* New York: Ballantine Books.

Shoemaker, P. J., and S. D. Reese. (1996). *Mediating the message: Theories of influence on mass media content,* 2nd ed. White Plains, NY: Longman.

Sloan, W. D., and J. D. Startt. (1996). *The media in America: A history,* 3rd ed. Northport, AL: Vision Press.

Smethers, J. S. (1998). "Cyberspace in the curricula: New legal and ethical issues," *Journalism & Mass Communication Educator,* 52, no. 4 (Winter):15–23.

Smith, L. D. (1998). University of Nebraska, Memorandum, "Executive Memorandum No. 16, Policy for Responsible Use of University Computers and Information Systems, January 6.

Smolla, R. A. (1992). *Free speech in an open society.* New York: Alfred A. Knopf.

Sproull, L., and S. Kiesler. (1991). *Connections.* Cambridge, MA: MIT Press.

Stamm, K. R., and W. B. Pearce (1971). "Communication behavior and coorientational relations," *Journal of Communication,* 21:210–211.

Star, S. L., ed. (1995). *The cultures of computing.* Cambridge, MA: Blackwell Press.

Stevenson, N. (1995). *Understanding media cultures: Social theory and mass communication.* London: Sage.

Strate, L., R. Jacobson, and S. B. Gibson, eds. (1996). Communication and cyber-space. Cresskill, NJ: Hampton Press.

Sunstein, C. R. (1995). "Emerging media technology and the First Amendment: The First Amendment in cyberspace," *Yale Law Journal,* (May): 1757–1804.

_____. (1993). *Democracy and the problem of free speech.* New York: Free Press.

Swingewood, A. (1998). *Cultural theory and the problem of modernity.* New York: St. Martin's Press.

Taylor, D. A., and I. Altman. (1987). "Communication in interpersonal relation-ships: Social penetration processes," in M. E. Roloff and G. R. Miller, eds., *Interpersonal processes: New directions in communication research.* Newbury Park, CA: Sage.

Van Alstyne, W. W. (1984). *Interpretations of the First Amendment.* Durham, NC: Duke University Press.

Wallace, J., and M. Green. (1997). "Bridging the analogy gap: The Internet, the printing press and freedom of speech," *Seattle University Puget Sound Law Review,* 20 (Spring):711, 732.

West, T. G. (1998). "The decline of free speech in twentieth-century America: The view from the founding," in K. L. Grasso and C. R. Castillo, eds., *Liberty under law: American constitutionalism, yesterday, today and tomorrow,* 2nd ed. Lanham, MD: University Press of America, 1998.

Williams, R. (1966). *Communications.* London: Chatto & Windus.

Williams Jr., W. (1998). "The impact of ownership rules and the Telecommunica-tions Act of 1996 on a small radio market," *Journal of Radio Studies,* 5, no. 2 (Summer):8–18.

Wise, J. M. (1997). *Exploring technology and social space.* Thousand Oaks, CA: Sage.

Woolpert, S., C. D. Slaton, and E. W. Schwerin, eds. (1998). *Transformational politics: Theory, study, and practice.* Albany: State University of New York Press.

Wrobel, L. A., and E. M. Pope. (1995). *Understanding emerging network services, pricing, and regulation.* Boston: Artech House.

Yoder, A. (1996). *Pirate radio: The incredible saga of America's underground, illegal broadcasters.* Solana Beach, CA: HighText Publications.

Mass Media Sources

Associated Press. (1999). "Internet pornography sites thriving" (August 2).

_____. (1999). "FCC makes Internet calls long-distance" (February 26).

_____. (1999). "Anti-abortion web verdict" (February 3).

_____. (1999). "Judge orders removal of Pope web site" (January 9).

_____. (1998). "Judge backs student's web rights" (December 29).

_____. (1998). "Tablets may be earliest writing" (December 12).

_____. (1998). "Judge delays Internet-decency law" (November 24).

_____. (1998). "Computerized records not open to publisher" (October 1).

_____. (1998). "JonBenet cybersleuths" (September 19).

_____. (1998). "Arlo Guthrie in cyberspace" (August 30).

_____. (1998). "Vatican computer office to link bishops, diplomats" (August 22).

_____. (1998). "Foreign countries selling unique Internet suffixes (August 10).

_____. (1998). "Two teen hackers plead guilty in Pentagon case" (July 30).

_____. (1998). "China to try computer engineer" (July 29).

_____. (1998). "Internet confessor enters not guilt plea" (July 19).

_____. (1998). "FCC scales back on school Internet hookup subsidies" (June 13).

_____. (1998). "Business booming on Net" (April 15).

_____. (1998). "Internet broadcasting business flourishing" (March 16).

Barbineck, M. (1998). "Oprah Winfrey beats big beef," Associated Press (February 26).

Biskupik, J. (1999). "High court upholds law banning 'obscene' e-mail: Justices deny First Amendment protection," *Washington Post*, p. A-K2 (April 20).

Breslau, K. (1997). "A Capital cyber clash: A beltway libel suit could make Internet history," *Newsweek* (October 20).

Bridis, T. (1998). "It's official! AOL buys Netscape," Associated Press (November 24).

Brouwer, G. (1999). "Crips, Bloods in the web 'hood,'" *Salon Magazine* (February 26), at http://www.salonmagazine.com.

Chronicle of Higher Education. (1998). "China imposes Internet restrictions," p. A-61 (January 9).

CNN Interactive. (1999). "AOL bans 10-year-old for Internet prank, then backs off" (February 2).

_____. (1998). "Dr. Laura drops lawsuit over nude pictures; Alyssa Milano wins suit over nude Internet photos" (December 23).

_____. (1998). "School to teacher: Impeachment lesson fine, but leave out sex" (December 9).

Derk, J. (1998). "Internet put to test," Evansville, *Indiana Courier Online* (September 13).

Electronic Media. (1999). "Hot sites," p. 18 (February 8).

Estes, A. (1999). "Report: Net increases hate groups," Associated Press (February 25).

Evans, H. M. (1997). "Freedom for what?" Twentieth Annual Frank E. Gannett Lecture (December 10).

Grady, D., and J. Gimple. (1998). "Virtual barbarians at the gate," *Public Relations Strategist* (Fall).

Guernsey, L. (1998). "Scholars at meeting debunk technology's potential to foster Utopia—or Apocalypse," *Chronicle of Higher Education*, p. A-23 (November 20).

Haring, B. (1998). "You can't stop the music on the Net," *USA Today*, p. 5-D (November 4).

Harmon, A. (1998). "Online trail to an offline killing," *New York Times*, p. A-1 (April 30).

Hibler, D. J. (1998). "Attack on my tenure is free speech issue," *Omaha World-Herald*, p. 23 (March 5).

Huffstutter, P. J. (1998). "Obeying court order, AOL reveals subscriber's name," *Los Angeles Times*, p. D-1 (July 18).

Johnston, D. C. (1997). "E-mail porn invades a childhood," New York Times News Service (December 7).

Kaggwa, L. (1998). "Field of technology law booming," *Omaha World-Herald*, p. 1-M (July 19).

Kiernan, V. (1998). "Use of 'cookies' in research sparks a debate over privacy," *Chronicle of Higher Education*, p. A–31 (September 25).

Kirst, S. (1998). "Chain-letter hoax harasses professor," Newhouse News Service (July 5).

Komarrow, S. (1998). "Candidates set foot on campaign cybertrail," *USA Today*, p. 19-A (November 4).

Kunde, D. (1999). "Sounding off has risks," *Dallas Morning News*, in *Omaha World-Herald*, p. 1-G (February 14).

———. (1998). "Secrets never safe in office e-mail," *Dallas Morning News*, in *Omaha World-Herald*, p. 1-G (August 2).

Kurtz, H. (1999). "Matt Drudge cuts radio deal with ABC," *Washington Post*, p. C–1 (July 8).

Los Angeles Times News Service. (1998). "AOL gives name of newspaper employee with critical Web site" (July 18).

McAleavy, Y. (1999). "Principal files suit to fight e-mail," *Bergen Record* web site (February 23).

McCollum, K. (1998). "NYU sues proprietor of 'dorm cam' sex site," *Chronicle of Higher Education*, p. A-20 (July 31).

———. (1998). "Web site features motion pictures from the Spanish-American War," *Chronicle of Higher Education*, p. A-36 (April 10).

———. (1998). "Scholars turn unwanted e-mail into a lesson in the culture of the Internet," *Chronicle of Higher Education*, p. A-29 (January 9).

Mindich, D. T. Z. (1999). "The dredge report: Matt Drudge is the face of bad news," *Ottawa Citizen*, p. A-17 (July 23).

Morrison, K. G. (1998). "Savvy constituents pull Congress to the web," *Omaha World-Herald*, p. 1 (March 7).

Moseley-Braun, C. (1998). "Protecting our children on the Internet," *Albion (Illinois) Journal Register*, p. 4 (May 6).

Murphy, C. (1998). "Words tacked on web tell tales," New York Times News Service (December 28).

Murphy, D. (1998). "Disgruntled workers web site," Scripps Howard News Service (November 1).

New York Times News Service. (1998). "Hyde admits long-ago affair" (September 17).

O'Donnell, J. J. (1998). "Tools for teaching: Personal encounters in cyberspace," *Chronicle of Higher Education*, p. B-7 (February 13).

Plotnikoff, D. (1998). "Someone watching over you," *San Jose Mercury News*, in *Omaha World-Herald*, p. 1-G (November 29).

Powers, J. (1998). "Ghoulpools big business on the Internet," *Boston Globe*, reprinted in *Omaha World-Herald*, p. 1-E (July 12).

Ryan, M. (1998). "He fights dictators with the Internet," *Parade Magazine*, p. 12 (August 23).

San Jose Mercury News Service. (1998). "Dr. Laura making waves on Web" (October 28).

Scripps Howard News Service. (1998). "Nuremberg files on the Net" (November 14).

Sixel, L. M. (1998). "Free speech goes only so far," *Houston Chronicle*, in *Omaha World-Herald*, p. 11-G (August 16).

Smith, J. (1998). "Software lets adults control access to the Web," *Detroit News*, p. F-13 (February 2).

Smith, L. D. (1998). Executive memorandum #16, University of Nebraska (January 6).

Stroh, M. (1998). "Managing Internet addresses is big, complicated business," *Baltimore Sun*, in *Omaha World-Herald*, p. extra 3 (October 28).

Tahmincioglu, E. (1999). "Big brother may be listening, watching on the job," *St. Petersburg Times*, in *Omaha World-Herald*, p. 13-G (February 14).

Tedesco, R. (1998). "Clinton tape gets a little (re)play online," *Broadcasting & Cable*, p. 52 (September 28).

Thomas, K. (1998). "Message from mom: 'WhatRUsaYiNg?'" *USA Today*, p. 5-D (December 9).

USA Today. (1998). "Microsoft on trial," p. 1-A (October 16–18).

_____. (1998). "Study: More Net use is more depressing," p. 1 (August 30).

Valdmanis, T., and P. Davidson. (1999). "Justice Department feasts eyes on Microsoft bust-up," *USA Today*, p. 1-B (July 29).

Wall Street Journal Reports. (1997). "The Internet," Section R (December 8).

Washington Post News Service. (1998). "Virginia library barred from software filtering" (November 24).

_____. (1996). "Phony web site raises serious issues" (March 10).

Wilson, R. (1998). "U. of Wisconsin considers proposal to ease limits on faculty speech," *Chronicle of Higher Education*, p. A-14 (October 2).

Yagoda, B. (1998). "I have reservations about computers and e-mail. How about you?" *Chronicle of Higher Education*, p. B-6 (February 13).

Young, J. R. (1998). "Technorealists hope to enrich debate over policy issues in cyberspace," *Chronicle of Higher Education*, p. 23 (April 3).

Index